CONTENTS

Part IV: Quantitative Skills

PETERSON'S®

MASTER THE™ ACCUPLACER® TESTS

CONTENTS

Part I: Preparing for the Exam

Part II: Diagnosing Strengths and Weaknesses

Part III: Reading and Writing Skills

Part V: Practice Tests

CONTENTS

Credits

Excerpt from "Address by Honorable William C. Redfield, Secretary of Commerce, at Regional Chairmen of the Highway Transport Committee Council of National Defense Highway Transport Committee, Bulletin 4" by William C. Redfield (October 1918)

Excerpt from *The Analysis of Mind* by Bertrand Russell (1921)

Excerpt from "How Did Cool Become Such a Big Deal?" by David Skinner from *Humanities* (July/August 2014)

Excerpt from *A Daughter of the Samurai* by Etsu Inagaki Sugimoto (1925)

Excerpt from *Calculus Made Easy* by Silvanus Thompson (1910)

Review of "Overview – SSRI Antidepressants" by UK National Health Service (February 2021)

Excerpt from *Draft of a Plan for Beginning Animal Sanctuaries in Labrador* by William Wood (1913)

BEFORE YOU BEGIN

OVERVIEW

WHY YOU SHOULD USE THIS BOOK

Peterson's *Master the™ ACCUPLACER® Tests* is designed by educators and test experts to fully prepare you for test-day success. In this book, we provide in-depth information about the structure of the ACCUPLACER, the content areas addressed, and the question types you can expect to see on the exam. This book provides a thorough overview of major topics in reading, writing, and math to help you focus your study time and review important concepts in preparation for the exam. As you learn more about the ACCUPLACER's format and structure, you'll gain the confidence you need to do your best on test day.

This helpful guide includes the following:

ESSENTIAL TEST INFORMATION

We take the stress out of planning for your placement exam by providing all the information you'll need to know in one place—including how the ACCUPLACER is used, how to register, and even what to bring on the day of the exam. We've got you covered!

COMPREHENSIVE COVERAGE OF THE ACCUPLACER TEST FORMAT

After using this book, you'll know the structure and format of the ACCUPLACER from start to finish and have all the information you'll need for success on test day.

THOROUGH TEST TOPIC REVIEW

You'll get a thorough review of *every topic* tested on the ACCUPLACER and help creating an effective study plan. We'll cover the content areas and question types you'll encounter on the exam, so you can be confident that you're prepared on test day.

PLENTY OF REALISTIC TEST QUESTION PRACTICE

Most topic chapters in this book contain realistic practice with questions just like those you'll encounter during the actual exam. In addition, you can customize your preparation based on your target test.

Take a full-length diagnostic exam to help you determine your strengths and weaknesses and target your study time effectively. Then, build your confidence by taking a full-length practice exam, which you can use to strengthen your test-taking skills and get comfortable with the format and structure of the actual exams. There's no better way to practice for the big day!

EXPERT TIPS, ADVICE, AND STRATEGIES

Our test prep professionals know what it takes to do your best on the ACCUPLACER exam—you'll get the expert tools and strategies that have proven to be effective on exam day so that you'll be calm, cool, and collected when you take the ACCUPLACER.

We know that doing well on your exam is important, both to you and your family—and we're here to help you through every step of your journey. Consider this book your all-in-one test preparation package to get you through the placement exam and into the classes you need to succeed in college.

HOW THIS BOOK IS ORGANIZED

This book covers everything you need to do your best on the ACCUPLACER. It contains up-to-date information, hundreds of practice questions, and solid test-taking advice. Here's how you can use it to familiarize yourself with the exam format and develop a study plan that meets your needs.

How to Navigate This Book

Part I: Part I provides a comprehensive overview of what's on the ACCUPLACER. You'll learn what kinds of questions to expect and how they look, how the tests are scored, and numerous learning strategies and study skills to help you make the most of your prep time.

Part II: Part II provides you the opportunity to try your hand at sample questions from the exam. The ACCUPLACER diagnostic test can show you where your skills are strong and where to focus your study time.

Part III: Part III covers the reading and writing skills tested on the ACCUPLACER. In these chapters, you'll learn how to approach the reading placement test, the writing placement test, and the WritePlacer essay exam.

Part IV: Part IV covers topics that you should expect to see on the math placement tests. Here, you can get a refresher on arithmetic, algebra, geometry, statistics, and more. Use the results from the diagnostic test to help you pinpoint which chapters might be most helpful to you.

Part V: Part V contains two practice tests for the ACCUPLACER. Take at least one to see how you improve after you've taken the diagnostic test and spent time studying any areas in need of improvement.

HOW TO USE THIS BOOK

Diagnostic Test Method

One way to use this book is to start with a diagnostic test for the ACCUPLACER. A diagnostic test is a test that helps you understand your strengths and weaknesses on the exam. It "diagnoses" the skills that need the most improvement.

In this method, you take a diagnostic test first and then use the results to develop a study plan. The diagnostic test will give you a sampling of the kinds of questions you are likely to see on the test, and it will show you where you might need to focus your test-prep efforts.

Once you've taken the diagnostic test, score yourself to see your strengths and weaknesses. How did you do? Make a list of your strong and weak areas. If you scored well on math but poorly on reading, then you can count math as a strength. Your reading skills, on the other hand, will need some work. Rank the different sections in terms of your strongest and weakest skills.

Use your ranking list to develop your study plan. Your plan should prioritize boosting your weaker skills. You don't need to spend as much time brushing up on your strengths. However, you should plan to spend *some* time on "strong skills" exercises—just to stay in shape.

Once you've got a study plan, put it to work. Read about the ACCUPLACER in Part I. Then, focus on improving your weak skills by studying the sections in Parts III and IV. After you've reviewed the content sections, take a practice test or two in Part V. This test should show an improvement in your score!

Front-to-Back Method

Another way to use this book is the front-to-back method. In this method, you work through the book the way it is organized.

Start at Part I of the book and carefully read through the information on the ACCUPLACER. This will help you understand the exam and how it's scored. Next, take the diagnostic test in Part II. Then, study the content sections in Parts III and IV. If you know your stronger and weaker skills, you might devote extra time to sections where you need the most improvement.

After you've reviewed the content, take a practice test in Part V. Taking a practice test will help you be more prepared on exam day. Even if you somehow don't improve your score between the diagnostic test and practice test, the process of taking each can itself help increase your score. This is because you become more familiar with the test format each time you try, which increases your confidence.

After you complete each test, review your answers with the explanations provided. If you still don't understand how to answer a certain question, you might ask a teacher for help. A review session with a friend might prove helpful too.

 FYI

For access to additional interactive lessons, instructional videos, and timed practice tests, go to **petersons.com/accuplacer.**
Use coupon code ACCU2023 for 25% off your first digital purchase.

SPECIAL STUDY FEATURES

Peterson's *Master the*™ *ACCUPLACER*® *Tests* was designed to be easy to use so that you can locate the information you need. It includes several features to make your preparation easier.

OVERVIEW

Each review chapter begins with a bulleted overview listing the topics that will be covered in the chapter. You know immediately where to look for a topic that you need to work on.

SUMMING IT UP

Each chapter ends with a point-by-point summary that captures the most important points.

KNOWLEDGE CHECKS

At the end of most chapters, you'll find a Knowledge Check, which is a short quiz designed to test your understanding of the concepts presented throughout the chapter. Use the Knowledge Checks to see how well you're able to apply the information you've learned from the chapter and to get a sense of what to expect on the actual exam. In Chapter 6: Strategies for the WritePlacer® Exam, you'll find information about the test along with a sample prompt and essay in lieu of a Knowledge Check.

BONUS INFORMATION

In addition, be sure to look throughout the book for the following test prep tools:

- **FYI:** FYIs (for your information) highlight critical information about the format of the ACCUPLACER.

- **TIP:** Tips draw your attention to valuable concepts, advice, and shortcuts for tackling the tests or your study time.

- **ALERT:** Whenever you need to be careful of a common pitfall or test-taker trap, you'll find an Alert. This information reveals and helps eliminate the wrong turns many people take on the exam.

QR CODES

Throughout this book, you'll find QR codes that link to free supplemental video content. These videos are designed to provide you with focused lessons on specific topics. If you find yourself struggling with a specific concept, look for a QR code in the section or chapter for additional instruction.

Strategies for Managing Test Anxiety

As part of your preparation for the ACCUPLACER, you might find it helpful to keep the following strategies in mind if you struggle with test anxiety.

1 **Be prepared.** Research what you will need to bring or have with you on test day. The night before, make sure you have everything you need in one place. Decide on the outfit you will wear. Be comfortable but look put together to boost confidence.

2 **Eat smart.** Plan to eat a balanced meal before your exam. Have something with a combination of healthy fats, protein, and carbs. Avoid caffeine if it makes you jittery and avoid sugary items that will spike your energy level—it won't last, and you'll be worse for it as you work through your exam.

3 **Focus only on the test.** Don't plan any other activities on test day or attempt to squeeze the test in between other plans.

4 **Arrive rested, relaxed, and on time.** Plan to arrive a little bit early. Leave plenty of time for any unexpected delays. This still applies if you're taking the test from home: get set up early.

5 **If the test is proctored, ask questions if there are any instructions you do not understand.** Make sure that you know exactly what to do. In the test room, the proctor will provide the instructions you must follow when taking the examination. If something is unclear, ask for clarification.

6 **Follow instructions exactly during the exam.** Even though you won't have to worry about time restrictions, you still want to make sure everything is done according to testing protocol. Follow any instructions you're given and don't gloss over details in the directions.

7 **Maintain a positive attitude.** Remain calm—you know yourself best and which strategies or techniques will help you ease any test anxiety. Remember that a can-do attitude creates confidence, and confidence is key.

PETERSON'S® PUBLICATIONS

Peterson's publishes a full line of books—career preparation, education exploration, test prep, and financial aid. Peterson's books are available for purchase online. Visit **petersonsbooks.com** for more information. Sign up for one of our online subscription plans and you'll have access to our entire test prep catalog of more than 150 exams *plus* instructional videos, flashcards, interactive quizzes, and more! Our subscription plans allow you to study as quickly as you can or as slowly as you'd like. For more information, and discounted access to practice for placement exams like the ACCUPLACER, go to **petersons.com/accuplacer.**

GIVE US YOUR FEEDBACK

Peterson's publications can be found at your local bookstore and library, high school guidance offices, college libraries and career centers, and at **petersonsbooks.com.** Peterson's books are now also available as ebooks.

We welcome any comments or suggestions you may have about this publication. Your feedback will help us make educational dreams possible for you—and others like you.

YOU'RE WELL ON YOUR WAY TO SUCCESS!

Remember that knowledge is power. By using this book, you will be studying the most comprehensive guide available.

The *first step* to feeling prepared and ready to do your best on the ACCUPLACER is to know the structure and format of the exam you're going to take inside and out, including all the basics you need to know.

We *know* you're eager to get to the test practice and review, but taking the time to develop a thorough understanding of the ACCUPLACER from top to bottom will help you know what to expect so that you can be confident and prepared on test day. Let's get started!

Good luck!

PART I
PREPARING FOR THE EXAM

1 | ACCUPLACER®
Format and Questions

CHAPTER

ACCUPLACER®
Format and Questions

ACCUPLACER® FORMAT & QUESTIONS

OVERVIEW

What to Know about the ACCUPLACER®

What to Expect on the ACCUPLACER®

The WritePlacer® Essay Exam

Summing It Up

Before you jump with both feet into preparing for your exam, this chapter offers a useful preview of what the ACCUPLACER is, how schools use the results, how the test is administered, the kinds of subjects and questions that will be covered, and anything else you might need to know about the ACCUPLACER. Once you have a firm grasp of what to expect, you'll be ready to start preparing for your exam in the chapters that follow.

WHAT TO KNOW ABOUT THE ACCUPLACER®

The ACCUPLACER is a placement test designed to place high school seniors into dual enrollment classes and newly enrolled college students into the appropriate college courses. The array of tests included under the ACCUPLACER comprises five multiple-choice placement exams that cover reading, writing, and math, plus the WritePlacer essay exam, which assesses a student's readiness for college-level writing. Many colleges and universities require students to take all six exam sections, while others may pick and choose which sections best help them evaluate incoming students. For instance, some schools may opt for just the writing placement exam, others for just the WritePlacer essay exam, while still others may require you to do both. If you can't find out which specific sections will be required for you, your best bet is to prepare for all of them. The ACCUPLACER is especially useful for college applicants who don't have recent SAT or ACT scores but want to show experience or proficiency in certain subjects to receive credit for certain introductory courses, such as English composition or math.

Why the ACCUPLACER Matters

In preparing for the ACCUPLACER, you should focus on reviewing concepts you have already learned instead of trying to teach yourself new, more advanced concepts. Doing too well on the exam means you might get placed into courses that are too advanced for your skill level. On the other hand, doing poorly on the exam means you might get placed in classes that are not challenging enough for you, which could result in you wasting time on (and paying tuition for) content that you've already mastered. As such, the best course of action is to learn the format and structure of the exam while brushing up on concepts you know you've already learned. As you prepare, focus on building your test-taking strategies and developing tools to help manage any test anxiety you might have.

How to Register

To register for the exam, go to the College Board's ACCUPLACER Student Portal and use the Test Center Locator to find a test center near you. Depending on the institution where you want to take the exam, registration fees may vary. If you have a documented disability, you can also request accommodations. Be sure to contact your individual testing center for more information about how to register for the ACCUPLACER and how to request accommodations.

What to Bring (and Not Bring) on Test Day

What you should and should not bring will vary depending on the institution where you plan to take the exam. Be sure to bring a photo ID with you. Do **not** bring the following items to the test center: phones, tablets, dictionaries, cameras, watches or smart watches, food or drinks, paper, rulers, protractors, or listening devices such as Bluetooth headphones, etc. Contact your test center for more information on what you can and cannot bring with you on test day.

How the Test Is Scored

The five multiple-choice sections of the exam each have a score range of 200–300 and are divided into five score bands, while the WritePlacer is scored on a scale of 1–8. The score bands for multiple-choice sections are as follows:

- 200–236
- 237–249
- 250–262
- 263–275
- 276–300

At the end of each answer and explanation section in the diagnostic test in Chapter 2, there will be a chart you can use to score yourself according to the ACCUPLACER test standards. Each score band describes a student's estimated level of proficiency. For example, someone who scores a 240 on the reading portion of the exam can likely identify the purpose of a sample text if it is explicitly stated. In contrast, someone who scored a 276 or above on the reading portion has successfully demonstrated complex reading skills, such as identifying the central thesis statement of a text or evaluating an author's use of evidence to support claims. An institution can use a student's performance on the ACCUPLACER to determine whether that student should be enrolled in a remedial composition class, placed in a first-year composition class, or given credit for a first-year composition class.

ACCUPLACER for English Language Learners

The ACCUPLACER English as a Second Language (ESL) Tests are designed to help assess English language learners' proficiency in reading skills, language use, sentence meaning, and listening. Some institutions may require English language learners to take the ACCUPLACER English as a Second Language Tests in lieu of the college placement ACCUPLACER tests. For more information, please visit the College Board website.

COMPANION Tests

COMPANION tests are provided for test takers with documented disabilities who are unable to take the online version of the ACCUPLACER. These tests are available in paper-and-pencil format as well as on compact discs, in braille, and in large print. COMPANION tests consist of the same five multiple-choice placement tests on reading, writing, and math as well as the WritePlacer essay exam. However, they typically have 1.5 to 2 times as many items as the corresponding computer-adaptive tests. Contact your individual test center for details on registering for the COMPANION test.

WHAT TO EXPECT ON THE ACCUPLACER®

The ACCUPLACER is a computer-adaptive test, meaning you complete the exam on a computer and the test adapts to your estimated proficiency by presenting you with questions that represent various levels of difficulty. The ACCUPLACER is also untimed, so you can take as long as you need to complete each section.

In this chapter, we provide a brief overview of each section on the test along with sample questions. By learning about the different sections and question types on the exam, you can go into the ACCUPLACER knowing what to expect. Throughout this book, we will cover the sections of the exam and the different question types in depth so that you can be confident your ACCUPLACER results will be an accurate representation of your knowledge and abilities.

FYI

Throughout this chapter, we will provide the correct answer to a sample question, along with an explanation as to why the answer choice is correct or incorrect. These answer explanations are provided to assist you in your study prep. Note that explanations like these will not appear on the actual exam.

The Reading Placement Test

On the reading ability section of the ACCUPLACER, there are 20 multiple-choice questions divided up as follows:

- One literary passage followed by four questions
- One informational set of two paired passages followed by four questions
- 10–12 informational passages with one question per passage
- 1–2 "fill-in-the-blank" vocabulary questions

Passages on the ACCUPLACER range from 75 to 400 words in length and will be informative/explanatory, argumentative, or narrative in nature. Passages cover a wide range of topics, including literature, literary nonfiction, careers, history, social studies, humanities, and science.

On this section of the exam, you'll be tested on your ability to do the following tasks.

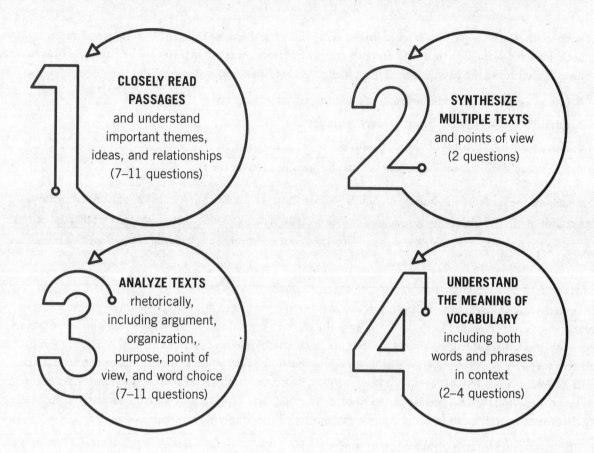

1 CLOSELY READ PASSAGES and understand important themes, ideas, and relationships (7–11 questions)

2 SYNTHESIZE MULTIPLE TEXTS and points of view (2 questions)

3 ANALYZE TEXTS rhetorically, including argument, organization, purpose, point of view, and word choice (7–11 questions)

4 UNDERSTAND THE MEANING OF VOCABULARY including both words and phrases in context (2–4 questions)

The directions for ACCUPLACER reading ability questions will resemble the following example:

Directions for Questions 1–18: Read the passage(s) below and answer the question(s) based on what is stated or implied in the passage(s) and in any introductory material that may be provided.

Here, we have provided you with two samples of reading passages like those that will appear on the ACCUPLACER. Each is followed by a sample question.

A large proportion of the people who are behind bars are not convicted criminals but are people who have been arrested and are being held until their trial in court. Experts have often pointed out that this detention system does not operate fairly. For instance, a person who can afford to pay bail usually will not get locked up. The theory of the bail system is that the person will make sure to show up in court when they are expected to show; otherwise, their bail will be forfeited, meaning the person will lose the money they posted for the bail. Sometimes, a person who can show that they are a stable citizen with a job and a family will be released on "personal recognizance" (without bail). The result is that the well-to-do, the employed, and those with families can often avoid the detention system. The people who do wind up in detention tend to be the poor, the unemployed, the single, and the young.

1. Suppose that two people were booked on the same charge at the same time and that the same bail was set for both. Person 1 was able to post bail and was released. Person 2 was not able to post bail and was held in detention. The writer of the passage would most likely feel that this result is

   A. unfair, because it does not have any relation to guilt or innocence.

   B. unfair, because Person 1 deserves severe punishment.

   C. fair, because Person 1 is obviously innocent.

   D. fair, because the law should be tougher on poor people than on the rich.

   The correct answer is A. This question requires you to identify the author's point of view and anticipate how the author might feel in response to a related scenario. As such, you can determine from the text that the author would feel this situation is unfair because a person's financial situation has no bearing on their guilt or innocence.

Roller derby got its start in the 1930s and since has evolved to form a culture all its own. While it might not seem revolutionary by today's standards, roller derby played a critical role in evolving American assumptions about the capabilities of women as athletes. For one, roller derby was and remains an aggressive, high impact, full-contact sport in which players are prone to injury due to the very physical nature of competition. While roller derby is primarily associated with women today, it afforded both sexes equal opportunities at its outset, leveling the playing field between men and women. The rules and expectations were the same for both, meaning that women participants in roller derby were considered the equals of their male counterparts.

In roller derby, two teams each skate laps around a track for two 30-minute intervals called "jams." While a roller derby team consists of fifteen skaters, each team has only five players on the track at a time—one "jammer" designated by a star on their helmet and four blockers who help protect the jammer. To score points for their team, the jammer must lap members of the other team, meaning complete a full loop to pass them on the track. This means that blockers are uniquely tasked with both offense and defense, since they must assist their own jammer in lapping opposing teams while also blocking the opposing jammer from passing them. As a result of all the jostling and jockeying to pass, derby is known for its physical skirmishes, a trait reflected in derby participants' colorful nicknames, such as "Helmet-Bash Heidi" and "Debbie Destructor."

2. The author's primary purpose in this passage is to

   A. analyze the historical impact of roller derby.

   B. discuss some of the most impactful roller derby athletes.

   C. clarify how roller derby got its start.

   D. explain how roller derby is played and why its emergence was important.

   The correct answer is D. Questions about the author's purpose are related to questions about the main idea of the passage and what the author was intending to convey to the reader. In this case, the author wrote the passage to explain how roller derby is played and why its emergence was important.

For more information on how to approach the reading placement test and the types of questions and passages you can expect to encounter, see Chapter 3.

1

The Writing Placement Test

The writing placement test consists of 25 multiple-choice questions that require test takers to edit and revise drafts of nonfiction texts. You will be tested on your ability to improve a text so that it more effectively develops, organizes, and conveys ideas and so that it conforms to proper conventions of syntax, usage, and punctuation. You will be given one literary nonfiction text accompanied by 5 questions and 4 informational passages with 5 questions each.

Here is a sample writing text with directions, followed by three sample questions.

Directions: Read the following early draft of an essay and then choose the best answer to the question or the best completion of the statement.

(1) Scholars study the phenomenon of collective memory to better understand how groups of people remember and engage with the past. (2) Collective memory refers to the experiences and memories that are shared by a group of people and passed down through generations. (3) In the United States, there are many public memorials to commemorate a variety of important events, like the 9/11 Memorial in New York City or the USS *Arizona* Memorial in Pearl Harbor, Hawaii. (4) Memorials provide insight into how a country collectively remembers people and events and how those events have shaped history and national identity.

(5) Sometimes, people disagree on how a certain event or experience should be commemorated. (6) Most war memorials in the United States pay tribute to those who served and died in war with towering white columns or heroic sculptures depicting the strength and bravery of service members. (7) However, the Vietnam Veterans Memorial, designed by American architect Maya Lin, broke the mold. (8) More than 58,000 names are etched into the walls; commemorating those who died in the war. (9) The black granite has a mirror-like effect, so people looking at the wall can see their own reflections and consider their part in the conflict or in history at large.

(10) The Vietnam War was controversial in and of itself, and the memorial was no different. (11) The design for the memorial did not overtly celebrate the war effort but rather encouraged viewers to draw their own conclusions about the reality of the war. (12) Many people protested the memorial's message, or lack thereof, and a more traditional bronze statue depicting three soldiers was added to the entrance of Lin's Vietnam War memorial. (13) For many, the Vietnam War was a source of shame; for others, it was still important to acknowledge the sacrifice made by those who fought.

(14) Today, the Vietnam Veterans Memorial is viewed as a groundbreaking and deeply moving structure. (15) In the past, war had been seen as a necessary evil, one that required sacrifice and heroism in the face of death and destruction. (16) But as reactions to the Vietnam Veterans Memorial demonstrate, American attitudes toward war are evolving as more people question the necessity and purpose of modern-day conflicts. (17) The war in Iraq was also controversial, and many Americans believed it did not have a clear purpose. (18) Accordingly, our collective memory, the way we decide to commemorate the experience of war, has also changed, prompting us to reimagine our country's relationship to war.

1. Which is the best version of the underlined portion of sentence 8 (reproduced below)?

   More than 58,000 names are etched into the <u>walls; commemorating</u> those who died in the war.

   A. (as it is now)

   B. walls. Commemorating

   C. walls, commemorating

   D. walls (commemorating

   > **The correct answer is C.** A comma is the best choice to set off a participial phrase when it comes at the end of the sentence. Choices A and B make the phrase "commemorating those who died in the war" into a fragment. Choice D would require a second parenthesis at the end of the sentence.

2. The writer is considering adding the following sentence.

   Lin's winning design for the memorial consisted of two black granite walls, partially buried in the earth, that meet at a 125-degree angle to form a "V" shape.

   Which is the most logical placement for the sentence?

   A. After sentence 7

   B. After sentence 8

   C. After sentence 9

   D. After sentence 12

   > **The correct answer is A.** Sentence 7 introduces Maya Lin as the winning architect and sentence 8 starts to give specific details about the memorial. The sentence the writer wants to insert gives an overall picture of the memorial's design and would help link the two ideas, so the most logical placement is after sentence 7.

3. Which sentence blurs the focus of the last paragraph and should therefore be deleted?

   A. Sentence 14

   B. Sentence 15

   C. Sentence 17

   D. Sentence 18

   > **The correct answer is C.** Sentence 17 unnecessarily introduces another example of a modern conflict that Americans disagreed on, taking the focus off the Vietnam War and directing attention to the more recent past. Generally, a writer should avoid introducing new evidence into the conclusion and should instead focus on summarizing the main points that have already been covered in the essay.

For more information on the writing placement test, see Chapter 4.

The Mathematics Placement Tests

On the ACCUPLACER, there are three multiple-choice math placement tests: the first covers arithmetic; the second covers quantitative reasoning, algebra, and statistics; and the third covers advanced algebra and functions. In this book, we have separated mathematics practice materials into chapters according to the test section they are most likely to appear on, but note that some math skills (like linear equations) may appear in more than one test section.

 You will not be able to bring a calculator with you to the exam; however, because the ACCUPLACER is a computer-adaptive exam, certain questions are configured for the use of a calculator. In these situations, a calculator icon will appear in the upper right-hand corner of your screen. In this book, for the three mathematics sections, feel free to use a calculator when you see this icon appear just as you would on your computer-based exam.

The Arithmetic Placement Test

The arithmetic placement test consists of 20 questions. You'll be tested on your knowledge of and skills in the following areas:

- Whole number operations (3–5 questions)
- Fraction operations (3–5 questions)
- Decimal operations (3–5 questions)
- Percents (3–5 questions)
- Number comparisons and equivalents (3–5 questions)

Questions will require you to compute the answers to various math problems, apply the order of operations, estimate and round as needed, compare and order values and recognize equivalent values presented in different formats, and apply mathematical problem solving to real-world contexts.

Here are two sample questions that cover topics you might expect to see on the arithmetic placement test.

1. Which of the following fractions is equivalent to $-7\frac{2}{3}$?

   A. $-\frac{9}{3}$

   B. $-\frac{19}{3}$

   C. $-\frac{23}{3}$

   D. $-\frac{72}{3}$

The correct answer is C. To change any mixed number to an improper fraction, multiply the denominator by the whole number, add that product to the numerator, and then take the result and report it over the original denominator. If there is a negative sign, ignore it until you report your answer. So, in this case:

$$-7\frac{2}{3} = \frac{(7 \cdot 3)+2}{3}$$
$$= \frac{21+2}{3}$$
$$= \frac{23}{3}$$
$$= -\frac{23}{3}$$

2. Chris has 75 apples, but 32% of them are bruised. How many apples without bruises does Chris have?

   A. 24

   B. 32

   C. 43

   D. 51

The correct answer is D. First, figure out how many apples are bruised, then subtract that amount from the total amount of apples. We know that 32% of 75 is 24 because 0.32(75) = 24. This means that 24 of the apples are bruised. So 75 – 24 = 51, which means that 51 apples are not bruised.

For more information on what will be covered on the arithmetic placement test, see Chapter 7.

The Quantitative Reasoning, Algebra, and Statistics Placement Test

The quantitative reasoning, algebra, and statistics placement test consists of 20 questions. You'll be tested on your knowledge of and skills in the following areas:

- Rational numbers (1–3 questions)
- Ratio and proportional relationships (3–4 questions)
- Exponents (2–3 questions)
- Algebraic expressions (2–3 questions)
- Linear equations (2–4 questions)
- Linear applications and graphs (2–4 questions)
- Probability and sets (1–3 questions)
- Descriptive statistics (1–3 questions)
- Geometry concepts for Pre-Algebra (1–2 questions)
- Geometry concepts for Algebra 1 (1–2 questions)

Questions will require you to work with rational numbers, use proportional reasoning, create linear expressions and equations, understand probability and set notation, interpret graphs, and apply mathematical problem solving to real-world contexts.

Here are two sample questions that cover topics you might expect to see on the quantitative reasoning, algebra, and statistics placement test.

1. Which two lines are parallel?

   A. $x + 3y = 6$ and $-3x + y = 2$

   B. $2x + 4y = 16$ and $-2x + 4y = 6$

   C. $x - 2y = 6$ and $6x - 3y = 24$

   D. $2x - 8y = 16$ and $-3x + 12y = 6$

The correct answer is D. If two lines are parallel, their equations will have the same value for the slope, m. Write each of the equations above in slope-intercept form to find the slopes of the

equations. The two equations for choice D can be written in slope-intercept form as follows:

$$2x - 8y = 16$$
$$-2x + 2x - 8y = -2x + 16$$
$$-8y = -2x + 16$$
$$\frac{-8y}{-8} = \frac{-2x + 16}{-8}$$
$$y = \frac{1}{4}x - 2$$

$$-3x + 12y = 6$$
$$3x - 3x + 12y = 3x + 6$$
$$12y = 3x + 6$$
$$\frac{12y}{12} = \frac{3x + 6}{12}$$
$$y = \frac{1}{4}x + \frac{1}{2}$$

2. A bag contains 3 blue marbles, 7 red marbles, and 5 yellow marbles. If Joanne picks 1 marble from the bag at random, what is the probability that it will be blue?

   A. $\frac{1}{5}$

   B. $\frac{1}{4}$

   C. $\frac{3}{4}$

   D. $\frac{4}{5}$

The correct answer is A. Use the probability formula: Probability $= \frac{\text{desired events}}{\text{possible events}}$. There are 15 marbles (3 blue + 7 red + 5 yellow) in the bag, so there are 15 possible events. The favorable event is selecting a blue marble. There are 3 chances for this because there are 3 blue marbles in the bag. Plug these numbers into the probability formula, and you get $\frac{3}{15}$ or $\frac{1}{5}$.

See Chapter 8 for more information on how to approach the quantitative reasoning, algebra, and statistics placement test.

Questions will require you to work with a range of equations and functions and may assess your ability to apply mathematical problem solving to real-world contexts.

Here are two sample questions that cover topics you might expect to see on the arithmetic placement test.

1. Find the factors of $x^2 - x - 6$.

   A. $(x - 3)(x + 2)$

   B. $(x + 3)(x + 2)$

   C. $(x - 2)(x + 3)$

   D. $(x - 6)(x + 1)$

The correct answer is A. To find the factors of a quadratic, use reverse FOIL. This quadratic is already written in standard form, $ax^2 + bx + c$.

Set up two sets of parentheses and determine the first terms, which should be the two factors of x^2: x and x.

$$(x)(x)$$

Now find factors of the c term (-6) that add up to the b term (-1). Since 6 is negative, these two factors will have different signs. The larger factor should be negative because, after adding the other factor, the result must be negative (-1). Factors of -6 are:

$$-6, -3, -2, -1, 1, 2, 3, 6.$$

The two factors of -6 that add up to -1 are -3 and 2. Therefore, the factors of the quadratic are:

$$(x - 3)(x + 2)$$

You can check the work by using FOIL on the factors to verify whether the result is the quadratic:

$$(x-3)(x+2) = x^2 - 3x + 2x - 6$$
$$= x^2 - x - 6$$

The Advanced Algebra and Functions Placement Test

The advanced algebra and functions placement test consists of 20 questions. You'll be tested on your knowledge of and skills in the following areas:

- Linear equations (2–3 questions)
- Linear applications and graphs (2–3 questions)
- Factoring (1–2 questions)
- Quadratics (2–3 questions)
- Functions (2–4 questions)
- Radical and rational equations (1–3 questions)
- Polynomial equations (1–3 questions)
- Exponential and logarithmic equations (1–3 questions)
- Geometry concepts for Algebra 1 (1–2 questions)
- Geometry concepts for Algebra 2 (1–2 questions)
- Trigonometry (1–3 questions)

2. Which of the following matches the value of x when $f(x) = \dfrac{1}{2}$ in the given function?

$$f(x) = \frac{3}{2}x - 4$$

A. $-\dfrac{13}{4}$

B. -1

C. $\dfrac{5}{3}$

D. 3

The correct answer is D. Plug $\dfrac{1}{2}$ in for $f(x)$ in the equation:

$$f(x) = \frac{3}{2}x - 4$$
$$\frac{1}{2} = \frac{3}{2}x - 4$$

Then, solve for x.

$$\frac{1}{2} = \frac{3}{2}x - 4$$
$$\frac{1}{2} \times 2 = \left(\frac{3}{2}x - 4\right) \times 2$$
$$1 = 3x - 8$$
$$1 + 8 = 3x - 8 + 8$$
$$9 = 3x$$
$$\frac{9}{3} = \frac{3x}{3}$$
$$3 = x$$

See Chapter 9 for more information on how to approach the advanced algebra and functions placement test.

THE WRITEPLACER® ESSAY EXAM

The WritePlacer is an essay exam designed to test your ability to effectively convey and develop ideas in writing. For the essay exam, you will be asked to read a short passage and then respond to a prompt on a related issue. In your response, you must clearly identify and develop your point of view on the issue at hand. You will be evaluated on the following criteria:

- Purpose and focus
- Organization and structure
- Development and support
- Sentence variety and style
- Mechanical conventions
- Critical thinking

Depending on your proficiency in each of these six dimensions, your essay will be a given a holistic score between 1 and 8, with 4 considered the threshold score for college-level readiness. Here, we've provided a sample prompt similar to what you might see on the exam.

Passage

> The COVID-19 pandemic upended our lives in numerous ways. I went into lockdown as myself but emerged as a completely different person, unrecognizable to myself. Suddenly, everything that I knew about life, about my family and my relationships, my work and my identity had changed. Everything mattered and nothing mattered. The world as I knew it was gone, and a new reality had taken its place.

Assignment

Has the COVID-19 pandemic made us more isolated or more connected to one another?

Plan and write a multiparagraph essay (approximately 300–600 words) in which you develop your point of view on the above question. Support your position with reasoning and examples taken from your reading, studies, experience, or observations.

For more information on how to approach the WritePlacer essay exam, see Chapter 6.

SUMMING IT UP

- The ACCUPLACER is designed to assess students' readiness for college-level classes in writing and math. To prepare for the ACCUPLACER, focus on learning the structure and format of the exam, and brush up on topics and concepts you've already mastered.

- The ACCUPLACER is an untimed computer-adaptive assessment that consists of five multiple-choice tests on reading, writing, and math. Additionally, the ACCUPLACER also includes the WritePlacer essay exam, which evaluates your writing abilities.

- The reading placement test consists of 20 multiple-choice questions. You will be given passages and asked to read closely for important themes, ideas, and relationships. You will also be asked to analyze texts rhetorically, synthesize multiple texts and points of view, and understand the meaning of vocabulary in context.

- The writing placement test consists of 25 multiple-choice questions. You will be asked to edit and revise nonfiction texts so that they more effectively develop, organize, and convey ideas and so that they conform to proper conventions of syntax, usage, and punctuation.

- The arithmetic placement test consists of 20 multiple-choice questions. You'll be tested on your knowledge of whole number operations, fraction operations, decimal operations, percents, and number comparisons and equivalents.

- The quantitative reasoning, algebra, and statistics placement test consists of 20 multiple-choice questions. You'll be tested on your knowledge of the following:
    - Rational numbers
    - Ratio and proportional relationships
    - Exponents
    - Algebraic expressions
    - Linear equations
    - Linear applications and graphs
    - Probability and sets
    - Descriptive statistics
    - Geometry concepts for Pre-Algebra
    - Geometry concepts for Algebra 1

- The advanced algebra and functions placement test consists of 20 multiple-choice questions. You'll be tested on your knowledge of the following concepts:
  - Linear equations
  - Linear applications and graphs
  - Factoring
  - Quadratics
  - Functions
  - Radical and rational equations
  - Polynomial equations
  - Exponential and logarithmic equations
  - Geometry concepts for Algebra 1
  - Geometry concepts for Algebra 2
  - Trigonometry

- The WritePlacer essay exam requires you to read a short passage and respond to the issue at hand in a 300–600-word essay. Your essay will be evaluated on the following six dimensions:
  1. Purpose and focus
  2. Organization and structure
  3. Development and support
  4. Sentence variety and style
  5. Mechanical conventions
  6. Critical thinking

You will be given a holistic score between 1 and 8, with 4 being the threshold for college readiness.

PART II
DIAGNOSING STRENGTHS AND WEAKNESSES

2 | ACCUPLACER® Diagnostic Test

CHAPTER

PART II

DIAGNOSTIC MATH

ACCUPLACER®
Diagnostic Test

ACCUPLACER® DIAGNOSTIC TEST

DIAGNOSTIC TEST

This diagnostic test is designed to help you recognize your strengths and weaknesses. The questions cover information from all the different sections of the ACCUPLACER. Use the results to help guide and direct your study time. At the end of each answer and explanation section, you'll find a chart to help you score yourself according to the ACCUPLACER test standards.

ANSWER SHEET: ACCUPLACER® DIAGNOSTIC TEST

Reading

1. Ⓐ Ⓑ Ⓒ Ⓓ   5. Ⓐ Ⓑ Ⓒ Ⓓ   9. Ⓐ Ⓑ Ⓒ Ⓓ   13. Ⓐ Ⓑ Ⓒ Ⓓ   17. Ⓐ Ⓑ Ⓒ Ⓓ
2. Ⓐ Ⓑ Ⓒ Ⓓ   6. Ⓐ Ⓑ Ⓒ Ⓓ   10. Ⓐ Ⓑ Ⓒ Ⓓ   14. Ⓐ Ⓑ Ⓒ Ⓓ   18. Ⓐ Ⓑ Ⓒ Ⓓ
3. Ⓐ Ⓑ Ⓒ Ⓓ   7. Ⓐ Ⓑ Ⓒ Ⓓ   11. Ⓐ Ⓑ Ⓒ Ⓓ   15. Ⓐ Ⓑ Ⓒ Ⓓ   19. Ⓐ Ⓑ Ⓒ Ⓓ
4. Ⓐ Ⓑ Ⓒ Ⓓ   8. Ⓐ Ⓑ Ⓒ Ⓓ   12. Ⓐ Ⓑ Ⓒ Ⓓ   16. Ⓐ Ⓑ Ⓒ Ⓓ   20. Ⓐ Ⓑ Ⓒ Ⓓ

Writing

1. Ⓐ Ⓑ Ⓒ Ⓓ   6. Ⓐ Ⓑ Ⓒ Ⓓ   11. Ⓐ Ⓑ Ⓒ Ⓓ   16. Ⓐ Ⓑ Ⓒ Ⓓ   21. Ⓐ Ⓑ Ⓒ Ⓓ
2. Ⓐ Ⓑ Ⓒ Ⓓ   7. Ⓐ Ⓑ Ⓒ Ⓓ   12. Ⓐ Ⓑ Ⓒ Ⓓ   17. Ⓐ Ⓑ Ⓒ Ⓓ   22. Ⓐ Ⓑ Ⓒ Ⓓ
3. Ⓐ Ⓑ Ⓒ Ⓓ   8. Ⓐ Ⓑ Ⓒ Ⓓ   13. Ⓐ Ⓑ Ⓒ Ⓓ   18. Ⓐ Ⓑ Ⓒ Ⓓ   23. Ⓐ Ⓑ Ⓒ Ⓓ
4. Ⓐ Ⓑ Ⓒ Ⓓ   9. Ⓐ Ⓑ Ⓒ Ⓓ   14. Ⓐ Ⓑ Ⓒ Ⓓ   19. Ⓐ Ⓑ Ⓒ Ⓓ   24. Ⓐ Ⓑ Ⓒ Ⓓ
5. Ⓐ Ⓑ Ⓒ Ⓓ   10. Ⓐ Ⓑ Ⓒ Ⓓ   15. Ⓐ Ⓑ Ⓒ Ⓓ   20. Ⓐ Ⓑ Ⓒ Ⓓ   25. Ⓐ Ⓑ Ⓒ Ⓓ

Arithmetic

1. Ⓐ Ⓑ Ⓒ Ⓓ   5. Ⓐ Ⓑ Ⓒ Ⓓ   9. Ⓐ Ⓑ Ⓒ Ⓓ   13. Ⓐ Ⓑ Ⓒ Ⓓ   17. Ⓐ Ⓑ Ⓒ Ⓓ
2. Ⓐ Ⓑ Ⓒ Ⓓ   6. Ⓐ Ⓑ Ⓒ Ⓓ   10. Ⓐ Ⓑ Ⓒ Ⓓ   14. Ⓐ Ⓑ Ⓒ Ⓓ   18. Ⓐ Ⓑ Ⓒ Ⓓ
3. Ⓐ Ⓑ Ⓒ Ⓓ   7. Ⓐ Ⓑ Ⓒ Ⓓ   11. Ⓐ Ⓑ Ⓒ Ⓓ   15. Ⓐ Ⓑ Ⓒ Ⓓ   19. Ⓐ Ⓑ Ⓒ Ⓓ
4. Ⓐ Ⓑ Ⓒ Ⓓ   8. Ⓐ Ⓑ Ⓒ Ⓓ   12. Ⓐ Ⓑ Ⓒ Ⓓ   16. Ⓐ Ⓑ Ⓒ Ⓓ   20. Ⓐ Ⓑ Ⓒ Ⓓ

Quantitative Reasoning, Algebra, and Statistics

1. Ⓐ Ⓑ Ⓒ Ⓓ   5. Ⓐ Ⓑ Ⓒ Ⓓ   9. Ⓐ Ⓑ Ⓒ Ⓓ   13. Ⓐ Ⓑ Ⓒ Ⓓ   17. Ⓐ Ⓑ Ⓒ Ⓓ
2. Ⓐ Ⓑ Ⓒ Ⓓ   6. Ⓐ Ⓑ Ⓒ Ⓓ   10. Ⓐ Ⓑ Ⓒ Ⓓ   14. Ⓐ Ⓑ Ⓒ Ⓓ   18. Ⓐ Ⓑ Ⓒ Ⓓ
3. Ⓐ Ⓑ Ⓒ Ⓓ   7. Ⓐ Ⓑ Ⓒ Ⓓ   11. Ⓐ Ⓑ Ⓒ Ⓓ   15. Ⓐ Ⓑ Ⓒ Ⓓ   19. Ⓐ Ⓑ Ⓒ Ⓓ
4. Ⓐ Ⓑ Ⓒ Ⓓ   8. Ⓐ Ⓑ Ⓒ Ⓓ   12. Ⓐ Ⓑ Ⓒ Ⓓ   16. Ⓐ Ⓑ Ⓒ Ⓓ   20. Ⓐ Ⓑ Ⓒ Ⓓ

Advanced Algebra and Functions

1. Ⓐ Ⓑ Ⓒ Ⓓ   5. Ⓐ Ⓑ Ⓒ Ⓓ   9. Ⓐ Ⓑ Ⓒ Ⓓ   13. Ⓐ Ⓑ Ⓒ Ⓓ   17. Ⓐ Ⓑ Ⓒ Ⓓ
2. Ⓐ Ⓑ Ⓒ Ⓓ   6. Ⓐ Ⓑ Ⓒ Ⓓ   10. Ⓐ Ⓑ Ⓒ Ⓓ   14. Ⓐ Ⓑ Ⓒ Ⓓ   18. Ⓐ Ⓑ Ⓒ Ⓓ
3. Ⓐ Ⓑ Ⓒ Ⓓ   7. Ⓐ Ⓑ Ⓒ Ⓓ   11. Ⓐ Ⓑ Ⓒ Ⓓ   15. Ⓐ Ⓑ Ⓒ Ⓓ   19. Ⓐ Ⓑ Ⓒ Ⓓ
4. Ⓐ Ⓑ Ⓒ Ⓓ   8. Ⓐ Ⓑ Ⓒ Ⓓ   12. Ⓐ Ⓑ Ⓒ Ⓓ   16. Ⓐ Ⓑ Ⓒ Ⓓ   20. Ⓐ Ⓑ Ⓒ Ⓓ

READING

20 Questions

Directions for Questions 1–18: Read the passage(s) below and answer the question(s) based on what is stated or implied in the passage(s) and in any introductory material that may be provided.

In this passage, Jane Eyre, 10, confronts John Reed, the son of the family that has been charged with taking care of the orphan Jane. In this scene, the narrator has just introduced John and his bullying tendencies.

(1) Habitually obedient to John, I came up to his chair: he spent some three minutes in thrusting out his tongue at me as far as he could without damaging the roots: I knew he would soon strike, and while dreading the blow, I mused on the disgusting and ugly appearance of him who would presently deal it. **(2)** I wonder if he read that notion in my face; for, all at once, without speaking, he struck suddenly and strongly.

(3) "That is for your impudence in answering mama awhile since," said he, "and for your sneaking way of getting behind curtains, and for the look you had in your eyes two minutes since, you rat!"

(4) Accustomed to John Reed's abuse, I never had an idea of replying to it; my care was how to endure the blow which would certainly follow the insult.

(5) "What were you doing behind the curtain?" he asked.

(6) "I was reading."

(7) "Show the book."

(8) I returned to the window and fetched it thence.

(9) "You have no business to take our books; you are a dependent, mama says; you have no money; your father left you none; you ought to beg, and not to live here with gentlemen's children like us, and eat the same meals we do, and wear clothes at our mama's expense. **(10)** Now, I'll teach you to rummage my bookshelves. Go and stand by the door, out of the way of the mirror and the windows."

(11) I did so, not at first aware what was his intention; but when I saw him lift and poise the book and stand in act to hurl it, I instinctively started aside with a cry of alarm: not soon enough, however; the volume was flung, it hit me, and I fell, striking my head against the door and cutting it.

(12) "Wicked and cruel boy!" I said. **(13)** "You are like a murderer—you are like a slave driver—you are like the Roman emperors!"

(14) "What! what!" he cried. **(15)** "Did she say that to me? **(16)** Did you hear her, Eliza and Georgiana? **(17)** Won't I tell mama? but first—"

(18) He ran headlong at me: I felt him grasp my hair and my shoulder: he had closed with a desperate thing. **(19)** I felt a drop or two of blood from my head trickle down my neck, and was sensible of somewhat pungent suffering: these sensations for the time predominated over fear, and I received him in frantic sort. **(20)** I don't very well know what I did with my hands, but he called me "Rat! Rat!" and bellowed out aloud. **(21)** Aid was near him: Eliza and Georgiana had run for Mrs. Reed, who was gone upstairs: she now came upon the scene, followed by Bessie and her maid Abbot. **(22)** We were parted: I heard the words "Dear! dear! What a fury to fly at Master John!"

(23) "Did ever anybody see such a picture of passion!"

(24) Then Mrs. Reed subjoined—

(25) "Take her away to the red-room, and lock her in there." **(26)** Four hands were immediately laid upon me, and I was borne upstairs.

Adapted from Charlotte Brontë, *Jane Eyre*. Originally published in 1847.

1. The point of view from which this passage is narrated is best described as a(n)

   A. young child communicating her emotions and perceptions in the first person.

   B. third-person narrator aware of every character's emotions.

   C. adult reflecting on her youth in the first person.

   D. third-person narrator focused on a single perspective.

2. The word "pungent" as used in sentence 19 most nearly means

   A. pleasant.

   B. odorous.

   C. pervasive.

   D. latent.

3. The narrator's tone and word choices suggest that the "red-room" mentioned in sentence 25 is a place of

   A. refuge.

   B. safety.

   C. sanctuary.

   D. punishment.

4. Based on the passage, the relationship between the narrator and John Reed can best be described as

   A. an abused child and abusive child.

   B. resentment from an adopted child toward a biological child.

   C. a healthy sibling rivalry.

   D. a parent and a disobedient child.

Passage 1

The following passage is adapted from a biography of the French writer Honore de Balzac.

Balzac worked hard. His habit, at this time, was to go to bed at six in the evening and sleep till twelve, and after, to rise and write for nearly twelve hours at a stretch, imbibing coffee as a stimulant through these spells of composition. What recreation he took in Paris was at the theatre or at the houses of his noble acquaintances, where he went to gossip of an afternoon. It was exhausting to lead such an existence; and even the transient fillips given by the coffee were paid for in attacks of indigestion and in abscesses which threw him into fits of discouragement.

Balzac's too great absorption in his writing forced him more than once to go into the country and recuperate his health. His iron constitution was not able always to resist the demands continually made upon it; and his abuse of coffee only aggravated the evil. To Laure he acknowledged that this beverage refused to excite his brain for any time longer than a fortnight; and even the fortnight was paid for by horrible cramps in the stomach, followed by fits of depression, which he suffered when suddenly deprived of his beloved drink. In his "Treatise of Modern Stimulants" he describes its peculiar operation upon himself. "This coffee," he says, "falls into your stomach, and straightway there is a general commotion. Ideas begin to move like the battalions of the Grand Army on the battlefield, and the battle takes place. Things remembered arrive full gallop, ensign to the wind. The light cavalry of comparisons deliver a magnificent, deploying charge; the artillery of logic hurry up with their train and ammunition; the shafts of wit start up like sharp-shooters. Similes arise; the paper is covered with ink; for the struggle commences and is concluded with torrents of black water, just as a battle with powder."

Adapted from Frederick Lawton, *Balzac*. Originally published in 1910.

Passage 2

Doctors have differed in relation to the sanitary properties of coffee. We will omit all this, and devote ourselves to the more important point, its influence on the organs of thought.

There is no doubt but that coffee greatly excites the cerebral faculties. Any man who drinks it for the first time is almost sure to pass a sleepless night.

Sometimes the effect is softened or modified by custom, but there are many persons on whom it always produces this effect, and who consequently cannot use coffee.

I have said that the effect was modified by use, a circumstance which does not prevent its having effect in another manner. I have observed persons whom coffee did not prevent from sleeping at night, need it to keep them awake during the day, and never failed to slumber when they had taken it for dinner. There are others who are torpid all day when they have not taken their cup in the morning.

The loss of sleep caused by coffee is not painful, for the perceptions are very clear, and one has no disposition to sleep. One is always excited and unhappy when wakefulness comes from any other cause. This, however, does prevent such an excitement, when carried too far, from being very injurious.

Formerly only persons of mature age took coffee. Now every one takes it, and perhaps it is the taste which forces onward the immense crowd that besiege all the avenues, and of the temple of memory.

Coffee is a more powerful fluid than people generally think. A man in good health may drink two bottles of wine a day for a long time, and sustain his strength. If he drank that quantity of coffee he would become imbecile and die of consumption. I saw at Leicester square, in London, a man whom coffee had made a cripple. He had ceased to suffer, and then drank but six cups a day.

All fathers and mothers should make their children abstain from coffee, if they do not wish them at twenty to be puny dried up machines. People in large cities should pay special attention to this, as their children have no exaggeration of strength and health, and are not so hearty as those born in the country.

Adapted from Jean Anthelme Brillat-Savarin, *The Physiology of Taste*.
Translated by Fayette Robinson from the 1854 Paris edition and originally published in 1803.

5. The main purpose of paragraph 2 in Passage 1 is to offer

   A. narration.

   B. justification.

   C. exemplification.

   D. illustration.

6. Based on paragraph 2 in Passage 2, which is the most likely definition of the word "excites?"

   A. To promote a state of increased energy

   B. To cause strong feelings and emotions

   C. To bring out or give rise to

   D. To express happiness and joy

7. Which choice best describes the relationship between the two passages?

   A. Passage 1 mainly discusses coffee's effect on an individual, while Passage 2 mainly discusses coffee's effect on children.

   B. Passage 1 presents a personal perspective on coffee use, while Passage 2 presents a general perspective on coffee use.

   C. Passage 1 focuses on France, while Passage 2 focuses on all of Europe.

   D. Passage 1 is an objective report, while Passage 2 is a more subjective report.

8. Given the evidence in both passages, with which statement would the authors of both passages most likely agree?

   A. Coffee is a plague on society.

   B. Coffee can generate useful energy.

   C. Coffee, like any drug, should be regulated or outlawed.

   D. Coffee can be an instigator of artistic achievement.

2

To calculate a fare, ride-hailing apps rely on mobile devices for determining the vehicle's movements and travel time, and to access the company's proprietary software. In contrast, traditional taxis have hardware components installed that measure time and distance and feed the data to a taximeter. The National Institute of Standards and Technology (NIST) recently published a draft set of standards created by a NIST-led working group that proposes measurements and procedures that states could adopt for equal and fair regulations for both software-based ride-hailing services and traditional taxi services.

If adopted, the standards should help ensure that ride-hailing vehicles and taxis provide accurate data for ride distance and time, and therefore, accurate fares.

"For me, the most difficult aspect of developing the new standard was that we are not using a physical measuring system located in the vehicle to measure the distance, but are relying on the company's software, as well as satellite- and cellular-based networks," said NIST's John Barton, technical advisor to the group that developed the proposed code. "There's no precedent for determining the accuracy of the combination of GPS and a ride-hailing company's software to determine travel distance," he added.

For example, both types of transportation services are evaluated based on distance traveled and time elapsed—measurements that can be traced back to NIST standards. Regulatory officials compare a certified measurement of distance and/or time to information obtained from receipts for the ride-hailing vehicles and to displayed information on taximeters. Inspectors also check for any violations of other portions of the standards, such as improper information posted in the cars or broken displays.

The standards also address how information such as base fares and rates for time and distance is presented to operators and riders, and how the devices and systems are designed.

Adapted from "New Standard Aims to Ensure Accurate Fares in Both Ride-Hailing Technology and Traditional Taxi Services" February 15, 2018. National Institute of Standards and Technology.

9. Which of the following does the author offer as evidence to support the claim in the second paragraph that "If adopted, the standards should help ensure that ride-hailing vehicles and taxis provide accurate data for ride distance and times, and therefore, accurate fares."

   A. "For example, both types of transportation services are evaluated based on distance traveled and time elapsed—measurements that can be traced back to NIST standards." (paragraph 4)

   B. "Regulatory officials compare a certified measurement of distance and/or time to information obtained from receipts for the ride-hailing vehicles and to display information on taximeters." (paragraph 4)

   C. "Inspectors also check for any violations of other portions of the standards, such as improper information posted in the cars or broken displays." (paragraph 4)

   D. "The standards also address how information such as base fares and rates for time and distance is presented to operators and riders, and how the devices and systems are designed." (paragraph 5)

In the summer of 2021, during a mission to excavate sections of the ancient Mayan city, Palenque, archeologists found a partial visage of an ancient statue in which a chin, nose, and parted mouth are visible. In 2022, researchers from Mexico's National Institute of Anthropology and History (INAH) asserted that the partial statue shows the likeness of Hun Hunahpu, the Mayan god associated with maize.

Maize, or corn, is indigenous to the areas of Central America the Maya had inhabited. It was not only a staple of the Mayan diet but also a critical symbol of the Maya people's spiritual relationship with the earth. Perhaps most importantly, the Mayans believed that humankind itself had come from maize, since their creation folklore included the idea that humans had been fashioned by the gods using white and yellow corn. In short, maize was linked to virtually all aspects of Mesoamerican culture.

Because of the god's association with such an important resource, the Maya worshipped Hun Hunahpu devoutly. Beliefs associated with Hun Hunahpu included the idea that every autumn, when the harvest came, the god would be decapitated, only to be reborn when spring came. This deep connection to the cycle of life and death as well as the changing of the seasons meant both Hun Hunahpu and the maize with which they were associated were central to Mayan concepts of time itself.

10. In this passage, the relationship between paragraph 2 and paragraph 3 can best be described by noting that paragraph 2

   A. offers evidence to support the claim that it would be useful to devote more time and resources to further excavations in Palenque, which in paragraph 3 the author relates to the archaeological significance of Hun Hunahpu.

   B. questions the assertions made by researchers at the INAH to set up a counterclaim about the significance of the archaeological findings in paragraph 3.

   C. details the importance of Hun Hunahpu in Mayan culture in order to emphasize why maize would have been significant to the Maya in paragraph 3.

   D. details the importance of maize in Mayan culture in order to emphasize why Hun Hunahpu would have been significant to the Maya in paragraph 3.

The following is excerpted from an editorial in a journal on higher learning and education.

On both an educational and sociocultural level, students who spend at least a month living and learning overseas glean much from the tapestry of experiences they weave while adapting to prolonged exposure to a culture. The longer a student is embedded in a cultural paradigm that is different than the one in which they were socialized, so multiplies the benefit for the student. Given the countless benefits of such opportunities, colleges would do well to bolster their international programs by providing an array of such opportunities to appeal to a diverse range of students.

Yet there can be no doubt that study abroad experiences are often limited only to those privileged enough to afford them. There seems to be pervasive thinking among college administrations that despite the benefits to students, these sorts of experiences are "extra" and therefore low priority when it comes to financial aid funding. This sort of thinking is outdated, and universities need to divert more resources to ensuring equity of opportunity for study abroad experiences within their student populations. The university benefits from providing more students such opportunities, since the casual learning that accompanies lived experience is valid and prepares students better for a career in a global society than traditional schooling alone. For this reason, it would also be smart for corporations who wish to hire well-rounded graduates to invest in scholarship programs that help promising students from less-advantaged backgrounds go abroad.

11. Which of the following would be a fair summary of the author's argument in this passage?

   A. Since studying abroad helps make students well-rounded, corporations who wish to hire well-rounded graduates should take responsibility for providing equitable financial aid opportunities for international learning programs.

   B. Since studying abroad helps make students well-rounded, universities should work harder to make sure these kinds of opportunities are available to all students, not just those who can afford them.

   C. The benefits that come from studying abroad are not worth the exorbitant costs involved in funding these opportunities.

   D. While it is nice for students to study abroad, these types of experiences are ultimately "extra" and should be a low priority when it comes to financial aid.

Cool is still cool. The word, the emotional style, and that whole flavor of cultural cachet remains ascendant after more than half a century. It is, according to linguistic anthropologist Robert L. Moore, the most popular slang term of approval in English. Moore says cool is a counterword, which is a term whose meaning has broadened far beyond its original denotation. For a millennium or so, cool has meant low in temperature, and temperature itself has long been a metaphor for psychological and emotional states (a cool reception, hot-headed). Chaucer, [as] the Oxford English Dictionary tells us, used [the word] cool to describe someone's wit, Shakespeare to say, "More than cool reason ever comprehends."

But starting around the 1930s, cool began appearing in American English as an extremely casual expression to mean something like "intensely good." This usage also distinguished the speaker, italicizing their apartness from mainstream culture. As its popularity grew, cool's range of possible meanings exploded. Pity the lexicographer who now has to enumerate all the qualities collecting in the hidden folds of cool: self-possessed, disengaged, quietly disdainful, morally good, intellectually assured, aesthetically rewarding, physically attractive, fashionable, and on and on. Cool as a multipurpose slang word grew prevalent in the fifties and sixties, Moore argues, displacing swell and then outshowing countless other informal superlatives such as groovy, smooth, awesome, phat, sweet, just to name a few. Along the way, however, it has become much more than a word to be broken down and defined. It is practically a way of life.

Originally published by David Skinner as "How Did Cool Become Such a Big Deal?" in the July/August 2014 edition of *Humanities* magazine, a publication of the National Endowment for the Humanities.

12. This passage most strongly suggests that the word "cool"

   A. is an outdated trend.

   B. is an adjective that describes something low in temperature.

   C. is hard to describe yet easily understood.

   D. only has one clear definition.

The preliminary terror, which chokes off most students from even attempting to learn calculus, can be abolished once and for all by simply stating what is the meaning—in common-sense terms—of the two principal symbols that are used in calculus.

These dreadful symbols are:

(1) *d*, which merely means "a little bit of."

Thus *dx* means a little bit of *x*; or *du* means a little bit of *u*. Ordinary mathematicians think it more polite to say "an element of," instead of "a little bit of." Just as you please. But you will find that these little bits (or elements) may be considered to be indefinitely small.

(2) ∫, which is merely a long *S*, and may be called (if you like) "the sum of."

Thus ∫ *dx* means the sum of all the little bits of *x*; or ∫ *dt* means the sum of all the little bits of *t*. Ordinary mathematicians call this symbol "the integral of." Now any fool can see that if *x* is considered as made up of a lot of little bits, each of which is called *dx*, if you add them all up together you get the sum of all the *dx*'s, (which is the same thing as the whole of *x*). The word "integral" simply means "the whole." If you think of the duration of time for one hour, you may (if you like) think of it as cut up into 3,600 little bits called seconds. The whole of the 3,600 little bits added up together make one hour.

When you see an expression that begins with this terrifying symbol, you will henceforth know that it is put there merely to give you instructions that you are now to perform the operation (if you can) of totalling up all the little bits that are indicated by the symbols that follow.

That's all.

Adapted from Silvanus Thompson, *Calculus Made Easy*. Originally published in 1910.

---

13. The perspective in this passage is generally that of a(n)

   A. expert simplifying a complex subject.

   B. academic adding to the literature on the subject.

   C. mathematician who admires alternative viewpoints.

   D. scientist studying a complex subject.

In recent years, anyone that has ever sat down next to a teen driver in the car, whether as a friend, a parent, or a driver's ed instructor, has likely been vigilant in ensuring that the teen first sets down their phone before taking to the road. When they do forget, one would hope that anyone else in the car would remind them, as texting and driving is the most common cause of fatal car accidents in the US. Thankfully, this information has been widely promoted since the dawn of the mobile phone, so statistics show that teens are increasingly more cautious about phone use while driving.

Despite the fact that most people who imagine a distracted driver are probably placing a teen at the wheel in their mind's eye, it is actually adult drivers who are at the highest risk for using mobile devices behind the wheel. A study shown in *USA Today* writes that while 98 percent of adults say they know texting and driving is unsafe, a whopping 49 percent of adults admit to nonetheless texting behind the wheel. In comparison, only 43% of teens admit to the same. Still, while teens may be less likely to text and drive, it's still true that a higher percentage of fatal car crashes involve distracted teens behind the wheel. It seems that the example must be set by adults first if there is any hope of quelling this unfortunate reality that affects all those on the road.

14. Of the following, which is the most accurate and descriptive title for the passage?

   A. "The Misconceptions of Teen Texting and Driving"
   B. "Adult Texting and Driving: A Menace"
   C. "The Dangers of Texting and Driving"
   D. "Teen vs. Adult Habits"

Sweden has been widely recognized for decades as one of the most socially advanced countries in the world not only for their economy, civil rights, and citizen worldliness but also for their approach to parental leave. While the US delegates decisions on parental leave to individual employers and companies, Sweden and other Nordic countries implement family friendly policies for new parents that provide ample support to workers at all levels. Swedish parents have access to 480 days total of paid parental leave, 390 of which they are entitled to 80% of their given salary and the remaining 90 to a flat rate. At least one parent in the family unit, which includes the father, is required to take 90 days of paid leave. Expectant childbearing parents with labor-intensive, strenuous jobs are entitled to further benefits before and after childbirth, and these same policies apply to parents who adopt, which has the added benefit of giving same-sex couples equal share in the benefits that come with parenthood.

Contrarily, American workers are given on average six weeks of somewhat paid leave with an equivalent to a less than 3-week salary. This benefit is also directly targeted at expectant mothers, leaving fathers without any benefits surrounding their newfound parenthood. It should be acknowledged, however, that while the American government has yet to take notice of such disparities in paid parental leave policies, corporations such as Apple, Bank of America, and more have implemented far more substantial parental leave policies that extend across the board to all eligible employees. There has been an upsurge in American business advocating for and implementing Scandinavian work-life balance policies, using their legal freedoms to make the change they'd like to see at the federal level. Still, the differences between Scandinavian parental policies and their American counterparts, while gaping, have been recognized by American businesses, and word of mouth has begun to spark the necessary changes.

15. With which of the following statements would the author most likely agree?

  A. American parental leave policies are without fault.

  B. Parental leave policies in the United States are no better or worse than Sweden's.

  C. The American government should adopt parental leave policies similar to Sweden's.

  D. Neither Sweden nor the US has adoption-friendly parental leave policies.

The Federal Communications Commission (FCC) is responsible for monitoring all radio waves and broadcasting media in the US. One of their policies requires broadcasting stations to be cognizant of something called the equal time rule in order to maintain their license. This policy requires all non-cable and radio stations to grant equal opportunities for airtime and advertising to registered candidates running for public office; the rates must be equal between candidates beginning forty-five days before a primary election and sixty days before a general election. A request for equal opportunity under this rule must be submitted within one week of the day an opportunity is initially given to the first candidate. For instance, if a talk show host were to grant 13 minutes and 7 seconds to a Republican candidate in the general election, then that same time must be granted to the Democratic candidate running opposite them so long as the campaign submits the request within one week of the day the other candidate appears on air.

---

16. The author uses the talk show host example to

  A. advocate for talk show hosts.

  B. convey the scope of the FCC's reach in broadcasting.

  C. give an example of the equal time rule in action.

  D. provide visualization for the role of the FCC on TV.

Labrador retrievers are known for their affectionate, outgoing personalities that have helped them retain their title as the top-rated dog breed in America since 1991. Praised as the ideal family dog, Labrador retrievers have a long history of companionably serving their humans. While the name Labrador retriever was coined in England, the breed itself originates from Newfoundland, though it is always assumed that the name is derived from the province of Labrador in Canada. In fact, they were originally christened Lesser Water dogs, as they are the combination of small water dogs and Newfoundlands. Intended as fishing dogs, for their fur was short and their paws webbed, these dogs were bred as excellent swimmers, runners, and eventually hunting dogs. In the 1830's, English nobility, such as the Earl of Malmesbury and Duke of Buccleuch, saw the breed in action and decided to take them back to England, shifting the breed closer to the role of a "family dog." By this time, the Labrador retriever had received its new name, and the breed became an aristocrat's dog. That was until farmers and hunters from the United States learned of the breed in the early 1900s and began incorporating the dogs into their everyday lives. By 1917, the Labrador retriever was recognized by the American Kennel Club and has since grown to become the adoring and adorable companion we all know and love.

17. The primary purpose of this passage is to

    A. provide historical background for a beloved, famous dog breed.

    B. disprove common misconceptions made about Labrador retrievers.

    C. advocate for the use of Labrador retrievers as hunting dogs.

    D. explain the appeal of Labrador retrievers as pets.

Typical airport runways have a length running between 8,000 and 13,000 feet. Planes must take off at the end of the runway, so many commercial pilots look for "distance remaining markers." A distance remaining marker that bears the number "4" indicates 4,000 feet left on the runway, while a "3" indicates 3,000 feet and so on. Understanding these and other visual cues associated with safe takeoffs and landings is part of the basic career training that hopeful pilots receive before ever setting foot inside a cockpit.

18. The information in the passage indicates that

    A. there are no airport runways that run under 13,000 feet.

    B. the longest airport runway is 13,000 feet.

    C. a distance remaining marker indicates how far the plane has traveled on the runway.

    D. a distance remaining marker bearing the number 7 indicates that the plane has 7,000 feet remaining to travel before takeoff.

Directions for Questions 19 and 20: The following sentences have a blank indicating that something has been left out. Beneath each sentence are four words or phrases. Choose the word or phrase that, when inserted in the sentence, best fits the meaning of the sentence as a whole.

19. The construction on the job had lasted forever, and the homeowners were not _____ the work, so they fired the contractor.

    A. signified by

    B. satisfied with

    C. unpleased with

    D. livid with

20. The fact that the language was not rigid appealed to the young student; since it was flawed, there was less pressure to learn it _____.

    A. impeccably

    B. impetuously

    C. impecuniously

    D. inconveniently

WRITING

25 Questions

Directions: Read the following early essay drafts and then choose the best answer to the question or the best completion of the statement.

(1) The last fifty years have seen a slew of zombie-related media, starting with George Romero's 1968 *Night of the Living Dead*. (2) Books such as *Pride and Prejudice and Zombies*; *World War Z*; and *The Walking Dead* showcase the cultural influence of zombies, as their presence is now in everything from satires to graphic novels. (3) This recent infatuation might be the natural progression of a series of real scientific mysteries that give a little truth to the zombie myth. (4) Because a number of diseases may offer insight into zombie-like behavior and perhaps the spark of imagination that has seen the proliferation of all things zombie.

(5) Let's begin with an obscure tribe in the highlands of Papua New Guinea, located northeast of Australia. (6) In the 1930s, a group of Australian gold miners surveying the area discovered close to 1 million people living there. (7) One tribe, in particular, interested medical researchers. (8) The Fore tribe only numbered 11,000 or so, and yet each year close to 200 of them died from a disease they called kuru, which translated meant "shivering" or "trembling." (9) People attributed it to sorcery or witchcraft. (10) But one researcher, a medical anthropologist from the City University of New York named Shirley Lindenbaum, noticed that the disease primarily affected women and children younger than 8 years old. (11) At first, the researchers thought a genetic cause, but they eliminated this because it afflicted women in the same social group, but not genetic group. (12) What Lindenbaum discovered was that it had to do with funerals. (13) In many villages, in an act of love and grief, villagers cooked and consumed the dead person. (14) Lindenbaum theorized that this cannibalism was causing this mysterious disease. (15) The hypothesis proved correct, it is caused by an infectious protein found in brain tissue, which the Fore people would eat as part of the funerary ritual. (16) Biologists injected chimpanzees with infected brain matter; the chimpanzees grew ill and died. (17) It wasn't a virus, a bacterium, a fungus, or a parasite. (18) Rather, it was a twisted protein, capable of compelling normal proteins on the surface of nerve cells to contort just like them. (19) The so-called prions—or proteinaceous infectious particles—would misfold enough proteins to kill pockets of nerve cells in the brain, making the brain like a sponge, and causing a loss of control of the nervous system. (20) Hence, there is a connection between eating human brains and a strange disease that makes people shake and twitch, similar to popular manifestations of zombies.

(21) Such a tale is not unique. (22) In England, in the early 2000s, cases of so-called Mad Cow Disease had people in a panic. (23) Mad Cow Disease is an iteration of prion disease, a progressive, fatal neurological disorder resulting from infection from a prion. (24) It appears that Mad Cow Disease was caused when farmers fed cattle ground up bone and flesh from cows. (25) Essentially, cows were cannibalizing themselves and developing a neurological disease similar to kuru. (26) When people ate the cows, they developed a similar disease. (27) 231 cases of Mad Cow Disease were reported worldwide as of 2018.

(28) Both of these cases resulted from cannibalism of a sort and turned people and cows into zombie like creatures. (29) Perhaps it is this that has given writers the impetus to begin telling zombie stories, a popular genre today.

1. Which choice most effectively combines sentences 3 and 4 (reproduced below) at the underlined portion?

   This recent infatuation might be the natural progression of a series of real scientific mysteries that give a little truth to the zombie myth. Because a number of diseases may offer insight into zombie-like behavior and perhaps the spark of imagination that has seen the proliferation of all things zombie.

   A. (as it is now)

   B. zombie myth. As a number

   C. zombie myth—a number

   D. zombie myth; a number of

2. Which is the best version of the underlined portion of sentence 10 (reproduced below)?

   But one researcher, a medical anthropologist from the City University of New York named Shirley Lindenbaum, noticed that the disease primarily affected women and children younger than 8 years old.

   A. (as it is now)

   B. the disease primarily effected

   C. the disease's primary affect

   D. the disease's primary effect

3. Which is the best version of the underlined portion of sentence 15 (reproduced below)?

   The hypothesis proved correct, it is caused by an infectious protein found in brain tissue, which the Fore people would eat as part of the funerary ritual.

   A. (as it is now)

   B. correct, because it is

   C. correct, but it is

   D. correct: it is

4. Sentence 16 is reproduced below.

   Biologists injected chimpanzees with infected brain matter; the chimpanzees grew ill and died.

   The writer is considering adding the following text at the beginning of the sentence.

   To further test this hypothesis,

   Should the writer make this addition there?

   A. Yes, because it elaborates on the claim made at the end of the sentence.

   B. Yes, because it allows a transition from sentence 15.

   C. No, because it introduces details that are irrelevant to the paragraph's focus.

   D. No, because it fails to explain what a hypothesis is.

5. Which sentence blurs the focus of the third paragraph and should therefore be deleted?

   A. Sentence 21

   B. Sentence 23

   C. Sentence 24

   D. Sentence 27

(1) In 2010 Matthew Crawford, who holds a doctorate in political philosophy, wrote an unlikely *New York Times* bestseller called *Shop Class as Soulcraft: An Inquiry into the Value of Work*. **(2)** In it, Crawford writes, "I would like to speak up for an ideal that is timeless but finds little accommodation today: manual competence, and the stance it entails toward the built, material world." **(3)** Crawford, essentially, was lamenting the loss of the world of workers. **(4)** In the last fifty years the United States has seen a decline in manual workers, so much so that many employers are decrying their inability to fill jobs. **(5)** Crawford, and others like him, is pushing for the redefining of education to better suit the desires and needs of society, part of which can happen at the end of a vocational education. **(6)** This essay will consider vocational training at the secondary level.

(7) The 1990 Perkins Act defines vocational education as "organized educational programs offering a sequence of courses which are directly related to the preparation of individuals in paid or unpaid employment in current or emerging occupations." **(8)** A vocational education might come in one of three settings, at a comprehensive secondary school, area vocational schools, and full-time vocational high schools. **(9)** Vocational courses are categorized as agriculture, business, marketing, health, occupational home economics, trade, industry, technical, and communications. **(10)** Full-time vocational schools enroll about 10% of secondary students. **(11)** 97% of students will complete at least one vocational education course in their high school career, according to the National Center for Education Statistics.

(12) As the demand for highly skilled workers have increased, so too has the demand for vocational training. **(13)** Michael Bloomberg, in 2008 as the mayor of New York City, addressed vocational training, wanting it to offer a springboard for students not dedicated to a college path. **(14)** In his State of the City 2008 Address, he said, "This year, we're going to begin dramatically transforming how high school students prepare for technical careers in a number of growing fields. **(15)** Traditionally, such career and technical education has been seen as an educational dead-end. **(16)** We're going to change that. **(17)** College isn't for everyone, but education is." **(18)** Businesses have echoed this sentiment. **(19)** According to the Associated General Contractors of America, 75% of construction companies in the United States cannot find qualified workers. **(20)** The Bureau of Labor Statistics predicts that one-third of all new jobs through 2022 will be in construction, health care, or personal care. **(21)** A final statistic, this one from the US Department of Education, states that there will be 68% more jobs in infrastructure-related fields (think bridges and roads) in the next five years than there are people to fill them.

(22) It might be time, as Matthew Crawford stated, to rethink our notion of the value of work as opposed to the value of a college degree. **(23)** 30 million jobs in the United States with an average pay of $55,000 don't require a bachelor's degree.

6. The writer is considering adding the following text between sentences 3 and 4.

   Matthew Crawford was not alone in his lament of the decline of workers.

   Should the writer make this addition?

   A. Yes, because it moves from a specific person's critique to a more general critique.

   B. Yes, because it adds necessary details.

   C. No, because it blurs the focus of the paragraph.

   D. No, because it fails to explain what Crawford's lament is.

7. Which is the best decision regarding sentence 6 (reproduced below)?

   This essay will consider vocational training at the secondary level.

   A. Leave it as it is now.

   B. Revise it to "This essay will consider vocational training."

   C. Revise it to "A consideration of vocational training at the secondary level will be considered in this essay."

   D. DELETE it

8. Which is the best version of the underlined portion of sentence 8 (reproduced below)?

   A vocational education might come in one of <u>three settings, at a comprehensive</u> secondary school, area vocational schools, and full-time vocational high schools.

   A. (as it is now)

   B. three settings; at a comprehensive

   C. three settings: at a comprehensive

   D. three settings—at a comprehensive

9. Which is the best version of the underlined portion of sentence 12 (reproduced below)?

   As the demand for highly skilled workers <u>have</u> increased, so too has the demand for vocational training.

   A. (as it is now)

   B. has

   C. are

   D. was

10. Which is the most logical placement for sentence 23 (reproduced below)?

    30 million jobs in the United States with an average pay of $55,000 don't require a bachelor's degree.

    A. Where it is now

    B. After sentence 5

    C. After sentence 11

    D. After sentence 15

(1) We've all been there. (2) You're driving down a highway, maybe you're running late maybe you're not, you crest a hill and there you see it: a line of red taillights indicating that your about to descend into traffic.

(3) Traffic might seem simple at first—too many cars in too little space—but the science behind traffic jams is anything but simple. (4) The study of traffic flow is a subset of mathematics and civil engineering. (5) In order to assess traffic flow, these people study the interaction among all types of travelers—pedestrians, bicyclists, and drivers—and the infrastructure they utilize, such as highways, signs, traffic signals, and the like. (6) Traffic is complex, and is as dependent on human behavior as the number of vehicles or the roadway. (7) Humans react, which means that three drivers driving the same speed across a three lane highway may inhibit drivers and cause traffic, though the road in front of them is vehicle free. (8) Likewise, an impatient person cutting in and out of traffic could cause an accident leading to worse traffic, or a small accident becomes a major traffic jam as everyone else tries to get a look at the accident. (9) Also, humans cannot drive at a constant speed, and continuous speeding and slowing contributes to traffic. (10) There are actual mathematical principles involved in studying this and certain threshold parameters for defining traffic. (11) Stable flow, for example, is considered to be 12–30 vehicles per mile. (12) Once a road has more than 30 vehicles per mile traffic flow becomes unstable and a minor incident can result in major backup. (13) If vehicle density hits 185–250 vehicles per mile, you've encountered a traffic jam.

(14) While not as bad as some countries, traffic problems are also bad in the United States. (15) According to a report from 2001, Moscow is the worst in the world, followed by Istanbul and Bogotá. (16) In Bogotá, drivers lost 272 hours due to congestion, or 11.3 days. (17) One analytics firm, INRIX, releases an annual Global Traffic Scorecard, which pulls data from 300 million sources and over five million miles of road around the world. (18) In the most recent report, Boston ranked as the worst congested city in the United States, followed by Washington, D.C. (19) According to this report, drivers in Boston lost 164 hours in rush hour traffic. (20) This is the equivalent of almost a week (6.8 days) of their lives. (21) Boston was one of only two cities in the United States that landed in the top 20 of cities in the world.

(22) Technology has tried to answer the traffic problem. (23) One solution is a variable speed limit: when traffic density gets too high, an electronic speed limit sign can lower the speed limit in 5 MPH increments to optimize road space. (24) Today's apps, such as Waze and Google Maps, can help you avoid traffic by redirecting your route around it.

11. Which is the best version of the underlined portion of sentence 2 (reproduced below)?

    You're driving down a highway, maybe you're running late maybe you're not, you crest a hill and there you see it: a line of red taillights indicating that your about to descend into traffic.

    A. (as it is now)

    B. you're about to

    C. one is about to

    D. ones about to

12. In context, which is the best version of the underlined portion of sentence 5 (reproduced below)?

    In order to assess traffic flow, these people study the interaction among all types of travelers—pedestrians, bicyclists, and drivers—and the infrastructure they utilize, such as highways, signs, traffic signals, and the like.

    A. (as it is now)

    B. they

    C. researchers

    D. some

13. Which is the best version of the underlined portion of sentence 14 (reproduced below)?

    While not as bad as some countries, traffic problems are also bad in the United States.

    A. (as it is now)

    B. the United States also has bad traffic problems.

    C. traffic problems plague the United States.

    D. the United States sees its share of traffic problems.

14. Which is the most logical placement for sentence 17 (reproduced below)?

    One analytics firm, INRIX, releases an annual Global Traffic Scorecard, which pulls data from 300 million sources and over five million miles of road around the world.

    A. Where it is now

    B. After sentence 14

    C. After sentence 15

    D. After sentence 21

15. Which is the best version of the underlined portion of sentence 22 (reproduced below)?

    Technology has tried to answer the traffic problem.

    A. (as it is now)

    B. to uncover

    C. to remedy

    D. to solve

(1) The psychological study of motivation is a difficult research area: difficult to define the word, difficult to study the behavior, and made more difficult today as new technology disrupts how many psychological studies are conducted.

(2) One of the difficulties researchers of motivation have is defining it. (3) A consideration of the etymology of the word will tell you that motivation comes from the Latin *movere*, which means to move. (4) Ultimately, this definition simplifies an otherwise complex subject. (5) Researchers who study motivation typically define it as a set of interrelated desires, goals, needs, values, and emotions that explain behavior initiation, direction, and intensity. (6) It has been said that motivation is about energizing action and direction, as Ronnel King and Dennis McInerney define it in *Culture and Motivation: The Road Travelled and the Way Ahead*.

(7) The difficulty of studying motivation has diminished in recent years as new technologies have led to a schism in the research field, with some researchers who study motivation using the traditional methods of researchers—field notes, surveys, observation, interviews, artifact review—and those who adopt a neuroscientific framework, researchers who study the neurological and physiological bases of motivation utilizing technology such as functional magnetic resonance imaging (fMRI) machines. (8) Though their subject matter overlaps, striking differences exist in terms of training, journals, research methodology, acceptable evidence, and units of analysis. (9) The difference in research methodology can be striking. (10) A traditional researcher studying the motivation of a student would have observed the student in and out of a classroom, would have interviewed the student, and would have considered the interactions of the student with peers and teachers. (11) The cognitive neuroscientist, on the other hand, would have observed the student in a laboratory setting, with the student donning an electroencephalographic (EEG) cap or laying on a bed inside an fMRI machine. (12) These data will show changes in cerebral blood flow, event related waveforms, and reaction times while the student is presented with various stimuli, such as images or incentives. (13) With the first researcher, the situation is more authentic, but prone to the biases of the researcher; with the second researcher, the situation is inauthentic, but the data quantifiable, and less biased. (14) Both of these types of researchers offer valuable insights into the motivation of people, but a question for the future of the research area is how might these two groups communicate to offer a more robust understanding of motivation.

(15) Cognitive neuroscientists could take understandings of traditional motivation research and study them from a neuroscientific framework. (16) For example, one interesting study on motivation that linked identity and motivation was the simple use of noun wording, because nouns signal who we are, how we identify. (17) Noun wording is saying, for example, "I am a baseball player" rather than "I play baseball." (18) The study on noun wording, performed by Bryan, Walton, Rogers, and Dweck, asked participants how much they cared about being a voter (noun wording) or how much they cared about voting (verb wording). (19) Those participants who identified with the noun wording were more likely to vote in an upcoming election. (20) To extend this, identifying with a group can also be motivating, as another study found. (21) In this study, students who were identified as part of a numbers group showed greater persistence in completing a math problem than an individual identified as a numbers person. (22) It seems that membership in a group can be motivating. (23) This research was conducted by Walton, Cohen, Cwir, and Spencer in 2012. (24) This is just a small sampling of the veins of research conducted in motivation.

16. In context, which is the best version of the underlined portion of sentence 4 (reproduced below)?

    Ultimately, this definition simplifies an otherwise complex subject.

    A. (as it is now)

    B. Nevertheless,

    C. However,

    D. At the same time,

17. Which is the best version of sentence 6 (reproduced below)?

    It has been said that motivation is about energizing action and direction, as Ronnel King and Dennis McInerney define it in Culture and Motivation: The Road Travelled and the Way Ahead.

    A. Leave it as it is now.

    B. Motivation gets talked about as energizing action and direction, as Ronnel King and Dennis McInerney define it in _Culture and Motivation: The Road Travelled and the Way Ahead._

    C. Ronnel King and Dennis McInerney define it in _Culture and Motivation: The Road Travelled and the Way Ahead_ as energizing action and direction.

    D. In _Culture and Motivation: The Road Travelled and the Way Ahead,_ Ronnel King and Dennis McInerney define it as energizing action and direction.

18. Which is the best decision regarding the underlined portion of sentence 7 (reproduced below)?

    The difficulty of studying motivation has diminished in recent years as new technologies have led to a schism in the research field, with some researchers who study motivation using the traditional methods of researchers—field notes, surveys, observation, interviews, artifact review—and those who adopt a neuroscientific framework, researchers who study the neurological and physiological bases of motivation utilizing technology such as functional magnetic resonance imaging (fMRI) machines.

    A. (as it is now)

    B. has been mitigated

    C. has been exacerbated

    D. has been prevalent

19. Which is the best decision regarding the opening of sentence 10 (reproduced below)?

    A traditional researcher studying the motivation of a student would have observed the student in and out of a classroom, would have interviewed the student, and would have considered the interactions of the student with peers and teachers.

    A. (as it is now)

    B. And yet,

    C. However,

    D. For example,

20. Which choice most effectively combines sentences 23 and 24 (reproduced below) at the underlined portion?

    This research was conducted by Walton, Cohen, Cwir, and Spencer in 2012. This is just a small sampling of the veins of research conducted in motivation.

    A. in 2012, and this is

    B. in 2012, just a

    C. in 2012, this is

    D. in 2012, yet this is

(1) Though I had a fine education—private high school, college, graduate school—I emerged, at twenty-three, without the ability to write, stymied by simple grammatical matters such as a comma splice, a grammatical flaw made embarrassingly clear by a college professor in a graduate level English course; or more weighty matters such as specificity, saying that glowy thing when I meant lightning bug. (2) How I managed to graduate might be an indictment of the educational system, which seems to suffer the slings and arrows of everyone, or it might be more personal, a celebration of sloth: for twenty years I did what I had to do, nothing more. (3) So it was a strange undertaking, an odyssey in the purest sense of the word, when I decided that to find purpose and insure my future I should become a writer.

(4) My literary rejections are legion. (5) They came on small slips of paper and standard 8 1/2 by 11 sheets; they came in blues and reds; they had trite messages ("Not for this magazine"); they had kind handwritten words ("Loved your writing, please send us something else"); they destroyed me, they elevated me. (6) I egotistically sent my first journalistic idea to *Esquire* magazine because this was where the big boys played. (7) My meekness marked each word of the query letter: "I have run with the bulls and eaten the heart of a killed bull in Pamplona and can tell this story to your reader." (8) This half-fabulation and half-truth was littered with stylistic inconsistencies and extraordinarily stale thought. (9) The editor summarily rejected it without a peep.

(10) Cowed by rejection after rejection, with the advice of my mentor the writer Roland Merullo in my head, I sat down to learn to write and spent ten years writing, averaging three hours a day, most days, and even took up the teaching of writing. (11) Those three hours, over a ten-year time period, equated to 10,950 hours of practice. (12) My teaching of writing at the time was an ironic position, as deep inside I still knew little about writing, my presence in front of students a farce. (13) I did get them to love writing as much as I did, but struggled to find words to help them on their own journey, as I still knew little.

21. Which is the most logical placement for sentence 4 (reproduced below)?

    My literary rejections are legion.

    A. Where it is now
    B. After sentence 5
    C. After sentence 8
    D. After sentence 9

22. Sentence 6 is reproduced below.

I egotistically sent my first journalistic idea to Esquire *magazine because this was where the big boys played.*

The writer is considering adding the following text at the end of the sentence.

like the famous authors Hemingway, Mailer, Updike

Should the writer make this addition here?

A. Yes, because it provides specific examples.

B. Yes, because it establishes historical precedent.

C. No, because it introduces details that are irrelevant to the paragraph's focus.

D. No, because it fails to explain who these names are.

23. In sentence 7 (reproduced below), the writer wants to echo their sentiment from sentence 6. Which version of the underlined portion best accomplishes that goal?

My <u>meekness</u> marked each word of the query letter: "I have run with the bulls and eaten the heart of a killed bull in Pamplona and can tell this story to your reader."

A. (as it is now)

B. deference

C. hubris

D. attitude

24. Which is the best version of the underlined portion of sentence 8 (reproduced below)?

This half-fabulation and half-truth was littered with stylistic inconsistencies and <u>extraordinarily</u> stale thought.

A. (as it is now)

B. extremely

C. powerfully

D. DELETE it

25. Which sentence blurs the focus of the last paragraph and should therefore be deleted?

A. Sentence 10

B. Sentence 11

C. Sentence 12

D. Sentence 13

ARITHMETIC

20 Questions

> **Directions:** Choose the best answer. Use the space provided for any calculations.

1. Which of the following correctly orders the values below from least to greatest?

$$\frac{3}{100}, 0.33, 0.3$$

   A. $\frac{3}{100}, 0.3, 0.33$

   B. $0.33, 0.3, \frac{3}{100}$

   C. $0.3, \frac{3}{100}, 0.33$

   D. $\frac{3}{100}, 0.33, 0.3$

2. What is 25% of 80%?

   A. 20%

   B. 31.25%

   C. 32%

   D. 200%

3. What is $12.52, rounded to the nearest dollar?

   A. $10

   B. $12

   C. $12.50

   D. $13

4. Which of the following is equivalent to $\frac{5}{2} \times \frac{8}{7}$?

   A. $\frac{35}{16}$

   B. $\frac{20}{14}$

   C. $\frac{51}{14}$

   D. $\frac{20}{7}$

5. Camille wants to work $37\frac{1}{2}$ hours this week. She has worked $24\frac{3}{4}$ hours. How many more hours must Camille work this week to achieve her target of $37\frac{1}{2}$ hours?

   A. $12\frac{1}{4}$

   B. $12\frac{3}{4}$

   C. $13\frac{1}{4}$

   D. $13\frac{3}{4}$

6. What is the product of 16 and 18?

   A. 2

   B. 34

   C. 228

   D. 288

7. What is 8,740 + 685?

   A. 8,055

   B. 8,336

   C. 9,325

   D. 9,425

8. $\left(\dfrac{1}{4}\right)^3 + \dfrac{3}{4} \times \dfrac{1}{2} =$

   A. $\dfrac{49}{128}$

   B. $\dfrac{25}{64}$

   C. $\dfrac{7}{16}$

   D. $\dfrac{4}{72}$

9. $1.2^2 - 0.26 \times 0.2 =$

   A. 0.092

   B. 0.236

   C. 0.92

   D. 1.388

10. If the tax on a $30 item is $1.95, what percent is the tax rate?

    A. 15.40%

    B. 6.50%

    C. 5.85%

    D. 0.07%

11. A, B, C, and D are numbers. We are given that A > B, B = C, and C < D. Which of the following statements must be true?

    A. A = D

    B. B > D

    C. C < A

    D. D > A

12. Which of the following is equivalent to $\dfrac{26}{65}$?

    A. 0.26

    B. 0.4

    C. 0.5

    D. 0.65

13. 16 is 20% of what number?

    A. 3.2

    B. 32

    C. 80

    D. 320

14. If Sam buys 8.7 pounds of wheat flour and 3.33 pounds of corn flour, what is the total weight of the flour that Sam buys, in pounds?

    A. 4.20 lb.

    B. 11.03 lb.

    C. 11.04 lb.

    D. 12.03 lb.

15. A train car seats 72 passengers. If a train has 15 cars, how many passengers can the train carry?

    A. 870

    B. 1,070

    C. 1,080

    D. 7,560

16. Which of the following correctly orders the values below from greatest to least?

    $$0.45, 4.5\%, \dfrac{9}{2}$$

    A. $\dfrac{9}{2}$, 0.45, 4.5%

    B. 0.45, 4.5%, $\dfrac{9}{2}$

    C. 0.45, $\dfrac{9}{2}$, 4.5%

    D. 4.5%, 0.45, $\dfrac{9}{2}$

17. The fraction $\dfrac{80}{1,000}$ is equivalent to which decimal value?

   A. 0.8

   B. 0.08

   C. 0.008

   D. 0.0008

18. If $\dfrac{7}{5} \div \dfrac{1}{8} = f$, then the value of f is between which of the following pairs of numbers?

   A. 6 and 9

   B. 10 and 11

   C. 11 and 12

   D. 12 and 15

19. 35% of what number is equal to 21?

   A. 60

   B. 167

   C. 600

   D. 735

20. What is the value of 1.03×5.6?

   A. 0.5768

   B. 1.133

   C. 5.768

   D. 11.33

QUANTITATIVE REASONING, ALGEBRA, AND STATISTICS

20 Questions

Directions: In the following questions, work out each problem and mark the letter that corresponds to the correct answer. The answers and explanations will follow. You are only permitted to use a calculator where indicated by a symbol ( ).

1. The last five questions on Perry's math quiz include two true/false and three multiple-choice questions; the multiple-choice questions each have four choices, with one correct choice. Because time has run out, Perry answers these five questions by randomly guessing. What is the probability that Perry will answer all five questions incorrectly?

   A. $\dfrac{1}{256}$

   B. $\dfrac{27}{256}$

   C. $\dfrac{27}{64}$

   D. $\dfrac{11}{16}$

2. In Natasha's aquarium, the ratio of goldfish to guppies is 5 to 3. In Roy's aquarium, the ratio of goldfish to guppies is 7 to 4. If Natasha's aquarium has 10 goldfish, whose aquarium has more guppies?

   A. Natasha's aquarium has more guppies.

   B. Roy's aquarium has more guppies.

   C. Natasha's aquarium and Roy's aquarium have an equal number of guppies.

   D. Not enough information is provided to determine which aquarium has more guppies.

3. What is the distance between the points (1, 9) and (13, 4) in the *xy*-plane?

   A. $\sqrt{7}$

   B. -7

   C. 7

   D. 13

4. Which monomial below is a factor of $2x^2 + 4x - 30$?

   A. $(x - 3)$

   B. $(x - 5)$

   C. $(2x - 3)$

   D. $(2x + 6)$

5. Which of the following steps should be used to solve $11 = \dfrac{x}{8} - 3$?

   A. Multiply both sides by 8, then add 3 to both sides.

   B. Add 3 to both sides, then multiply both sides by $\dfrac{1}{8}$.

   C. Subtract 11 from both sides, then multiply both sides by 8.

   D. Add 3 to both sides, then multiply both sides by 8.

6. The perimeter of a given square must be more than 600 feet and less than 800 feet. Let l equal the length in feet of one side of the square. Which inequality below satisfies the stated requirements?

   A. $150 \leq l \leq 200$

   B. $150 < l < 200$

   C. $600 < l < 800$

   D. $10\sqrt{6} < l < 20\sqrt{2}$

7. Which of the following is NOT equivalent to $a^2 \times a^{-3}$ $(a \neq 0)$?

   A. a^{-1}

   B. $\dfrac{1}{a}$

   C. $\dfrac{a^2}{a^3}$

   D. a^{-6}

8. Which of the following linear equations is satisfied by all the x, y pairs listed in the table?

x	y
$3\dfrac{1}{2}$	-2
4	2
12	0

   A. $y = 4x + 12$

   B. $y = 4x - 12$

   C. $y = -4x + 12$

   D. $y = -\dfrac{5x}{2} + 12$

9. Which of the scatterplots below suggests a strong negative correlation between the two variables shown?

A.

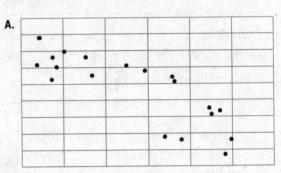

B.

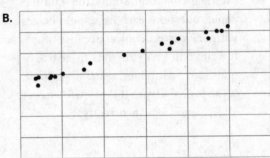

C.

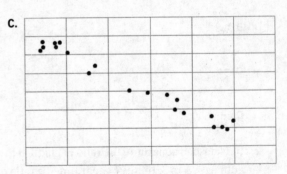

D.

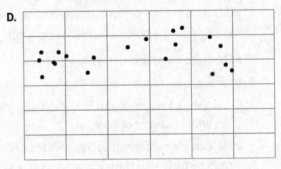

10. What is the median value of the data set shown below?

    {20.37, 6.12, 17.58, 10.08, 14.94, 21.45, 9.18}

    A. 10.08
    B. 13.79
    C. 14.25
    D. 14.94

11. If the area of a circle is 9π square inches, what is its diameter?

    A. 3 inches
    B. 3 square inches
    C. 6 inches
    D. 9 inches

12. What is the interquartile range of the data set represented by the box plot shown below?

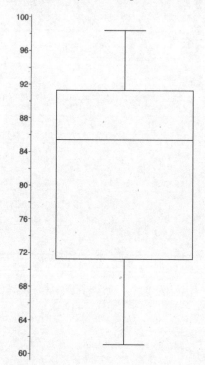

    A. 20
    B. 37
    C. 71
    D. 85

13. What is the area of the triangle shown below?

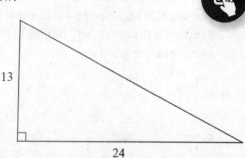

    A. 78
    B. 156
    C. 312
    D. 624

14. Which expression below is equal to $2\frac{1}{2}$?

    A. $\dfrac{6}{2} - \dfrac{-3}{|6|}$

    B. $\dfrac{-6}{2} - \dfrac{-3}{|6|}$

    C. $\dfrac{|-6|}{2} + \left|\dfrac{-3}{6}\right|$

    D. $\dfrac{|-6|}{2} + \dfrac{-3}{|6|}$

15. Which of the following is equivalent to $\left(\dfrac{x^3}{y}\right)^2$?

    A. $x^5 y$
    B. $x^6 y^2$
    C. $x^6 y^{-2}$
    D. $\dfrac{x^6}{y}$

16. If a stack of 16 bricks is 4 feet high, how high will a stack of 10 bricks be?

    A. 2 feet
    B. 2 feet and 3 inches
    C. 2 feet and 6 inches
    D. 40 feet

17. Briana rolls 2 six-sided dice, one red and one green. The sides of each die are numbered 1 through 6. What is the probability that the number on the red die will be greater than the number on the green die?

    A. $\dfrac{1}{3}$

    B. $\dfrac{5}{12}$

    C. $\dfrac{1}{2}$

    D. $\dfrac{5}{6}$

18. Which of the following is equivalent to $12 + 3(2 \div 3 - 6)$?

    A. −80

    B. $-\dfrac{71}{3}$

    C. −4

    D. 10

19. If a phone weighs 129 grams, what is its weight in kilograms?
    (1 kilogram = 1,000 grams)

    A. 0.0129 kg

    B. 0.129 kg

    C. 1.29 kg

    D. 129,000 kg

20. A homeowner spends $42,000 to remodel a kitchen and a bathroom. The homeowner spends twice as much on the kitchen as on the bathroom. Let k be the amount in dollars that it cost to remodel the kitchen, and let T be the total spent in dollars. Which equation below represents the total cost of the remodel?

    A. $T = 3k$

    B. $T = \dfrac{3}{2}k$

    C. $T = \dfrac{2}{3}k$

    D. $T = k + \dfrac{1}{2}$

ADVANCED ALGEBRA AND FUNCTIONS

20 Questions

Directions: In the following questions, work out each problem and mark the letter that corresponds to the correct answer. The answers and explanations will follow. You are only permitted to use a calculator where indicated by a symbol (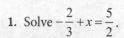).

1. Solve $-\dfrac{2}{3}+x=\dfrac{5}{2}$.

   A. $x=\dfrac{7}{5}$

   B. $x=\dfrac{10}{6}$

   C. $x=\dfrac{11}{6}$

   D. $x=\dfrac{19}{6}$

2. Which of the following is the equation of the line that passes through the point (–1, 2) and is parallel to the line shown below?

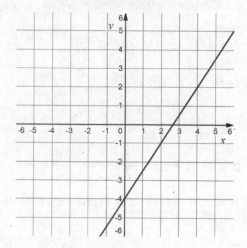

   A. $y=\dfrac{3x+7}{2}$

   B. $y=\dfrac{3x}{2}-4$

   C. $y=\dfrac{2}{3}x+\dfrac{8}{3}$

   D. $y=\dfrac{-2x}{3}+\dfrac{4}{3}$

3. Which of the following expressions is equivalent to $2x^2 - 20x + 42$?

   A. $2(x - 7)(x - 3)$

   B. $(x - 7)(x + 3)$

   C. $(x - 7)(x - 6)$

   D. $(x + 7)(2x + 6)$

4. If $f(g)=\sqrt[3]{g-7}$, what is $f(-20)$?

   A. 3

   B. –3

   C. $-\sqrt{27}$

   D. Undefined

5. Solve for x.
   $$\dfrac{2}{x-5}-\dfrac{1}{x+5}=\dfrac{4}{x^2-25}, x \neq 5 \text{ and } x \neq -5.$$

   A. $x = -11$

   B. $x=-\dfrac{1}{3}$

   C. $x = 10$

   D. There is no real solution.

6. Three of the expressions below are equivalent. Which expression is NOT equivalent to any of the others?

   A. $(x + 1)(x - 6)(2x - 1)$

   B. $2x^3 - 11x^2 - 7x + 6$

   C. $x(x(2x - 11) - 7) + 6$

   D. $(x - 11)(x^2 - 7x) + 6$

7. A patient consumes a 400-milligram dose of aspirin. The amount of aspirin in the patient's system decreases by one half every 3 hours. Which of the following equations gives the amount in milligrams of aspirin in the bloodstream, a, after h hours?

   A. $a = 400\left(\dfrac{1}{2}\right)^{3h}$

   B. $a = 400\left(\dfrac{1}{2}\right)^{\frac{h}{3}}$

   C. $a = 400\left(\dfrac{3}{2}\right)^{h}$

   D. $a = 400\left(\dfrac{h}{3}\right)^{\frac{1}{2}}$

8. What is the length of the hypotenuse of a right triangle with leg lengths 5 and 12?

   A. -17

   B. $\sqrt{17}$

   C. 13

   D. 17

9. What is 240° in radians?

   A. $\dfrac{4\pi}{3}$

   B. $\dfrac{2\pi}{3}$

   C. $\dfrac{\pi}{12}$

   D. 12π

10. If $-6x^2 + 5 = y + 2$ and $y = 0$, then which equation below is true?

    A. $x = \sqrt{-\dfrac{1}{2}}$

    B. $x = \dfrac{1}{\sqrt{2}}$

    C. $x = \sqrt{\dfrac{5}{6}}$

    D. $x = \dfrac{1}{2}$

11. Which of the following equations is linear?

    A. $\dfrac{2}{3A} + 5 = -5\dfrac{1}{3}x$

    B. $4^m = -16$

    C. $(4.62 \times 10^{-6})p = 0.0484$

    D. $4x^2 + 15 = 19$

12. Which system of inequalities is represented by the graph below?

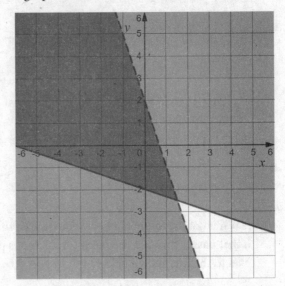

    A. $y \le -3x + 2;\ y > -\dfrac{1}{3}x - 2$

    B. $y < -\dfrac{1}{3}x + 2;\ y \ge -3x - 2$

    C. $y < -3x - 2;\ y \ge -\dfrac{1}{3}x + 2$

    D. $y < -3x + 2;\ y \ge -\dfrac{1}{3}x - 2$

13. Which of the following expressions is equivalent to $-x^3 - 2x^2 + 8x$?

    A. $-x(-x + 2)(x - 4)$

    B. $x(x - 2)(-x + 4)$

    C. $-x(x - 2)(x + 4)$

    D. $-x^2(x - 2) + 8$

14. What are the domain and range of the

    real-valued function $y = \left| \dfrac{x}{x-1} \right|$?

    A. domain = $\{y \mid y \geq 0\}$; range = $\{x \mid x \neq 1\}$
    B. domain = $\{x \mid x \neq 1\}$; range = $\{y \mid y \geq 0\}$
    C. domain = all real numbers; range = $\{y \mid y \geq 0\}$
    D. domain = $\{x \mid x \neq 1\}$; range = $\{y \mid y > 0\}$

15. Given parallel lines p and q, and that m$\angle A = 65°$, what is the measure of $\angle B$?

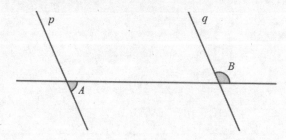

    A. 15°
    B. 65°
    C. 115°
    D. 245°

16. Which is a solution of the system of equations below?

    $$3x + y = 6$$
    $$3x^2 - y = 0$$

    A. $x = 1, y = 3$ or $x = -2, y = 12$
    B. $x = 1, y = 3$ or $x = 3, y = -3$
    C. $x = -1, y = 3$ or $x = -2, y = 12$
    D. $x = -1, y = 9$ or $x = -2, y = 12$

17. What is the domain of $f(x) = \sqrt[4]{6 - 2x}$?

    A. $x < 6$
    B. $x > -3$
    C. $x < 3$
    D. $x \leq 3$

18. The graph of $y = f(x)$ is shown below.

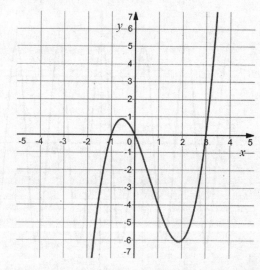

    Which of the following equations could define $f(x)$?

    A. $f(x) = x^3 - 2x^2 - 3x$
    B. $f(x) = -x^3 + 2x^2 + 3x$
    C. $f(x) = x^3 + 2x^2 - 3x$
    D. $f(x) = x^2 + 2x - 3$

19. If $2\log_5 x = \log_5 4$, then which of the following must be true?

    A. $5^x = \dfrac{625}{2}$
    B. $\log_5 x = \log_5 2$
    C. $x = 2$
    D. $x = 2$ or $x = -2$

20. Which equation is graphed here?

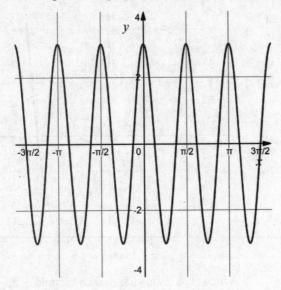

A. $y = 3\cos 2x$

B. $y = 3\cos 4x$

C. $y = 3\sin\left(x + \dfrac{\pi}{2}\right)$

D. $y = 3\sin 2x$

ANSWER KEYS AND EXPLANATIONS
Reading

1. C	5. D	9. A	13. A	17. A
2. C	6. A	10. D	14. A	18. D
3. D	7. B	11. B	15. C	19. B
4. A	8. B	12. C	16. C	20. A

1. **The correct answer is C.** The narrator is continuously self-reflective, which is an adult trait. If she were communicating via the persona of a young child, she would only be aware of her fear of John and would not be able to narrate the context within which his bullying occurred.

2. **The correct answer is C.** Of the options you're given, only two are synonymous with *pungent*—*odorous* (choice B) and *pervasive*. *Pervasive*, meaning "intense" or "inescapable," best matches the context in which the word *pungent* is used in the passage.

3. **The correct answer is D.** Throughout this passage, the narrator details the ways in which she is bullied by the family. John Reed, in quoting the mother, calls the narrator a "dependent," again suggesting that the narrator is a burden, a person worthy of punishing. Toward the end of the passage, she is "locked" in the red-room, which suggests a prison cell, not a place of refuge (choice A), safety (choice B), or sanctuary (choice C).

4. **The correct answer is A.** John Reed clearly demonstrates abusive behavior—in his antipathy, in his bullying, in his throwing the book at Jane, in his running "headlong" at her, "grasp[ing]" her hair and shoulder." Also, the narrator explicitly states that she felt bullied. In addition, it is clear that both of them are children as John Reed says to Jane "… you are a dependent, mama says; you have no money; your father left you none; you ought to beg, and not to live here with gentlemen's children like us, and eat the same meals we do, and wear clothes at our mama's expense."

5. **The correct answer is D.** This paragraph illustrates the effect of Balzac's "abuse of coffee," causing "horrible cramps" and "fits of depression."

6. **The correct answer is A.** The difficulty of this question lies in choosing, in context, the best definition of *excites*, for all the answers are correct usages of the word. The writer states that coffee "excites the cerebral faculties." The reader must choose the best answer for something that agitates the brain and that causes "sleepless nights." The expressions in choices B, C, and D are all characteristics of *excites*, but the best choice, based on the contextual evidence of "sleepless nights," is choice A because increased energy would contribute to sleepless nights.

7. **The correct answer is B.** The first passage, which offers an extended quotation from Balzac's writing, focuses on the effect of coffee on the one man, while the second passage focuses on all of society. While the first passage does speak about coffee's effect on an individual, choice A is incorrect because the writer discusses coffee's use throughout society, not just on children in the second passage. This is evident when he writes "I have observed persons," "one is always excited," and "a man in good health," portraying his wide range in considering coffee users. Choice C is incorrect because the first passage makes no mention of place names, and the second passage mentions Leicester Square in London; there is no evidence offered that Passage 1 is set in France, and it would be too broad an inference to go from one city or country to all of Europe. Choice D is incorrect because both passages are subjective. Passage 1 tells of Balzac's life and quotes extensively

from an essay Balzac wrote that is ripe with figurative language, and the last eight lines of Passage 1 are an extended metaphor—indications of the subjectivity of the writing.

8. **The correct answer is B.** In Passage 1, Balzac compares the effects of coffee to a "Grand Army" on the battlefield, galloping and giving rise to "similes" and "torrents of black water." Passage 2 details the positive effects of coffee, such as that it "excites the cerebral faculties" and makes perceptions "clear." We can safely conclude that the authors would both agree that coffee can generate useful energy.

9. **The correct answer is A.** Choice A is the only statement that provides evidence for the claim that adopting standards will ensure accurate fares. By saying that "both types of transportation services are evaluated based on distance traveled and time elapsed," the author is emphasizing how accurate recording of two data points—distance traveled and time elapsed—will allow for standardization and, consequently, accuracy of fares. Choices B and C are not directly concerned with accurate fares. Choice D addresses how new standards will address the problem but does not offer evidence of solving the problem.

10. **The correct answer is D.** The purpose of paragraph 2 is to detail the importance of maize in Mayan culture as a way of emphasizing Hun Hunahpu's importance to the Maya. Accordingly, the author expands upon Hun Hunahpu's importance to the Maya in the paragraph that follows.

11. **The correct answer is B.** Choice B is the only summary that adequately restates the author's main idea, which is that since international programs help make students more well-rounded, universities should invest more resources to make these opportunities available to a wider array of students.

12. **The correct answer is C.** The author delineates many of the "possible meanings" of *cool*, such as "self-possessed, quietly disdainful, morally good," and then further states that it has "become much more than a word to be broken down and defined." If the word does not need to be defined, it is

universally understood, making choice C the best answer. Choice A is incorrect because the author specifically states that "cool" has become a "way of life" and, starting in the 1930s and continuing today, has been embraced by culture. Choice B is incorrect because it restates the definition of *cool* as a temperature, which the author outlines in paragraph 1, but then details how it has broadened to mean something "intensely good" and is no longer simply an indication of temperature. Choice D is incorrect as the author states "cool's range of possible meanings exploded."

13. **The correct answer is A.** Thompson sets out to simplify calculus, a subject that induces "terror" and which "chokes off most students from even attempting" it. He then states that he will "abolish" this fear and offer "common sense" to understand it, all indications that he is an expert simplifying a complex subject.

14. **The correct answer is A.** The primary focus of the passage is the idea that while teens are suspected to be the prime culprits of texting while driving, adults are actually more likely to be the ones doing so. Therefore, "The Misconceptions of Teen Texting and Driving" is the best of the options you're given. All of the other titles are either too broad or do not address the main idea of the passage.

15. **The correct answer is C.** The author spends the majority of paragraph 1 listing Swedish parental leave policies and why they are sound. They then contrast Sweden's policies with the comparatively less accommodating policies of the US in paragraph 2. The author also praises corporations for "implementing Scandinavian work-life balance policies" and suggests that these new policies may "spark the necessary changes" needed at the federal level. Consequently, you can infer that the author would agree with the sentiment that the US should borrow parental leave policy ideas from Sweden.

16. **The correct answer is C.** The author uses the talk show host example to provide a real-life example of how the equal time action rule is deployed.

17. **The correct answer is A.** The primary purpose of this passage is to provide historical background on Labrador retrievers as a breed. There is no attempt to disprove common misconceptions about Labradors (choice B) or advocate for the use of Labradors as hunting dogs (choice C). You might be able to infer from what's written why Labradors appeal to people (choice D), but this is not the primary purpose of the passage.

18. **The correct answer is D.** The passage provides you with enough information to understand that a distance remaining marker bearing the number 7 would indicate that the plane has 7,000 feet remaining to travel before takeoff. None of the other answers can be supported by the details of the passage.

19. **The correct answer is B.** If the homeowners were not satisfied with the work, firing the contractor would be a logical conclusion.

20. **The correct answer is A.** *Impeccably* means "in accordance with the highest standards." Learning that the language is "flawed" and, therefore, imperfect would reduce the pressure to learn it impeccably.

Score Yourself: Diagnostic Test

At the end of each section, add up the total number of questions you answered correctly, then compare your score against the chart, which provides a rough approximation of where you might land within the scoring band for the ACCUPLACER.

Reading

Total Number of Correct Answers: _____/20

Total # of Correct Answers	Approximate ACCUPLACER Score	This score corresponds with a test taker who…
8 or fewer	200–236	shows a beginner's knowledge and skills for college and career readiness
9–11	237–249	demonstrates skills and knowledge using somewhat difficult to moderately difficult texts by drawing inferences, locating a passage's purpose, integrating ideas from multiple texts, and using context clues to understand common words
12–14	250–262	demonstrates skills and knowledge with moderately difficult texts by understanding implicit information, determining the function of a passage's parts, making connections between texts, and using context clues to understand academic words
15–17	263–275	demonstrates skills and knowledge with moderately difficult to difficult texts by identifying the effects of word choice on tone, understanding point of view, making complex connections between texts, and using context clues to understand academic terms as well as uncommon and figurative language
18–20	276–300	shows advanced skills and knowledge with difficult to highly difficult texts by determining the complex function of part of a passage, identifying nuanced or challenging claims and counterclaims, and understanding an author's reasoning and use of evidence

Writing

1. D	6. A	11. B	16. C	21. A
2. A	7. D	12. C	17. D	22. A
3. D	8. C	13. B	18. C	23. C
4. B	9. B	14. B	19. D	24. D
5. D	10. A	15. D	20. D	25. B

1. **The correct answer is D.** The use of a semicolon to connect the sentences indicates that sentence 4 is of equal importance to sentence 3, which is appropriate in this case. Sentence 4 is not only necessary but integral to understanding the development of the writer's essay as this excerpt details two diseases that might offer insight. Choice A results in an incoherent sentence 4. Choice B repeats the incoherence of the original sentences, substituting the word *as* for *because*. An em dash, as used in choice C, is typically used for parenthetical information.

2. **The correct answer is A.** *Affect* is primarily a verb, and in this sentence, it is used correctly to convey that the disease is acting upon women and children. *Effect* is most commonly used as a noun meaning "the result or impact of something, or an outcome." Knowing the meaning and grammatical usage of similar sounding words will aid in choosing the correct answer in the proper context.

3. **The correct answer is D.** A colon can be used to explain or define, as it does in this case. The colon is used after an independent clause to explain why the hypothesis proved correct. Choice A leaves us with a comma splice. Choice B is incorrect because the word *because* is a subordinating conjunction used with a causal relationship. In this case, the relationship is defining rather than cause and effect; further, no comma is necessary. Choice C is incorrect because the word *but* is used for ideas that contrast, which is not the case in this sentence.

4. **The correct answer is B.** The addition of the phrase "To further test this hypothesis" creates a logical transition between sentence 16 and sentence 15, which explained the accuracy of the stated hypothesis. Sentence 16 then serves to further support

Lindenbaum's hypothesis by discussing the outcomes of animal testing with the infected brain matter in question. Choice A is incorrect because no claim is made at the end of the sentence, but rather a fact is stated: "the chimpanzees grew ill and died." Choice C is incorrect because the details are relevant to the paragraph's focus, which is the process that scientists went through to uncover this disease. Choice D is incorrect because the writer can reasonably assume that a person reading about this disease would be familiar with the word *hypothesis*. In addition, the writer has previously used the word *hypothesis*; if the author felt it needed to be defined, then they would have done so then.

5. **The correct answer is D.** Sentence 27 should be deleted as it moves away from the focus of this paragraph, which is how mad cow disease develops; it instead tells about the number of worldwide cases. Sentence 21 transitions from the previous paragraph, specifically about the Fore tribe and kuru, and moves the reader into the third paragraph, which is another example of a similar disease, making kuru "not unique." Sentence 23 explains the connection between mad cow disease and kuru, which are both caused by the prion protein. Sentence 24 tells how the cows were infected while also paralleling the narrative of the Fore tribe.

6. **The correct answer is A.** This sentence is necessary to help the reader transition from Matthew Crawford's critique to the wider critique of a lack of workers; it also successfully transitions by repeating the word *lament*. Choice B is incorrect because the sentence is not adding any details. Choice C is incorrect because the sentence doesn't blur the focus of the paragraph; it actually helps cohesion and the

shift from one man's critique to an industry critique. Choice D is incorrect because Crawford's lament has already been established.

7. **The correct answer is D.** A sentence such as this calls attention to the writing and should therefore be deleted. This eliminates choice A. Choices B and C essentially do the same thing as the original sentence. Choice B broadens the scope of the sentence by removing the restriction of "secondary level," while choice C merely makes the sentence wordier and changes it to the passive voice.

8. **The correct answer is C.** This question is asking a writer to properly use a colon to introduce a list after an independent clause. Choice A makes improper use of a comma before the items in the list. Choice B is an incorrect use of a semicolon, which generally needs to join two independent clauses. An em dash, as used in choice D, is incorrect because "at a comprehensive secondary school, area vocational schools, and full-time vocational high schools" is a necessary addition to this sentence, clearly illustrating the three settings where one would find vocational schooling.

9. **The correct answer is B.** The word *has* correctly agrees with the subject *demand*. The difficulty of this question lies in the proximity of the noun *workers* to the verb *have*, which might trick a person into selecting *have* (choice A). *Are* (choice C) is an incorrect verb choice. *Was* (choice D) changes the meaning of the introductory clause.

10. **The correct answer is A.** Leaving the sentence where it is provides the most logical placement, as it offers evidence of sentence 22's claim about rethinking the value of work. To move it after sentence 5 (choice B) is illogical as the case for the value of work has yet to be made, so the evidence would be out of place. To move it after sentence 11 (choice C) would not logically follow the progression of that paragraph, which informs the reader about what vocational training is and where a student might encounter it. Placing it after sentence 15 (choice D) disrupts the quote from Michael Bloomberg.

11. **The correct answer is B.** This question asks a reader to properly identify the correct version of the pronoun and the correct contraction/possessive. The best answer is "you're about to," which is the correct pronoun *you*, combined and contracted with the verb *are*. Choice A is the possessive *your*, which is incorrect. Choices C and D change the pronoun from *you* to *one*, creating a pronoun shift from the *you* used earlier in the sentence.

12. **The correct answer is C.** This question asks a reader to fix the ambiguous pronoun "these people." In this sentence, it is unclear who "these people" are. Choices A, B, and D do not make the pronoun any less ambiguous. Inserting the word *researchers* helps to clear up who is performing the study.

13. **The correct answer is B.** As it stands, this sentence has a dangling modifier, for it is unclear to what "while not as bad as some countries" refers. To clarify this, move the modified noun, "the United States" (choice B), closer to the modifying phrase. Choice C does not fix the dangling modifier. Choice D is not the best answer because, while the modifier is fixed, it doesn't use the word *also*, which makes the relationship between the first and second half of this sentence clearer.

14. **The correct answer is B.** The only logical choice is to place sentence 17 after sentence 14, before all of the facts and data from the study are presented. To leave this sentence where it is now makes it abruptly enter a paragraph that has already been discussing the study in the previous two sentences. To move it after sentence 21 does not fix this problem but makes it worse by placing it at the end of a paragraph that has pulled data from the study. To move it after sentence 15 does not fix the problem either, as it will now come after the fact was presented that "Moscow is the worst in the world, followed by Istanbul and Bogotá."

15. **The correct answer is D.** The difficulty of this question lies in a slight nuance of word choice. "To answer" (choice A) might sound correct, but a close look at the sentence reveals that something was a "problem." Problems get solved, so "to solve" makes

more sense. "To uncover" (choice B) doesn't work because the problem has already been "uncovered." "To remedy" (choice C) would be the best answer if the problem was medical in nature.

16. **The correct answer is C.** This question asks a reader to carefully consider the best transition word or conjunction from sentence 3 to 4. Though it's easy to define motivation as "to move," as sentence 3 does, it "simplifies an otherwise complex subject" as sentence 4 says. Sentence 5 then expands the definition exponentially, delivering on the promise of complexity from sentence 3. In context, then, choice C is the best answer because the word *however* suggests a contrast—in this case a contrast between simplicity and complexity. *Ultimately* (choice A) means "finally or in the end" or "at a basic level." In context, there has been no final definition of *motivation*, nor is it basic; rather, *motivation* is described as complex and difficult to define. *Nevertheless* (choice B) means "in spite of that." The previous sentence gives the etymology of the word *motivation*, so there's nothing to be in spite of. Choice D is incorrect because nothing is occurring at the same time.

17. **The correct answer is D.** A writer must properly signal into a paraphrase, put the words in the best order, and cite the authors and book, all while using the best verb. Choice D does this properly: it puts the authors closest to the action verb *define* so it is clear that they are doing the action. Additionally, this change also maintains a proper paraphrase of the source material. The sentence as it is lacks concision. Choice B uses passive voice. Choice C puts the book between the word *define* and the definition, making this choice confusing.

18. **The correct answer is C.** A careful reading of the sentence will show that the problem has worsened, or "has been exacerbated," as new technologies led to a "schism in the research field." *Exacerbate* means "make a bad situation worse." The bad situation has been previously explained—the unclear way motivation is defined—and this is worsened as new technologies have split researchers. In the context of sentence 7, "has diminished" (choice A) and "has

been mitigated" (choice B) are incorrect because the difficulty has not decreased or been reduced; rather, as the result of "new technologies," it has increased. Choice D, "been prevalent," is an odd sentence construct using an inexact word. *Prevalent* means "widespread in a particular area or at a particular time."

19. **The correct answer is D.** The question is asking for the best way to transition from sentence 9 to sentence 10. Since sentence 10 serves to illustrate the statement made in sentence 9 by using an example, the phrase "for example" is the best choice. Although grammatically correct, choice A is not the best answer since the lack of a transitional phrase makes sentence 10 sound abrupt. Choices B and C both imply a contradiction or contrast from one sentence to the next, which is not the case.

20. **The correct answer is D.** Choice D correctly identifies the relationship between the first and second sentence. The word *yet* contrasts with the first sentence—the single research study—with the multiple other studies out there, while also emphasizing the fact that there are many more studies. While choice A is grammatically correct, it does not emphasize the relationship between the first and second sentences. Choice B unnecessarily repeats the phrase "just a." Choice C creates a comma splice.

21. **The correct answer is A.** The author makes a claim—that they had a lot of rejections—and then supplies ample evidence in sentences 5, 6, and 9 to support that claim. Offering the claim after the evidence (choices B, C, and D) would impede the reader from seeing the relationship between the claim and the proof.

22. **The correct answer is A.** The examples in the proposed text illustrate who "the big boys" are while also supporting the idea that the author was egotistical, comparing their experience to three of the most famous writers of the twentieth century. Choice B is incorrect because the writer, who doesn't make it as a writer by the end of this excerpt, wouldn't have precedent with three writers who did make it. The details are relevant to the paragraph's focus, which emphasizes the writer's egotism, making choice

C incorrect. It can be assumed that a reader who chooses a personal essay about a writer's journey would be familiar with three famous authors from the twentieth century, so choice D is incorrect.

23. **The correct answer is C.** This paragraph focuses on the author's ego. The author writes about egotism and wants to play where "the big boys" play, implying their grand thoughts. *Hubris* means "excessive pride or self-confidence," making it the best word to keep this paragraph cohesive. The use of "meekness" (choice A) works against the egotism alluded to by the author. There is no "deference" (choice B) as the author doesn't defer to anyone. While *attitude* (choice D) may work to imply a way of being, this word doesn't capture the ego that the writer has.

24. **The correct answer is D.** With the limited context, it becomes difficult to choose between the adverbs offered by choices A, B, and C. Depending on the situation, they can act as synonyms. Thus, eliminating the adverb (choice D) serves concision and creates greater parallelism with the phrase "stylistic inconsistencies" (adjective + noun).

25. **The correct answer is B.** Sentence 11, doing the arithmetic for the hours spent, is interesting but does little to develop the topic of the paragraph or the theme of the excerpt. The other sentences are all relevant to the theme. Sentence 10 tells of the narrator's dedication to writing. Sentence 12 details the irony of a person who doesn't identify as a good writer becoming a writing teacher. Sentence 13 reinforces the idea of the author identifying as a bad writer who, nevertheless, was able to instill a love of writing in their students.

Writing

Total Number of Correct Answers: _____/25

Total # of Correct Answers	Approximate ACCUPLACER Score	This score corresponds with a test taker who…
9 or fewer	200–236	shows a beginner's knowledge and skills for college and career readiness
10–13	237–249	demonstrates skills and knowledge using somewhat difficult to moderately difficult passages and contexts by revising basic development and organization issues, using mostly effective language, and correcting basic mechanics errors
14–17	250–262	demonstrates skills and knowledge with moderately difficult to difficult passages and contexts by revising development and organization, using effective language, and correcting basic mechanics errors
18–21	263–275	demonstrates skills and knowledge with difficult passages and contexts by revising development and organization, using effective language, and correcting most mechanics errors
22–25	276–300	shows advanced skills and knowledge with difficult to highly difficult passages and contexts including sophisticated revision of development and organization, using highly effective language, and correcting most or all mechanics errors

Arithmetic

1. A	5. B	9. D	13. C	17. B
2. A	6. D	10. B	14. D	18. C
3. D	7. D	11. C	15. C	19. A
4. D	8. B	12. B	16. A	20. C

1. **The correct answer is A.** Write all three numbers as fractions with a common denominator of 100:

$$\frac{3}{100}; 0.33 = \frac{33}{100}; \text{ and } 0.3 = \frac{30}{100}$$

Now we can better see that:

$$\frac{3}{100} < \frac{30}{100} < \frac{33}{100}$$

So:

$$\frac{3}{100} < 0.3 < 0.33$$

2. **The correct answer is A.** 25% of 80% is 25% of 0.8, or 0.25×0.8. The result of that multiplication is 0.2, which is equivalent to 20%.

3. **The correct answer is D.** To round to the nearest dollar, check the digit to the right of the decimal point. If that digit is 5 through 9, increase the digit in the ones place by 1 and remove the decimal point and all digits to the right of it. If the digit to the right of the decimal point is 0 through 4, simply remove the decimal point and all digits to the right of it. In $12.52, the digit to the right of the decimal is 5, so increase the 2 in the ones place to 3 and remove 0.52. The result is $13.

4. **The correct answer is D.** Multiply and reduce:

$$\frac{5}{2} \times \frac{8}{7} = \frac{5 \times 8}{2 \times 7} = \frac{40}{14} = \frac{20}{7}$$

5. **The correct answer is B.** Rewrite the mixed numbers as fractions:

$$37\frac{1}{2} = \frac{75}{2} \text{ and } 24\frac{3}{4} = \frac{99}{4}$$

To find the number of additional hours Camille must work, calculate the difference between the number of hours she has worked and the hours she wants to work. Using a common denominator of 4:

$$\frac{75}{2} - \frac{99}{4} = \frac{150}{4} - \frac{9}{4} = \frac{51}{4}$$

Convert $\frac{51}{4}$ to a mixed number:

$$\frac{51}{4} = \frac{48}{4} + \frac{3}{4} = 12 + \frac{3}{4} = 12\frac{3}{4}$$

6. **The correct answer is D.** The product of two numbers is the result obtained when the numbers are multiplied. To multiply 16 and 18, first recognize that $16 \times 18 = (10 + 6) \times 18 = (10 \times 18) + (6 \times 18)$. Perform the multiplication within parentheses to get $10 \times 18 = 180$ and $6 \times 18 = 108$. Add these results to get $180 + 108 = 288$.

7. **The correct answer is D.** Moving from right to left: the sum in the ones place is $0 + 5 = 5$. In the tens place, $4 + 8 = 12$; record 2 in the tens place and carry 1 to the hundreds place. In the hundreds place, $1 + 7 + 6 = 14$; record 4 in the hundreds place and carry 1 to the thousands place. In the thousands place, add the carried 1 to 8 to get 9. So $8,740 + 685 = 9,425$.

8. **The correct answer is B.** Following order of operations, first evaluate the expression with an exponent, $\left(\frac{1}{4}\right)^3$, to get:

$$\left(\frac{1}{4}\right)^3 + \frac{3}{4} \times \frac{1}{2} = \left(\frac{1}{4} \times \frac{1}{4} \times \frac{1}{4}\right) + \frac{3}{4} \times \frac{1}{2}$$

$$= \frac{1}{64} + \frac{3}{4} \times \frac{1}{2}$$

Multiply before performing addition:

$$\frac{1}{64}+\frac{3}{4}\times\frac{1}{2}=\frac{1}{64}+\frac{3}{8}$$

Finally, use a common denominator of 64 to solve:

$$\frac{1}{64}+\frac{3}{8}=\frac{1}{64}+\frac{24}{64}=\frac{25}{64}$$

9. **The correct answer is D.** Following the order of operations, first evaluate the expression with an exponent:

$$1.2^2-0.26\times0.2=(1.2\times1.2)-0.26\times0.2$$
$$=1.44-0.26\times0.2$$

Then, multiply before performing subtraction:

$$1.44-0.26\times0.2=1.44-0.052=1.388$$

10. **The correct answer is B.** To determine what percent of 30 is 1.95, divide 1.95 by 30 and multiply by 100:

$$\frac{1.95}{30}\times100=0.065\times100=6.5$$

So 1.95 is 6.5% of 30, which means that 6.5% is the tax rate.

11. **The correct answer is C.** We are given that B = C, which means that we can replace B with C in any true equation or inequality, and it will remain true after the substitution. If we replace B with C in the given inequality A > B, we have A > C, which is equivalent to C < A. Choice A is not always true. While A *might* be equal to D, it is not necessarily. For instance, if A = 3, B = 1, C = 1, and D = 2, then the three statements given in the problem are true, but A ≠ D. Choice B is not true. If C < D and B = C, then B < D. Choice D may be true in certain instances but not necessarily always true. For example, it would be untrue if A = 3, B = 1, C = 1, and D = 2.

12. **The correct answer is B.** First, simplify the fraction by dividing the numerator and denominator by the greatest common factor, 13:

$$\frac{26}{65}=\frac{2}{5}$$

To convert $\frac{2}{5}$ to a decimal number, multiply the numerator and denominator by 2:

$$\frac{2}{5}=\frac{4}{10}=0.4$$

13. **The correct answer is C.** To say 20% of a number x equals 16 means 20% $\bullet$ x = 16. Since 20% is equivalent to 0.20, we need to find the value of x that makes $0.20x = 16$ true. Divide both sides of the equation by 0.20 to get $x=\frac{16}{0.20}=\frac{160}{2}=80$, meaning that 16 is 20% of 80.

14. **The correct answer is D.** Adding the weights of the two types of flour gives 8.7 + 3.33 = 12.03.

15. **The correct answer is C.** To determine the number of passengers on the train, multiply the number of cars by the number of passengers in each car:

$$15\times72=1,080$$

16. **The correct answer is A.** To compare the numbers, convert them to fractions with the same denominator:

$$0.45=\frac{45}{100}=\frac{450}{1,000}$$
$$4.5\%=\frac{4.5}{100}=\frac{45}{1,000}$$
$$\frac{9}{2}=\frac{4,500}{1,000}$$

Listing greatest to least results in:

$$\frac{9}{2}=\frac{4,500}{1,000}>0.45=\frac{450}{1,000}>4.5\%=\frac{45}{1,000}$$

17. **The correct answer is B.** The fraction can be expressed as follows:

$$\frac{80}{1,000}=\frac{8}{100}=0.0800=0.08$$

The digit two places to the right of the decimal point represents hundredths.

18. **The correct answer is C.** To perform division on two fractions, invert the divisor (fraction to the right of the division sign) and multiply the two fractions.

$$\frac{7}{5} \div \frac{1}{8} = \frac{7}{5} \times \frac{8}{1}$$

$$= \frac{56}{5}$$

$$= 11\frac{1}{5}$$

The number $11\frac{1}{5}$ is between 11 and 12.

19. **The correct answer is A.** We need to find the value of x that makes $0.35x = 21$ true. Divide both sides of the equation by 0.35:

$$x = \frac{21}{0.35} = \frac{2,100}{35} = 60$$

20. **The correct answer is C.** First, multiply the tenths place of 5.6 by 1.03:

$$0.6 \times 1.03 = 0.618$$

Next, multiply the ones place of 5.6 by 1.03:

$$5 \times 1.03 = 5.15$$

Add these two products to obtain the correct answer:

$$0.618 + 5.15 = 5.768$$

Arithmetic

Total Number of Correct Answers: _____/20

Total # of Correct Answers	Approximate ACCUPLACER Score	This score corresponds with a test taker who…
8 or fewer	200–236	shows a beginner's knowledge and skills for college mathematics, including basic skills with addition, subtraction, multiplication, and division of whole numbers; the ability to identify fractions and decimal values; converting fractions to decimals; and putting numbers in order from least to greatest
9–11	237–249	demonstrates skills and knowledge with addition, subtraction, and multiplication of decimals; addition and subtraction of fractions; and the ability to solve one-step application problems
12–14	250–262	demonstrates skills and knowledge with adding, subtracting, multiplying, and dividing whole numbers and decimals in solving multi-step application problems; solving one-step fraction problems; and taking percentages
15–17	263–275	demonstrates skills and knowledge with using order of operations with decimals and whole numbers, solving multi-step fraction problems, solving one-step percent application problems, and converting fractions to decimals with rounding
18–20	276–300	demonstrates skills and knowledge with using order of operations on fractions, mixed numbers, and improper fractions; solving multi-step percentage application problems; and ordering numbers based on computational results

Quantitative Reasoning, Algebra, and Statistics

1. B	5. D	9. C	13. B	17. B
2. D	6. B	10. D	14. D	18. C
3. D	7. D	11. C	15. C	19. B
4. A	8. C	12. A	16. C	20. B

1. **The correct answer is B.** The probability that Perry will answer a true/false question incorrectly by guessing is $\frac{1}{2}$. The probability that he will guess incorrectly on a multiple-choice question is $\frac{3}{4}$ because three of the four choices are incorrect. Because answering each question is an independent event, multiply the probability of answering each question incorrectly to get the probability of answering all five incorrectly. There are two true/false and three multiple-choice questions, so the product of the probabilities is:

$$\frac{1}{2} \times \frac{1}{2} \times \frac{3}{4} \times \frac{3}{4} \times \frac{3}{4} = \frac{27}{256}$$

2. **The correct answer is D.** In order to determine the number of guppies based on the given ratios, we need to know something about the quantity of fish in *both* aquariums. Based on the ratio of 5 goldfish to 3 guppies, and given that there are 10 goldfish in Natasha's aquarium, Natasha has 6 guppies in her aquarium. We are given no information about the number of fish in Roy's aquarium.

3. **The correct answer is D.** To find the distance between points (x_1, y_1) and (x_2, y_2), use the distance formula:

$$D = \sqrt{(x_2 - x_1)^2 + (y_2 - y_1)^2}$$

In the given case:

$$D = \sqrt{(13-1)^2 + (4-9)^2}$$
$$= \sqrt{(12)^2 + (-5)^2}$$
$$= \sqrt{144 + 25}$$
$$= \sqrt{169}$$
$$= 13$$

4. **The correct answer is A.** First, factor a 2 out of the given expression:

$$2x^2 + 4x - 30 = 2(x^2 + 2x - 15)$$

Then, factor the quadratic:

$$2(x^2 + 2x - 15) = 2(x - 3)(x + 5)$$

The factors of $2x^2 + 4x - 30$ are 2, $(x - 3)$, and $(x + 5)$. Only choice A lists one of these factors.

5. **The correct answer is D.** Adding 3 first puts the constant term on the left side; then, multiplying by 8 removes the coefficient from x (that is, it makes the coefficient equal to 1).

6. **The correct answer is B.** The perimeter of a square with sides of length l is $4l$. To satisfy the stated conditions, the inequality $600 < 4l < 800$ must be true. Dividing by 4 yields $150 < l < 200$.

7. **The correct answer is D.** In general, $a^m \times a^n = a^{m+n}$. Observe that choice D, a^{-6}, does not equal $a^{2+(-3)} = a^2 \times a^{-3}$. So a^{-6} is not equivalent to $a^2 \times a^{-3}$.

8. **The correct answer is C.** First, find the slope of the line that passes through two of the points. You can select any two points, so choose those that have values that are easy to work with.

$$\frac{\Delta y}{\Delta x} = \frac{12 - 4}{0 - 2} = -\frac{8}{2} = -4$$

The slope of the line is –4. This allows you to eliminate all answers but choice C. However, if there were multiple choices still remaining, you would need to determine the y-intercept of the line. The y-intercept is where the line crosses the y-axis. You can substitute coordinates for one point on the line into the equation $y = -4x + b$, substituting the y-coordinate for y and the x-coordinate for x and solving for b. This would yield a y-intercept of 12.

Such information can also be seen in the table, (0, 12). Thus, the equation for the line is $y = -4x + 12$.

9. **The correct answer is C.** Observe that a line could be drawn through the points such that all of the points would lie fewer than one unit distant from the line. That suggests a strong correlation. Because the line would have negative slope, the correlation is negative.

10. **The correct answer is D.** The median is the middle value. In this set of seven data points, it is the number in the set such that three values in the set are less than the number and three values in the set are greater than the number. Sort the set from smallest to largest value to see that 14.94 is the number in the middle:

$$\{6.12, 9.18, 10.08, 14.94, 17.58, 20.37, 21.45\}$$

11. **The correct answer is C.** The formula for the area of a circle is Area $= \pi r^2$, where r is the radius of the circle. We are given $\pi r^2 = 9\pi$. Divide both sides by π to get $r^2 = 9$. That means $r = 3$ or $r = -3$, but the radius of a circle must be a positive. The diameter of a circle is 2 times the circle's radius, so a circle of radius 3 inches has a diameter of 6 inches.

12. **The correct answer is A.** The third quartile is indicated by the horizontal line at the top of the box at 91. The first quartile is the horizontal line at the bottom of the box at 71. The difference, $91 - 71 = 20$, is the interquartile range.

13. **The correct answer is B.** The formula for the area of a triangle is Area $= \frac{1}{2} \times B \times H$, where B is the length of the base of the triangle and H is the height of the triangle. In the triangle shown, $B = 24$ and $H = 13$. The area of the triangle is $\frac{1}{2} \times 24 \times 13 = 156$.

14. **The correct answer is D.** Simplify the absolute value symbols first:

$$\frac{|-6|}{2} + \frac{-3}{|6|} = \frac{6}{2} + \frac{-3}{6} = \frac{6}{2} - \frac{3}{6}$$

Use the common denominator, 6, to perform the subtraction:

$$\frac{6}{2} - \frac{3}{6} = \frac{18}{6} - \frac{3}{6} = \frac{15}{6}$$

This simplifies to $2\frac{1}{2}$.

15. **The correct answer is C.** Rewrite the expression, simplifying and combining exponents where possible:

$$\left(\frac{x^3}{y}\right)^2 = (x^3 y^{-1})^2$$
$$= (x^3)^2 \cdot (y^{-1})^2$$
$$= x^{3 \cdot 2} \cdot y^{-1 \cdot 2}$$
$$= x^6 y^{-2}$$

16. **The correct answer is C.** Given that a stack of 16 bricks is 4 feet high, the height of 1 brick is $4 \div 16 = \frac{1}{4}$ foot. Therefore, the height of 10 bricks is:

$$\frac{1}{4} \times 10 = \frac{10}{4} = 2\frac{2}{4}$$

Convert $\frac{2}{4}$ feet to inches by multiplying by 12:

$$\frac{2}{4} \times 12 = \frac{24}{4} = 6$$

A stack of 10 bricks will be 2 feet and 6 inches high.

17. **The correct answer is B.** There are $6 \times 6 = 36$ possible outcomes when 2 six-sided dice are rolled. In 6 of these outcomes, the number on the red die and number on the green die are equal. That leaves 30 out of 36 outcomes in which the numbers on the two dice are not equal. In half of these 30 outcomes, the number on the red die will be greater. So the probability that the number on the red die will be greater than the number on the green die is as follows:

$$\frac{1}{2} \times \frac{30}{36} = \frac{15}{36} = \frac{5}{12}$$

18. The correct answer is C. Following order of operations, first perform the operations inside the parentheses (in this case, division before subtraction) as follows:

$$12 + 3(2 \div 3 - 6) = 12 + 3\left(\frac{2}{3} - 6\right)$$
$$= 12 + 3\left(\frac{2}{3} - \frac{18}{3}\right)$$
$$= 12 + 3\left(\frac{-16}{3}\right)$$

Next, perform multiplication, then addition:

$$12 + 3\left(\frac{-16}{3}\right) = 12 + (-16) = -4$$

19. The correct answer is B. To convert grams to kilograms, divide by 1,000 by moving the decimal three places to the left.

$$129.0 \div 1,000 = 0.1290 = 0.129$$

20. The correct answer is B. We are given that the kitchen costs twice as much as the bathroom to remodel, which means that the cost to remodel the bathroom is half the cost of the kitchen, or $\frac{1}{2}k$. That means the total cost is computed as follows:

$$T = k + \frac{1}{2}k$$
$$= \left(1 + \frac{1}{2}\right)k$$
$$= \frac{3}{2}k$$

Quantitative Reasoning, Algebra, and Statistics

Total Number of Correct Answers: _____/20

Total # of Correct Answers	Approximate ACCUPLACER Score	This score corresponds with a test taker who demonstrates skills and knowledge with…
8 or fewer	200–236	identifying graphs; adding, subtracting, and multiplying integers; and identifying coordinates on an xy-plane
9–11	237–249	identifying linear equations and inequalities; finding the value of a variable in a linear equation; evaluating rational and radical expressions; and solving one-step problems with rate, ratio, proportion, and conversion
12–14	250–262	finding solutions to systems of equations and inequalities; solving problems by creating and using a system of linear equations; solving multi-step problems with rate, ratio, and conversion; and making connections between visual representations and algebraic equations
15–17	263–275	finding the slope and y-intercept of a parallel line, evaluating exponents, calculating conditional probability, and interpreting the y-intercept in context
18–20	276–300	finding the slope and y-intercept of a perpendicular line, calculating the input of a non-linear function, comparing means and medians of data sets, solving complex perimeter and area problems, and understanding absolute value

Advanced Algebra and Functions

1. D	5. A	9. A	13. C	17. D
2. A	6. D	10. B	14. B	18. A
3. A	7. B	11. C	15. C	19. C
4. B	8. C	12. D	16. A	20. B

1. **The correct answer is D.** Start by isolating the variable to the left side of the equation by adding $\frac{2}{3}$ to both sides. This results in $x = \frac{5}{2} + \frac{2}{3}$, rewritten as $x = \frac{15}{6} + \frac{4}{6}$, which equals $\frac{19}{6}$.

2. **The correct answer is A.** The slopes of parallel lines are equal. The slope of the line in the graph is $\frac{3}{2}$. Therefore, the equation of any line parallel to the line shown is $y = \frac{3}{2}x + b$. To find the equation of such a line passing through (–1, 2), substitute 2 for y and –1 for x and solve for b:

$$2 = \frac{3}{2}(-1) + b$$

This simplifies to $b = \frac{7}{2}$. So the equation of the line that passes through the point (–1, 2) with slope $\frac{3}{2}$ is $y = \frac{3}{2}x + \frac{7}{2}$, which can also be written as $y = \frac{3x+7}{2}$.

3. **The correct answer is A.** Factor $2x^2 - 20x + 42$ by first factoring out 2 to get $2(x^2 - 10x + 21)$; then factor the quadratic inside the parentheses to get $2(x - 7)(x - 3)$.

4. **The correct answer is B.** Substitute for the variable g:

$$f(-20) = \sqrt[3]{-20 - 7} = \sqrt[3]{-27} = -3$$

5. **The correct answer is A.** Note that $(x - 5)(x + 5) = x^2 - 25$. Multiply both sides of the given equation by $(x - 5)(x + 5)$ to get $2(x + 5) - (x - 5) = 4$. Solving for x yields $x = -11$.

6. **The correct answer is D.** Start by using FOIL on choice A. This yields $2x^3 - 11x^2 - 7x + 6$. Notice that this is the same cubic polynomial present in choice B, meaning that either choice C or D matches choices A and B. Choice D is easier to FOIL. It yields $x^3 - 18x^2 + 77x + 6$, which is not equivalent to the expressions in choices A, B, and C—by implication. Without distributing, you may also notice that there is no way to get a 2 coefficient on the x^3 term, thus removing the need for calculation.

7. **The correct answer is B.** An exponential function can be written in the form $y = ab^t$, where a is the initial amount, b is the growth or decay factor, and t is time (the number of periods). For the aspirin problem, replace y with a, the amount of aspirin remaining in the bloodstream. The initial amount is given as 400, so $a = 400b^t$. The decay factor is $\frac{1}{2}$ because the amount of aspirin decreases by one half, which gives the equation $a = 400\left(\frac{1}{2}\right)^t$. The amount of aspirin decreases by half every 3 hours, and the number of 3-hour periods in h hours is $\frac{h}{3}$. This gives the final equation $a = 400\left(\frac{1}{2}\right)^{\frac{h}{3}}$.

8. **The correct answer is C.** To find the hypotenuse of a right triangle, use the Pythagorean theorem: $a^2 + b^2 = c^2$, where a and b are legs of the triangle and c is the hypotenuse.

$$= \sqrt{5^2 + 12^2}$$
$$= \sqrt{25 + 144}$$
$$= \sqrt{169}$$
$$= 13$$

9. **The correct answer is A.** To convert degrees to radians, multiply the degree measure by $\frac{\pi}{180°}$. In this case:

$$240°\left(\frac{\pi}{180°}\right) = \frac{4\pi}{3}$$

2

10. **The correct answer is B.** Substitute 0 for y in the first equation $-6x^2 + 5 = 2$. This simplifies to $x^2 = \dfrac{-3}{-6}$ or $x = \sqrt{\dfrac{1}{2}}$, which can also be expressed as $x = \dfrac{1}{\sqrt{2}}$.

11. **The correct answer is C.** The equation $(4.62 \times 10^{-6})\,p = 0.0484$ is linear because the variable p is multiplied by a constant.

12. **The correct answer is D.** The dashed line is the graph of $y = -3x + 2$. It is dashed because the corresponding inequality, $y < -3x + 2$, is strictly *less than* (not *less than or equal to*), so values on the line are excluded. The area below (to the left of) the line is shaded because values of y less than the values on the line satisfy the inequality. The solid line is the graph of $y = -\dfrac{1}{3}x - 2$. It is solid because the corresponding inequality, $y \geq -\dfrac{1}{3}x - 2$, is *greater than or equal to*, so values on the line are included. The area above the line is shaded because values of y greater than or equal to the values on the line satisfy the inequality. The darker shaded area represents values of x and y that satisfy both inequalities.

13. **The correct answer is C.** Factor $-x^3 - 2x^2 + 8x$ by first factoring out $-x$ to get $-x(x^2 + 2x - 8)$; then, factor the quadratic inside the parentheses to get $-x(x - 2)(x + 4)$.

14. **The correct answer is B.** The domain of the rational expression $\dfrac{x}{x-1}$ excludes $x = 1$ because that would make the denominator 0. The absolute value function can assume any positive value or 0 (when $x = 0$).

15. **The correct answer is C.** Refer to the figure below.

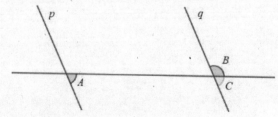

Angles A and C are corresponding angles, so they are congruent:

$$m\angle C = m\angle A = 65°$$

Angle C and angle B are supplementary, so:

$$m\angle C + m\angle B = 180°$$

Hence:

$$m\angle B = 180° - 65° = 115°$$

16. **The correct answer is A.** The first equation is equivalent to $y = -3x + 6$, so substitute $-3x + 6$ for y in the second equation to get $3x^2 - (-3x + 6) = 0$. This factors to $3(x - 1)(x + 2) = 0$, so $x = 1$ or $x = -2$. Substitute those x values into $y = -3x + 6$ to get the solutions $(1, 3)$ and $(-2, 12)$. Choice B is incorrect because $(3, -3)$ does not satisfy the second equation. Choice C is incorrect because $(-1, 3)$ does not satisfy the first equation. Choice D is incorrect because $(-1, 9)$ does not satisfy the second equation.

17. **The correct answer is D.** Because the index, 4, is even, the radicand, $6 - 2x$, must be nonnegative. Hence $6 - 2x \geq 0$. Subtract 6 from both sides to get $-2x \geq -6$. Dividing both sides by -2 and reversing the inequality (because of division by a negative number) yields $x \leq 3$.

18. **The correct answer is A.** Factor $x^3 - 2x^2 - 3x$ by first factoring out x:

$$x^3 - 2x^2 - 3x = x(x^2 - 2x - 3)$$

Then, factor the quadratic inside the parentheses:

$$x(x^2 - 2x - 3) = (x - 3)(x + 1)x$$

The roots of this polynomial are 3, -1, and 0, and we see that $(-1, 0)$, $(0, 0)$, and $(3, 0)$ are points on the graph. Also, because the x^3 term is positive, the value of y should increase in the positive direction as x increases, as the graph shows.

19. **The correct answer is C.** We are given that $2\log_5 x = \log_5 4$, so $\log_5 x^2 = \log_5 4$. The second equation implies that $x^2 = 4$, so x could equal 2 or -2. However, because the question includes $\log_5 x$, x, the argument of the logarithm, must be greater than 0. So, $x = 2$.

20. **The correct answer is B.** The graph shown is the graph $y = \cos x$ with amplitude increased from 1 to 3 and period compressed from 2π to $\dfrac{\pi}{2}$. In general, a graph of $y = a \cos cx$ is a cosine graph with amplitude a and period $\dfrac{2\pi}{c}$. To get the given graph, substitute 3 for a and 4 for c, which results in $y = 3 \cos 4x$.

Advanced Algebra and Functions

Total Number of Correct Answers: _____ /20

Total # of Correct Answers	Approximate ACCUPLACER Score	This score corresponds with a test taker who demonstrates skills and knowledge with...
8 or fewer	200–236	calculating the output of a linear function, applying rules of exponents when simplifying expressions, solving quadratic equations, and using exponential functions
9–11	237–249	solving linear equation systems, connecting tables to equations, using factoring to rewrite polynomials, and solving rational and radical equations
12–14	250–262	connecting graphs and equations, rewriting rational expressions, solving problems using triangle properties, and using simple trigonometric ratios
15–17	263–275	adding and subtracting rational expressions, solving complex radical equations, solving exponential equations in one variable, relating the solutions of a system of a linear and nonlinear equation in two variables to the graphs of the system
18–20	276–300	connecting graphs, tables, and algebraic relationships involving absolute value; solving quadratic equations in one variable; solving problems using trigonometric functions; and evaluating logarithmic equations

PART III
READING AND WRITING SKILLS

CHAPTER

Reading Comprehension

READING COMPREHENSION

OVERVIEW

During the reading section of your ACCUPLACER exam, you'll be presented with passages and questions that test your ability to understand what you read. The questions examine not only how well you comprehend what you read but also how well you interpret a passage's meaning and the author's intent. These questions also test your ability to draw conclusions based on what you've read. Since the ACCUPLACER is not a timed test, you do not need to worry about how fast you read. Instead, you should focus on reading closely to maximize comprehension. In this chapter, we'll discuss strategies for improving reading comprehension, expanding your vocabulary, and reading closely based on the comprehension questions you are given. We'll also discuss eight different categories of common reading comprehension questions, all of which are likely to show up on your ACCUPLACER reading exam.

UNDERSTANDING THE ACCUPLACER® READING SECTION

On the ACCUPLACER reading placement test, you'll be presented with passages and asked to respond to questions about them. Two passage sections (one literary passage and one set of two paired informational passages) will be followed by four questions. The remaining 10–12 informational passages will be followed by one question each, for a total of 13–15 passages and 20 questions. You will also likely be given at least one vocabulary question that asks you to fill in a missing blank in a provided sentence.

Here is an example of a reading passage and question set as they are likely to appear on the ACCUPLACER. Since we haven't provided you with an explanation of the answer, consider this your first practice question. What would be your justification for the indicated correct answer, and how might you arrive at it if you weren't sure?

EXAMPLE

In the US, enduring customs around weddings include purchasing an engagement ring, tossing the bouquet, cutting the cake as a couple, having a first dance, or even making sure you have "something old, something new, something borrowed, and something blue" for good luck. Outside the US, there are myriad other cultural wedding traditions. One common type involves rituals to ward off evil spirits. In Germany, ahead of a wedding, guests will throw porcelain dishes on the ground to scare off spirits during what's called a "Polterabend." In Norway, brides believe that sporting elaborate gold and silver crowns with tinkling accessories and reflective charms does the trick. Armenian couples place lavash flatbread on their shoulders to keep the spirits at bay, while in Scotland, newlyweds are covered in molasses, feathers, grass, or anything else that's messy to make them less attractive to nefarious forces. It's also said that if an Irish bride wants to avoid being kidnapped by evil faeries, she must keep one foot on the dance floor during her entire first dance.

Other practices are about bringing good luck to the newlyweds. In China, this means hiring a woman to attend to the bride as she travels to the wedding. Venezuelan couples will sneak away before the reception is over; if they can do so without being caught, it's considered very fortuitous! In other cultures, good luck wedding rituals are loaded with symbolic meanings. For instance, in Wales, the bride will offer a cutting of myrtle from her own bouquet to each bridesmaid as a symbol of love.

From this passage, we can infer that

A. Norwegians are more traditional about weddings than Americans are.

B. numerous world cultures have traditionally believed in evil spirits.

C. the most common reason for observing a wedding tradition involves bringing the couple good luck.

D. wedding traditions are outdated.

Reading Passages on the ACCUPLACER

The informational passages you encounter could be about science, the humanities, history, social studies, or careers, among other topics. The literary passage generally focuses on either prose fiction or literary narratives, such as excerpts from memoirs. The passages come in four different lengths: very short (75–100 words), short (150–200 words), medium (250–300 words), and long (350–400 words). Passages on the ACCUPLACER reading comprehension section typically follow one of three writing modes.

 TIP

Capitalize on ACCUPLACER's lack of a time limit and take the time to read closely. If you do, you'll likely be able to answer the questions without having to return to the passage except to double check your answers.

NARRATIVE

The purpose of the text is to tell a story, often by narrating an experience. It may focus on providing a play-by-play of how certain actions took place; describing an object, place, person, or time period in detail; relaying information about events that have already occurred; or some combination of all three.

INFORMATIVE/EXPLANATORY

The purpose of the text is to explain a concept or inform the reader on a topic. It may focus on explaining key details of a concept or event, defining terms, or providing the reader with information.

ARGUMENTATIVE

The purpose of the text is to make an argument. The author might focus on making a specific argument, persuading the reader to agree with their point of view, or convincing the reader to consider their analysis effective.

Since the focus of this book is familiarizing you with the ACCUPLACER exam, we've made every effort to replicate the formatting of reading passages as they appear on the ACCUPLACER. However, be aware that the reading passages on your exam day may look slightly different than how they are presented here. If this is the case, don't worry! The key to preparing for a reading exam is recognizing how to address certain question types when they come up and learning to pull necessary information from a given reading passage. By practicing with this book, you will be well on your way to tackling any reading passage that might come up on the ACCUPLACER, no matter how it is formatted.

Remember that like the rest of the test, the reading section on the ACCUPLACER is computer-adaptive. This means that as you answer questions, the passage difficulty (and accompanying questions) will likely change to suit your skill level. If you are struggling, you might notice the passages and questions getting easier and/or shorter. Conversely, if you're doing well, you might notice a considerable hike in the difficulty and/or length of what you're reading. Be aware of this tendency and recognize that some passages may take you more time and effort to complete. This is a normal part of the ACCUPLACER testing process and part of the reason you are not given a time limit. Since this book cannot replicate computer-adaptivity, we have included a range of passages and questions so that you can practice with a variety of difficulty levels.

3

Another reminder is that the lack of time limit on the ACCUPLACER is a huge benefit to you as a test taker. Instead of measuring how quickly and efficiently you can read, as timed reading exams do, this exam focuses on your overall reading comprehension. Whether you tend to read quickly or slowly, you have the freedom to move through the passages and questions at a pace that suits you. This is especially important to remember when you are confronted with a difficult passage that seems daunting; instead of panicking, remember that you can take your time to work through it.

Reading Comprehension Questions on the ACCUPLACER

The questions that follow your passages are multiple choice with four answer choices each. There are 20 reading questions on the computer-adaptive version of the test. Reading questions typically address one of four categories.

RHETORIC

These questions focus on the structure of the passage and the choices the author has made in crafting the text. For these questions, test takers must think analytically to consider the rhetorical effect of what has been written. Questions from this section measure your ability to do the following: determine the effect of specific words and phrases and why the author chose them; analyze language use and rhetorical strategies deployed in the text; describe the structure of the whole text; analyze how part of the text relates to the structure of the whole; determine the author's point of view, style, mode of writing, and perspective; determine a text's tone or mood; determine the purpose of the passage as a whole or a section of the text; analyze the author's argument, including any claims and counterclaims; and recognize how the author uses (or fails to use) evidence to support their argument. This category accounts for 35–55% of the questions on the reading exam.

INFORMATION AND IDEAS

These questions focus on the content of the passage, including any details given and any concepts described. Questions from this category measure your ability to do the following: identify the main idea and purpose of the text; identify supporting details; accurately respond to questions based on details of the text; identify a reasonable summary of the text; recognize different types of explicit and implicit relationships within the text, such as comparisons, contrasts, cause and effect, and sequential relationships; and draw reasonable inferences based on the content of the text. This category accounts for 35–55% of the questions on the reading exam.

VOCABULARY

These questions require test takers to identify the meaning of words and phrases as used in the context of a passage or a provided sentence with an indicated blank space for a missing word or phrase. This category accounts for 10–20% of questions on the reading exam.

SYNTHESIS

These questions require test takers to synthesize information from more than one text at a time. You may be asked to perform skills related to any of the other categories, with a primary focus being your ability to recognize how one text relates to another. Generally, these questions are found with the set of two paired informational texts that receives four questions. This category accounts for 10% of questions on the reading exam. Note that synthesis questions may have overlapping aims with other categories, such as asking you to identify a strong summary of the two texts (Information and Ideas) or determine how each author approaches their rhetoric differently.

BUILDING VOCABULARY TO INCREASE COMPREHENSION

Before we break down the different question types, let's take a moment to address vocabulary in terms of reading comprehension. Vocabulary and reading comprehension are closely related. You can't grow your vocabulary without reading, and you can't comprehend a text without a firm grasp of the words the author is using. Both for the reading section and other parts of the ACCUPLACER, such as the writing section, you'll need a strong vocabulary. Here are some ways you can build vocabulary expansion into your overall exam prep.

Keep a Word Log

First off, read material that is more challenging. The key is to find material with words that are new or unfamiliar to you.

Next, write down the words that you don't understand. Once you have a good list of unfamiliar words, look up the definitions in a dictionary and write them down for future reference. Focus on learning a few words at a time so that you can learn them well.

Third, try to use the word yourself in a sentence or in conversation. Practice using the word by creating your own sentences and writing them down in a notebook. This will help you get a sense of how to use the word in different contexts while cementing the word and its meaning into your vocabulary. Take note of the contexts in which you often see or use a word. Getting familiar with the topics and situations in which certain words are used will help you feel more confident and self-assured when you integrate new words into your vocabulary.

Study Root Words, Prefixes, and Suffixes

You can increase your vocabulary by learning about the structure of words. This will help you figure out the meanings of unfamiliar words when you encounter them.

English words have recognizable parts that often come from Latin or Greek. Generally, there are three basic types of word parts:

1. **Roots** are the basic elements of a word that determine its meaning. Many derive from Latin and Greek and must be combined with prefixes, suffixes, or both.

2. **Prefixes** attach to the beginning of a root word to alter its meaning or to create a new word.

3. **Suffixes** attach to the end of a root word to change its meaning, help make it grammatically correct in context, or form a new word. Suffixes often indicate whether a word is a noun, verb, adjective, or adverb.

Sometimes, depending on the word, it can be difficult to parse out whether a word part is a prefix or a root word. However, the key takeaway here is that certain word parts carry meaning that is recognizable no matter what the word is. Knowing the meaning of part of a word can help you infer the meaning of the word.

To aid you in your learning, we've compiled some frequently used root words, prefixes, and suffixes. These tables are by no means comprehensive, but they should help you get started on breaking down the words you see often or encounter when reading, including while preparing for your exam.

Scan this QR code to watch a video on word parts.

COMMON PREFIXES

Prefix	Meaning	Example
Anti-	Against	Antifreeze, antibacterial
Bene-	Good	Benefit, benevolent
De-	Opposite	Deactivate, derail
Dis- *Dys-*	Not	Disagree, dysfunctional
En- *Em-*	Cover	Encode, embrace
Extra-	Beyond	Extraterrestrial, extracurricular
Fore-	Before	Forecast, forehead
Il- *Im-* *In-* *Ir-* *Non-* *Un-*	Not	Illegitimate, impossible, inexcusable, irregular, nonstop, nonsense, unable, undefined
Inter-	Between	Intergalactic, interpret, intermediary
Mal-	Bad, badly	Malicious, malnourished, malfunction
Mis-	Wrongly	Mistake, misinterpret, misnomer
Over-	Over, more, too much	Overlook, oversee, overachieve, overcast
Pre-	Before	Prefix, prevent, predict, prehistoric, prejudice
Re-	Again	Revision, reimagine, return
Trans-	Across	Transatlantic, transverse, transport

COMMON ROOTS

Root	Meaning	Example
Aqu *Hydr*	Water	Aqueous, aquarium, hydrate, hydrotherapy
Aud	Hear	Auditory, audio, audible
Biblio	Book	Bibliophile, bibliography
Chrono	Time	Chronological, chronology
Chrom	Color	Monochromatic, chromosome
Circ	Round	Circle, circus
Geo	Earth	Geography, geomagnetic
Juris	Law	Jurisdiction, jurisprudence
Junct	Join	Conjunction, juncture
Log *Logue*	Speaking, speech	Epilogue, eulogy, dialogue
Photo	Light	Photosynthesis, photography, photon
Scribe	Write	Describe, prescribe, inscribe
Sect	Cut	Dissect, sector
Volve	Roll, turn	Involve, evolve, revolve

COMMON SUFFIXES		
Suffix	**Meaning**	**Example**
-able *-ible*	Capable	Agreeable, collectible
-al	Pertaining to	Logical, magical, criminal
-ance *-ence*	Indicating a state or condition; indicating a process or action	Clearance, ignorance, evidence, patience
-ent	Causing, promoting, or doing an action; one who causes or does something	Different, absorbent, student, agent, deterrent
-fy *-ize* *-ate* *-en*	Cause to be	Classify, diversify, realize, contextualize, create, communicate, awaken, sharpen
-ious *-ous*	Characterized by; full of	Nutritious, delicious, simultaneous, nervous
-ism	Belief, act	Catholicism, plagiarism
-ity	State or quality of being	Enmity, ability, responsibility
-less	Without	Homeless, restless, countless
-let	Small	Booklet, piglet
-or *-er* *-ist*	A person who is or does something	Benefactor, investigator, driver, teacher, chemist, narcissist
-ship	Position held	Friendship, citizenship, allyship, ownership
-tion *-sion* *-ment*	Action or instance of something	Liberation, concentration, admission, decision, achievement, bereavement
-y	Quality of	Thirsty, wintry

KEY CONCEPTS FOR READING ON THE ACCUPLACER®

There are a lot of different ways to approach a reading exam. For many exams you've taken in the past, it's likely you focused on reading quickly and getting through as many questions as possible in an allotted amount of time to maximize your score. On the ACCUPLACER, while you *do* want to score as well as you can, you have to modify your approach slightly to suit the purpose of the exam and take advantage of the lack of time constraints.

As we've discussed before, ACCUPLACER is all about accurately placing you in courses that match your abilities. While you want to achieve as high a score as possible for your skill level, you don't want to do so at the expense of accurately reflecting your genuine capabilities. Doing so could mean being placed in a course that is too advanced for you to keep up. Conversely, you also don't want to slack off or speed through the reading section and end up placed in a course that bores you to tears. You don't need to stress yourself out trying to perfect every single reading skill all at once before the big test. But you *can* practice the skills you need for the reading comprehension section so that on exam day you can show the best you are capable of and minimize anxiety.

Develop a Routine for Approaching Passages

When approaching a reading passage on the ACCUPLACER, we suggest beginning your preparation by performing the tips we provide here in the recommended order. As you practice, feel free to develop a different strategy that works for you personally. Try to identify which aspects of reading exams you struggle with most: understanding passages, reading questions, narrowing down answer options when guessing, etc. Then, use that information to develop exam day strategies that suit your needs.

Glance at the Passage for the Main Idea

Glance quickly through the passage to get the gist of what it's about. Look for key words or names that repeat and see if there are any concepts or terms that stand out. This part should be done quickly.

Read the Questions before the Passage

Since you have the luxury of time for your exam, we suggest beginning by reading the questions thoroughly. If the computerized test allows you to look at more than one question at a time for a given passage, do so. After you've glanced at the passage long enough to know what it's about, read the question(s) closely. Pay attention to how the question is phrased so you know exactly what it is asking. For easier questions, you may be able to venture a tentative guess that you can then confirm or change after reading. Knowing the topic of a question in advance will help you zero in on the most important parts of the passage for answering it.

Closely Read the Passage One Time

Since you have time to read the passage closely, do so. Don't just skim through it looking for your answer. Instead, take the time to read the passage closely so you can recognize any nuances that might help you land on the most accurate answer. While reading closely helps you develop a more sophisticated understanding than simply skimming a passage does, your goal isn't to memorize every single fact in the passage since it will contain much more information than what you need. Instead, aim to understand the "big picture" concepts at play while also reading actively to locate the answers to your questions. Slow down and focus more when you find reading sections with relevant information.

Answer the Question, Then Verify against the Passage

Having previewed your question(s), you will likely be able to answer them after close reading. That said, make sure you read the question again to refresh your memory on what is being asked. Once you have an answer, go back to the section of the passage that is relevant to the question and verify that you are correct before moving on. If you are struggling with finding an answer, move on to the next two steps.

As Needed, Draw Conclusions Based on Information in the Passage

Remember: while every question can be answered with information in the passage, not every answer will be explicitly stated in the passage. You might be asked to infer or predict something, or you might be asked about something else an author won't usually state directly, like tone, mood, or point of view. When a question asks you what the author has implied or asks you about the tone of the passage, you must use what you've read to draw your own conclusions. To do so, you might ask yourself some analytical questions, like "What would I not understand had I not read this passage?" or "What conclusions can I draw that aren't stated directly but are still clear to me now that I've read?" In some situations, an "If/Then" construction can be a good way to do this: "If ____ is true/false, then ... what comes next?"

Skim and Scan to Make a Guess If You Aren't Sure

If you truly can't figure out an answer, skim the passage for keywords that relate to your answer options. This will help you either find the answer or find other information that can help you eliminate incorrect answer choices. There's no penalty for guessing on the ACCUPLACER, so once you've done your best to narrow down answer choices, make a guess and move on to the next passage or question.

Some Other Reminders and Advice

Here are a few other things to keep in mind if you want to tackle reading passages like a pro.

1 **Predict the Answer after Reading the Question:** After you reread a question, make a prediction about what the answer should be based on what you know from the passage. If you see that answer or similar among the available choices, there's a good chance that it's correct.

2 **Read All Your Answer Choices:** Don't just mark down the first answer that seems correct. Instead, make sure you read each answer choice and eliminate those you know are incorrect before choosing the *best* answer. Some answers may be similar, and you need to evaluate each one before moving on.

3 **Eliminate Wrong Answers:** There is only one right answer for each question, which means that there is a good reason why the right answer is correct and why each of the incorrect answers are wrong. Any answer that contradicts information in the passage (unless that's what the question is looking for) is incorrect, so you can eliminate those from consideration. After taking the steps to predict an answer and read all the answer choices, you should be able to narrow down your options. At that point, even if you haven't settled on one answer, you've done a lot of work to increase your likelihood of guessing correctly.

4 **Stick to the Passage:** Avoid involving personal or emotional judgments when finding your answers. Even if you disagree with the author or spot a factual error in the passage, you must answer based on what's stated or implied in the text. Similarly, even if you have outside knowledge of a topic, answer based only on what's written in front of you. An answer can be true in the sense that it reflects something about the real world, but if it's not supported by the passage, it's incorrect.

5 **Don't Worry If You Don't Know the Topic:** To put all test takers on a level playing field, test writers choose approachable reading passages on a variety of topics. Some will be a little harder for you than others, but all are designed to be understood by a general audience. You probably have not seen the reading material before, but you're not being tested on your knowledge of the topic. Instead, you're being tested on how well you can comprehend what you read and answer the questions.

TIP

While reading the whole passage closely is recommended, don't waste your time on rereading irrelevant technical details or breaking down information that the questions don't ask about. If you are struggling with part of the passage and it's clear that that section does not relate to your question(s), move on.

Comprehension Questions to Practice Close Reading

Thus far, we've discussed that the best way to address reading questions is to take the time to read the passage closely. One way to maximize comprehension while reading is to keep some basic comprehension questions in mind as you go. When practicing for your exam, pay attention to the kinds of questions that get asked and work on adjusting your reading to figure out that information preemptively. If you know what topics test makers tend to ask about, you'll have a better chance of easily locating the information you need.

To proactively build comprehension, ask yourself some of the following questions while reading:

- What is the author's main point, their tone/mood, and their purpose for writing?
- What ideas are central or most important?
- What are some of the most important supporting details related to the main point?
- What is the purpose of each different paragraph, and how do they work together to form an overall whole?
- Which words or phrases stand out or repeat?
- What did I learn about this topic?
- Is this a story or does it discuss an opinion? Does it inform me about a topic? Attempt to persuade me? Argue for a particular course of action?
- What can I predict about this passage?
- What conclusions can I draw after reading?

Practice asking and answering these questions as you read until looking for these things in an exam passage simply becomes second nature.

EIGHT COMMON QUESTION TYPES (WITH PRACTICE!)

This section covers the eight most common types of questions that are likely to come up on the ACCUPLACER. Here, we have separated them into various study categories, but know that certain question types will map more explicitly to the four question categories on the ACCUPLACER (Information and Ideas, Rhetoric, Vocabulary, and Synthesis) than others.

The most common types of reading exam questions address test takers' reading abilities along the following lines:

1 **Main Idea Questions**: Require you to identify the main idea of a text, including central themes or arguments and an author's overall purpose, as well as the ability to summarize either.

2 **Supporting Detail Questions**: Require you to demonstrate your comprehension of supporting details in the passage and the ability to identify information related to those details through close reading.

3 **Vocabulary Questions**: Require you to demonstrate word comprehension and the ability to define vocabulary words or phrases based on the context in which they are used within a passage or sentence.

Inference Questions: Test your ability to draw logical inferences and conclusions from ideas and details presented in the passage.

 Tone, Style, and Language Use Questions: Test your ability to identify the author's tone, style, and use of language to accomplish an explicit purpose, as well as any other rhetorical choices they make including those related to word choice, writing mode, and structure of claims and counterclaims.

 Organization and Logic Questions: Test your ability to identify and evaluate how a passage's organization and logic help an author meet their purpose, including the ability to recognize how a passage is structured and why.

 Opinion and Argument Questions: Ask you to evaluate the rhetoric authors use to express opinions and arguments, including how that rhetoric relates to an author's point of view and mode of writing as well as their ability to support claims and counterclaims.

 Synthesis Questions: Ask you to synthesize information between two passages, including recognizing the relationship between two texts and where two authors converge and contrast in their claims as well as summarizing both individual texts and their combined impact or message.

In the sections that follow, we'll discuss each of these question types, offer tips on how to address them, and give you a chance to practice your skills with passages. At the end of this section, you'll find a graphic model demonstrating how multiple question types relate to details from a single informational passage.

Main Idea Questions

The main idea of a passage is the primary point the text is trying to convey to readers. In argumentative writing, it will be the author's main opinion or argument. You can think of the main idea as the overall message

an author is trying to send by writing a passage. Often, the quickest way to identify the main point is to read the first and last sentences of the first and last paragraphs of a passage. Otherwise, the main point should be evident after close reading.

QUESTIONS TO ASK YOURSELF: MAIN IDEA

- What is the author telling the reader?
- What does the author want readers to take away from the passage?
- What would be a good title for this passage?
- Why did the author write this passage?
- How could this passage be summarized in one sentence?

Main idea questions will sometimes be explicit, asking "What is the main idea of this passage?" Other common types of main idea questions involve choosing an appropriate passage title or identifying the passage's overall purpose. No matter the approach, you can be prepared for any main idea question if you summarize the most important "takeaway" from the passage whenever you finish reading. Try and do so in a single statement, such as by completing sentences like "This passage was about _____." or "The author wants the reader to know that _____." Having this main idea in mind should make it easier to identify correct answers to both main idea questions and questions that are related to them, such as supporting detail questions and questions about organization and logic.

Addressing Main Idea Questions

One of the fastest ways to eliminate incorrect answers to main idea questions is by looking for choices that are either too specific or too general. To demonstrate, let's say you read a passage, and when you finish, you mentally summarize the main idea as follows: "This passage was about how squid develop over the course of their entire life." Then, you are faced with the following common type of main idea question.

What might be the best title for this passage?

A. "Squid Mating Habits"

B. "The Life Cycle of Squid"

C. "Animals of the Ocean"

D. "The Evolution of Squid"

Since a passage's title should reflect its main idea, you are looking for the answer that is most like your summary of the passage's main idea. In this case, "The Life Cycle of Squid" does the trick. Having already identified the main idea, the correct answer should hopefully stand out the second you read it. If it doesn't, remember to check for answers that are too vague or too specific. "Squid Mating Habits" (choice A) reflects a topic that relates to the life cycle of squid and may even have been addressed in part of your passage but is too specific to encompass the main idea you identified, which included the stages of a squid's entire life. Meanwhile, "Animals of the Ocean" (choice C) is far too vague a title for a passage that talks about squid specifically.

Once you have eliminated options that are too specific or vague, the remaining incorrect option(s) will usually address something that either wasn't mentioned in the passage or that is slightly off topic from the passage. In this case, "The Evolution of Squid" (choice D) is related to the main idea you identified but not directly so since the evolution of a species is different than its life cycle.

FYI

Even if a test question doesn't use the words "main idea," it might still be asking for the main idea. If you have identified the main idea for yourself, then you shouldn't be too caught off guard no matter how the question is phrased.

Addressing Questions about the Author's Purpose

One common subset of main idea questions specifically addresses the author's purpose for writing the text. You might also be asked questions related to the author's purpose for certain paragraphs when you encounter questions on rhetoric. In short, the author's purpose is the reason the author has written the passage. While the main idea is about *what* is in the passage—the information the author wants you to know—the purpose is about *how* the author is presenting that information and *why* they've chosen the rhetoric they did.

QUESTIONS TO ASK YOURSELF: AUTHOR'S PURPOSE

- Why did the author write the information they did in the way they did?

- What verbs describe what the author is doing in this passage?

- Is the author trying to convince the reader to believe something?

- Is the author making an argument for or against a particular idea or course of action?

- Is the author sticking to factual information?

- Is this passage written for a particular audience?

- Is the author telling a story?

- Why has the author chosen the words they used or phrased things the way they did?

Questions that deal with the author's purpose are easy to spot because they usually contain the word *purpose*. The question might appear as "The author's main purpose in this passage is to…" and ask you to choose the answer that best matches how the author communicates the passage's main idea. An author's purpose can generally be expressed as a *to* + verb expression, with common purposes being to inform, explain, or argue.

As with main idea questions, state for yourself what the author's purpose is whenever you finish reading a passage. Whatever verb you choose to describe the author's purpose (or a synonym for it) is likely to pop up in your answer options later. To illustrate, let's say you read a passage and you decide after reading that the author's purpose was to compare the typical diets of alligators and crocodiles. Therefore, you know you're looking for an answer that includes the word *compare* or whatever is closest to it. You are then given a seemingly vague question:

EXAMPLE

The author's purpose in this passage is to

   A. praise.

   B. criticize.

   C. contrast.

   D. illustrate

If you have already determined that the author's purpose is to compare, you will easily spot that choice C is the correct answer since *contrast* is used as a synonym for *compare* when discussing an author's purpose. Sometimes, two answers may seem plausible. For instance, you might convince yourself that such a comparison illustrates (choice D) the differences between the animals' diets. However, always choose the answer that *best* expresses the author's purpose. *Contrast* is a more specific description of the author's purpose, which you determined was to compare the diets of two similar but different species.

 TIP

If a question asks about the author's purpose, focus on the active verbs in the answer choices. Sometimes, you can automatically eliminate some incorrect choices by noting what the author *didn't* do.

The following table provides a list of verbs commonly used to describe an author's purpose.

COMMON VERBS TO DESCRIBE AN AUTHOR'S PURPOSE	
Purpose Verbs	**In a reading passage, this looks like the author is…**
inform educate teach	providing information to educate a reader on a topic, often (but not always) while gesturing to credible support.
persuade argue convince	convincing the reader to agree with an opinion or point of view.
amuse entertain	entertaining the reader with an interesting, inventive, or humorous topic.
compare contrast	showing the similarities or differences between ideas or known facts.
describe	using the five senses and other descriptive details to portray the characteristics or qualities of a topic.
explain (information) clarify break down	making an idea or issue clearer through description, details, or a breakdown of how something works or occurs.
discuss examine consider	examining different angles or perspectives of a topic or argument.
analyze evaluate assess	conducting a detailed analysis of numerous facts, quantities, or perspectives impacting an issue or topic, most often using credible support.
critique criticize	expressing disapproval for a topic, issue, or the perspective of another person.
praise celebrate	expressing approval for a topic, issue, or the perspective of another person.
tell narrate explain (as a story)	using a narrative (storytelling) approach to entertain, relay ideas, or explain a topic using figurative details.
quantify	employing statistics, facts, and other quantifiable data to "place a number" on something that is otherwise a concept.
summarize	providing a summary of a topic.

Test Yourself 1: Main Idea

Directions: Read the passage below and then answer the three main idea questions that follow. After you've selected each answer, read the answer explanations to check yourself.

The following is adapted from a textbook for pre-med students.

Selective serotonin reuptake inhibitors, or SSRIs, are commonly known simply as "antidepressants," though they are not the only kind of antidepressant that exists. Compared with other antidepressants, SSRIs are more commonly prescribed because they tend to cause fewer overall side effects in the general population. Most people who take SSRIs do so as treatment for depression, though others may do so in combination with forms of talk therapy related to generalized anxiety disorder, post-traumatic stress disorder (PTSD), obsessive-compulsive disorder (OCD), or other mental health afflictions.

Serotonin is a neurotransmitter found in serum and blood platelets. Common thinking around serotonin is that it's a "good mood" chemical that plays a vital role in regulating emotions, focus, and sleep—if you're feeling calm, happy, or at ease, it's probably because your serotonin levels are stable. In people with depression or other mental health concerns, it can be difficult to keep serotonin levels stable. When coupled with the fact that mental health disorders can also affect hormones, other neurotransmitters, and the body's physical sensations, it's clear why a medication that can help regulate serotonin would be beneficial. This is where SSRIs come in.

SSRIs work by ensuring the brain has enough serotonin even in individuals who have trouble keeping levels stable. According to the United Kingdom National Health Service (NHS), "After carrying a message, serotonin is usually reabsorbed by the nerve cells (known as 'reuptake'). SSRIs work by blocking ('inhibiting') reuptake, meaning more serotonin is available to pass further messages between nearby nerve cells." This explains the "R" and "I" in the term SSRIs; these types of drugs are reuptake inhibitors. Since there is less serotonin reuptake, more serotonin sticks around, making it easier to combat issues caused by decreased serotonin. While low serotonin isn't necessarily the cause of all mental health concerns treated by SSRIs, studies show that increasing serotonin levels is a positive therapeutic intervention for many. Though SSRIs aren't without their side effects, which the NHS notes include gastrointestinal issues, feelings of dizziness or blurred vision, and a suite of side effects related to reproductive wellness, for many who suffer from mental health struggles, the benefits of this type of therapy outweigh potential side effects.

Citation: UK National Health Service, 2021. "Overview - SSRI Antidepressants." *NHS*. February 15, 2021.
https://www.nhs.uk/mental-health/talking-therapies-medicine-treatments/medicines-and-psychiatry/ssri-antidepressants/overview/.

1. What is the best title for this passage?

   A. "What is an Antidepressant?"

   B. "Are You Feeling Depressed?"

   C. "Antidepressants"

   D. "How SSRI Antidepressants Work"

2. The author's purpose in writing this passage is to

   A. narrate their experience taking SSRIs.

   B. praise SSRIs for being so effective.

   C. educate the reader about what SSRIs are and how they work.

   D. summarize scientific studies about the efficacy of SSRIs.

3. The main idea of this passage is that SSRIs

   A. are safe for most individuals to take daily.

   B. work by inhibiting serotonin reuptake, thereby helping the brain retain more serotonin.

   C. produce numerous side effects, including gastrointestinal issues and dizziness.

   D. can be used to treat OCD, PTSD, and anxiety as well as depression.

Answers

1. **The correct answer is D.** The passage focuses specifically on SSRI antidepressants and how they work, so the best title for the passage is "How SSRI Antidepressants Work." Choice C is too vague, and the others don't suit the passage's main idea.

2. **The correct answer is C.** The author's purpose in this passage is to educate the reader about what SSRIs are and how they work.

3. **The correct answer is B.** This passage is focused on how SSRIs work, so you need only identify which response concerns how SSRIs work.

Supporting Detail Questions

Supporting details, or supporting ideas, are pieces of information that help the reader understand the author's main idea or argument. Generally, they offer background or necessary context. These sentences might provide examples, facts, statistics, quotations, related stories, descriptions, or lots of other information to support the main idea and purpose.

Quite often, questions about supporting details won't look like reading questions at all. Remember, though, these questions are on a reading exam, so they will never ask about anything you can't answer using the details of the reading passage(s) alone. Don't be thrown off if you get a question that looks like it's from history, science, math, or any other subject besides reading. Instead, assume the question is asking about something you can answer by finding the relevant sentence(s) in the passage.

QUESTIONS TO ASK YOURSELF: SUPPORTING DETAILS

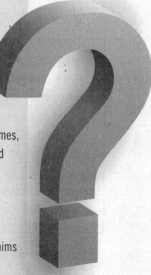

- What information does the author provide?
- How is that information used to support and explain the main idea and purpose?
- Are there any important names, concepts, or words repeated multiple times?
- How do smaller details in the passage add up to a bigger picture?
- What claims and counterclaims does the author make to support their main argument?

Supporting detail questions will look wildly different depending on the topic of the reading passage; in other words, don't expect to see something like "What are the supporting details in this passage?" Instead, detail questions will ask you about the passage's content. For example, if the passage is informing you about different cultural theories prominent in the field of sociology, a details question might ask, "Which of the following is *not* a tenet of postcolonial theory?" Or "In this passage, the author compares Foucault's theories on power to…" It's your job to scan back through the passage and choose the right answer based on the details provided. You will never be asked a question about supporting details that requires you to have outside knowledge of a subject.

Test Yourself 2: Supporting Details

Directions: Read the passage below and then answer the three supporting detail questions that follow. After you've selected each answer, read the answer explanations to check yourself.

There are few figures from Slavic folklore considered as formidable or intriguing as Baba Yaga. Loosely translated, her name is said to mean something like "Grandmother Witch," though this only partially encompasses her being. Baba Yaga is also a cannibal, goddess figure, fairy godmother, trickster, and villain, popping up in stories to terrorize heroes only to inadvertently provide them with the skills or items they require to complete their journey. Perhaps most importantly, Baba Yaga is a figure who symbolizes transformation, affording her further associations with birth, death, and transitional life phases like puberty.

There are numerous telltale characteristics that let you know Baba Yaga is in a story, even when she is not mentioned by name. For one, she lives in a hut in the woods that rests on chicken legs, which act like moveable stilts to hold the hut aloft. Because the house can move around the forest and turn itself in any direction, Baba Yaga is thought to always potentially be around the corner. This status gives her a frightening mystique. Her hut is not her only means of transport, however, as she can also fly around using a mortar and pestle. Because she is associated with fertility, the mortar and pestle are said to symbolize her male and female sides. When traveling this way, she uses a broom to sweep away the tracks left behind; some scholars believe this is partially why we associate brooms with witches today. The primary way she threatens people is by kidnapping them and planning to eat them, though in most stories, they escape before she can feast.

1. Of the following, which is NOT a term used to describe Baba Yaga?

   A. Goddess

   B. Trickster

   C. Witch

   D. Vampire

2. To get around, Baba Yaga travels by

   A. flying broomstick.

   B. mortar and pestle.

   C. teleportation.

   D. floating.

3. The passage states that Baba Yaga is associated with all the following EXCEPT:

   A. Death

   B. Puberty

   C. Fertility

   D. Marriage

Answers

1. **The correct answer is D.** Though vampires are indeed said to come partially from Slavic folklore, it is not one of the terms used to describe Baba Yaga.

2. **The correct answer is B.** As paragraph 2 states, in addition to having a moving hut that walks on chicken feet, "[Baba Yaga] can also fly around using a mortar and pestle."

3. **The correct answer is D.** The passage never mentions Baba Yaga being associated with marriage.

Vocabulary Questions

For some vocabulary questions on ACCUPLACER, you will be given a standalone sentence with a blank space where a word or phrase is missing. In this case, your task is to choose the word or phrase that best fulfills the intended meaning of the whole sentence. When vocabulary questions come up after passages, you usually won't have to identify word definitions directly, as is common on other vocabulary tests. Instead, you'll be asked to identify a synonym for a word used in the passage that matches the context in which it was used in the passage. Remember that a synonym is a word with the same meaning. You must consider how the word is used in the passage and then choose the answer that most nearly matches that same contextual meaning.

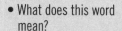
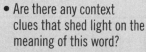

QUESTIONS TO ASK YOURSELF: VOCABULARY

- What does this word mean?

- Are there any context clues that shed light on the meaning of this word?

- Which of these answer options means the same thing or something close?

Sometimes, a question or answer option will present you with a short phrase instead of a single word, so don't be thrown off if you notice this. For instance, "in a little bit" is a perfectly suitable synonym for *soon*, even if one is a phrase and the other a word. Remember, too, that building vocabulary and studying word parts can help you tackle unknown words when you encounter them or eliminate answer choices that are less likely to be correct.

⚠ **ALERT**

Vocabulary-in-context questions don't always ask for the most common meaning of a word. Instead, look for the meaning that best fits the context in which the word was used in the passage.

Test Yourself 3: Vocabulary

Directions: Read the passage below and then answer the three vocabulary questions that follow. After you've selected each answer, read the answer explanations to check yourself.

The biggest of all species within the genus *Bathynomus* is the giant isopod, or *B. giganteus*. They may look like bugs, but giant isopods are not ocean insects. Rather, like crabs and shrimp, they're crustaceans. You might not expect a somewhat scary looking bottom dweller crustacean to get much love, but it seems the internet at large has given the giant isopod a new reputation. Thanks to the popularity of digital forms of communication like memes, the giant isopod has become recognizable to a wider swath of the general population, including a dedicated subset of isopod fans who insist these little guys are quite cute.

Giant isopods truly are sizable; their average length is between 7.5 and 14.2 inches, but scientists have found specimens as long as 2.5 feet! Their outer shells are usually brown or a pale lilac. Some researchers speculate that isopods evolved to be so massive to withstand the ocean's immense pressure. These carnivorous scavengers typically gorge themselves on the corpses of dead animals that fall to the ocean floor but are also adapted to forgo eating for long periods of time. One interesting adaptation isopods share with felines is what's called a tapeum, meaning a reflective layer towards the back of the eye that increases their ability to see in the dark. However, this only helps giant isopods so much—they have weak eyesight and often must depend on their antennae to augment their navigational abilities.

1. As used in the final sentence of paragraph 1, the word "subset" most nearly means

   A. team.
   B. portion.
   C. neighborhood.
   D. company.

2. As used in the third sentence of paragraph 2, the word "withstand" most nearly means

   A. endure.
   B. prolong.
   C. avoid.
   D. create.

3. As used in the last sentence of paragraph 2, the word "augment" most nearly means

   A. agree with.
   B. negate.
   C. camouflage.
   D. amplify.

Answers

1. **The correct answer is B.** In paragraph 1, the term *subset* is used to refer to a portion of people from within a larger group (fans of giant isopods).

2. **The correct answer is A.** To withstand something, such as in this case the ocean's pressure, means to endure, tolerate, or defy it.

3. **The correct answer is D.** The verb *augment* means "to amplify, strengthen, reinforce, or expand."

Inference Questions

You make an inference when you conclude something based on ideas in the passage. Generally, the answer won't be stated directly in the passage. Instead, you are looking for a reasonable conclusion that could be drawn from the information given. For instance, if the passage mentioned that field geologists must often spend long periods of time camping alone or in small groups, you could infer that camping skills are *most likely* a job requirement for field geologists even if the passage didn't say so directly. You don't have enough information to know if this is for sure the case, but it's a logical conclusion you could draw from what you read.

Inference questions are therefore asking you to "do something" with what you've just read. For example, you might be asked to make a prediction about what happens next or to compare ideas in two paired passages with each other. Similarly, you may also be asked to give an interpretation of what you've read or to identify a situation that is most like the one described in the passage. Additionally, questions might ask you to infer about the author's attitude or why figures within a narrative make the choices they make.

Inference questions will sometimes be blunt and ask you "Which of the following can you infer from this passage?" But these questions might also ask you things like "With which of these statements would the author of this passage most likely agree?" or "Based on this passage, what is the protagonist likely to do next?" They may also resemble supporting detail questions, such as by asking you to identify which statement *might* be true in light of another detail from the passage. All of these are asking you to infer since the answer to the question is not stated directly in the passage—you can only make a logical prediction. Of all the reading comprehension abilities the ACCUPLACER tests, this one relies the most on your critical thinking skills. You may have to think a little to find your answer, but remember that at their core, inference questions are asking you what you can figure out from the information you've been given, so you shouldn't have to work too hard to make your answer fit.

QUESTIONS TO ASK YOURSELF: MAKING INFERENCES

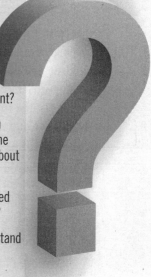

- What can the reader predict based on the information presented in the passage?

- How are ideas in the passage alike and different?

- What information is given about the characters in the story and how they feel about the situation?

- What information is implied but isn't explicitly stated?

- What might readers understand to be true or false after reading this passage?

Test Yourself 4: Inferences

Directions: Read the passage below and then answer the three inference questions that follow. After you've selected each answer, read the answer explanations to check yourself.

Essentially all children are naturally endowed with curiosity, a sense of wonder about the world, and a need for nurturing and play. Similarly, almost all children around the world greet the first day of school with a mix of anticipation and trepidation. To ease these concerns and make the transition to schooling a little easier, different countries engage in a panoply of back-to-school traditions.

If you were a 6-year-old headed to your first day of school in Germany, you would likely do so with a giant paper cone in tow. These cones, called *Kindertüte*, are fun-filled goodie bags containing candy, toys, school supplies, and anything else a child might need to have a joyful first day. Even though the treats are nice, the Kindertüte are more about celebrating and communicating to children that they are entering a new stage of life. Japanese parents do something similar, gifting their children a new backpack and sometimes a new desk to use at home to mark the first day of school. As in Germany, these presents are intended to help the child understand that they are embarking on a new chapter in their development.

Many cultures mark the first day of school with a celebration. In Kazakhstan, children start school at the age of 7. Their first day is called Tyl Ishtar, which means "Initiation into Education," and to celebrate it, parents will invite family and friends to a giant feast at their home. During this feast, the school-bound child is expected to recite the names of their grandfathers going back seven generations to honor their ancestry. Other first day celebrations are more about giving children an opportunity to get to know one another. In Saudi Arabia, the first few days of school contain no lessons, instead giving children a chance to share food and play games. In parts of Indonesia, the first day is treated as an orientation to help children intentionally develop friendships meaningful enough to last through their schooling years.

1. From this passage, we can infer that
   A. children do not start school until after age 7 in Japan.
   B. there are no back-to-school traditions in the United States.
   C. Japanese and German children are culturally considered more mature once school starts.
   D. children in Japan are commonly homeschooled.

2. From paragraph 3, we can infer that

    A. children's friendships aren't considered meaningful in Kazakhstan.

    B. children's friendships aren't considered meaningful in Indonesia.

    C. families in Kazakhstan have traditionally followed a patriarchal structure.

    D. families in Indonesia have traditionally followed a matriarchal structure.

3. From this passage, we can infer that

    A. around the world, children do not always start school at the same age.

    B. around the world, children always start school at the same age.

    C. German families take the first day of school more seriously than families in other countries do.

    D. Indonesian students have more respect for their teachers than students in other places do.

Answers

1. **The correct answer is C.** Paragraph 2 mentions how both Germany and Japan consider the start of school an important life stage transition for children. Consequently, it would be logical to infer that the start of school is considered an advancement in a child's maturity in these cultures.

2. **The correct answer is C.** On the first day of school, children in Kazakhstan are expected to honor their ancestors by reciting the names of their grandfathers going back seven generations. Since they are expected to recite the names of grand*fathers*, we can infer that families in Kazakhstan have traditionally followed a patriarchal structure.

3. **The correct answer is A.** In different parts of the passage, you are told that German children start school at 6 while children in Kazakhstan start at 7. Therefore, you can infer that around the world, children do *not* always start school at the same age.

Tone, Style, and Language Use Questions

Tone, style, and language use are all related in that they focus on the choices an author makes to best fulfill their purpose. Questions from these categories tend to focus especially closely on rhetoric, including word choice, style, tone, mood, mode of writing, genre, and use of figurative language. The following sections cover some of the most common topics that tend to come up in questions on tone, style, and language use.

Author's Tone or Mood Questions

The term *tone* describes both an author's attitude toward the topic and the attitude they assume in writing about it. In fictional or literary narratives, tone is more often described using the term *mood*. Questions

about tone might provide you with a few adjectives and ask you to pick which one best describes the tone of the passage, or they might ask you to make a conclusion based on the tone. As with the author's purpose, taking a moment to determine the tone of the passage while reading will make it easier to answer questions such as "What is the author's tone?" If in doubt, eliminate the answer options that seem least correct first.

Point of View Questions

An author's point of view is their position, opinion, belief, or angle regarding a topic. For example, an author might be for or against an idea, or an author might be stating ideas from personal experience. They may also be taking a position or making an argument from a particular perspective. These questions can

QUESTIONS TO ASK YOURSELF: TONE, STYLE, AND LANGUAGE USE

- How does the author feel about this topic?

- What is the genre or style of the passage?

- What do the author's word choices communicate to the reader about their tone or their stance on the topic?

- What position is the author taking in this passage?

- How does the author use language for comparisons, descriptions, or meaning?

- What sort of non-literal language exists in the passage to communicate figurative ideas?

- What are the different methods the author uses to make their ideas and point of view clear?

sometimes look like main idea questions since they also concern the primary argument or idea an author is trying to get across. Therefore, you can use the same techniques you use with main idea questions to address most questions about an author's point of view. Alternatively, in narrative passages, questions about point of view might refer to the narrator's point of view, such as first person vs. third person. A point of view question might ask "What position does the author take in this debate?" or "From whose perspective is this story narrated?" It might also ask you to complete a sentence, such as "We can assume that the author of this passage agrees that..."

Figurative Language Questions

An author uses figurative language to draw comparisons, enhance descriptions, or create deeper meaning. In short, the term "figurative language" describes language that is meant to communicate without being taken literally. It often makes a comparison, creates an image, or otherwise highlights a fundamental quality about a being, object, or situation. Questions about figurative language can pop up anywhere, but they're especially common following literary passages.

The following table lists some common types of figurative language. A question about language use might point out one of these figures of speech and ask you about it, or it might point to a sentence and ask you to identify the type of figurative language used.

COMMON TYPES OF FIGURATIVE LANGUAGE AND FIGURES OF SPEECH

Term	Definition	Examples
Simile	A comparison between two objects or ideas using *like* or *as*.	• The lighthouse beacon was **as** bright **as** the sun. • My bedroom looks **like** a landfill.
Metaphor	A comparison that substitutes literal language for an analogy for another object or idea; usually uses a form of *is*.	• My math teacher **is** a monster! • Some say I **am** a shark in the courtroom. • That restaurant has always **been** a ghost town.
Hyperbole	An overtly exaggerated statement for figurative effect.	• I'm so hungry that I could **eat a horse**! • The **entire galaxy** stops to listen to her stories.
Imagery	Using vivid descriptions to create an image in a reader's mind, often involving adjectives, adverbs, and references to the five senses.	• The sun's **warm, bright** rays came **bursting** through the window as she **quickly** drew the **heavy velvet** curtain. • I **felt goosebumps** as a **biting cold whooshed across my skin**—my **clumsy** brother had left the door open for the **blustering winter wind** to **whip back** in.
Irony	When an author says something that is the opposite of what they mean or that involves a contradiction between expectation and reality. In literary texts, it can also be situations that create irony for a character.	• A character in a play tells their new friend Morgan that they wish they could speak to their brother, but the audience knows that Morgan is their brother in disguise. • A marriage counselor files for divorce. • A character in a story freezes to death in the desert.
Personification	When an object or animal is given human-like qualities.	• I'm so tired that **my bed is calling me.** • The **ocean swallowed** the tiny ship whole. • **My cat** always **flirts** with visitors.
Aphorism	A witty statement or saying that highlights a general truth	• Pride comes before a fall. • Finders keepers, losers weepers. • She's her mother's daughter.
Idiom	A group of words that make sense together phrasally because of their association with a common saying	• Getting to my house is a **piece of cake.** • My husband finally **saw the light** about that ugly paint color. • The flu left Sonja feeling **under the weather**.
Analogy	A comparison between two things made for the purpose of adding clarity or offering an example; they often use simile, metaphors, or idioms to do so	• Finding a job is like **finding a needle in a haystack**. • This summer has been a **rollercoaster of emotions.** • My kitten is a **wrecking ball**, crashing into everything.

Test Yourself 5: Tone, Style, and Language Use

Directions: Read the passage below and then answer the three questions that follow, which address the author's tone/mood, style, word choice, or use of language. After you've selected each answer, read the answer explanations to check yourself.

The following excerpt is adapted from a short story by Willa Cather entitled "The Sculptor's Funeral." In this scene, the sculptor's coffin is being delivered to his hometown in preparation for his funeral.

(1) The coffin was got out of its rough box and down on the snowy platform. **(2)** The townspeople drew back enough to make room for it and then formed a close semicircle about it, looking curiously at the palm leaf which lay across the black cover. **(3)** No one said anything. **(4)** The baggage man stood by his truck, waiting to get at the trunks. **(5)** The engine panted heavily, and the fireman dodged in and out among the wheels with his yellow torch and long oilcan, snapping the spindle boxes. **(6)** The young Bostonian, one of the dead sculptor's pupils who had come with the body, looked about him helplessly. **(7)** He turned to the banker, the only one of that black, uneasy, stoop-shouldered group who seemed enough of an individual to be addressed.

(8) "None of Mr. Merrick's brothers are here?" he asked uncertainly.

(9) The man with the red beard for the first time stepped up and joined the group. "No, they have not come yet; the family is scattered. The body will be taken directly to the house." **(10)** He stooped and took hold of one of the handles of the coffin.

(11) "Take the long hill road up, Thompson—it will be easier on the horses," called the liveryman as the undertaker snapped the door of the hearse and prepared to mount to the driver's seat.

(12) Laird, the red-bearded lawyer, turned again to the stranger: "We didn't know whether there would be anyone with him or not," he explained. **(13)** "It's a long walk, so you'd better go up in the hack." **(14)** He pointed to a single, battered conveyance, but the young man replied stiffly: "Thank you, but I think I will go up with the hearse. If you don't object," turning to the undertaker, "I'll ride with you."

(15) They clambered up over the wheels and drove off in the starlight up the long, white hill toward the town. **(16)** The lamps in the still village were shining from under the low, snow-burdened roofs; and beyond, on every side, the plains reached out into emptiness, peaceful and wide as the soft sky itself, and wrapped in a tangible, white silence.

Adapted from Willa Cather, "The Sculptor's Funeral." Originally published in 1905.

1. From the final paragraph of the passage, we can infer that this story most likely takes place during the

   A. spring.

   B. summer.

   C. autumn.

   D. winter.

2. By saying that the family can't pick up the coffin because they are "scattered," the red-bearded man means that the family is

   A. too depressed to be up to the task.

   B. living in different places far from the town.

   C. mostly dead already.

   D. estranged from the dead sculptor.

3. Based on this excerpt, the mood of the story would best be described as

   A. somber.

   B. romantic.

   C. quixotic.

   D. whimsical.

Answers

1. **The correct answer is D.** Context clues like "snow-burdened roofs" and plains that are "wrapped in a tangible, white silence" assure the reader that there is snow on the ground, so this story most likely takes place in winter.

2. **The correct answer is B.** Saying that the sculptor's family is "scattered" is a figurative way of saying that they are living in different places far from the town.

3. **The correct answer is A.** The mood of this story is somber, meaning "solemn and serious." *Romantic* (choice B) and *whimsical* (choice D) both point to a much more lighthearted story, while *quixotic* (choice C) means "extravagant or idealistic," so it does not match the mood.

Organization and Logic Questions

A passage's organization includes how the information in the passage is arranged and whether that arrangement is logical. It is also about the transition between ideas and how smoothly those transitions are executed. An organized passage will follow a logical train of thought, using transitions and topic sentences when moving between ideas to guide the reader and show how all are related to an overall purpose or main idea. Disorganized passages, on the other hand, tend to jump around between topics without providing adequate transitions or integrating new topics into the context of older ones. You can trust that each of the passages you read on the ACCUPLACER will be well organized, but you should be prepared to

answer questions about *how* the author chose to organize the passage. You should also be prepared to identify a reasonable summary of a passage, which usually involves not just recognizing the main idea of the passage but also the sequence and structure through which the author has conveyed their message.

The term *logic* refers to a reasonable way of thinking about something that makes sense. Logical ideas are organized, direct, ordered, and readily accessible to a reader with reasonable knowledge of the topic. By contrast, ideas are illogical if they are disorganized, jumbled, confusing, or unreasonable. All the reading passages you'll see should be logical, understandable, and clear. As with questions about organization, you will be tested less on whether the passage is logical or not and more on what logic it uses to justify its claims or ideas. It's up to you to decipher how each passage is organized, how the author has logically arranged their ideas, and how the author might logically build on what is already written if they were to do so.

Organization and logic questions might ask you to choose how a particular section is organized. Questions might read something like "Which option best describes the organization of sentences 6–12?" or "Why does the author begin with the example in paragraph 1?" Questions might also ask you to describe the organizational strategy of an entire passage: "This passage is organized in _____ order." The passage might be presented in order of time (known as chronological or sequential order), in a step-by-step order, in order of importance, in physical order (known as spatial order), or something else. Still other questions might ask you about hypothetical writing that isn't included, such as "Which of the following would make a logical topic for a hypothetical paragraph 5?" In each case, you're being asked to identify why the author constructed their passage the way they did and how they might expand on it, if they were to do so.

You may also be asked how the author's purpose relates to the organization of a passage, such as in questions like "What is the purpose of paragraph 3?" While a question like this does require you to understand the author's purpose, it is also asking you to figure out how the placement of that particular paragraph logically relates to ideas that came before and after it. Similarly, you might be asked what sort of information could be

QUESTIONS TO ASK YOURSELF: ORGANIZATION AND LOGIC

- How are the ideas in this passage arranged—are they in order of importance, time, or a different pattern?

- Does the author use transitions and topic sentences to guide the reader through their argument?

- How does the organization of the passage affect its logic?

- If the passage were to continue, what might logically come next?

- If the passage is an excerpt, what might have logically come before it?

- How does the author use (or fail to use) evidence to support claims and counterclaims?

- Does the passage as presented follow a logical train of thought?

added to a passage that would logically match its current organization, such as in a question like "What would be a logical topic for a hypothetical new paragraph between paragraphs 1 and 2?" or "Which of the following additional pieces of evidence would best support the author's purpose?"

 FYI -

Test sections on the ACCUPLACER are sometimes interconnected and questions on organization and logic are a good example of how. While you will likely be asked about how a passage is organized on the reading placement test, you will also be asked to correct issues with logic and organization on the writing placement test. Similarly, the WritePlacer essay will evaluate your ability to deliver organized, logical writing. Therefore, studying the concept for one section of the exam will likely help you when it comes up elsewhere too.

One other type of organization question involves the author's use of research, evidence, quotations from experts, and facts. When authors include such information, they are doing so to show that they are credible sources who have used credible research to make their claims. This type of construction is often called an "appeal to credibility." You may be asked a question like, "In which of the paragraphs does the author appeal to a credible source?" You can also expect to be asked questions about the kind of evidence used to support claims. These and any other questions related to providing credible support tend to fall under the umbrella of organization and logic.

Test Yourself 6: Organization and Logic

Directions: Read the passage below and then answer the three questions that follow, which address the author's organization and logic. After you've selected each answer, read the answer explanations to check yourself.

Sometimes referred to as the Godmother of Rock n' Roll, Sister Rosetta Tharpe is an example of a Black woman who shaped history but didn't end up as famous as most of her male contemporaries. Born in Cotton Plant, Arkansas, she was the daughter of Willis Atkins and Katie Bell Nubin Atkins, a mandolin-playing singer who was also an evangelist for the Church of God in Christ. As a result of her mother's influence, Tharpe's early musical inspiration came primarily from gospel music. To aid in her mother's efforts, Tharpe began singing and playing the guitar as young as four years old.

By the time Tharpe was six years old, she was performing regularly with her mother and was adept at combining secular music styles with the gospel styles popular in religious music. While she was a gifted singer, it was Tharpe's virtuoso skill on the guitar that from such a young age paved her path to fame. Not only could Tharpe easily find various chords and tones, but she was also able to manipulate the strings to produce individual notes, melodies, and riffs, as well as combine chords unexpectedly to produce new sounds. Very few women played guitar at the time, let alone young Black women, so Tharpe was something of an anomaly. Her experimentation with the capabilities of the guitar as an instrument proved foundational to rock n' roll music as a genre.

Over the years, Tharpe gathered new influences from sources like blues and jazz, then integrated aspects of those sounds and styles into her own work, creating a hybrid sound that would set the stage for later developments in rock n' roll and other musical genres. When Tharpe was eventually signed to Decca Records in 1938, it didn't take long for her to become a sensation. To avoid alienating her divergent fan bases, Tharpe would record gospel music for the religious crowd and more up-tempo songs for her growing (and largely white) secular audience. She continued to find success this way for the rest of her career, which ended with her death in 1973.

1. The author's purpose in paragraph 1 is to

    A. talk about Sister Rosetta Tharpe's musical influences.

    B. clarify how Sister Rosetta Tharpe's talents developed by singing in the church gospel choir.

    C. introduce rock n' roll music as a genre.

    D. offer background on Sister Rosetta Tharpe's early childhood.

2. The author wants to add a fourth paragraph. What would be a logical topic for this hypothetical paragraph 4?

    A. Distinctive guitar sounds of Sister Rosetta Tharpe's era

    B. How Sister Rosetta Tharpe influenced music before her death

    C. How Sister Rosetta Tharpe continued to influence music after her death

    D. The long-term influence of gospel music on popular music

3. This passage is organized

    A. to provide step-by-step information.

    B. according to relevance of topic.

    C. in spatial order.

    d. in chronological order.

Answers

1. **The correct answer is D.** The first paragraph offers background on Sister Rosetta Tharpe's parents and her early childhood.

2. **The correct answer is C.** Since paragraph 3 ends by mentioning Sister Rosetta Tharpe's death in 1973, the most logical next move would be to discuss how she continued to influence music after her death. All the other topics would be better suited to other sections of the passage if they were to be inserted.

3. **The correct answer is D.** Since the passage starts with Sister Rosetta Tharpe's birth and ends with her death, it is organized in chronological order.

Opinion and Argument Questions

When an author clarifies their own beliefs, viewpoints, or judgments, they are expressing an opinion. When an author takes a side in a debate, presents a plausible perspective on a researched subject, or tries to convince you to agree with their opinion, they are making an argument. If an author is making an argument, you should be able to identify the argument and how it's organized as well as any support given for that

ALERT

A statement being true doesn't necessarily mean it's a correct answer. Make sure that the answer choice you select answers the question that is asked. Several answer choices might be true, but only one will be the answer to the question.

QUESTIONS TO ASK YOURSELF: OPINION AND ARGUMENT

- Is this passage fact or opinion?
- What is the author's opinion and why?
- What is the author's argument?
- What strategies does the author use to convince readers to agree with the argument?
- Is the author sticking to their own ideas or are they supporting their thoughts with outside information or sources?
- From whose perspective is the author speaking and to which intended audience?
- Does the author seem to have any bias that might cloud the logic of their argument?

argument, such as related facts or examples. You should also be able to identify any claims the author makes and counterclaims they address.

A question dealing with opinion might take the form "Which of these choices best expresses the author's opinion?" For argument questions, you might be presented with several arguments and asked to consider "Which of these statements best summarizes the author's argument in this passage?"

Test Yourself 7: Opinion and Argument

Directions: Read the passage below and then answer the three questions that follow, which address the author's argument. After you've selected each answer, read the answer explanations to check yourself.

Teenagers today are not receiving adequate educations in financial literacy, and it is having an undue impact on their adult lives. On top of that, common advice given to teenagers encourages them to embark on risky financial endeavors that they are too young to fully understand. An 18-year-old is not even considered responsible enough to purchase alcohol, yet our culture believes they have the wherewithal to make a sound and informed decision concerning five-figure student loans. If the culture isn't going to change to be less financially predatory toward young people, then school curricula must change to incorporate a far greater degree of financial literacy training before students graduate high school.

Besides it simply being the ethical thing to do in today's world, there are numerous benefits for young people who learn financial literacy starting in high school or earlier. Knowing how to make money, save money, and make wise financial decisions is empowering for teens, allowing them to feel like they're in control of their financial futures. Furthermore, not providing this type of education leaves young people anxious and ill-equipped. As Geoffrey Bellamy notes in his book *Guiding Teens Toward Financial Success*, when young people don't receive financial literacy education, "they struggle to maintain good credit scores, are unable to save enough money to buy a home or prepare for retirement, and have no idea how to invest." Equipping teens with financial literacy ensures they enter the world with more confidence and avoid falling into bad habits that will be harder to break when they're in a financial hole later. This can protect them, too, such as by making it easier for them to keep a savings fund for emergencies and making them aware of common financial pitfalls, such as gambling and pyramid schemes.

1. The author's main argument in this passage is that

   A. financial literacy training should begin in early adulthood.

   B. young people deserve more financial literacy training before they graduate high school.

   C. teenagers are usually bad with money.

   D. it's becoming harder and harder to save money.

2. With which of the following statements would the author likely agree?

   A. No one should ever take out student loans.

   B. Credit scores are an unfair way to determine who deserves loans.

   C. Teenagers should not have to pay taxes until age 18.

   D. High school students should be taught how to financially plan for their retirement.

3. Which quotation from the passage best expresses the author's argument?

   A. "…common advice given to teenagers encourages them to embark on risky financial endeavors…" (Paragraph 1)

   B. "…school curricula must change to incorporate a far greater degree of financial literacy training…" (Paragraph 1)

   C. "Knowing how to make money, save money, and make wise financial decisions is empowering…" (Paragraph 2)

   D. "Furthermore, not providing this type of education leaves young people anxious and ill-equipped." (Paragraph 2)

Answers

1. **The correct answer is B.** As is often the case with argumentative passages like this one, the author summarizes their argument in the final sentence of the first paragraph: "If the culture isn't going to change to be less financially predatory toward young people, then school curricula must change to incorporate a far greater degree of financial literacy training before students graduate high school."

2. **The correct answer is D.** Since the author's main idea is that young people should get more financial literacy education before they graduate high school, you can infer that the author would agree with the idea of teaching high school students how to start planning for their eventual retirement.

3. **The correct answer is B.** The second quotation comes from the author's thesis statement, which is a type of statement that summarizes an author's argument.

Synthesis Questions

When you are asked to address more than one passage at a time, such as in the paired set of informational passages you'll encounter on the ACCUPLACER, you must use all the skills you've deployed in the sections prior simultaneously. Paired passages are all about synthesizing information. The verb *synthesize* in this context means "to combine a number of elements into a coherent whole." Your task then is to figure out how the passages make sense together rather than just on their own.

The good news is that when synthesizing information from multiple passages simultaneously, you're not actually reading any differently. You should approach reading the paired passages in the same way you would solo passages in any other section. The challenge lies in looking for relationships between the texts, recognizing where they agree and diverge, and practicing your inference and summary skills so you can express that relationship clearly.

If you can identify the main idea, purpose, and supporting details of each passage, you should have what you need to synthesize information between the two.

QUESTIONS TO ASK YOURSELF: SYNTHESIZING INFORMATION FROM MULTIPLE PASSAGES

- How could each passage be summarized individually?
- How could passages be summarized together?
- In which ways do the authors agree and disagree?
- What are some key concepts or ideas that come up in both passages?
- How might looking at both passages provide deeper understanding than just looking at one or the other?
- If the authors of both passages were to debate each other, what topics might come up?
- How do the passages represent two different perspectives on the same topic?

Test Yourself 8: Synthesis

Directions: Read the passages below and then answer the three questions that follow, which address your ability to synthesize information from two related passages. After you've selected each answer, read the answer explanations to check yourself.

Passage 1 is adapted from "When Modern Eurasia Was Born," published by the University of Copenhagen, which focuses on how immigration patterns leading up to and during the Bronze Age contributed to the demographics of modern Eurasia. Passage 2 is adapted from "European invasion: DNA reveals the origins of modern Europeans," by Alan Cooper and Wolfgang Haak.

Passage 1

The re-writing of the genetic map began in the early Bronze Age, about 5,000 years ago. From the steppes in the Caucasus, the Yamnaya Culture migrated principally westward into North and Central Europe, and to a lesser degree, into western Siberia. Yamnaya was characterized by a new system of family and property. In northern Europe the Yamnaya mixed with the Stone Age people who inhabited this region and along the way established the Corded Ware Culture, which genetically speaking resembles present-day Europeans living north of the Alps today.

Later, about 4,000 years ago, the Sintashta Culture evolved in the Caucasus. This culture's sophisticated new weapons and chariots were rapidly expanding across Europe. The area east of the Urals and far into Central Asia was colonized around 3,800 years ago by the Andronovo Culture. The researchers' investigation shows that this culture had a European DNA background.

During the last part of the Bronze Age, and at the beginning of the Iron Age, East Asian peoples arrived in Central Asia. Here it is not genetic admixture we see, but rather a replacement of genes. The European genes in the area disappear.

These new results derive from DNA analyses of skeletons excavated across large areas of Europe and Central Asia, thus enabling these crucial glimpses into the dynamics of the Bronze Age. In addition to the population movement insights, the data also held other surprises. For example, contrary to the research team's expectations, the data revealed that lactose tolerance rose to high frequency in Europeans, in comparison to prior belief that it evolved earlier in time (5,000–7,000 years ago).

Passage 2

What we have found is that, in addition to the original European hunter-gatherers and a heavy dose of Near Eastern farmers, we can now add a third major population: steppe pastoralists. These nomads appear to have "invaded" central Europe in a previously unknown wave during the early Bronze Age (about 4,500 years ago).

This event saw the introduction of two very significant new technologies to western Europe: domestic horses and the wheel. It also reveals the mysterious source for the Indo-European languages.

The genetic results have answered several contentious and long-standing questions in European history. The first big issue was whether the first farmers in Europe were hunter-gatherers who had learnt farming techniques from neighbours in southeast Europe, or did they instead come from the Near East, where farming was invented? The genetic results are clear: farming was introduced widely across Europe in one or two rapid waves around 8,000 years ago by populations from the Near East—effectively the very first skilled migrants.

At first the original hunter-gatherer populations appear to have retreated to the fringes of Europe: to Britain, Scandinavia and Finland. But the genetics show that within a few thousand years they had returned, and significant amounts of hunter-gatherer genomic DNA was mixed in with the farmers 7,000 to 5,000 years ago across many parts of Europe.

But there was still a major outstanding mystery. Apart from these two groups, the genomic signals clearly showed that a third—previously unsuspected—large contribution had been made sometime before the Iron Age, around 2,000 years ago. But by whom?

We have finally been able to identify the mystery culprit, using a clever new system invented by our colleagues at Harvard University. Instead of sequencing the entire genome from a very small number of well-preserved skeletons, we analysed 400,000 small genetic markers right across the genome. This made it possible to rapidly survey large numbers of skeletons from all across Europe and Eurasia.

This process revealed the solution to the mystery. Our survey showed that skeletons of the Yamnaya culture from the Russian/Ukrainian grasslands north of the Black Sea, buried in large mounds known as kurgans, turned out to be the genetic source we were missing.

1. Which choice best describes the relationship between Passage 1 and Passage 2?

   A. Both passages show conflicting claims about the migrations.

   B. Both passages describe different scientific methodologies.

   C. Passage 2 provides supplementary information to Passage 1.

   D. Passage 2 is written from a different perspective than Passage 1.

2. Based on information in the passages, which of the following statements could be made about scientific inquiry?

   A. DNA evidence showed why many Europeans are lactose intolerant.

   B. Genetic research can provide valid historical information.

   C. Evidence showed that the steppe pastoralists introduced horses and the wheel to Western Europe.

   D. Scientific investigation can provide evidence about human history not obtainable through other means.

3. How do the passages illustrate the contributions of DNA evidence to scientific inquiry?

   A. Both passages provide examples of how DNA evidence enabled scientists to fill in gaps in their knowledge about human migrations.

   B. Both passages describe how DNA analysis is used in scientific investigations.

   C. Both passages imply that DNA evidence can solve evolutionary questions.

   D. Both passages show how scientists solved the mysteries of DNA evidence.

Answers

1. **The correct answer is C.** When reading paired passages, you will encounter questions that ask you to examine the relationship between the passages. On your first reading, you probably noticed that the two passages do not contradict one another, nor do they show different points of view. This means you can eliminate choices A and D. Since both passages describe scientific studies and what scientists were able to learn from them and both describe using DNA as the methodology, choice B cannot be correct. By process of elimination, choice C must be the best answer. The second passage adds to the information in the first, which makes the information in Passage 2 supplementary to the information shown in Passage 1.

2. **The correct answer is D.** This question asks you to compare the two passages and look for a topic that is not directly discussed, but one that is implicit within it—the nature of scientific inquiry. While choices A and C are true, neither one answers the question. Choice B is also true, but it doesn't address the nature of scientific investigations; it is simply a general statement that could apply to many texts. Choice D, however, states a fact about scientific inquiry that can be gleaned from the text: Both passages describe how scientists were able to use DNA data to answer questions they were unable to address before the use of DNA testing was available.

3. **The correct answer is A.** In paired passages, you will encounter questions that ask you to compare or contrast information presented explicitly in the passages. Both passages illustrate how DNA has been used to answer questions about human migration patterns—questions that had been unresolved before the ability to use DNA as evidence for such studies. Neither passage gives details about the actual scientific methodology as both are focused on the results, so you can eliminate choice B as a possible correct answer. Choices C and D are not correct interpretations of the passages, so you can eliminate these choices as well.

Bringing Your Reading Comprehension Skills Together

You now know all the most important reading comprehension topics and skills that are likely to be covered on the ACCUPLACER. As a reminder, these include the following:

- Author's Main Idea and Purpose
- Supporting Details
- Vocabulary in Context
- Making Inferences
- Author's Style, Tone/Mood, Language Use, and Word Choice
- Organization and Logic of Passage

- Determining Opinion and/or Argument
- Synthesizing Information from Multiple Passages

On the next page, you'll find a sample reading passage with a graphic illustration of how different parts of a passage relate to multiple question types we have discussed here. Keep in mind that you might get a question on the exam that doesn't seem to fall into any of these categories, but don't panic! If you're reading closely and actively for understanding, you can tackle any reading comprehension question that is thrown at you. Rest assured that the information you need to answer a question will always be found in the passage, so rely on the reading comprehension abilities you've built to find the right answer.

NOTES

Example Reading Passage with Sample Questions

Directions: Read the passage and note how the numbered sections relate to the numbered sample questions on the opposite page. The numbers are there to help you identify how different types of questions relate to a single passage and where in the passage you would find the answer. Try to answer the questions for yourself. Then, check your answers against the answer key. As a challenge, imagine yourself in the role of an editor for this book. What sort of explanations would you write to show how and why the correct answers are correct?

Sometimes, you can knock a vocabulary question out before you even begin reading by previewing the sentence that contains it.

Note that previewing the first and last sentence of the first and last paragraphs would allow you to answer at least two questions before even reading the full passage!

Michelangelo Buonarroti's *David* is arguably the most famous statue in the world. Michelangelo sculpted the 17-foot biblical figure from marble be-

❶ tween 1501 and 1504 to grace the Pallazo Vecchio, a public square near some government buildings. Today, a replica stands in its initial location and

❷ Michelangelo's original is featured at the Galleria dell'Academia in Florence, Italy.

In his left hand, David carries a sling reminiscent of the biblical story

❸ in which he slays a giant. This detail means that Michelangelo was likely picturing David as a left-handed person. However, art historians note that

❹ it is David's right hand that presents a bigger mystery. First, it seems oversized compared to the otherwise proportionate statue. Second, the fingers appear to be curled around a mystery object. Art historians note that the veins in the right hand are prominent, suggesting that whatever David is holding, he's clutching it tightly.

There is some speculation that the oversized structure of the right hand is purely symbolic and meant to remind viewers of David having a "strong

❺ hand" in his later years as a king. Others suggest it could be as simple as David holding the stone that he will use to slay a foe with his sling. Still others suggest he could be holding a second weapon entirely. Whatever the case may be, there is no way of knowing what exactly Michelangelo imag-

❻ ined David gripping in his right hand, so the answer remains one of the art world's greatest mysteries.

1 INFERENCES

From paragraph 1, we can infer that

- **A.** in the 16th century, all Italian art was required to have a religious context.
- **B.** it took more than a decade to sculpt *David*.
- **C.** *David* was not considered a masterpiece of sculpture until it was moved to a museum.
- **D.** the government in Michelangelo's time was at least somewhat tied to the Christian church.

2 SUPPORTING DETAILS

Where is the original *David* located today?

- **A.** Museo di Michelangelo
- **B.** Pallazo Vecchio
- **C.** Galleria dell'Academia
- **D.** Sistine Chapel

3 VOCABULARY

As used in the first sentence of the second paragraph, the word "reminiscent" most nearly means

- **A.** bashful.
- **B.** elusive.
- **C.** mindful.
- **D.** remindful.

4 ORGANIZATION AND LOGIC

The author's purpose in paragraph 2 is to

- **A.** critique Michelangelo's artistic execution.
- **B.** narrate Michelangelo's creative process.
- **C.** clarify a prominent reason that art historians still speculate about the statue.
- **D.** summarize recent findings about the importance of the statue.

5 TONE, STYLE, AND LANGUAGE USE

The author's use of the phrase "strong hand" in paragraph 3 figuratively references the idea that David might have been a(n)

- **A.** firm, decisive leader.
- **B.** renowned athlete.
- **C.** impulsive, hot-headed warrior.
- **D.** celebrated artist.

6 MAIN IDEA

The main idea of this passage is that

- **A.** *David* is the most important statue of all time.
- **B.** art historians remain divided as to what the David figure is holding in his right hand.
- **C.** art historians determined that the David figure is holding a weapon in his left hand.
- **D.** *David* is a proportionately oversized work, and its size reflects its symbolic meanings.

ANSWER KEY

| 1. D | 2. C | 3. D | 4. C | 5. A | 6. B |

SUMMING IT UP

- The reading section on the ACCUPLACER consists of 20 questions and does not have a time limit. This section includes the following:

  - One literary passage followed by four questions
  - A set of two paired informational passages followed by four questions
  - 10–12 standalone passages with a question each
  - 1–3 vocabulary questions, in which you must choose a missing word or phrase from a given sentence

- The questions you will encounter on the reading comprehension section could be about the following:

  - Identifying Main Idea and Author's Purpose
  - Finding Supporting Details for Main Idea
  - Analyzing Vocabulary in Context
  - Making Inferences
  - Explaining Author's Style, Tone, Mood, Use of Language, and Word Choice
  - Indicating Author's Organization and Logic
  - Determining Opinions and Arguments
  - Synthesizing Information from Multiple Passages

- Read the questions before you begin closely reading a passage, then actively pay attention while reading to determine the location of relevant information.

- Pay attention to what the passage isn't saying. You might be asked to infer or predict something that isn't directly stated.

- If you're stumped, try to eliminate incorrect answer choices before making a guess and moving on.

READING COMPREHENSION

20 Questions

> **Directions for Questions 1–18:** Read the following passage(s) and answer the related question(s) based on what is stated or implied in the passage(s) as well as any provided introductory material.

This passage is excerpted from a memoir written by the daughter of a samurai. In this passage, she recalls some of her observations as a young woman who grew up in feudal Japan before moving to an American suburb with her family at the turn of the 20th century.

(1) The standards of my own and my adopted country differed so widely in some ways, and my love for both lands was so sincere, that sometimes I had an odd feeling of standing upon a cloud in space and gazing with measuring eyes upon two separate worlds. (2) At first I was continually trying to explain, by Japanese standards, all the queer things that came every day before my surprised eyes; for no one seemed to know the origin or significance of even the most familiar customs, nor why they existed and were followed. (3) To me, coming from a land where there is an unforgotten reason for every fashion of dress, for every motion in etiquette—indeed, for almost every trivial act of life—this indifference of Americans seemed very singular.

(4) Mother was a wonderful source of information, but I felt a hesitation about asking too many questions, for my curiosity was so frequently about odd, trifling, unimportant things, such as why ladies kept on their hats in church while men took theirs off; what was the use of the china plates which I saw hanging on the walls of some beautiful houses; why guests are taken to the privacy of a bedroom and asked to put their hats and cloaks on the *bed*—a place that suggested sleep or sickness; why people make social calls in the *evening*—the time of leisure in Japan; what originated the merriment and nonsense of Hallowe'en and April Fool's days, and why such a curious custom exists as the putting of gifts in stockings—*stockings*, the very humblest of all the garments that are worn.

(5) It seemed strange to me that there should never be any hint or allusion to these customs in conversation, in books, or in newspapers. (6) In Japan, tradition, folklore, and symbolism are before one all the time. (7) The dress of the people on the streets; the trade-mark on the swinging curtains of the shops; the decorations on chinaware; the call of the street vender; the cap of the soldier; the pleated skirt of the schoolgirl: each points back to some well-known tale of how or why. (8) Even the narrow blue-and white towel of the jinrikisha man and the layer lunch-box of the workman bear designs suggesting an ancient poem or a bit of folklore, as familiar to every Japanese child as are the melodies of Mother Goose to the children of America.

From Etsu Inagaki Sugimoto, *A Daughter of the Samurai*. Originally published in 1925

1. The contrast the author sets up between feudal Japan and suburban America can best be described as one of

   A. old traditions vs. new traditions.

   B. awareness of the history of traditions vs. lack of awareness about the origin of traditions.

   C. adherence to traditions vs. refusal of traditions.

   D. indifference to traditions vs. meticulous observation of traditions.

2. The author uses descriptive, figurative language in sentence 1 to

   A. help the reader understand what it felt like to balance existing in two cultural paradigms simultaneously.

   B. allude to the frustration the author felt about not understanding American customs.

   C. question the purpose for engaging in American customs like removing one's hat in church.

   D. vividly describe how the Japanese language affected her understanding of American concepts.

3. A reasonable inference one can draw from this passage is that

   A. religious customs are a primary source of long-standing traditions globally.

   B. the author did not enjoy her childhood in Japan compared with her life in the United States.

   C. the author did not enjoy her time in the United States compared with her life in Japan.

   D. in the United States, holidays are closely linked with traditions and customs.

4. As used at the end of sentence 3, the word "singular" most nearly means

   A. peculiar.

   B. solitary.

   C. lonesome.

   D. outstanding.

The following passages represent two perspectives regarding debates around the legalization of schedule I psychedelics for use in clinical research regarding their therapeutic effects.

Passage 1

Ever since the federal government classified psychedelic drugs as schedule I substances in 1973, meaning it was illegal to possess them, it has been difficult for the scientific community to engage in meaningful clinical research about the potential efficacy of these substances in treating a wide range of physical and psychological conditions. Today, this policy is widely regarded as the reason that scientists do not yet have a more nuanced understanding of the therapeutic benefits of psychedelics, which are increasingly proving to be myriad. Luckily, sentiments seem to be shifting in favor of valuing scientific inquiry over outdated notions of propriety regarding what is and is not suitable for therapeutic use. For instance, Oregon now allows researchers freedom to investigate clinical application of psilocybin despite it still being classified as a schedule I psychedelic. Researchers who champion this application of psilocybin are hopeful that further research will highlight potential benefits of psilocybin use for the therapeutic treatment of suicidality, post-traumatic stress disorder, addiction, and depression, among others. One can expect that as psychedelic advocacy increases among medical researchers, so too will the potential for a wide range of therapeutic treatments that have heretofore been cut off from potential discovery. As the benefits of such therapies become clearer and demand for psychedelic therapy increases, we can expect the pace of clinical psychedelic research to rightfully accelerate accordingly.

Passage 2

There can be no doubt that further research needs to be done regarding the potential therapeutic benefits of psilocybin. When considering the promising results researchers have already had regarding such life-altering issues as post-traumatic stress disorder, complex childhood trauma, and suicidal ideations, it is obvious that any headway researchers can make in finding ways to alleviate these issues for patients is a net positive. That said, there is undeniably a tradeoff that must occur when considering schedule I psychedelics as therapeutic interventions, especially as concerns patients who have already demonstrated psychological issues or a propensity toward addiction. Regardless of how governmental interventions have historically prevented research of the depth and rigor necessary to better understand how to safely use psychedelics, the fact remains that researchers are largely in uncharted territory when it comes to therapeutic applications of psychedelics generally and psilocybin specifically.

For one, there can be no doubt that any drug, no matter how beneficial, represents the potential for addictive behavior. Schedule II drugs like dextroamphetamine (more commonly known as Adderall) are widely available and have been linked not only with habit-forming behavior in patients who take them legally but also with addictive behavior in those for whom the drug is not prescribed. The takeaway is that even proper therapeutic applications of schedule I psychedelics are not without dangers of abuse by patients and non-patients alike. Should schedule I drugs like psilocybin become available, there is a strong likelihood that some who take them will form addictions and that the drugs will be more easily reachable by those who wish to abuse them recreationally. This is not to say that the likelihood of abuse precludes the potential benefits of clinical investigations into the therapeutic positives of such drugs, only that those who enthusiastically endorse more widespread access to these substances may unintentionally gloss over these dangers in their quest for scientific innovation. Any approach to research on use of psilocybin and other psychedelics for medicinal purposes would do well to take a long view rather than rushing to make these treatments widely available immediately. Protocols for controlling access to the drugs, as well as rigorous testing to ensure undue side effects are accounted for, must be foremost in the process.

5. The rhetorical stance the author takes in Passage 1 suggests that they are

   A. against the legalization of schedule I psychedelics for possession in clinical research settings.

   B. perplexed as to why scientists have not bothered to investigate therapeutic uses of psilocybin in the past.

   C. enthusiastic about the potential benefits of allowing clinical researchers to conduct experiments using schedule I psychedelics.

   D. wary of the potential pitfalls that might come from conducting clinical experiments using psilocybin.

6. Given the claims made in the passages, both authors would most likely agree that

 A. there is no way to conduct research on schedule I substances safely.

 B. the potential negative side effects of psilocybin and other schedule I substances would likely outweigh any potential therapeutic benefit the drugs might hold.

 C. psilocybin and other schedule I psychedelics should be clinically researched for potential therapeutic benefits.

 D. psilocybin and other schedule I psychedelics should not be clinically researched for potential therapeutic benefits.

7. Which summary best describes the relationship between the two passages?

 A. Passage 1 is in favor of clinical research on schedule I psychedelics, while Passage 2 is opposed to clinical research on schedule I psychedelics.

 B. Passage 1 is in favor of clinical research on all psychedelics, while Passage 2 argues that some psychedelics (such as psilocybin) are too dangerous to be deserving of reclassification for research settings.

 C. Passage 1 primarily considers the potential benefits of clinical research on psychedelics for therapeutic purposes, while Passage 2 focuses exclusively on the potential negative impact of using such substances therapeutically.

 D. While the authors of both passages recognize that research into the therapeutic benefits of psychedelics is necessary, the author of Passage 2 cautions that research needs to be thorough, controlled, and not rushed.

8. The author of Passage 2 includes the example about dextroamphetamine to

 A. illustrate how existing legal drugs have been shown to be habit-forming and how their availability increased addiction issues among patients with prescriptions and the general population alike.

 B. show the similarities between dextroamphetamine and psilocybin since both affect chemicals in the brain.

 C. question the validity of psilocybin treatment for psychiatric conditions since dextroamphetamine proved to be of limited therapeutic value.

 D. offer an example of an existing drug that should be on the list of schedule I substances so that it can be better regulated.

The following is adapted from an essay by an ecological researcher.

There are numerous downsides to traditional grass lawns. For one, all the chemicals and fertilizers people use to keep them green don't stay put; instead, sprinklers and rainwater make them run off lawns and into sewers, where they end up polluting streams, rivers, lakes, and the ocean, wreaking havoc on the local ecosystem. Those same chemicals can also harm pets, such as by seeping into their paws when they hang out in the yard. Lawns are also typically unused or rarely used spaces, yet every house having one makes it harder for municipalities to create enough housing for increasing populations. Add to that the amount of water that keeping lawns green uses up and you have a serious problem. According to the Environmental Protection Agency, as much as 30% of the average American household's water use goes to the lawn alone. If you cut out the grass lawn, you're also saving thousands of gallons of water a year.

It is imperative that people consider more eco-friendly alternatives to the traditional grass lawn. One alternative involves mowing less often (or not at all) to allow native grasses and plants to be restored. This effect is all the better when homeowners plant noninvasive local plants that thrive in the climate. Similarly, turning some of the turf into planting ground for edible plants is a way to make more economical use of lawn space, especially if you plant things that might help others in your community, like fruit trees. Another method is xeriscaping, which is a fancy term for landscaping that requires little to no water. This often involves using hardy desert plants like succulents within rock arrangements to create a visually appealing lawn with minimal or no grass. Traditional lawns just aren't worth it when so many eco-friendly alternatives exist.

9. Based on the claims in the passage, which of the following is NOT a social or ecological concern associated with green grass lawns?

   A. Grass lawns use up a significant amount of water.
   B. Fertilizers and other lawn chemicals can hurt pets.
   C. Runoff from lawns pollutes streams and rivers.
   D. Fertilizers and other lawn chemicals can pollute the air.

Rather than an idyllic place for specters to cohabitate, a "ghost town" is a town that has long since been left abandoned or uninhabited. While buildings and other artefacts remain as proof of the life that once lit up the streets, ghost towns are generally empty, decaying, and proverbially returning to nature. There are roughly 3,800 ghost towns in the United States alone, many of which exist because they were founded during gold rushes or periods of thriving industrial development, then abandoned when those industries became no longer lucrative or necessary.

10. As used in the last sentence of the passage, the word "lucrative" most nearly means

   A. profitable.

   B. expensive.

   C. habitable.

   D. safe.

Throughout his March 2018 *Smithsonian Magazine* article "Do Trees Talk to Each Other?" journalist Richard Grant recounts German forester and author Peter Wohlleben demonstrating various ways that trees communicate in nature. For instance, Wohlleben takes Grant to a pair of beech trees and shows that their leaves avoid intruding on each other's space. Grant quotes Wohlleben saying, "These two are old friends. They are very considerate in sharing the sunlight, and their root systems are closely connected. In cases like this, when one dies, the other usually dies soon afterward, because they are dependent on each other." Instead of trees being isolated individuals, as scientists long thought, the article says new evidence points toward an opposite truth. Trees are communal, participating in communicative activities like sharing water and nutrients, using root networks to send distress signals to one another about unfavorable conditions like disease, pests, or drought, and even keeping old stumps alive after a tree has fallen. Wohlleben even pushes his theory into the realm of personification, emphasizing how mother trees have been known to "suckle their young" by sending sugar to their roots to stimulate healthy growth.

Adapted from Grant, Richard. 2018. Review of *Do Trees Talk to Each Other?, Smithsonian Magazine*, March 2018. https://www.smithsonianmag.com/science-nature/the-whispering-trees-180968084/.

11. The author's purpose in this summary paragraph is to

   A. theorize new ways for humans to communicate with trees.

   B. persuade the reader to care more about ecological concerns that affect trees.

   C. list the different examples Wohlleben gave Grant that demonstrate trees being communicative.

   D. debate whether the findings Wohlleben showed Grant truly prove that trees communicate.

The Nehiyawak, more commonly known to English speakers as the Cree people, are the largest group of indigenous peoples in Canada. More than 350,000 people in Canada identify as having Cree ancestry. There are also a few pockets of Cree in the United States, such as on the Rocky Boy Indian Reservation in Montana. Of those with Cree ancestry, only about 96,000 still speak the language. Consequently, efforts are being made to preserve the Cree language, alongside many other indigenous languages, so that they won't be lost to the ravages of time. For instance, members of the James Bay Cree community founded an annual language symposium in 2018, and local governments in Cree communities have passed resolutions to support the preservation of language and culture by investing in community education on the topic.

Young people with Cree backgrounds are also working in their own way to protect the history of their people. For instance, there are numerous influencers on platforms like TikTok, Twitter, and Instagram who are working to inform their followers about their culture. A common message among them is the idea that indigenous culture isn't a relic of the past but rather a living, breathing aspect of their identities. They want to remind people that they exist and are still contributing their unique perspectives on art, culture, politics, and society to the world. By sharing traditional costumes, music, and dances as well as speaking on their experiences, these young influencers show that the Cree First Nations are still and always have been an integral part of Canadian life.

12. Which of the following pieces of evidence from the passage best supports the author's implicit claim that preservation of Cree language and culture is a modern issue?

   A. 350,000 people in Canada identify as having Cree ancestry.

   B. Young influencers are using TikTok and other social media platforms to discuss Cree issues.

   C. Different Cree communities have different governments that tackle issues in their own way.

   D. There is a Cree language symposium held each year in the James Bay Cree community.

Renowned scientist Rosalind Franklin's most groundbreaking discovery was that of the structure of DNA. However, she is equally well known for being a prime example of a woman who suffered sexist intellectual theft in the scientific community. Having acquired skills in both x-ray diffraction and crystallography, Franklin was the first to apply these skills to the study of DNA fibers, representing a fundamentally novel application of x-ray diffraction. During her experiments, Franklin managed to take a photograph that played a pivotal role in scientists' early understanding of DNA structure. Specifically, Franklin determined that DNA had a dry form, known as the A form, and a wet form, known as the B form. The photograph Franklin took, known as Photograph 51, showed the B form clearly enough to help solidify this new knowledge about DNA, but getting it also meant Franklin was exposed to more than 100 hours of x-ray radiation. While there is no definitive proof, many speculate that Franklin's radiation exposure ultimately played a role in her developing terminal cancer when she was only 37 years old.

Frustratingly, as is the case for many women in the history of science, it took many years for the scientific community to give Franklin the recognition she deserved. Drawing on her research, other scientists tried to claim her discoveries as their own. For instance, a colleague of Franklin's named Maurice Wilkins shared Photograph 51 with another scientist, James Watson, without Franklin's permission. Wilkins and Watson, along with scientist Francis Crick, went on to use the information gleaned from the photograph as the basis of their own famous DNA model. Effectively, this meant that the three men published groundbreaking knowledge from Franklin's discovery without affording her proper credit beyond a measly footnote. It wasn't until many years later that this intellectual theft was recognized by the wider scientific community and scientific history properly amended to restore credit to Franklin.

13. The author's purpose in the second paragraph is to

   A. highlight how the men Franklin worked with took credit for her discoveries.

   B. argue against the narrative that Franklin had her work stolen.

   C. enumerate the problems women face in the sciences.

   D. discredit the findings published by Wilkins, Watson, and Crick.

This passage is adapted from a historical document describing the Berlin Wall.

The wall was an imposing landmark. It was built of concrete right in the middle of the city and topped with barbed wire. It had a strip of "no man's land" in the center that was patrolled by attack dogs and included land mines and massive barriers. During the 28 years that armed guards watched over the wall, more than 100,000 East German citizens tried to escape using such innovative methods as digging tunnels, ziplining, performing suitcase contortion, and even flying hot air balloons. Tragically, more than 600 were not successful and lost their lives while attempting to escape.

14. Which of the following was NOT a type of deterrent used to keep people from crossing the Berlin Wall?

   A. Armed guards

   B. Grenades

   C. Attack dogs

   D. Barbed wire

Picture this: You're a young, established revolutionary poet in the Soviet Union during Stalin's reign, living through a period that will later be called the "Great Terror" or "Great Purge" by historians. During this period, anyone who speaks out against Stalin or the atrocities they've witnessed is rounded up and sent to harsh labor camps in Siberia called *gulags*. As a poet, you know the importance of words for preserving history, but it's too dangerous to write your ideas down—someone might find them and report you, which would essentially be a death sentence. What would you do?

This is the exact dilemma Anna Akhmatova found herself in during the Great Purge between 1936 and 1938 when as many as 750,000 people were executed and another million were interred in gulags by Stalin's Soviet government. Akhmatova knew she was being closely watched by secret police because she was a known political agitator; her own husband had been framed and killed, and her son had been arrested and tortured at various points. All eyes were on her, so even a single scrap of paper containing a single critical line would have been enough for Akhmatova to end up facing execution.

So, what did Akhmatova do to make sure she and her poetry survived this period? She never kept a single writ-ten word. Instead, Akhmatova would create lines of poetry on paper, memorize them, then burn the scraps of paper. She regularly recited the parts she had already memorized so she could keep building on the poem over time. Akhmatova titled the poem "Requiem," and it became one of the only surviving pieces of Russian litera-ture written about Stalin's Great Purge while it was occurring.

15. Which is the best title for this passage?

   A. "Women Writers in Stalin's Soviet Union"

   B. "Why is Poetry Important to History?"

   C. "A Biography of Anna Akhmatova"

   D. "Anna Akhmatova's 'Requiem' and the Great Purge"

The following is excerpted from an art history textbook analyzing the impact of different contemporary artists.

What makes a painting a painting, and what makes a photograph a photograph? If you've ever seen works by the contemporary German artist Gerhard Richter, then you'll know that the answer to that question isn't as straightforward as it seems.

After acquiring formal training in painting through his teen years and early adulthood, Richter became fascinated with the interplay between abstract art and photorealism. More specifically, he was interested in blurring the lines between photographs and paintings—what would it mean if you could make a painting that looked just like a photograph? How would people know it was a painting? Would it matter that it was a painting and not a photograph if people couldn't tell the difference? Questions like these drove Richter to experiment. He created abstract but realistic oil paintings meant to look exactly like motion-blurred or unfocused photographs in hopes of convincing viewers to grapple with these same questions.

16. The author's purpose in paragraph 1 is to

    A. set up a critique of Gerhard Richter's art.

    B. introduce the topic by discussing Gerhard Richter's personal biography.

    C. pose a rhetorical question that helps introduce the main idea.

    D. transition from earlier writing to a new topic.

The following excerpt is adapted from an account of the scientific contributions of John Snow, a prominent figure in the history of epidemiology and public health.

Snow was born in York on 15 March 1813, one of eight children in a family of modest means. He apprenticed with a surgeon-apothecary in Newcastle from 1827 to 1833, and there witnessed the first epidemic of cholera in the UK. He then moved to London, qualified as physician in 1843 and set up general practice in Soho. Early in his career he became interested in the physiology of respiration in recognition of the major problem of asphyxia of the newborn.

These interests led him to be invited to witness one of the first applications of ether anesthesia in the UK in December 1846. He immediately recognized the importance of ambient temperature and within one month published tables of the vapor pressure of ether. This initiated an important line of research on instruments for administering anesthetics and led to his becoming the most prominent authority on anesthesia in the UK. He administered chloroform to Queen Victoria at the birth of Prince Leopold in 1853.

The second great cholera epidemic arrived in London in 1848, and many attributed its cause to an atmospheric "effluence" or "miasma." Snow's firsthand experience of the disease in 1832, combined with studies of respiration, led him to question miasma theories and to publish the first edition of *On the Mode of Communication of Cholera* in 1849, in which he proposed that cholera was attributable to a self-replicating agent which was excreted in the cholera evacuations and inadvertently ingested, often, but not necessarily, through the medium of water.

17. This passage is organized

    A. in chronological order.

    B. in spatial order.

    C. to offer step-by-step information.

    D. to put the most important information up front.

Nicholas Wegner of NOAA Fisheries' Southwest Fisheries Science Center in La Jolla, California, is lead author of a new paper on the opah, or moonfish. He and his coauthor, biologist Owyn Snodgrass, discovered that the opah has the unusual ability to keep its body warm, even in the cold depths of the ocean. An excerpt on their findings follows.

Wegner realized the opah was unusual when a coauthor of the study, biologist Owyn Snodgrass, collected a sample of its gill tissue. Wegner recognized an unusual design: Blood vessels that carry warm blood into the fish's gills wind around those carrying cold blood back to the body core after absorbing oxygen from water.

The design is known in engineering as "counter-current heat exchange." In opah it means that warm blood leaving the body core helps heat up cold blood returning from the respiratory surface of the gills, where it absorbs oxygen. Resembling a car radiator, it's a natural adaptation that conserves heat. The unique location of the heat exchange within the gills allows nearly the fish's entire body to maintain an elevated temperature, known as endothermy, even in the chilly depths.

"There has never been anything like this seen in a fish's gills before," Wegner said. "This is a cool innovation by these animals that gives them a competitive edge. The concept of counter-current heat exchange was invented in fish long before we thought of it."

---

18. Which of the following statements most accurately summarizes what makes the opah different from other cold climate fish?

    A. Opah do not require warm blood to function in cold temperatures since their bodies are uniquely adapted to function even when their blood is cooled by dips in environmental temperatures.

    B. Due to a natural adaptation in which warm blood vessels from the opah's core transfer heat to blood vessels carrying cold blood from the gills, opah can maintain their body temperatures even in extremely chilly conditions.

    C. Due to a natural adaptation, opah can centralize heat to their gills where it's needed most while maintaining cold temperatures throughout the rest of their bodies, effectively paralyzing part of their body to conserve heat.

    D. Opah gills are uniquely shaped to insulate the rest of the body from cold temperatures, allowing them to heat their bodies through rapid movement of the gill structure.

Directions for Questions 19 and 20: The following sentences have a blank indicating that something has been left out. Beneath each sentence are four words or phrases. Choose the word or phrase that, when inserted in the sentence, best fits the meaning of the sentence as a whole.

---

19. My annoying stepsister considers it her destiny in life to _____ me.

    A. perturb

    B. germinate

    C. perforate

    D. rebate

20. Henrietta's new assistant has a more businesslike manner than her _____ in the position.

    A. precedent

    B. ancestor

    C. successor

    D. predecessor

ANSWER KEY AND EXPLANATIONS

1. B	**5.** C	**9.** D	**13.** A	**17.** A
2. A	**6.** C	**10.** A	**14.** B	**18.** B
3. D	**7.** D	**11.** C	**15.** D	**19.** A
4. A	**8.** A	**12.** B	**16.** C	**20.** D

1. **The correct answer is B.** The author makes it clear that Americans do have and keep traditions and customs since she spends most of the second paragraph listing American traditions she has observed being carried out. However, she also notes in sentence 6 that "In Japan, tradition, folklore, and symbolism are before one all the time," whereas in the US, people don't seem to be as aware of where their traditions and customs come from or why they observe them. While the author does mention "indifference" in sentence 3, contextual clues reveal that the indifference to which the author refers is that of knowing the history and purpose of traditions and customs, not indifference to the traditions themselves.

2. **The correct answer is A.** Context clues reveal that the author uses the descriptive metaphor of "standing upon a cloud in space and gazing with measuring eyes upon two separate worlds" to figuratively relay to the reader what it felt like to balance her understanding of and socialization within two cultures simultaneously.

3. **The correct answer is D.** The only inference that can be supported by the text is that holidays in the United States are closely linked with traditions and customs. This is because a fair amount of time is spent in sentence 4 questioning why Americans engage in certain holidays (Halloween, April Fool's Day) or holiday traditions (hanging stockings at Christmas).

4. **The correct answer is A.** All the answer options represent potential definitions for the word *singular*, but only *peculiar* is synonymous with its use in the passage.

5. **The correct answer is C.** Different context clues support the inference that the author's rhetorical stance is one of enthusiasm for the potential benefits that could come from allowing clinical researchers to conduct experiments on schedule I psychedelics. Consider, for instance, this quotation: "Luckily, sentiments seem to be shifting in favor of valuing scientific inquiry over outdated notions of propriety regarding what is and is not suitable for therapeutic use." Both the use of the word *luckily* as well as the contrast between "scientific inquiry" and "outdated notions of propriety" reveal the author's perspective that the government's choice to limit researchers' access to schedule I psychedelics was not only a mistake but an example of old-fashioned thinking. This point of view is echoed in the final sentence when the author suggests that this type of research will "rightfully" accelerate as people realize the potential benefits of therapeutic psychedelic use.

6. **The correct answer is C.** The key to understanding how to answer this question lies in the second paragraph of passage 2, when the author states: "This is not to say that the likelihood of abuse precludes the potential benefits of clinical investigations into the therapeutic positives of such drugs, only that those who enthusiastically endorse more widespread access to these substances may unintentionally gloss over these dangers in their quest for scientific innovation." Contextually, the author is saying that while they do agree with some researchers (like the author of Passage 1) that schedule I psychedelics should be researched further, they advocate that a great degree of caution should be taken in the process. Therefore, one place where the two authors *do* seem to agree is in their shared stance that more research on these substances is needed.

7. **The correct answer is D.** The summary that best synthesizes information from both passages is the one that states that while both authors recognize that research into the therapeutic benefits of psychedelics is necessary, the author of passage 2 cautions that research on schedule I psychedelics like psilocybin needs to be thorough, controlled, and not rushed.

8. **The correct answer is A.** The author of passage 2 discusses dextroamphetamine as an example of an existing legal drug that has been shown to be habit-forming and that increased addiction issues among patients and the general population alike when it became available for therapeutic use. This example helps them set up their concerns about what might happen should research of schedule I psychedelics be rushed.

9. **The correct answer is D.** While it is possible that some studies have shown a correlation between fertilizer use and air pollution, it is not mentioned in this passage.

10. **The correct answer is A.** Something that is lucrative is profitable.

11. **The correct answer is C.** The purpose of the paragraph is to list all the different examples of tree communication that Wohlleben gave Grant while he was writing the article.

12. **The correct answer is B.** The author mentions young influencers using modern forms of social media like TikTok, Twitter, and Instagram to support their implicit claim that preservation of Cree culture is an ongoing, modern issue. Choices A and C do not directly relate to the preservation of Cree language and culture. Choice D captures a current concern for Cree language but does not speak directly to the preservation of broader culture as choice C does.

13. **The correct answer is A.** The author's purpose in paragraph 2 is to highlight how the men Franklin worked with took credit for her discoveries. While the author does point out that this is a problem faced by women in science, choice C is incorrect because listing those problems is not the purpose of the paragraph. The passage does the opposite of choice B, since it argues that Franklin's work was indeed stolen. Choice D might have thrown you if you mistook the word *discredit* to mean something like "criticized" when in fact it means "disprove," which the author does not do—Wilkins, Watson, and Crick may well have published accurate information, but the problem is that they used Franklin's discovery without her permission.

14. **The correct answer is B.** Close reading reveals that grenades are never mentioned in the passage. However, land mines are, so if this question fooled you, make sure you're reading carefully and not confusing terms.

15. **The correct answer is D.** Remember, questions that ask for a passage's best title are simply main idea/author's purpose questions. If you have figured out that the author's purpose in this passage is to talk about Anna Akhmatova's "Requiem" and how it came about during the Great Purge, then it becomes clear that "Anna Akhmatova's 'Requiem' and the Great Purge" is the best possible title. Akhmatova is an important woman writer of the Stalin era, but you would expect a passage entitled "Women Writers in Stalin's Soviet Union" (choice A) to discuss more than just one writer. "Why is Poetry Important to History?" (choice B) relates to the passage but does not express the main idea. While we learn about Akhmatova, the reader is not given the type of background information or depth traditional to a biographical passage, so the title "A Biography of Anna Akhmatova" (choice C) would not be accurate.

16. **The correct answer is C.** If you know that the first sentence "What makes a painting a painting, and what makes a photograph a photograph?" is a rhetorical question, then you likely spotted that the purpose of paragraph 1 is to pose a rhetorical question that helps introduce the main idea. If you didn't, you could also find the correct answer through a process of elimination. You know that paragraph 1 is being used as an introduction to Richter, so you can first eliminate any options

that do not reflect an introduction (choice D). You can eliminate choice A because there is no attempt to critique Richter's art in the passage. The passage is not thorough enough to be a biography, so you can also eliminate choice B, leaving you with choice C as the correct answer.

17. **The correct answer is A.** The first paragraph begins with Snow's birth, the second addresses events that began in 1846, and the third addresses events that began in 1848, so the excerpt is in chronological order. You may have noted that the second paragraph mentions events that occurred after 1848, but don't be thrown! In paragraph 2, the author focuses on Snow witnessing the first use of ether as anesthesia and then within that paragraph mentions some related events that came later; however, if you pay attention to the broader topic and purpose of each paragraph, you'll recognize that the passage as a whole is still organized according to chronological order.

18. **The correct answer is B.** Only choice B correctly summarizes what makes opah different from other cold climate fish, which is that they have a unique circulatory system in which warmer blood vessels transfer heat to those with colder blood, regulating temperature for their entire bodies.

19. **The correct answer is A.** Here, you are looking for a synonym for *annoy* and *perturb* does the trick.

20. **The correct answer is D.** The person who held this job before the current assistant was her predecessor.

CHAPTER

The Writing Placement Test

THE WRITING PLACEMENT TEST

OVERVIEW

Understanding Expression of Ideas Questions

Approaching Expression of Ideas Questions
- Development Questions
- Organization Questions
- Effective Language Use Questions

Summing It Up

Knowledge Check: Writing (Expression of Ideas)

Answer Key and Explanations

The ACCUPLACER writing placement test consists of 25 multiple-choice questions based on five passages, including one literary passage and four informational passages. The multiple-choice questions fall into two categories: expression of ideas and standard English conventions. Expression of ideas questions test how well you can optimize expression by selecting words, phrases, and sentences that result in better organization, topic development, and use of language. Standard English conventions questions test your ability to select options that improve sentence structure, usage, and punctuation. In this chapter, we'll focus on how to approach the expression of ideas questions. In the following chapter, we'll address how to approach questions on standard English conventions.

UNDERSTANDING EXPRESSION OF IDEAS QUESTIONS

On the writing placement test, questions about expression of ideas will generally require you to analyze the passage's topic development, organization, and language use to make improvements for maximum impact. You should expect to see 14–16 questions that fall into this category. You may be asked to improve the wording or structure of the passage or strengthen the writer's point.

You will be given a multi-paragraph passage that includes several expression issues. These questions ask you to choose the best option that improves the expression. This could be an underlined portion of the passage that is reproduced after the question or 1–2 sentences you are asked to revise. Sometimes, expression of ideas questions will give you a sentence and ask you where it should fit into a passage, or the questions may tell you a revision the passage writer is considering and ask you if this is something the writer should do or not.

In answering these questions, you should always keep in mind the clarity, conciseness, and understandability of the passage and choose options that are going to make the passage most effective. Questions that concern development will ask you to revise things like main claims, topic sentences, details, and support and will also include questions about potentially removing information to keep the passage focused. Organization questions include revisions to the logic of the passage, including the order of information and effective use of introduction, conclusion, and transition phrases or sentences. Lastly, effective language use questions ask you to revise the passage with word choice in mind, including its precision, conciseness, style, tone, and syntax.

Here are some sample questions that concern expression of ideas. Keep in mind that the passages on the ACCUPLACER will be much longer than the passage in these sample questions, but these examples will still give you an idea of what these questions might ask.

EXAMPLE

> (1) There is a debate about whether early humans had the mental capacity to cook. (2) Though it may not seem sophisticated, cooking requires planning, an ability to interrupt gratification, and the complex use of tools.

Which option is the best version of the underlined portion of sentence 2 (reproduced below)?

Though it may not seem sophisticated, cooking requires planning, an ability to interrupt gratification, and the complex use of tools.

- **A.** (as it is now)
- **B.** apprehend
- **C.** delay
- **D.** restrain

The correct answer is C. Here, you must choose the word that makes the most sense in the context. The word you are looking for means "to hold off," and only *delay* conveys that sense. *Interrupt*, *apprehend*, and *restrain* don't make sense given the context of the sentence.

EXAMPLES

> **(1)** As Jupiter's volcanic moon, Io's surface composition is primarily sulfur and sulfur dioxide. **(2)** With literally hundreds of volcanoes dotting its surface, the tiny moon has a surprisingly substantial impact on the giant planet it orbits. **(3)** Since Io's orbit cuts through Jupiter's magnetic lines of force, and because the moon itself generates so much activity, it works like an electric generator, developing as much as 400,000 volts across its surface, per NASA's calculations. **(4)** This, in turn, creates lightning storms in Jupiter's upper atmosphere, which are powered by the ~3 million amperes of electrical current that pulse from Io across the planet's magnetic fields as if by superhighway.

Which choice best summarizes the main idea of the paragraph?

A. There are lightning storms on Jupiter caused by nearly 3 million amperes of electrical current.

B. Scientists do not yet know why Io is able to create such a huge degree of electricity despite its small size.

C. As a volcanic moon, the sulfur content on Io, one of Jupiter's moons, is significant.

D. Despite being a relatively small moon, Io's composition and orbit pathway allow it to have a big impact on Jupiter because of the electrical currents the moon generates.

The correct answer is D. The question asks you to determine which sentence best summarizes the main idea of the paragraph. Choices A and C contain ideas that are important to the paragraph, but they do not encompass the entire main idea. Choice B contains an inaccurate reading of the meaning of the paragraph. Choice D contains the crux of the paragraph: that Io, despite being a small moon, has a big impact on Jupiter because of the electrical current generated by its composition and orbit.

> **(1)** At the beginning of the Civil War, Harriet Tubman worked for the Union Army as a cook and nurse. **(2)** Later in the war, she shifted to a more decisive position as a spy and scout. **(3)** Tubman was the first woman to lead an expedition of armed fighters, and her leadership during a raid at Combahee Ferry resulted in the liberation of 700 enslaved people. **(4)** Tubman was born in Dorchester County, Maryland, around 1822.

The writer is considering deleting sentence 4. Should the writer delete this sentence?

A. Yes, because it fails to offer further biographical detail about Tubman.

B. Yes, because the sentence veers from the topic of Tubman's role in the war.

C. No, because the sentence provides valuable historical information about Tubman.

D. No, because the sentence provides a strong conclusion to the paragraph.

The correct answer is B. You are being asked if the sentence in question is relevant to the paragraph. In this case, basic information about where and when Tubman was born has little to do with a paragraph about her role in the Civil War and should be deleted.

APPROACHING EXPRESSION OF IDEAS QUESTIONS

Expression of ideas questions make up the bulk of the writing placement test on the ACCUPLACER. They will test your knowledge of writing and composition, particularly related to developing and supporting an argument, organizing and transitioning between ideas, and using language effectively. In this section, we'll look at examples of different types of questions you might expect to find on the writing placement test. Many of the concepts for any type of question are interrelated with concepts covered in Chapter 3: Reading Comprehension, such as the ability to identify the main idea and purpose of a text or to recognize how a

text ought to be organized. As such, feel free to revisit that chapter as needed. Some of the concepts we touch on here, especially those having to do with effective language use, are covered in more depth in Chapter 5: Conventions of Syntax, Usage, and Punctuation, so be sure to review the grammatical concepts addressed there if you have any questions. Because your writing abilities are also tested on the WritePlacer exam, you may find it helpful to review some of the concepts we cover in Chapter 6: Strategies for the WritePlacer Exam. In that chapter, we go into more depth on thesis statements, topic sentences and transitions, paragraph structure, and other concepts that can help you approach questions on the writing placement test.

Development Questions

Development questions require you to clearly understand the main idea or purpose of a text and to make revisions in accordance with that purpose. For these questions, you'll need to make revisions related to a text's proposition, support, or focus. Proposition questions revolve around how a text supports its central argument. As such, you will need to make revisions pertaining to central ideas, topic sentences, and claims in order to ensure that the text's ideas are conveyed appropriately. Support questions will focus on the supporting details, like examples, facts, and statistics, that are necessary to back up claims and ideas. Focus questions will ask you to add, revise, delete, or retain information as needed to ensure that the text stays on topic in accordance with its central purpose.

Example of a Proposition Question

Proposition questions test your ability to determine the central argument or main idea of a passage itself or of a paragraph within a passage. In other words, to answer these questions, you'll need a solid understanding of how arguments are established in the introduction of a text in the form of a thesis statement, reinforced in body paragraphs with claims and topic sentences, and restated in conclusions. In these questions, you'll need to make sure that claims and evidence are closely aligned, that thesis statements are well-supported and developed by body paragraphs, and that introductions and conclusions accurately forecast and summarize the body of a text.

EXAMPLE

> (1) On the tropical tree-lined streets of Nassau, old Victorian mansions and cathedrals stand among modern shops, internet cafés, and Vegas-style casinos. (2) Parliament Square in the heart of downtown displays the pastel-pink and green government buildings erected in the early 1800s. (3) These structures evoke the British colonial period, with such names as "The Houses of Parliament" and with such emblems of empire as the stately marble statue of Queen Victoria. (4) Further downtown, one finds Fort Charlotte, built in 1788, complete with dungeons and a moat. (5) Yet, in Nassau, such monuments to yesteryear fit right in among the modern-day bustle of taxi-cabs, motor scooters, and jitney buses.

The author is considering adding a topic sentence at the beginning of this paragraph. Which sentence would be the best fit?

A. Nassau, the capital city of the Bahamas, is a unique and exciting place.

B. Nassau, the capital city of the Bahamas, has embraced its role as a tourist destination.

C. Nassau, the capital city of the Bahamas, is a captivating mix of past and present-day features.

D. Nassau, the capital city of the Bahamas, has changed very little over the past two hundred years.

The correct answer is C. This type of question requires you to add a topic sentence that is supported by the rest of the paragraph. In other words, what is the primary takeaway of the paragraph, and which answer choice captures that idea best? You must look at the examples and ideas discussed throughout the rest of the paragraph and decide which sentence best summarizes them. Your best clue is probably the last sentence, which acts as a summary of sorts: Nassau is a blend of old and new features. As such, the correct answer is choice C.

Example of a Support Question

In support questions, your focus is on the use of evidence, specifically facts, details, and statistics, to back up claims. Similar to proposition questions, you must be able to identify main ideas and claims, but the emphasis is on the evidence used to support and develop those claims. You may be asked what type of evidence or example would be most persuasive as support. You may also be presented with additional evidence and asked to determine whether it would be advantageous to incorporate it into a specific sentence or paragraph. Regardless, you'll need to critically examine whether evidence can and should be used to bolster the argument being presented.

(1) In recent years, as droughts and water shortages have plagued the western United States, bottled water manufacturers have been subject to increased scrutiny. (2) These manufacturers are able to obtain permits at extremely affordable prices to extract groundwater, which they then bottle and sell back to consumers at a profit. (3) Environmentalists question why what should be a free and publicly available resource can be sold to private companies at such cheap prices, when it is clearly in the public interest to preserve sources of freshwater. (4) In some cases, bottled water companies have depleted waterways and aquifers in the states and regions in which they operate. (5) Plastic water bottles are also one of the largest sources of plastic waste. (6) In order to preserve existing supplies of freshwater and limit future plastic waste, states and local municipalities should protect their freshwater sources and stop issuing permits to bottled water companies.

Sentence 5 is reproduced below.

Plastic water bottles are also one of the largest sources of plastic waste.

The writer is considering adding the following text at the end of the sentence.

because most end up in landfills and very few are recycled.

Should the writer make this addition here?

A. Yes, because it provides evidence showing why plastic water bottles are a large source of waste.

B. Yes, because it argues in favor of recycling plastic water bottles instead of throwing them away.

C. No, because it draws attention away from the harm caused by bottled water companies.

D. No, because it takes the passage in a different direction.

The correct answer is A. In this question, you must determine what the text the writer is considering adding contributes to the idea in the sentence. In this case, the original sentence claims that plastic water bottles are a significant source of plastic waste. The text the writer is considering adding explains how plastic water bottles create waste since most are thrown away and not recycled. As such, this text is helpful for expanding on the sentence's claim. Choice B is incorrect because the additional text does not argue for recycling plastic water bottles; it actually explains that few bottles are indeed recycled, so producing less waste in the first place is the solution. Choice C is incorrect because this added information would provide more evidence, not less, of how bottled water companies cause harm. Choice D is incorrect because the sentence immediately following sentence 5 continues with the idea of "limit[ing] future plastic waste."

Example of a Focus Question

With focus questions, the key is to determine the central idea of the passage, or a specific paragraph of a passage, so that you can identify information that would or would not advance the main idea. Information that feels tangential or that introduces an unrelated idea is often the culprit in these questions. Similarly, you may encounter questions where you'll be given a sentence and asked where it would work best in a paragraph or passage. This will require you to examine the sample paragraph and see what's missing or what could be expressed more thoroughly with the addition of another sentence. However, you may be given a sentence that is unrelated or does not really fit within the paragraph. In these scenarios, you'll want to leave the paragraph as is to indicate that the sentence does not belong. In these questions, your goal is to first identify the organization of the paragraph and then determine whether the sample sentence fits and where it belongs.

EXAMPLE

---

(1) Emily Brontë's *Wuthering Heights* tells the story of the Earnshaw and Linton families. (2) The story at first revolves around the relationship between Catherine Earnshaw and Heathcliff, a young, orphaned boy adopted by the Earnshaws. (3) However, Catherine and Heathcliff's romance is doomed due to his low social status. (4) Emily Brontë was also a poet and was even respected by Emily Dickinson. (5) The tension between love and social expectations is one of many important and powerful themes. (6) The novel has become a literary classic for its portrayal of pain and heartbreak that span generations.

Which sentence blurs the focus of the paragraph and should be deleted?

- A. Sentence 1
- B. Sentence 2
- C. Sentence 3
- D. Sentence 4

The correct answer is D. Sentence 4 focuses on Emily Brontë as a person, not her book *Wuthering Heights*. The topic sentence sets up expectations for the reader that the paragraph will focus on the book itself, not necessarily the author.

Organization Questions

Organization questions focus more on your ability to improve a text's logical cohesion. You'll need to look at the structure of the text overall as well as its organization at the paragraph and sentence level to make sure that ideas are presented in a logical sequence. You'll also be asked to improve the beginnings or ends of passages or paragraphs by using transitional words, phrases, and sentences. The key with answering these types of questions is to make sure that ideas build off one another and that there is a clear justification for why ideas, sentences, or paragraphs are presented in a certain order.

Example of a Logical Sequence Question

When approaching a logical sequence question, you'll need to consider which answer choice facilitates the most logical flow and progression of ideas. The first step in answering these questions is to determine how the passage is organized: chronologically, process (step by step), cause and effect, problem and solution, etc. As you evaluate the answer options, consider whether certain information needs to be presented first in order to understand information that comes later. This can help you gain a better sense of how ideas must be developed over the course of the passage and the order in which they should appear so that the reader can follow along.

4

(1) Back in 1992, Mae Jemison became the first African American woman to ever travel to space. (2) Having trained as a doctor, engineer, and NASA astronaut, Jemison was more than ready for the job. (3) In fact, it was the culmination of a dream she had had ever since she was a child, back when she used to idolize Lieutenant Uhura on *Star Trek*, who was played by an equally groundbreaking African American woman named Nichelle Nichols.

(4) Despite the discrimination she experienced throughout her education, particularly later when she was often the only woman or African American student in some of her graduate school classes, Jemison pushed through to achieve her dreams. (5) While completing her undergraduate education at Stanford University and later attending Cornell Medical School, Jemison also somehow found time to engage in charitable work. (6) For instance, she led medical studies in Cuba and assisted at a refugee camp in Cambodia. (7) After graduating, she spent two years with the Peace Corps working as a medical officer in Africa.

(8) It wasn't until 1983, when Sally Ride became the first American woman in space, that Jemison truly set her sights on NASA. (9) She applied a few times to the astronaut program before finally being accepted in 1987. (10) After two years of rigorous training, Jemison was slated to join the STS-47 crew, who would head to space in 1992 aboard the space shuttle *Endeavor*.

(11) After hearing about how inspired Jemison was by Lieutenant Uhura growing up and that she was such a huge fan of the show, actor LeVar Burton invited Jemison to be the first real-life astronaut to ever appear in an episode of *Star Trek: The Next Generation*. (12) Jemison retired from NASA in 1993, but her space adventures weren't over. (13) She also went on to create a summer camp for children interested in space and wrote a children's book about her own life story called *Find Where the Wind Goes* in 2001.

Which is the most logical placement for sentence 12 (reproduced below)?

Jemison retired from NASA in 1993, but her space adventures weren't over.

A. Where it is now

B. After sentence 9

C. After sentence 10

D. The sentence does not fit in this passage.

The correct answer is C. To answer this question, you'll want to pay attention to the organization and structure of the passage. You'll notice that Jemison's achievements are discussed chronologically, so it would make the most sense for sentence 12 to be moved after sentence 10. This is especially noticeable when you observe the ending of sentence 12, which says that Jemison's space adventures weren't over. This makes for a smooth transition from Jemison's experience at NASA to her guest appearance on *Star Trek: The Next Generation*. In addition to noticing the overall structure of the passage, it can also be helpful to pay attention to the beginnings and ends of sentences to see how they build off the sentences that come before and after them.

Example of an Introductions, Conclusions, and Transitions Question

With questions on introductions, conclusions, and transitions, the focus is on how to use phrases or sentences to create a logical train of thought connecting ideas. This might involve adding in a word or a phrase to create a transition between two sentences or paragraphs. Alternatively, this might require you to add or revise an appropriate topic sentence to introduce a paragraph or a transition sentence to conclude a paragraph in order to connect ideas in a passage. Remember that we cover both topic sentences and transitions in more depth in Chapter 6: Strategies for the WritePlacer Exam, so be sure to look there for more information and examples.

EXAMPLE

(1) Gene editing is a relatively new technology that allows scientists to modify an organism's DNA. (2) By adding, removing, or replacing part of the genome, scientists can possibly prevent and treat myriad diseases in humans. (3) For example, sickle cell disease is an inherited red blood cell disorder that can lead to numerous painful and debilitating health complications, including infections and strokes. (4) Gene editing technology can offer palliative or even curative treatment for patients by correcting the genetic mutation responsible for sickle cell disease. (5) In fact, doctors were able to successfully use gene editing technology on a woman with sickle cell disease by taking cells from her bone marrow and editing a gene in the cells before infusing billions of those edited cells back into her body. (6) As a result, her symptoms have been alleviated, and she has experienced a significant increase in her quality of life.

(7) Though the applications of gene editing are still being explored, it is still a controversial area of inquiry. (8) Numerous scientists have raised concerns about the practice, noting an urgent need for more clear ethical guidelines around editing the human genome. (9) In addition to concerns about safety, scientists have also warned of the potential exploitation of gene editing for "human enhancement" and modern-day eugenics. (10) Still, others argue that gene editing is a critical tool for alleviating suffering from what could now be preventable devastating inherited diseases, like sickle cell disease, cystic fibrosis, and more. (11) Furthermore, the applications of gene editing could also be extended to cancer, which would be groundbreaking for the roughly 2 million people diagnosed with cancer every year in the United States alone. (12) While gene editing has the capacity to fundamentally change medicine as we know it, we must also proceed with caution to ensure that human dignity guides the ongoing debate over this revolutionary new technology.

The writer wants to add a conclusion at the end of the first paragraph. Which sentence most effectively summarizes the main idea of the first paragraph?

A. Patients with sickle cell disease tend to need blood transfusions frequently, so gene editing techniques could help alleviate some of the demand for healthy blood donors.

B. Gene editing techniques will likely not be helpful for those with certain types of diseases.

C. The short-term results of gene editing technology have shown significant promise for those with certain inherited diseases, though time will tell how effective such treatments will be in the long run.

D. Additionally, there are currently clinical trials for using gene editing techniques to target areas of the HIV genome to prevent virus replication and hopefully cure patients with HIV infections.

The correct answer is C. Remember that you are looking for the sentence that best summarizes the main idea of the first paragraph. As such, you want to avoid sentences that introduce new information, switch topics, or focus too closely on details. Choice B identifies a limitation of gene editing while choice D expands on the applications of gene editing, neither of which makes for an effective conclusion sentence to the paragraph. While choice A provides information that might be relevant to the focus of the paragraph, its placement as a conclusion sentence is questionable because it does not summarize the main idea of the passage—that gene editing can be a promising tool for preventing and curing a host of inherited diseases.

Effective Language Use Questions

Effective language use questions assess your ability to revise a text in accordance with several purposes: to improve precision and economy of word choice, to ensure consistency and appropriateness of style and tone, and to incorporate a variety of sentence structures. As you review the answer choices, you must consider the overall purpose of the text you're revising. In other words, the revisions you make must advance the purpose of the passage and should be consistent with the overall style, tone, and language use of the passage as a whole.

When approaching one of these questions, you'll need to consider which answer choice is the most effective and concise. It's also important to ensure that the answer choices fit with the style and tone used in the rest of the passage so that the revisions are consistent. Be sure to utilize a variety of sentence structures: simple, compound, complex, and compound-complex sentences. We'll cover sentence structure in depth in

Chapter 5: Conventions of Syntax, Usage, and Punctuation, so review those concepts as much as you need to in preparation for this portion of the writing placement test.

(1) On 6 June 1822, French Canadian fur trade voyageur Alexis St. Martin was accidentally shot in the stomach at an American Fur Company store on Michigan's Mackinac Island. (2) The blast left a gaping wound in St. Martin's abdomen. (3) St. Martin eventually recovered from the gruesome accident. (4) The wound never closed completely, leaving a small permanent opening in his stomach wall. (5) His surgeon, William Beaumont, began monitoring gastric secretions through this opening in St. Martin's body and keeping a meticulously detailed log of any noteworthy observations. (6) Beaumont, who would later become known as the father of gastric physiology, would attach various types of food to a string and suspend them through the hole. (7) Later, he would pull out the string to see what portion of the food had been digested. (8) During these experiments, Beaumont noticed that St. Martin's mood seemed to affect how quickly he digested food. (9) When St. Martin was grumpy, for instance, food broke down more slowly.

(10) These early observations provided the first clues of crosstalk between the brain and the gut. (11) Researchers later called this communication system the gut–brain axis. (12) Over the years, studies have revealed that the brain influences the gastrointestinal (GI) tract through several mechanisms. (13) Yet, only recently have scientists recognized the importance of a third component to the gut–brain axis: the trillions of bacteria, viruses, archaea, and eukaryotes that make up the gut microbiome. (14) In little more than a decade, researchers have uncovered compelling associations between gut bacteria and a host of neurological disorders and psychiatric conditions. (15) These include depression, anxiety, autism spectrum disorders (ASDs), and Parkinson's disease.

(16) Most of the early research has been conducted in rodents. (17) Germ-free mice—which are born in sterile conditions and free of all microorganisms—are popular for gut flora research because scientists can inoculate the mice with specific microbes and watch what happens. (18) Experiments with germ-free mice have yielded intriguing clues about the possible influence of the gut microbiome on behavior and neurodevelopment. (19) However, it is still unclear whether these findings are relevant to humans, so additional researchers are now beginning to probe the connection in humans. (20) Outside neuroscience, gut microbiome research in laboratory animals and humans is changing the way some environmental health scientists view the effects of environmental exposures on neurodevelopment and brain chemistry. (21) From the moment of birth—and possibly even earlier—our microbiomes begin to develop. (22) There is evidence that a healthy gut microbiome is important for brain development.

Example of a Precision Question

To answer precision questions effectively, you'll want to consider the author's purpose and make revisions to enhance the clarity of existing sentences. For instance, you could be asked to decide whether to incorporate modifiers into a sentence to provide additional context, to replace a word or phrase whose connotation doesn't quite fit the context of the sentence, or to replace a word or phrase that is too broad, general, or vague with something more specific.

EXAMPLE

Sentence 16 is reproduced below.

Most of the early research has been conducted in rodents.

The writer is considering adding to the sentence as follows.

Most of the early research on the microbiome–gut–brain axis has been conducted in rodents.

Should the writer make this addition?

A. Yes, because it clarifies which research is being discussed.

B. Yes, because it adds length to the sentence.

C. No, because the phrase the writer is considering adding is too wordy.

D. No, because the reader already knows which research is being discussed.

The correct answer is A. At times, you'll need to balance precision and concision, but if there is any aspect of the sentence that is unclear and additional information would provide clarity, then precision is the priority. This information is helpful here to clarify what research is being referenced, specifically research on the microbiome–gut–brain axis. Choice B is incorrect because adding length to a sentence isn't an inherently positive or negative thing, though you shouldn't need to sacrifice precision for concision. Choice C is incorrect because there isn't really a way to add the information using fewer words. Adding the information also helps avoids any confusion in case the reader mistakenly assumes the research has to do with the conditions or diseases mentioned in the previous sentence, which eliminates choice D.

Example of a Concision Question

In these questions, you can eliminate any answers that are redundant or that include unnecessary information. This often manifests as information that is already implied but is stated again in different words or as details that don't add anything of value to the passage. In these scenarios, your goal is to maximize word economy by determining what information the reader needs, how that information can be stated directly and concisely, and what information the reader can do without.

EXAMPLE

Which is the best decision regarding the underlined portion of sentence 5 (reproduced below)?

His surgeon, William Beaumont, began monitoring gastric secretions through this opening in St. Martin's body and keeping a meticulously detailed log of any noteworthy observations.

A. Leave it as it is now

B. Revise it to "and keeping a log of his observations."

C. Revise it to "and noting his observations."

D. DELETE it and end the sentence with a period

The correct answer is D. Whether or not William Beaumont kept a detailed log of his observations is of no consequence to the reader. However, one could infer from the word *monitoring* that Beaumont likely did take notes on his observations of St. Martin's body, which would also make the underlined phrase redundant. Because the underlined text is not essential for understanding the main idea of the sentence, that Beaumont observed St. Martin's gastric secretions through the opening in his body, the information can be deleted.

Example of a Style and Tone Question

To answer style and tone questions, you'll need to pay close attention to the stylistic choices the writer consistently makes throughout the passage. For instance, you'll want to observe the use of voice, verb tense and mood, word choice, and point of view throughout the passage. This will help you identify words, phrases, or sentences that significantly diverge from the author's style so that you can revise them appropriately.

EXAMPLE

Which is the best decision regarding the underlined portion of sentence 9 (reproduced below)?

When St. Martin was <u>grumpy</u>, for instance, food broke down more slowly.

- **A.** Leave it as it is now
- **B.** Revise it to "on a short fuse"
- **C.** Revise it to "irritable"
- **D.** Revise it to "violent"

The correct answer is C. This question asks you to consider the connotation of the word *grumpy*, which is a more informal or casual way of saying that someone is upset or annoyed. Because the rest of the passage reads in a more academic or formal manner, this word feels out of place. Therefore, you'd need to replace the word with a more appropriate synonym. The phrase "on a short fuse" (choice B) is too idiomatic and still too casual as a synonym for *grumpy*. The word *violent* (choice D) isn't quite a suitable replacement for the word *grumpy* and likely would misrepresent the author's purpose. Thus, *irritable* is our best and most appropriate option.

Example of a Syntax Question

Syntax questions require you to identify opportunities to combine simple sentences and vary the sentence structure used within a passage. For instance, instead of having two simple sentences in a row, you'll be asked to consider how to best combine the sentences. As such, you'll be expected to know how to join independent and dependent clauses and form compound, complex, and compound-complex sentences. For more information on this, be sure to review Chapter 5: Conventions of Syntax, Usage, and Punctuation.

EXAMPLE

Which choice most effectively combines sentences 3 and 4 (reproduced below) at the underlined portion?

St. Martin eventually recovered from the gruesome <u>accident. The wound </u>never closed completely, leaving a small permanent opening in his stomach wall.

- **A.** accident, and the wound
- **B.** accident; however, the wound
- **C.** accident; as a result, the wound
- **D.** accident-the wound

The correct answer is B. To effectively combine the two sentences, it's important to think about the relationship between them. Using a comma and the coordinating conjunction *and* (choice A) to connect the two sentences works but does not provide any additional context as to the relationship between the two ideas. Using a semicolon would also work, but with the transitional phrase "as a result" (choice C), this sets up a misleading cause-and-effect relationship between the two ideas. Choice D incorrectly utilizes a hyphen to join the two sentences together. Choice B best captures the relationship between the two ideas with the use of the word *however*, which expresses that while St. Martin did recover, he was left with a permanent wound.

SUMMING IT UP

- The ACCUPLACER writing placement test consists of 25 multiple-choice questions based on five passages of varying topics. You can expect 14–16 expression of ideas questions on the writing placement test. Questions about expression of ideas require you to analyze the passage's topic development, organization, and language use and make appropriate revisions in line with the author's purpose. Like the rest of the ACCUPLACER, there is no time limit on the writing placement test.

- Development questions require you to clearly understand the main idea or purpose of a text and to make revisions in accordance with that purpose. For these questions, you'll need to make revisions related to a text's proposition, support, or focus.

- Organization questions test your ability to improve a text's logical cohesion. You'll examine the structure of the text overall as well as both the paragraph- and sentence-level organization to ensure that ideas are presented in a logical sequence. You may also need to make revisions to the beginnings or ends of passages or paragraphs through the use of transitional words, phrases, and sentences.

- Effective language use questions require you to make revisions that reduce wordiness, ensure appropriate style and tone, and utilize various sentence structures.

KNOWLEDGE CHECK

WRITING (EXPRESSION OF IDEAS)

15 Questions

> **Directions:** Read the following early essay drafts and then choose the best answer to the question or the best completion of the statement.

(1) Australia is known for its biodiversity, including a wide array of marsupials. (2) While kangaroos, wallabies, and koalas are familiar to most people, there are other marsupials, like the Tasmanian devil, the wallaroo, and the bandicoot, that tend to be less understood outside of the land down under. (3) One example of a lesser-known marsupial is the quokka. (4) Sometimes called the "happiest animal in the world" due to its almost teddy bear-like appearance, these friendly, small, native Australian marsupials have round, stout bodies. (5) They usually grow to be about 16–21 in. (40–54 cm.) long and have coarse, brownish-grey fur.

(6) Their appearance is matched by a tendency to trust and be curious about humans—a tendency that has conservationists exerting great effort to remind tourists that it's still best not to feed or interact too closely with these wild animals! (7) A quokka's most charming feature is its face; with round ears and a habit of looking like they're grinning from ear-to-ear, quokkas always seem happy to make your acquaintance. (8) Visitors to quokka habitats like Rottnest Island, home of the largest quokka population in Australia due to its lack of predators, have been known to pose for pictures with the smiling animals.

(9) Quokkas are considered a vulnerable species. (10) For one, deforestation from commercial development and logging has contributed to slowly declining quokka populations. (11) Climate change, urbanization, and other environmental factors have displaced many animals from their own traditional habitats, meaning that new predators, like foxes, have moved into areas where quokkas used to safely roam free from threats. (12) Attacks from domestic animals like dogs and cats also pose a threat to quokkas, as do humans, who will sometimes cruelly (and illegally) hunt them for sport. (13) A number of celebrities and politicians have spoken out against "trophy hunting." (14) Habitat loss from natural events like wildfires also threatens quokkas.

(15) To support the development of a more robust quokka population in the future, conservationists are taking numerous measures, including using baiting techniques to curtail introduced predator populations, pushing for environmental protection measures, and monitoring existing quokka populations for changes.

1. Which is the most logical placement for sentence 6 (reproduced below)?

   Their appearance is matched by a tendency to trust and be curious about humans—a tendency that has conservationists exerting great effort to remind tourists that it's still best not to feed or interact too closely with these wild animals!

   A. Where it is now
   B. After sentence 1
   C. After sentence 7
   D. After sentence 8

2. In context, which is the best version of the underlined portion of sentence 9 (reproduced below)?

   Quokkas are considered a vulnerable species.

   A. (as it is now)
   B. Unfortunately, quokkas
   C. Similarly, quokkas
   D. Therefore, quokkas

3. Which is the best decision regarding the underlined portion of sentence 11 (reproduced below)?

   Climate change, urbanization, and other environmental factors have displaced many animals from their own traditional habitats, meaning that new predators, like foxes, have moved into areas where quokkas used to safely roam <u>free from threats</u>.

   A. Leave it as it is now
   B. Revise it to "without fear."
   C. Revise it to "free from the threats of humans and animals alike."
   D. DELETE it and end the sentence with a period

4. Which sentence blurs the focus of the third paragraph and should be deleted?

   A. Sentence 9
   B. Sentence 11
   C. Sentence 12
   D. Sentence 13

5. Sentence 14 is reproduced below.

   Habitat loss from natural events like wildfires also threatens quokkas.

   The writer is considering adding the following text at the end of the sentence.

   and will continue to do so as the climate changes.

   Should the writer make this addition there?

   A. Yes, because it provides an example of a natural event.
   B. Yes, because it establishes that there is an ongoing threat to quokkas.
   C. No, because it introduces details that are irrelevant to the paragraph's focus on threats to quokkas.
   D. No, because it fails to explain how climate change poses a threat to quokkas.

(1) Astronomers around the world contributing to the Event Horizon Telescope (EHT) collaboration celebrated in May 2022. (2) They finally achieved the impressive feat of capturing an image of Sagittarius A* (Sgr A*), the supermassive black hole at the center of the Milky Way. (3) While it may shock some to learn that there is a black hole so close to home, scientists have long guessed that there was such an object in the center of our galaxy. (4) They based these suppositions about Sgr A* (pronounced "sadge-ay-star") on their observation of gases and objects orbiting that spot at the center of the Milky Way.

(5) A research team working for the EHT produced the image by creating a composite of observations taken using an entire network of radio telescopes positioned around the globe. (6) Given the nature of black holes, the image of Sgr A* isn't a picture of the black hole itself so much as a representation of all the light that bends around it. (7) Think of the negative of a print photograph—by seeing how light moves around this massive object, you can see a representative of the object by way of the negative space the light's edges reveal. (8) Thus, the image shows a bright ring around a supermassive object that astronomers can presume is indeed Sgr A*.

(9) EHT is also known for another image of a black hole, what is often called the first image of a black hole ever recorded in human history. (10) The 2019 image shows M87*, a black hole in the Messier 87 galaxy. (11) Though much further away than Sgr A*, M87* is a much steadier black hole to observe than Sgr A*, which is surrounded by rapidly moving gases that make it hard to create a clear image. (12) According to EHT, advanced new tools capable of accounting for the difficulties in detecting Sgr A* have been developed through the collaboration of 300 researchers representing more than 80 worldwide institutes. (13) Their achievement is a momentous illustration of the possibilities fostered by worldwide scientific collaboration and a monumental discovery about the nature of our home galaxy.

6. Which choice most effectively combines sentences 1 and 2 (reproduced below) at the underlined portion?

   Astronomers around the world contributing to the Event Horizon Telescope (EHT) collaboration celebrated in May 2022. They finally achieved the impressive feat of capturing an image of Sagittarius A* (Sgr A*), the supermassive black hole at the center of the Milky Way.

   A. in May 2022 when they
   B. in May 2022 since they had
   C. in May 2022, for astronomers
   D. in May 2022, in that they

7. Which is the best version of the underlined portion of sentence 3 (reproduced below)?

   While it may shock some to learn that there is a black hole so close to home, scientists have long guessed that there was such an object in the center of our galaxy.

   A. (as it is now)
   B. awaited
   C. suspected
   D. hoped

8. Which is the best version of the underlined portion of sentence 7 (reproduced below)?

Think of the negative of a print photograph—by seeing how light moves around this massive object, you can see a <u>representative</u> of the object by way of the negative space the light's edges reveal.

A. (as it is now)

B. repercussion

C. demonstration

D. representation

9. Which is the best version of sentence 9 (reproduced below)?

EHT is also known for another image of a black hole, what is often called the first image of a black hole ever recorded in human history.

A. Leave it as it is now

B. EHT is also known for the first ever image of a black hole.

C. EHT is also known for another image of a black hole, the first image ever recorded of a black hole.

D. EHT is also known for the first image of a black hole in human history.

10. Which is the best version of sentence 12 (reproduced below)?

According to EHT, advanced new tools capable of accounting for the difficulties in detecting Sgr A* have been developed through the collaboration of 300 researchers representing more than 80 world-wide institutes.

A. Advanced new tools were being developed to account for the difficulties in detecting Sgr A* by 300 researchers representing more than 80 worldwide institutes who were collaborating, according to EHT.

B. To account for the difficulties in detecting Sgr A*, advanced new tools were developed through the collaboration of 300 researchers who represent more than 80 worldwide institutes, according to EHT.

C. According to EHT, at least 300 researchers representing more than 80 worldwide institutes collaborated to develop advanced new tools capable of accounting for the difficulties in detecting Sgr A*.

D. According to EHT, to account for the difficulties in detecting Sgr A*, the development of advanced new tools was made possible due to the collaboration of more than 300 researchers representing more than 80 worldwide institutes.

(1) A certain question has plagued zoologists for years now: How did giraffes end up with such long necks? (2) Their hearts must work overtime to get all that blood pumping up and down the great distance between their hearts and brains. (3) One of the reasons that scientists find this question intriguing is that long necks are not necessarily helpful to giraffes. (4) This is wildly inefficient because of the large amount of energy required simply to maintain blood pressure. (5) Scientists have long assumed that there must be a specific reason that giraffes have this trait; otherwise, the species would have likely evolved to have more efficient features.

(6) The most widely accepted theory has been that giraffes evolved this way to reach leaves on higher and higher trees, an adaptation that would have been crucial when drought or overgrazing meant lower foliage was picked over. (7) While this seems like a straightforward theory, there's a catch—research has been showing that giraffes don't necessarily go for the highest foliage they can reach, often seeming perfectly content to munch on lower-hanging leaves. (8) Another theory suggests that the length of the neck was a way for male giraffes to attract mates. (9) Female giraffes have the same average neck length. (10) This has also largely been considered speculation.

(11) By analyzing various archeological specimens of an ancient giraffoid (meaning "giraffe-like") creature with a helmet-shaped protrusion on its forehead that have been discovered in China over the last few decades, scientists believe they now have a new clue about how giraffes got their long necks. (12) The ancient creature, named *Discokeryx xiezhi* after the term for a unicorn figure from Chinese folklore, *xiezhi*, likely used this hard forehead protrusion to headbutt others of its kind when competing for mates.

(13) The search for high foliage likely did still play some role in helping giraffes evolve long necks. (14) The fossils suggest that as fighting between males became more complex, natural selection favored animals with the longest and strongest necks. (15) Giraffes aren't the only animals with long necks relative to their body sizes; ostriches, swans, and flamingos all have mysteriously long necks as well. (16) While there are some zoologists who are still skeptical of this theory, it adds new fodder to the discussion about how today's giraffes ended up with the features they have now.

11. Where is the most logical placement for sentence 2 (reproduced below)?

Their hearts must work overtime to get all that blood pumping up and down the great distance between their hearts and brains.

A. Where it is now

B. After sentence 3

C. After sentence 4

D. After sentence 5

12. In context, which is the best version of the underlined portion of sentence 5 (reproduced below)?

<u>Scientists</u> *have long assumed that there must be a specific reason that giraffes have this trait; otherwise, the species would have likely evolved to have more efficient features.*

A. (as it is now)

B. On the other hand, scientists

C. Therefore, scientists

D. Regardless, scientists

13. Which is the best version of the underlined portion of sentence 7 (reproduced below)?

While this seems like a straightforward theory, there's a catch—research <u>has been showing</u> that giraffes don't necessarily go for the highest foliage they can reach, often seeming perfectly content to munch on lower-hanging leaves.

A. (as it is now)

B. has shown

C. shows

D. had shown

14. Which sentence blurs the focus of the last paragraph and should be deleted?

A. Sentence 13

B. Sentence 14

C. Sentence 15

D. Sentence 16

15. The author is considering adding a topic sentence at the beginning of the last paragraph. Which sentence would be the best fit?

A. Consequently, scientists studying *Discokeryx xiezhi* fossil specimens believe giraffes' long necks evolved because of male-male combat between ancient giraffoid creatures becoming more intense and involving more of the neck over time.

B. By studying *Discokeryx xiezhi* fossil specimens, scientists have been able to arrive at fascinating conclusions about the nature of herd dynamics and the ongoing struggle for power between male giraffoid creatures.

C. Overall, it is unclear why giraffes' long necks evolved the way that they did, although there are many probable theories being explored by scientists today.

D. It is possible that we may never know why giraffes evolved such long necks and that it will remain one of earth's greatest mysteries.

ANSWER KEY AND EXPLANATIONS

1. C	4. D	7. C	10. C	13. B
2. B	5. B	8. D	11. B	14. C
3. D	6. A	9. B	12. C	15. A

1. **The correct answer is C.** Pay attention to how the sentence begins and ends. The phrase "their appearance" is at the beginning of the sentence, so logically, this sentence should follow a description of the quokka's appearance. If we place this sentence after sentence 7, it would also serve as a transition to the description of how visitors interact with the quokkas on Rottnest Island.

2. **The correct answer is B.** The word *unfortunately* signals a transition to a less pleasant topic, specifically how quokkas are a vulnerable species. The word *similarly* (choice C) does not adequately capture this shift in topic, while *therefore* (choice D) creates a misleading cause-and-effect relationship between the two paragraphs.

3. **The correct answer is D.** Because the sentence already states that quokkas are able to "safely roam," this implies that quokkas are free from threats. Therefore, this information is redundant and can be deleted from the sentence altogether.

4. **The correct answer is D.** Sentence 13 mentions that celebrities have spoken out against trophy hunting, which distracts the reader from the topic of current threats to quokkas.

5. **The correct answer is B.** By revising the sentence so that it says, "Habitat loss from natural events like wildfires also threatens quokkas and will continue to do so as the climate changes," the writer can provide context that supports the aforementioned idea that climate change poses a significant threat to quokka populations while clarifying that the issue will continue for the foreseeable future.

6. **The correct answer is A.** Because the first sentence ends with the phrase "in May 2022," the most effective option is to turn the second sentence into

a dependent clause beginning with *when* and join it with the first sentence.

7. **The correct answer is C.** The most precise word to use here is *suspected* considering that scientists often hypothesize based on available evidence as opposed to just making arbitrary guesses. Remember to consider the context of the sentence at large and the connotation of the word when determining which option is the best choice.

8. **The correct answer is D.** While *representative* and *representation* have similar meanings, a representative is typically a person. Instead, the best choice is *representation*, meaning "the description or portrayal of something."

9. **The correct answer is B.** As written, the sentence is wordy: notice the repetition of "image of a black hole" and the redundancy of "first" and "ever recorded in human history." As such, we can shorten this sentence to "EHT is also known for the first ever image of a black hole."

10. **The correct answer is C.** Notice that this sentence is in the passive voice while most of the passage uses the active voice. As such, the correct answer should be in the active voice and should place the researchers working on EHT in the subject position to be consistent with the rest of the passage.

11. **The correct answer is B.** Notice that sentence 3 references the question mentioned in sentence 1, so we know that sentence 2 should be moved so those two sentences can go next to each other. Because the sentence in question provides an example of how "long necks are not necessarily helpful to giraffes," it would work best after sentence 3.

12. **The correct answer is C.** The transition word *therefore* clearly establishes a cause-and-effect relationship between the ideas presented in the first

paragraph. The preceding sentences set up the idea that long necks have no immediate benefit to giraffes and seem to be a hindrance to them biologically. This leads scientists to believe that there must be some purpose for why giraffes have evolved to have such long necks.

13. **The correct answer is B.** "Has been showing" is in the present perfect progressive tense, but this isn't used anywhere else in the paragraph. To be consistent with the author's style, this verb phrase should be revised to the present perfect tense, "has shown," which is used frequently in the paragraph and throughout the passage.

14. **The correct answer is C.** Sentence 15 shifts focus by giving examples of other animals with long necks. Because this passage is focused on giraffes, this sentence should be deleted.

15. **The correct answer is A.** The topic sentence for the last paragraph should introduce the theory that scientists are entertaining and the rationale behind it. Choice A explains how the intensity of combat between male giraffes might necessitate longer necks, which accurately reflects the main idea of the paragraph. While choice B also mentions the ongoing power struggle between giraffes, it doesn't connect that idea to the need for longer necks.

CHAPTER

**Conventions of Syntax,
Usage, and Punctuation**

CONVENTIONS OF SYNTAX, USAGE

OVERVIEW

STANDARD ENGLISH CONVENTION QUESTIONS ON THE WRITING PLACEMENT TEST

As mentioned in the last chapter, the ACCUPLACER writing placement test consists of 25 multiple-choice questions based on five passages of varying topics. The multiple-choice questions fall into two categories: expression of ideas and standard English conventions. In the last chapter, we covered the expression of ideas questions. This chapter will cover the questions on standard English conventions, which test your ability to select options that improve sentence structure, usage, and punctuation.

Questions on standard English conventions require you to act as an editor and revise text so that it conforms to the standard rules for sentence structure and formation, punctuation, and usage. In most instances, you will be given a multi-paragraph passage that includes several errors, which may include some that you won't be asked about directly. These questions ask you to choose the best alternative to a potential error, identified as an underlined portion of the passage that is reproduced after the question. You can expect to see 9–11 questions in this category on the exam.

One of the skills tested is sentence structure, which includes questions about parallel structure, verb tense shifts, incomplete sentences, coordination, and subordination. Conventions of usage questions involve identifying correct possessives, nouns, and pronouns as well as common grammatical structures like subject-verb agreement. These questions will also include words that are often confused with each other, such as *its* and *it's*. Conventions of punctuation questions ask you to choose correct end-of-sentence and in-sentence punctuation, including periods, commas, apostrophes, parentheses, and hyphens.

SAMPLE STANDARD ENGLISH CONVENTION QUESTIONS

Here are some sample questions that concern standard English conventions.

EXAMPLE

(**1**) Scientists conducted a series of experiments with chimpanzees in the Democratic Republic of the Congo. (**2**) The results were astounding. (**3**) The conclusion, that chimpanzees would eventually learn to cook if provided an oven, could help explain how and when early humans began to cook there food.

1. Which choice most effectively combines sentences 1 and 2 (reproduced below) at the underlined portion?

   Scientists conducted a series of experiments with chimpanzees in the <u>Democratic Republic of the Congo. The results were astounding.</u>

   A. Democratic Republic of the Congo, and the results were astounding.

   B. Democratic Republic of the Congo, the results were astounding.

   C. Democratic Republic of the Congo the results were astounding.

   D. Democratic Republic of the Congo, but the results were astounding.

   The correct answer is A. Only choice A maintains the two sentences' meanings and combines them without creating a grammatical error. Choice B creates a comma splice, which is a form of a run-on sentence. Choice C incorrectly fuses the two sentences without the appropriate punctuation, creating a run-on sentence. Introducing *but* in choice D changes the meaning of the sentences by setting up a contrasting scenario.

2. Which option is the best version of the underlined portion of sentence 3 (reproduced below)?

   The conclusion, that chimpanzees would eventually learn to cook if provided an oven, could help explain how and when early humans began to cook there food.

   A. (as it is now)

   B. The conclusion—that

   C. The conclusion? That

   D. The conclusion that

   The correct answer is A. Leaving the sentence as is correctly creates a phrase in the middle of the sentence that is set off by two commas. Changing the comma to an em dash (choice B) would also require changing the comma after *oven* to an em dash to be correct. Using a question mark (choice C) does not conform to standard English conventions. Choice D is missing the first comma required after *conclusion* in order to set off the nonessential information in the middle of the sentence.

3. Which option is the best version of the underlined portion of sentence 3 (reproduced below)?

   The conclusion, that chimpanzees would eventually learn to cook if provided an oven, could help explain how and when early humans began to cook <u>there</u> *food.*

   A. (as it is now)

   B. they're

   C. their

   D. its

   The correct answer is C. *Their, there,* and *they're* are commonly confused words in English because they are homophones—words that sound alike but are spelled differently and have different meanings. *Their* is the possessive and is correct in this sentence because it refers to the humans' food. *There* (choice A) has multiple meanings and functions; usually, it means a direction, as in *over there,* which does not work in this sentence. *They're* (choice B) is a contraction for the words *they are* and would not fit into this context. While *its* (choice D) is a possessive, it is singular, and *humans* (the antecedent) is plural.

GRAMMAR

First, we'll do a quick recap of some important grammatical terminology you need to understand before we get into more complex topics related to sentence structure and formation, conventions of usage, and conventions of punctuation. The rules of grammar govern the ways in which parts of speech are organized in a sentence. There are rules concerning word endings, word order, and which words may be used together. You must know the parts of speech to follow the rules of grammar.

PARTS OF SPEECH

Type	Definition/Explanation
Noun	Nouns can be a person, place, thing, or idea. There are three types of nouns: 1. Common nouns, which are general 2. Proper nouns, which are specific 3. Collective nouns, which name groups of things Nouns have cases: A noun is in the nominative case when it is the subject of the sentence. **Example:** *Roberta* joined the band. A noun is in the objective case when it is the direct object, indirect object, or object of the preposition. **Example (direct object):** She built a *tree house*. **Example (indirect object):** Chananan sent *Kelsie* a message. **Example (object of the preposition):** The dog ran around *Jackson*. Possessive case is the form that shows possession. **Example:** The *queen's* crown was filled with rubies.
Verb	Verbs express action or a state of being. There are four major kinds of verbs: 4. **Transitive verbs** are action verbs and always have a direct object, which receives the action of the transitive verb. **Example:** The dog *broke* his tail. **Example:** The teacher *discussed* the reading. 5. **Intransitive verbs** are action verbs with no direct object. Some verbs can be either transitive or intransitive depending on their usage. **Example:** The glass *broke*. **Example:** Damien *cried*. 6. **Linking verbs** indicate a state of being and have no action. They link the subject to additional descriptive information. Examples include *is, are, was, were, be, am, taste, feel, seem,* etc. Certain verbs can be linking, auxiliary, or action verbs depending on their usage. **Example:** I *am* here. **Example:** He *looks* nervous. **Example:** The food *tastes* salty. 7. **Auxiliary** or **helping verbs** are used with an infinitive or participle to create a verb phrase. Auxiliary verbs always need a primary verb to function. Examples of auxiliary verbs include all forms of the verbs *to be, to have, to do,* and *to keep,* as well as *can, could, may, might, must, ought to, shall, will, would,* and *should.* **Example:** I *am reading* a book. **Example:** She *might take* a vacation. **Example:** He *should study* harder.

PARTS OF SPEECH

Type	Definition/Explanation

Adjective	Adjectives describe nouns and answer questions like *which one, what kind,* and *how many?* There are three uses of adjectives:
	
	 A **noun modifier** is usually placed before the noun it describes.
	
	     Example: Wanyi is a *smart* person.
	
	 A **predicate adjective** follows a stative or linking verb and modifies the subject.
	
	     Example: She is *happy.*
	     Example: I feel *sick.*
	
	 An **article** or **noun marker** points to a noun. The articles are *the, a,* and *an.*
	
	     Example: *The* teacher took *a* vacation to *an* island.

Pronoun	Pronouns substitute for a noun. The antecedent of the pronoun is the noun the pronoun replaces. A pronoun must agree with its antecedent in gender, person, and number. There are several types of pronouns:
	
	     Demonstrative pronouns: *this, that, these, those*
	     Indefinite pronouns: *all, any, nobody*
	     Interrogative pronouns: *who, which, what*
	     Personal pronouns: *I, you, we, me, him, her, us, they*

Adverb	An adverb modifies a verb, an adjective, or another adverb and answers the questions *why, how, where, when,* and *to what degree?* Many adverbs are easy to identify because they end in *-ly,* but there are other adverbs that do not have this ending.
	
	     Example: The cat *quickly* pounced on the mouse.
	     Example: I am doing *well.*
	     Example: The water swirled *clockwise* around the drain.

Preposition	Prepositions show position in time or space. Common prepositions include words like *around, in, over, under, during, after,* and *behind.* A preposition starts a prepositional phrase that usually shows the relationship between a noun or pronoun and the rest of the information in the sentence.
	
	     Example: The iguana sleeps *under the lamp.*
	     Example: She stood up *during the presentation.*
	     Example: *After the meeting,* we all went out for pizza.

Conjunction	Conjunctions join words, sentences, and phrases. The best way to remember the conjunctions is with the acronym FANBOYS: <u>f</u>or, <u>a</u>nd, <u>n</u>or, <u>b</u>ut, <u>o</u>r, <u>y</u>et, <u>s</u>o.
	
	     Example: Natilla *and* I went to class.
	     Example: He spent hours cleaning, *but* the house was still messy.
	     Example: Miguel didn't take the window seat, *nor* did Flavia.

SENTENCE STRUCTURE AND FORMATION

Now that you have an introduction to parts of speech, let's dive into concepts related to sentence structure and formation. On the ACCUPLACER, you'll be expected to understand sentence boundaries, and you will need to recognize and correct problems in coordination and subordination in sentences. This will require you to look at sample passages and recognize when independent clauses and dependent clauses have been joined together correctly or incorrectly and make revisions as needed. Here, we'll cover the different types of sentence structures and how to join independent and dependent clauses together in a variety of ways while avoiding common errors. You'll also be expected to know how to recognize and correct problems in modifier placement, parallel structure, verb tense, mood and voice, and word choice, so we'll take a look at these concepts as well.

There are four different kinds of sentence structures in English:

1. **Simple sentences** (an independent clause)
2. **Compound sentences** (two independent clauses joined together)
3. **Complex sentences** (an independent clause and at least one dependent clause)
4. **Compound-complex sentences** (at least two independent clauses and one dependent clause)

Compound, complex, and compound-complex sentences can technically have as many clauses as you want, as long as they are connected and punctuated correctly.

  Scan this QR code for a video about forming complex sentences.

Fragments

Basic Rule

Every sentence must have a subject (something to do the action) and a verb or predicate (the action) and express a complete idea. When all those items are present, you get an independent clause (another way of saying "a complete sentence"). A group of words that is missing one of these elements is called a sentence fragment or an incomplete sentence. If a group of words has a subject and verb but doesn't express a complete thought, it's a dependent clause.

There are two ways to correct incomplete sentences:

Add the fragment to the sentence that precedes it.

 Incorrect: Zoologists and wildlife biologists study animals and other wildlife. Including how they interact with their ecosystems.

 Correct: Zoologists and wildlife biologists study animals and other wildlife, including how they interact with their ecosystems.

 Explanation: The fragment is added to the sentence that precedes it by inserting a comma.

 Incorrect: By studying animal behaviors. Wildlife biologists seek to understand how animals interact with their ecosystems.

 Correct: Wildlife biologists seeks to understand how animals interact with their ecosystems by studying animal behaviors.

 Explanation: The fragment now serves as a prepositional phrase that modifies the rest of the sentence.

Add a subject and verb to the fragment.

 Incorrect: Considerable time studying animals in their natural habitats.

Correct: Wildlife biologists may spend considerable time studying animals in their natural habitats.

 Explanation: A subject (*wildlife biologists*) and verb (*may spend*) are added to the fragment.

Run-Ons and Comma Splices

Basic Rule

Complete sentences must be separated by a period, a comma and a coordinating conjunction, or a semicolon. A run-on sentence occurs when a writer fails to use either end-stop punctuation to divide complete thoughts or suitable conjunctions to join two ideas. When two independent clauses are joined only by a comma, you have an error called a comma splice.

The following rules will help you avoid and fix run-on sentences and comma splices:

 Divide the sentence using periods.

 Incorrect: Zoologists need a bachelor's degree for entry-level positions a master's degree is often needed for advancement.

Correct: Zoologists need a bachelor's degree for entry-level positions. A master's degree is often needed for advancement.

 Explanation: Inserting a period between *positions* and *A* corrects the run-on sentence by creating two independent clauses.

 Create a compound sentence by joining independent clauses using a comma and a coordinating conjunction such as *and*, *but*, or *so*.

 Incorrect: Zoologists need a bachelor's degree for entry-level positions a master's degree is often needed for advancement.

Correct: Zoologists need a bachelor's degree for entry-level positions, but a master's degree is often needed for advancement.

 Explanation: Remember that a comma is required when you use a coordinating conjunction to join two independent clauses.

3 Create a complex sentence by adding a subordinating conjunction—such as *because*, *although*, or *while*—making one of the independent clauses a dependent clause.

Incorrect: Zoologists need a bachelor's degree for entry-level positions a master's degree is often needed for advancement.

Correct (option 1): Zoologists need a bachelor's degree for entry-level positions although a master's degree is often needed for advancement.

Explanation: Adding the conjunction *although* between the two independent clauses corrects the run-on sentence by changing the second clause to a dependent clause and creating a complex sentence. Note: In general, commas are not required when the dependent clause follows the independent clause.

Correct (option 2): Although a master's degree is often needed for advancement, zoologists need only a bachelor's degree for entry-level positions.

Explanation: Adding the conjunction *although* and moving the second independent clause corrects the run-on sentence by changing the first clause to a dependent clause and creating a complex sentence. Note: Commas are required when the dependent clause precedes the independent clause.

4 Use a semicolon when ideas are closely related in meaning.

Incorrect: Zoologists and wildlife biologists study how animals and other wildlife interact with their ecosystems, these scientists work in offices, laboratories, or outdoors.

Correct: Zoologists and wildlife biologists study how animals and other wildlife interact with their ecosystems; these scientists work in offices, laboratories, or outdoors.

Explanation: Inserting a semicolon between the two independent clauses corrects the comma splice and creates a compound sentence.

Coordination and Subordination

Basic Rule

Coordinating and subordinating conjunctions are used to join phrases and clauses and form compound and complex sentences.

COMMON CONJUNCTIONS	
Coordinating conjunctions	**Subordinating conjunctions**
for, and, nor, but, or, yet, so	after, although, as, as if, because, before, even if, even though, if, if only, rather than, since, that, though, unless, until, when, where, whereas, wherever, whether, which, while

TIP

Remember that an independent clause is just a complete sentence. It has a subject and a verb and expresses a complete thought.

Basic Rule of Coordinating Conjunctions

Coordinating conjunctions are used to add items to a list and join independent clauses to make compound sentences. With items in a list, the last item in the list should be preceded by a coordinating conjunction.

 Independent clauses: There was a Treaty of Paris signed in 1763. There was also one signed in 1783. There was another signed in 1919.

 Joined: There were Treaties of Paris signed in 1763, 1783, and 1919.

When two clauses are joined, if the second remains an independent clause, a comma must be used before the coordinating conjunction. The coordinating conjunction signals that each clause carries the same weight while also creating a relationship between the ideas (additive, contrasting, or causal).

 Independent clauses: There was a Treaty of Paris signed in 1763. There was also one signed in 1783.

 Joined: There was a Treaty of Paris signed in 1763, but there was another Treaty of Paris signed in 1783.

Basic Rule of Subordinating Conjunctions

Subordinating conjunctions are added to an independent clause to make it a dependent clause.

A dependent clause establishes a place, a time, a reason, a condition, a concession, or a comparison for the independent clause—some form of extra information that clarifies the action of the independent clause. Dependent clauses have a subject and a verb but do not express a complete thought due to the subordinating conjunction. Because of that, the clause needs (or *depends* on) an independent clause to be grammatically correct. This also means that dependent clauses are subordinate to the information in the independent clause—meaning they're less important (offering extra information) and preceded by a subordinating conjunction. Dependent clauses can come before or after an independent clause, but if they're before, they must be separated from the independent clause by a comma. Review the list of subordinating conjunctions to identify dependent clauses more quickly. Let's look at some examples of subordinating conjunctions used to create dependent clauses.

 Independent clauses: A tax on imported goods from another country is called a tariff. A tax on imported goods from another country to protect a home industry is called a protective tariff.

 Joined: A tax on imported goods from another country is called a tariff while a tax on imported goods from another country to protect a home industry is called a protective tariff.

Here, the subordinating conjunction *while* was added to the second independent clause. The resulting dependent clause is then joined to the end of the first independent clause without using any punctuation.

A subordinating conjunction can also be used at the beginning of a sentence. The resulting dependent clause must be joined to an independent clause and separated by a comma.

Independent clauses: A tax on imported goods from another country is called a tariff. A tax on imported goods from another country to protect a home industry is called a protective tariff.

Joined: While a tax on imported goods from another country is called a tariff, a tax on imported goods from another country to protect a home industry is called a protective tariff.

Modifier Placement
Basic Rule

A modifier is a word, phrase, or clause that adds detail to a sentence. To avoid confusion, modifiers should be placed as close as possible to the things they modify. Examples of different modifiers are underlined in the sentences that follow.

1

Example: Within the field of marine biology, employment is highly competitive.

Explanation: The phrase "within the field of marine biology" modifies the subject of the sentence, which is *employment*. The word *highly* modifies our understanding of the competitive nature of finding employment.

Example: The abundant supply of marine scientists far exceeds the demands, and the number of federal and state government jobs is limited.

Explanation: *Abundant* modifies *supply*. *Marine* modifies *scientists*. *Federal, state, government,* and *limited* modify our understanding of *jobs*.

When the subject of a modifier is unclear or is not included in the sentence, it is considered a dangling modifier.

Incorrect: Not realizing that the job title of marine biologist rarely exists, *marine biology* is a term recognized by most people. (What is the first phrase modifying?)

Possible revision: Not realizing that the job title of marine biologist rarely exists, most people recognize the term *marine biology.*

Misplaced modifiers occur when a modifier is poorly placed and doesn't express the writer's intent accurately.

Incorrect: The term *marine biologist* is used to almost describe all of the disciplines and jobs that deal with the study of marine life, not just those that deal with the physical properties of the sea.

Possible revision: The term *marine biologist* is used to describe almost all of the disciplines and jobs that deal with the study of marine life, not just those that deal with the physical properties of the sea.

Parallel Structure

Basic Rule

Parallel structure is the repetition of a grammatical form within a sentence. When things are parallel, they are moving in the same direction. Parallel structure is a hallmark of effective writing and is often used to emphasize ideas and present compared items in an equal light. Coordinating conjunctions are often used in parallel constructions.

 Nonparallel structure: As a child, George Washington Carver enjoyed reading, learned about plants, and he made art.

 Parallel structure: As a child, George Washington Carver enjoyed reading, learning about plants, and making art.

In the first sentence, "George Washington Carver enjoyed reading" leads the reader to expect that the next items in the list will also be gerunds, verbs that end in *-ing*. However, the next items in the list are not in the same form: "learned about plants" is in the past tense while "he made art" is an independent clause. To resolve the issue with parallel structure, we need to pick one form of the word and stick to it. The easiest and most concise fix is to change the last two items to gerunds to match the first item, *reading*.

Issues with parallel structure are most noticeable in lists of things. It's important to remember that parallel structure applies to other parts of speech as well. To be grammatically correct, items that are being compared should be the same part of speech and used correctly in the structure of the sentence.

Verb Tense

Basic Rule

Use the same verb tense whenever possible within a sentence or paragraph. Do not shift from one tense to another unless there is a valid reason for doing so.

 Incorrect: The Magna Carta *was* signed in 1215 by King John of England and *has been* the first document of its kind to limit the power of the British monarchy.

 Correct: The Magna Carta *was* signed in 1215 by King John of England and *was* the first document of its kind to limit the power of the British monarchy.

Naturally, different verb tenses have different forms, but you will see some overlap. For example, even though the sentences "He was tall" and "He was running" both use the verb *was*, the former is a simple past tense verb while the latter is called the past progressive and uses *was*, a helping verb attached to the word *running*. Complete verbs can be individual words or consist of a helping verb (often a form of "to be," "to have," or "to do") and a main verb or a participle. Look out for those small verbs to decide which choice is best for the passage.

 ALERT - - - - - - - - - - - - - -

Different verb tenses have different forms, and there may be some overlap. It's important to select the choice that is the best for the passage.

When to Use the Perfect Tenses

Basic Rule: Present Perfect

Use *present perfect* for an action begun in the past and extended to the present.

1

Example: Scientists at NASA *have seen* an alarming increase in the accumulation of greenhouse gases.

Explanation: In this case, scientists at NASA *saw* would be incorrect. What they *have seen* (present perfect) began in the past and extends to the present.

Basic Rule: Past Perfect

Use *past perfect* for an action begun and completed in the past before some other past action.

2

Example: Despite their preparations, Lewis and Clark *had never encountered* the kinds of challenges that awaited them before their expedition.

Explanation: In this case, *never encountered* would be incorrect. The action *had never encountered* (past perfect) is used because it is referring to events prior to their expedition.

Scan this QR code to learn more about modifiers.

Basic Rule: Future Perfect

Use *future perfect* for an action begun at any time and completed in the future.

3

Example: When the American astronauts arrive, the Russian cosmonauts *will have been* on the International Space Station for six months.

Explanation: In this case, although both actions occur in the future, the Russian cosmonauts *will have been* on the space station before the American astronauts *arrive*. When there are two future actions, the action completed first is expressed in the future perfect tense.

Knowing when to choose between the simple (past, present, and future) and perfect tenses can be challenging as those choices often depend on the author's intended meaning. However, information presented in the sentence, like prepositional phrases or other modifiers, can help you decide which tense makes the most sense.

Tenses: Common Verbs

Refer to the following chart to familiarize yourself with some common verbs and their tenses.

COMMON VERBS AND THEIR TENSES						
Infinitive	Present	Past	Future	Present Perfect	Past Perfect	Future Perfect
to be	am	was	will be	have been	had been	will have been
to begin	begin	began	will begin	have begun	had begun	will have begun
to come	come	came	will come	have come	had come	will have come
to do	do	did	will do	have done	had done	will have done
to feel	feel	felt	will feel	have felt	had felt	will have felt
to get	get	got	will get	have gotten	had gotten	will have gotten
to go	go	went	will go	have gone	had gone	will have gone
to have	have	had	will have	have had	had had	will have had
to know	know	knew	will know	have known	had known	will have known
to leave	leave	left	will leave	have left	had left	will have left
to look	look	looked	will look	have looked	had looked	will have looked
to say	say	said	will say	have said	had said	will have said
to see	see	saw	will see	have seen	had seen	will have seen
to speak	speak	spoke	will speak	have spoken	had spoken	will have spoken
to study	study	studied	will study	have studied	had studied	will have studied
to take	take	took	will take	have taken	had taken	will have taken
to think	think	thought	will think	have thought	had thought	will have thought
to walk	walk	walked	will walk	have walked	had walked	will have walked
to write	write	wrote	will write	have written	had written	will have written

*Note: For consistency, all verbs are conjugated in the first-person singular.

Verb Mood

Basic Rule

Mood, as it relates to verb forms, refers to the kind of message the writer intends to communicate.

The indicative mood is the most common mood and is used to state facts or opinions.

EXAMPLE

Zora Neale Hurston's novel *Their Eyes Were Watching God* was forgotten for many years but is now considered a literary classic.

The imperative mood is used when a writer wants to give a directive or make a request. Though not stated, the subject of an imperative sentence is *you*.

EXAMPLES

Stop pretending that it doesn't matter.

George Washington peered across the Potomac as the frigid wind lashed his face. "Hurry!" he exclaimed. (*Peered* is in the indicative. *Hurry* is in the imperative.)

The subjunctive mood expresses a condition contrary to fact, a wish, a supposition, or an indirect command. Although it is going out of use in English, the subjunctive can still be seen in the following forms.

- To express a wish not likely to be fulfilled or impossible to be realized

EXAMPLE

I wish it *were* possible for us to approve his transfer at this time. (It is *not* possible.)

- In a subordinate clause after a verb that expresses a command, a request, or a suggestion

EXAMPLE

It was recommended by the White House *that* the Office of Homeland Security *be* responsible for preparing the statements.

- To express a condition known or supposed to be contrary to fact

EXAMPLE

If Ann *were* chosen to be our company's president, she would overhaul the marketing department.

- After *as if* or *as though*. In formal writing and speech, *as if* and *as though* are followed by the subjunctive, since they introduce as supposition something not factual. In informal writing and speaking, the indicative is sometimes used.

EXAMPLE

Before defecting to the British Army, Benedict Arnold talked as if he were a true American patriot. (He was not.)

Closely related to the subjunctive mood is the conditional mood. The conditional mood is used when making requests or statements that express under what condition something would happen. Signaled by such words as *would*, *could*, *should*, and *might*, the conditional mood is often used in connection with a phrase in the subjunctive mood and is preceded by the word *if*:

EXAMPLES

Had you followed the GPS directions, we would not have been lost.

The door might open if I jiggle the handle.

Avoid shifts in mood. Once you have determined the mood that properly expresses the passage's message, verify that the mood is sustained throughout the sentence or the paragraph. A shift in mood is confusing to the listener or reader; it indicates that the speaker or writer has changed their way of looking at the conditions.

 Incorrect: It is requested by the White House that a report of Congressional proceedings be prepared and copies *should be* distributed to all citizens. (*Be* is subjunctive; *should be*, indicative.)

 Correct: It is requested by the White House that a report of the Congressional proceedings *be* prepared and that copies *be* distributed to all citizens.

Verb Voice

Basic Rule

Voice tells us whether the subject of a sentence is the actor or is acted upon. There are two verb voices: active voice and passive voice. Active voice involves a subject that performs an action, which makes the meaning of the sentence clear and direct. Passive voice involves a subject that receives an action. While active voice is typically preferred over passive voice because it is more concise and straightforward, passive voice is sometimes necessary to describe an event or situation in which there is no clear agent or where the subject of the sentence is not important. However, be cautious when using the passive voice, as it is often used to deflect blame or avoid taking responsibility. Most of the time, sentences written in the passive voice can easily be revised so that they are in active voice.

 Passive voice: The speech was read carefully and deliberately. (Who is reading the speech?)

 Active voice: The politician read the speech carefully and deliberately.

 Passive voice: The decision was overturned by the courts.

 Active voice: The courts overturned the decision.

Word Choice

Word choice means using words in English correctly and effectively. Many English words are easily confused and misused because they have similar spellings, sounds, or meanings. Using the wrong word can have a negative effect on the clarity of your writing, so it's important to know some of the most commonly confused words and how to use them correctly. It's also important to build your vocabulary, such as by using the techniques discussed in Chapter 3: Reading Comprehension. Doing so affords you a wider variety of words from which to choose when writing.

Words that are homophones are pronounced the same but mean different things. For example, I might be *bored* in class, but I'm not *board* in class. *Bored* means to be dissatisfied with a tedious task while *board* means a piece of wood. Even though these words sound alike, their meanings are quite different.

There are also some words that don't have similar spellings or pronunciations, but it can still be difficult to decide which word to use. For example, when do you use *good* and when do you use *well*? *Good* is an adjective and describes a noun while *well* is an adverb that describes a verb. For example, I did *well* on the exam, but this pizza is *good*!

Here are some commonly misused words and examples of how to use them correctly.

accede—to agree with
We shall *accede* to your request for more evidence.

concede—to yield, but not necessarily in agreement
To avoid delay, we shall *concede* that more evidence is necessary.

exceed—to be more than
Federal expenditures now *exceed* federal income.

addition—the act or process of adding
In *addition* to a dictionary, she always used a thesaurus.

edition—a printing of a publication
The first *edition* of Shakespeare's plays appeared in 1623.

amount—applies to quantities that cannot be counted one by one
The review provided a vast *amount* of data.

number—applies to quantities that can be counted one by one
The farmer delivered a *number* of fruits.

breath—an intake of air
Before you dive in, take a very deep *breath*.

breathe—to draw in and release air
It is difficult to *breathe* under water.

breadth—width
The *breadth* and length of a square are equal.

access—availability
The lawyer was given *access* to the grand jury records.

excess—more than
The lab work revealed *excess* fluid.

accept—(v) to take an offer
The draft board will *accept* all seniors as volunteers before graduation.

except—(prep) excluding
All students *except* seniors will be called.

affect—(v) to influence
Your education will *affect* your future.

effect—(n) a result
The *effect* of the last war is still being felt.

adverse—unfavorable
He thought the medication was having an *adverse* effect on his health.

averse—disliking
Many students are *averse* to criticism from their classmates.

cite—quote or give credit
He was fond of *citing* the Scriptures.

sight—vision or looks
The *sight* of the wreck was appalling.

site—a place for a building or web page
The school board seeks a new school *site*.

complement—a completing part
The wine was an excellent *complement* to the dish.

compliment—expression of admiration
He *complimented* her sense of humor.

conscience—sense of right
His *conscience* prevented him from selfishness.

conscientious—meticulous or scrupulous
We all depend on him because he is *conscientious*.

conscious—aware
The injured woman was completely *conscious*.

decent—suitable
The *decent* thing to do is to admit your fault.

descent—going down
The *descent* into the cave was treacherous.

dissent—disagreement
Two of the nine justices filed a *dissenting* opinion.

desert—an arid area
The Sahara is a world-famous *desert*.

dessert—the final course of a meal
We had gelato for *dessert*.

can—able to
I *can* lift this chair over my head.

may—implies permission
You *may* leave after you finish your work.

capital—the city
Paris is the *capital* of France.

capitol—the building
We visited the *capitol* building on the tour.

coarse—vulgar or harsh
We were shunned because of his *coarse* behavior.

course—a path or study
The ship took its usual *course*.
I am taking an English *course*.

cent—a coin
One *cent* isn't enough to buy anything.

scent—an odor
The *scent* of roses is pleasing.

sent—past tense of send
We were *sent* to the rear of the balcony.

former—the first of two
The *former* half of the book was in prose.

latter—the second of two
The *latter* half of the book was in poetry.

its—belonging to "it"
The bicycle lost *its* front wheel.

it's—contraction for "it is"
It's more like a unicycle now.

principal—(adj.) chief or main; (n) leader; (n) a sum placed at interest

His *principal* supporters were enraged.

The school *principal* asked for test scores.

Her payment was applied as interest on the *principal*.

principle—a fundamental truth or belief
Humility was the guiding *principle* of Buddha's life.

 their—belonging to them
We took *their* books home.

there—in that place
Your books are over *there*.

they're—contraction for "they are"
They're going to the park.

 precede—to come before
The other symptoms *precede* a fever.

proceed—to go ahead
We can then *proceed* with our diagnosis.

 two—the numeral 2
There are *two* sides to every story.

to—in the direction of
We shall go *to* school.

too—more than or also
The weather is *too* hot.

AGREEMENT
Pronoun-Antecedent Agreement

A pronoun agrees with its antecedent in both person and number.

 Example: The archaeologists examined the fossilized bone with great care to make sure they didn't damage *it*.

 Explanation: The antecedent of the pronoun *they* is *archaeologists*. The antecedent of the pronoun *it* is bone.

Remember to use a singular verb when you refer to indefinite pronouns such as *everyone, everybody, each, every, anyone, anybody, nobody, none, no one, one,*

either, and *neither.* Some indefinite pronouns—*any, more, most, some*—will be singular or plural as dependent on usage. The pronouns *both, many, others,* and *several* will always need a plural verb for agreement.

EXAMPLES

Everyone seems to be enjoying the music.

Nobody is in the break room.

Most of the cake has been eaten.

Most attendees dressed appropriately.

Both are destined for success.

Many of us will be late.

Subject-Verb Agreement

Basic Rule

A verb agrees in number with its subject. A singular subject takes a singular verb. A plural subject takes a plural verb.

Let's take a look at an example.

Example: Choose the correct verb: (*is, am, are*)

Booker T. Washington, Frederick Douglass, and W.E.B. DuBois _____ all important historical figures.

Explanation: Remember that the verb must agree with the subject. Since the subject is plural—subjects joined by *and* are plural—a plural verb is needed. The correct response therefore should be:

Booker T. Washington, Frederick Douglass, and W.E.B. DuBois *are* all important historical figures.

Sometimes, the subject comes after the verb, but the rule still applies.

Example: Choose the correct verb: (*is, are*)

While the lecture has lasted two hours already, there _____ still three more speakers.

Explanation: *Are* is the correct verb choice since the subject *speakers* is plural and requires a plural verb.

There is one major exception to this rule. When the sentence is introduced by the word *there* and the verb is followed by a compound (double) subject, the first part of the subject dictates whether the verb should be singular or plural.

EXAMPLE

There is one American astronaut in the shuttle and four Russian astronauts in the space station.

When compound subjects are joined by *either-or* or *neither-nor*, the verb agrees with the subject closest to the verb.

Examples: Neither the violinist nor the other *musicians have had* much experience performing for an audience.

Neither you nor *I am willing* to make the sacrifices required of a professional musician.

Explanation: In the first example, *musicians* (plural) is closest to the verb; in the second example, *I* (singular) is closest to the verb.

To learn more about subject-verb agreement, scan this QR code.

TIP

The third person singular of most verbs ends in -*s*. For other forms, consider the following: I, we speak (first person); you speak (second person); he, she, it speaks (third person singular). Examples: He runs. She jogs. It jumps. The man sees. Jeremy laughs. The child walks. They eat.

Sometimes, a word or a group of words may come between the subject and the verb. The verb still must agree with the simple subject, and the simple subject is never part of a prepositional phrase.

EXAMPLE

Stephen King, the author of hundreds of best-selling novels, novellas, and short stories, *is* also a guitarist and singer in a band.

Collective Nouns

Collective nouns present special problems. A collective noun names a group of people or things. Although usually singular in form, it is treated as either singular or plural according to the sense of the sentence.

- A collective noun is treated as *singular* when members of the group act, or are considered, as a unit.

EXAMPLE

The citizens' *assembly is drafting* a petition that would seek to protect local aquifers from chemical run-off and hazardous waste.

- A collective noun is treated as *plural* when the members act, or are considered, as multiple individuals.

EXAMPLE

After one of the longest and most fabled droughts in baseball history, the *Boston Red Sox have* finally overcome the "Curse of the Bambino" to win another World Series.

COMMON COLLECTIVE NOUNS			
assembly	commission	crowd	minority
association	committee	department	number
audience	company	family	pair
band	corporation	firm	press
board	council	group	public
cabinet	counsel	jury	staff
class	couple	majority	United States

Logical Comparisons

Logical comparisons on the ACCUPLACER will test your ability to recognize and correct cases in which unlike terms are compared. Oftentimes, this looks like two unlike parts of speech being compared, for example, a verb and a noun, even if the ideas expressed are related or similar.

Let's look at an example.

EXAMPLE

Which option is the best version of the underlined portion of the sentence?

I prefer spring, when bright flowers begin to bloom and temperatures start to rise, to <u>experiencing winter</u> *with its bitter cold and early nights.*

A. NO CHANGE

B. enduring harsh winter weather

C. winter

D. when winter arrives

The correct answer is C. The speaker is comparing *spring* (a noun) with *experiencing winter*, a gerund phrase. To make this a logical comparison, we would need to revise the underlined phrase so that it is also a noun. While a gerund phrase is technically a noun, we can arrive at a more direct, logical comparison by replacing it with a noun. The only option that fits this criterion is *winter*.

CONVENTIONS OF PUNCTUATION

On the ACCUPLACER, you'll be expected to know how to use punctuation to communicate ideas effectively. For instance, as we've already discussed, it's important to understand how to use punctuation to formulate different types of sentences and to join phrases and clauses. On the exam, you will also be tested on your ability to use apostrophes with contractions and possessive nouns and pronouns. Certain questions will ask you to use punctuation to separate items in a series and to set off nonrestrictive and parenthetical elements in a sentence. You'll also need to study up on how to correctly use and recognize the incorrect use of commas, colons, semicolons, dashes, and ellipses. Finally, you may also be tested on whether certain punctuation is necessary, how to use hyphens, and which punctuation is appropriate to use at the end of a sentence. Here, we'll cover different types of punctuation—commas, semicolons, hyphens, em dashes, parentheses, ellipses, colons, apostrophes, and end-of-sentence punctuation—and the rules that govern them.

The Comma
Basic Rules

We use commas for a lot of things, but focus on separating the following:

- Independent clauses that are connected by a coordinating conjunction
- Introductory clauses and phrases
- Dependent and independent clauses
- Items in a series
- Nonessential and parenthetical elements
- Coordinate adjectives

Let's look at some examples:

- To separate independent clauses connected by a coordinating conjunction

EXAMPLE

Toni Morrison's first novel, *The Bluest Eye*, was published in 1970, and it received a rave review from *The New York Times*.

- To set off introductory clauses and phrases

EXAMPLE

The year after winning her Nobel Prize, Toni Morrison published the novel *Jazz*.

- To separate a leading dependent clause from an independent clause

EXAMPLE

While she was praised for her writing style and range of emotion, Toni Morrison was also celebrated for the attention she drew to racial tension in the past and present of the United States.

 FYI

If you pay attention to punctuation, it's likely you've noticed that not everyone puts the serial or Oxford comma before the *and* when separating three or more items in a list. On the ACCUPLACER, it's best to err on the side of including the Oxford comma.

 TIP

Nonessential and parenthetical elements (indicated by commas, parentheses, or em dashes) provide extra information that is not necessary for the meaning or grammatical correctness of a sentence. While each of these punctuation marks serves a similar purpose, the difference between them is one of emphasis.

- To separates three or more items in a list

EXAMPLE

In a span of 15 years, Toni Morrison won a National Book Critics Circle Award, the Pulitzer Prize, and the Nobel Prize for Literature.

- To separate nonessential and parenthetical elements from the main clause

EXAMPLE

Toni Morrison, who won the Nobel Prize in Literature in 1993, was a Professor Emeritus at Princeton University.

Last night, Toni Morrison began her lecture, titled "The Future of Time: Literature and Diminished Expectations," with a meditation on the nature of time and the human perception of progress.

- To separate coordinate adjectives that precede the noun they describe

EXAMPLE

Toni Morrison was rumored to be a fun, entertaining speaker.

When you have at least two adjectives describing a noun (e.g., "The tall, funny man" or "The cold and windy weather"), try separating the adjectives with a comma when their order can be reversed or when the conjunction *and* can be placed between them while still preserving the meaning of the phrase. If reversing the order or adding *and* disrupts the meaning of the phrase (e.g., "The giant hockey players" as "The hockey giant players" or "The giant and hockey players"), no comma is needed.

The Semicolon

Basic Rules

A semicolon (;) may be used to separate two complete ideas (independent clauses) in a sentence when the two ideas have a close relationship and are *not* connected with a coordinating conjunction.

EXAMPLE

"Inalienable rights" are basic human rights that many believe cannot and should not be given up or taken away; life, liberty, and the pursuit of happiness are some of those rights.

The semicolon is often used between independent clauses connected by conjunctive adverbs such as *consequently, therefore, also, furthermore, for example, however, nevertheless, still, yet, moreover,* and *otherwise.*

EXAMPLE

In 1867, critics thought William H. Seward foolish for buying the largely unexplored territory of Alaska for the astronomical price of $7 million; however, history has proven that it was an inspired purchase.

Here's a word of caution: Do not use the semicolon between an independent clause and a phrase or subordinate clause.

 Incorrect: While eating ice cream for dessert; Clarence and Undine discussed their next business venture.

 Correct: While eating ice cream for dessert, Clarence and Undine discussed their next business venture.

Similar to serial commas, semicolons are used to separate items in a list when the items themselves contain commas.

EXAMPLE

Some kinds of biologists study specific species of animals. For example, cetologists study marine mammals, such as whales and dolphins; entomologists study insects, such as beetles and butterflies; and ichthyologists study wild fish, such as sharks and lungfish.

The Hyphen
Basic Rules

A hyphen (-) is used to join words or parts of words together, especially compound adjectives that come before nouns or with compound words that aren't combined.

The cashier handed me a five-dollar bill.

My mother-in-law is flying in tomorrow.

Do not use hyphens with the adverb *very* or adverbs that end in *-ly*. When combining words with hyphens, do not use spaces before or after hyphens.

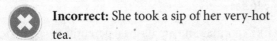

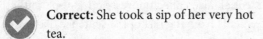

Incorrect: She took a sip of her very-hot tea.

Correct: She took a sip of her very hot tea.

Incorrect: He took his finely-aged wine to the party.

Correct: He took his finely aged wine to the party.

Use hyphens with compound numbers that modify nouns.

Amani bought sixty-five pencils.

When describing the age of someone or something, use two hyphens: one between the number and unit of time and one between the unit of time and the word *old*.

Dylan and Avery have a two-year-old child.

Cody adopted a 10-week-old puppy.

Words with certain prefixes require a hyphen to avoid confusion. Such prefixes may include *self-*, *ex-*, *mid-*, *all-*, *anti-*, *pre-*, and others.

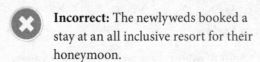

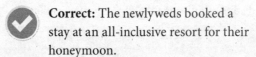

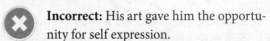

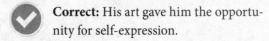

Incorrect: The newlyweds booked a stay at an all inclusive resort for their honeymoon.

Correct: The newlyweds booked a stay at an all-inclusive resort for their honeymoon.

Incorrect: His art gave him the opportunity for self expression.

Correct: His art gave him the opportunity for self-expression.

The Em Dash
Basic Rules

Em dashes (—) are used to set off parenthetical material that you want to emphasize. Dashes interrupt the flow of your sentence, thereby indicating a break in thought and calling attention to the information they contain. An em dash always precedes the nonessential information, so the aside must start later in the sentence.

Many consider Toni Morrison—winner of both the Pulitzer and Nobel Prizes in Literature—to be one of the greatest writers of her generation.

Benjamin Franklin's many intellectual pursuits—from printmaking to politics—exemplify his eclectic personality.

Em dashes can also be used to rename a nearby noun. Typically, a comma would be used to set off this information, but since it includes commas already, use an em dash.

Benjamin Franklin—a printer, writer, inventor, and statesman—was the son of a soap maker.

An em dash also indicates a list, a restatement, an amplification, or a dramatic shift in tone or thought.

Eager to write for his brother's newspaper, young Benjamin began submitting letters to the editor under the pseudonym Silence Dogood—they were a hit!

Parentheses
Basic Rules

Just like commas and em dashes, parentheses separate nonessential (also called nonrestrictive or parenthetical) elements from the rest of the sentence. Parentheses indicate that the enclosed information is less important or more tangential to the surrounding sentence. Parentheses must always come in pairs.

Toni Morrison's novel *Beloved* (1987) was made into a movie in 1998.

While at Princeton, Toni Morrison (the writer) established a special creative workshop for writers and performances called the Princeton Atelier.

Ellipses

Basic Rule

An ellipsis (…) is used to indicate the omission of one or more words, to represent a pause in thought, or to show when something is deliberately being left out. You can use an ellipsis to indicate that less relevant parts of a quotation have been removed to make the quotation more concise. In narrative writing, you can use ellipses to pause for dramatic effect or to show that a character's thoughts or dialogue are trailing off into silence.

EXAMPLES

In his speech "The Perils of Indifference," Elie Wiesel relies on rhetorical questions to invite the audience to consider the dangers of being indifferent, asking, "Why did some of America's largest corporations continue to do business with Hitler's Germany until 1942? […] It was documented that the Wehrmacht could not have conducted its invasion of France without oil obtained from American sources. How is one to explain their indifference?"

"I'm so tired. I can't keep my eyes open any-more…" she muttered as the anesthesia kicked in.

The Colon

Basic Rule

The colon (:) is used to precede a list, a long quotation, or a statement that illustrates or clarifies the earlier information.

EXAMPLES

There are only three nations that have success-fully landed spacecraft on the moon: the Soviet Union, the United States, and China.

In the United States, there are three branches of government: the Executive, the Legislative, and the Judicial.

Only use colons after independent clauses. Most commonly, that means that you won't use colons after a verb. Further, no introductory or connecting information should occur before or after a colon, such as *and* or *including*.

 Incorrect: The Louisiana Purchase included territory that would become: Montana, South Dakota, Nebraska, Kansas, Oklahoma, Arkansas, Louisiana, and Missouri.

 Correct: The Louisiana Purchase included territory that would become many of today's states: Montana, South Dakota, Nebraska, Kansas, Oklahoma, Arkansas, Louisiana, and Missouri.

The Apostrophe

Basic Rules

Apostrophes usually serve one of two purposes.

To indicate the possessive case of nouns: If the noun does not end in *s*—whether singular or plural—add an *'s*; if the noun ends in *s*, simply add the *'* after the *s*.

Note: Proper nouns are often an exception to this rule. On the ACCUPLACER, you might see names that end in -*s* pluralized by adding *'s*. What matters most is that your revisions and edits are consistent with the rest of the paragraph or passage you are given, so pay attention to other instances of apostrophe usage with names if you are unsure of what to do.

 Example 1: A car's headlights are typically wired in parallel so that if one burns out the other will keep functioning.

Example 2: The women's club sponsored many charity events.

Example 3: Charles Mingus's skill as a jazz musician is widely recognized.

To indicate a *contraction*—the omission of one or more letters: Place the apostrophe exactly where the missing letters occur.

Examples:

can't = cannot

it's = it is

we're = we are

End-of-Sentence Punctuation

Three types of punctuation are used to end a sentence: the period, the question mark, and the exclamation mark.

A period is used at the end of a sentence that makes a statement.

 Example: In 1620, the Pilgrims signed the Mayflower Compact.

A question mark is used after a direct question. A period is used after an indirect question.

Direct Question: Were The Federalist Papers written by James Madison, John Jay, or Alexander Hamilton?

Indirect Question: Profession Mahin wanted to know if you knew who wrote The Federalist Papers.

An exclamation mark is used after an expression that shows strong emotion or issues a command. It may follow a word, a phrase, or a sentence.

 Example: Koko the gorilla knew more than 1,000 sign-language signs and could communicate with humans. Amazing!

ALERT

Do not use apostrophes with possessive pronouns such as *yours, hers, ours, theirs,* and *whose*, which indicate possession already.

Unnecessary Punctuation

Unnecessary punctuation can break a sentence into confusing and illogical fragments. Here are some common mistakes to look out for.

- Don't use a comma alone to connect independent clauses. This is called a comma splice.

> ❌ **Incorrect:** Toni Morrison grew up in an integrated neighborhood, she did not become fully aware of racial divisions until she was in her teens.

> ✅ **Possible revision:** Toni Morrison grew up in an integrated neighborhood and did not become fully aware of racial divisions until she was in her teens.

- Don't use a comma between compound elements that are not independent clauses.

> ❌ **Incorrect:** In 1998, Oprah Winfrey, and Danny Glover starred in a film adaptation of Morrison's novel *Beloved*.

> ✅ **Possible revision:** In 1998, Oprah Winfrey and Danny Glover starred in a film adaptation of Morrison's novel *Beloved*.

- Do not use an apostrophe when making a noun plural.

> ❌ **Incorrect:** In 2006, *The New York Times Book Review* named *Beloved* the best American novel published in the last 25 year's.

> ✅ **Possible revision:** In 2006, *The New York Times Book Review* named *Beloved* the best American novel published in the last 25 years.

SUMMING IT UP

- The ACCUPLACER writing placement test will evaluate your ability to improve sentence structure, usage, and punctuation in a sample text.

- The following list summarizes the key conventions you need to remember to address most errors presented in the writing placement test:

  - Sentence Structure and Formation

    - **Fragments:** Every sentence must have a subject and a verb and express a complete idea. If a sentence is missing any one of those elements, it is incomplete.

    - **Run-ons and Comma Splices:** Connect complete sentences with proper punctuation.

    - **Combining Independent Clauses:** Use periods, a comma + FANBOYS, or a semicolon. You can also make an independent clause dependent with a subordinating conjunction to link sentences.

    - **Combining Dependent and Independent Clauses:** Place a comma after a dependent clause at the beginning of a sentence.

    - **Misplaced Modifiers:** Place modifiers (adjectives, adverbs, prepositional phrases) as close to the word they're modifying as possible.

    - **Parallel Structure:** Keep verbs and phrases in the same grammatical form when writing sentences.

    - **Verb Tense and Mood:** Keep consistent verb tense and mood within sentences and paragraphs unless otherwise justified.

    - **Voice:** Shift sentences to active voice (when the subject performs the action) rather than passive voice (when the subject of the sentence receives the action).

  - Punctuation

    - **Commas:** Separate independent clauses with a comma and FANBOYS; add a comma after an introductory phrase or leading subordinate clause; separate items in lists of three or more (including before the *and* before the final item); place commas around nonessential information to separate it from the main clause of a sentence.

- Em dashes: Indicate nonrestrictive or nonessential information with em dashes; these tangents, asides, and parenthetical statements follow em dashes and must be closed by another em dash—unless they finish the sentence.

- Semicolons: Use a semicolon to separate related independent clauses and items in a list where the items have commas.

- Hyphens: Use hyphens to combine words that form compound adjectives preceding the noun they modify, especially with compound numbers (seventy-three) or when describing ages of people or things (two-year-old child). Hyphens are also used for words with certain prefixes (mid-, anti-, etc.).

- Colons: Use a colon to indicate the start of a list or quotation or to add emphasis; colons must be preceded by an independent clause.

- Apostrophes: Indicate possession with an *'s* (or just an apostrophe after a noun that ends in an *-s*) or use an apostrophe to signal the contraction of two words into one (they + are = they're).

- Parentheses: Separate nonessential information of low importance from the rest of the sentence with a pair of parentheses.

- Ellipses: Use ellipses to indicate when parts of a quotation have been omitted or to indicate a pause.

- End-Stop Punctuation: End statements and indirect questions with periods; use question marks to end direct questions; end statements that indicate strong emotion or commands with an exclamation point.

○ Usage

- Pronouns: Pronouns must agree in case, number, and gender (where applicable) with their antecedent (the word they replace); it must be clear to which antecedent a pronoun applies when multiple possible antecedents are present.

- Subject-Verb Agreement: A verb must agree with its subject in number: singular when the subject is singular, plural when the subject is plural. Agreement occurs with the subject of a sentence—which may not necessarily be the word closest to the verb.

- Confused Words and Phrases: Select the word or phrase most appropriate to the situation, relying on common expressions and correct word choice for frequently confused words.

- Logical Comparisons: Make clear the objects being compared in a comparison; an object should be compared to an object of similar type.

KNOWLEDGE CHECK

WRITING (CONVENTIONS OF SYNTAX, USAGE, AND PUNCTUATION)

15 Questions

Directions: Read the following early essay drafts and then choose the best answer to the question or the best completion of the statement.

(1) Born in Pakistan on July 12, 1997, Malala Yousafzai was still just a teenager when she started changing the world. (2) Often known simply as "Malala," this young activist took the world by storm when she survived an assassination attempt at the tender age of 15, then goes on to tell her story to rally for change and publicly support the right for all girls in the world to receive an education.

(3) When Malala was growing up, the Pakistani Taliban instituted a prohibition on educating girls. (4) As the daughter of an activist and educator, Malala's family supported her when she decided to oppose this prohibition and go to school despite threats from the Taliban. (5) She was only 11 when she gave her first speech in defense of girls' education at a protest. (6) The speech was titled "How Dare the Taliban Take Away My Basic Right to Education?" and because press was in attendance, it got published throughout Pakistan. (7) During this time, the Taliban was routinely attacking girls for attending school and schools that dared to educate girls were bombed.

(8) Despite the danger her activism posed Malala continued to oppose the Taliban's restrictions, blogging for the BBC under an assumed name and making television appearances. (9) Her efforts were recognized in many ways; she received Pakistan's first ever National Youth Peace Prize. (10) However, it didn't protect her from being targeted by the Taliban. (11) Malala was shot in the head by a gunman from the Pakistani Taliban on October 9, 2012, when walking home from school.

(12) Miraculously, Malala survived this brutal attack, and it only made her more dedicated to her cause. (13) Following this heinous assault, a wave of worldwide protests in support of Malala also led Pakistan to adopt its first Right to Education Bill ensuring Pakistani girls access to education. (14) Since then, Malala has received numerous accolades for the activist work she continues to pursue. (15) The youngest person to ever receive the honor, the Nobel Peace Prize was awarded to 17-year-old Malala in 2014. (16) To share her side of the story, Malala also wrote a memoir entitled *I Am Malala: The Girl Who Stood Up for Education and Was Shot by the Taliban* in 2013.

1. Which is the best version of the underlined portion of sentence 2 (reproduced below)?

   Often known simply as "Malala," this young activist took the world by storm when she survived an assassination attempt at the tender age of 15, then __goes__ on to tell her story to rally for change and publicly support the right for all girls in the world to receive an education.

   A. (as it is now)

   B. was going

   C. went

   D. is going

2. Which is the best version of the underlined portion of sentence 7 (reproduced below)?

   During this time, the Taliban was routinely attacking girls for attending school and __schools that dared to educate girls were bombed__.

   A. (as it is now)

   B. bombing schools that dared to educate girls

   C. schools that dared to educate girls had been bombed

   D. will bomb schools that dared to educate girls

3. Which is the best version of the underlined portion of sentence 8 (reproduced below)?

   Despite the danger her activism __posed Malala__ continued to oppose the Taliban's restrictions, blogging for the BBC under an assumed name and making television appearances.

   A. (as it is now)

   B. posed—Malala

   C. posed; Malala

   D. posed, Malala

4. Which is the best version of the underlined portion of sentence 13 (reproduced below)?

   Following this heinous assault, a wave of worldwide protests in support of Malala also led Pakistan to adopt its first Right to Education Bill ensuring Pakistani __girls access__ to education.

   A. (as it is now)

   B. girl's access

   C. girls' access

   D. girls access'

5. Which is the best version of sentence 15 (reproduced below)?

   The youngest person to ever receive the honor, the Nobel Peace Prize was awarded to 17-year-old Malala in 2014.

   A. (as it is now)

   B. At 17 years old, the Nobel Peace Prize was awarded to Malala in 2014, making her the youngest person to ever receive the honor.

   C. At 17 years old, Malala received the Nobel Peace Prize, making her the youngest person in 2014 to receive the honor.

   D. Malala received the Nobel Peace Prize in 2014 at 17 years old, making her the youngest person to ever receive the honor.

(1) Invasive species wreaks havoc on ecosystems, and the emerald ash borer is no exception. (2) Emerald ash borers are brightly colored wood boring beetles that only attack ash trees. (3) Native to Asia, the emerald ash borer was first located in the United States in 2002 when it was spotted in Michigan. (4) The insect likely made its way over to the US by hitching a ride on a shipping crate or in wooden packing materials.

(5) Emerald ash borers are an invasive species in the US and Canada, killing up to 99% of ash trees in its path. (6) While adult emerald ash borers haven't done much damage, the larvae feed on the inner bark, making it difficult for the trees to get the proper nutrients. (7) Signs of an emerald ash borer infestation include: D-shaped exit holes, woodpecker feeding holes, bark deformities, yellowing foliage, and more.

(8) The most recent data suggest that emerald ash borers have been spotted in at least 35 states. (9) In states where emerald ash borers are widespread, there are often restrictions on the transport of firewood between counties since this is how the insects are likely to spread. (10) Residents with ash trees are encouraged to vaccinate they're trees against emerald ash borer infestation or else risk losing them to the invasive beetle. (11) In areas where infestation is likely or even inevitable, some cities and counties are taking preemptive action by either vaccinating trees or replacing ash trees with more resilient native species. (12) It's important that residents in affected areas keep an eye out for emerald ash borers or other invasive species and to notify the proper authorities of any sightings.

6. Which is the best version of the underlined portion of sentence 1 (reproduced below)?

   Invasive species wreaks havoc on ecosystems, and the emerald ash borer is no exception.

   A. (as it is now)
   B. Invasive species wreak
   C. Invasive species' wreak
   D. Invasive species' wreaks

7. Which is the best version of the underlined portion of sentence 5 (reproduced below)?

   Emerald ash borers are an invasive species in the US and Canada, killing up to 99% of ash trees in its path.

   A. (as it is now)
   B. it's
   C. its'
   D. their

8. Which is the best version of the underlined portion of sentence 7 (reproduced below)?

   Signs of an emerald ash borer infestation include: D-shaped exit holes, woodpecker feeding holes, bark deformities, yellowing foliage, and more.

   A. (as it is now)
   B. include, D-shaped
   C. include D-shaped
   D. include; D-shaped

9. Which is the best version of the underlined portion of sentence 10 (reproduced below)?

   Residents with ash trees are encouraged to vaccinate they're trees against emerald ash borer infestation or else risk losing them to the invasive beetle.

   A. (as it is now)
   B. their
   C. there
   D. his or her

10. Which is the best version of the underlined portion of sentence 12 (reproduced below)?

It's important that residents in affected areas keep an eye out for emerald ash borers or other invasive species and to notify the proper authorities of any sightings.

A. (as it is now)

B. will notify

C. ought to notify

D. notify

---

(1) In the animal kingdom, it's very common for like animals to group together. (2) For every species in which individuals tend to keep to themselves, there are a handful of others (including humans) instinctively programmed to stick by kin. (3) Scientists usually come up with special names to designate these groups. (4) These group names often vary based on the name, characteristics, or public reception of the species in question.

(5) Some of the names used to refer to a group of animals, are more familiar than others. (6) For instance, a group of deer, cows, sheep, or any other kind of cattle is generally referred to as a herd. (7) Groups of dogs, wolves, and other animals with canine features are typically called a pack, as are groups of mules. (8) Groups of swimming mammals are generally called a pod, as is the case with dolphins and whales. (9) The word *colony* is another common term for a group of animals. (10) It can refer to ants, bats, beavers, frogs, penguins, rabbits, rats, feral cats, and weasels, to name just a few.

(11) Scientists occasionally get creative when deciding what a group of animals should be called. (12) Often, this takes the form of alliteration, such as in a flamboyance of flamingos, a caravan of camels, a wisdom of wombats, a coalition of cheetahs, a shiver of sharks, or a pandemonium of parrots. (13) Other groups have dramatic names that allude to the unique characteristics of the species in question, as is the case with a quiver of cobras, a murder of crows, a thunder of hippopotami, a conspiracy of lemurs, or an ostentation of peacocks. (14) Still other terms make the groups of animals sound sophisticated; who wouldn't want to learn some wisdom from a parliament of owls or witness the majesty of a convocation of eagles!

---

11. Which is the best version of the underlined portion of sentence 5 (reproduced below)?

Some of the names used to refer to a group of animals, are more familiar than others.

A. (as it is now)

B. animals are

C. animals—are

D. animals…are

12. Which is the best version of the underlined portion of sentence 8 (reproduced below)?

Groups of swimming mammals are generally called a pod, as is the case with dolphins and whales.

A. (as it is now)

B. are generally called pod's

C. are generally called pods

D. is generally called a pod

13. Which choice most effectively combines sentences 9 and 10 (reproduced below) at the underlined portion?

The word colony *is another common term for <u>a group of animals. It can refer to</u> ants, bats, beavers, frogs, penguins, rabbits, rats, feral cats, and weasels, to name just a few.*

A. a group of animals, it can refer to

B. a group of animals … it can refer to

C. a group of animals-it can refer to

D. a group of animals; it can refer to

14. Which is the best version of the underlined portion of sentence 13 (reproduced below)?

Other groups have dramatic names that <u>allude</u> to the unique characteristics of the species in question, as is the case with a quiver of cobras, a murder of crows, a thunder of hippopotami, a conspiracy of lemurs, or an ostentation of peacocks.

A. (as it is now)

B. illude

C. elude

D. delude

15. Which is the best version of the underlined portion of sentence 14 (reproduced below)?

Still other terms make the groups of animals sound sophisticated; who wouldn't want to learn some wisdom from a parliament of owls or witness the majesty of a convocation of <u>eagles!</u>

A. (as it is now)

B. eagles.

C. eagles…

D. eagles?

ANSWER KEY AND EXPLANATIONS

1. C	4. C	7. D	10. D	13. D
2. B	5. D	8. C	11. B	14. A
3. D	6. B	9. B	12. C	15. D

1. **The correct answer is C.** To avoid shifting verb tenses from the past to the present, use *went* instead of *goes*.

2. **The correct answer is B.** Replacing the underlined phrase with "bombing schools that dared to educate girls" maintains the active voice and preserves parallel structure within the sentence.

3. **The correct answer is D.** Remember to use a comma after a dependent clause when it's at the beginning of a sentence.

4. **The correct answer is C.** To make a plural common noun possessive, add an apostrophe after the *s*.

5. **The correct answer is D.** As is, the original sentence has a misplaced modifier, as do choices B and C. Choice D corrects the misplaced modifier and presents the information clearly and in the active voice.

6. **The correct answer is B.** In this context, the word *species* is plural, so it requires a plural verb in order for the subject and the verb to agree.

7. **The correct answer is D.** *Its* seems to be referring back to the plural noun *emerald ash borers*; however, *it* is a singular pronoun, so it cannot have a plural antecedent. In order for the pronoun and antecedent to agree, *its* should be *their*.

8. **The correct answer is C.** While a colon can be used to introduce a list of things, an independent clause must precede the colon. As such, the colon must be removed. If the text before the colon said something like "The following are signs of an emerald ash borer infestation," then a colon could be used to introduce the list that follows.

9. **The correct answer is B.** The writer should be using *their* to indicate possession (the residents' trees) instead of *they're*, which is the contraction for *they are*.

10. **The correct answer is D.** To maintain parallel structure and match the form of the preceding verb *keep*, the writer can omit the *to* and simply write *notify*.

11. **The correct answer is B.** This comma is unnecessary. There is no need to use a comma to separate the subject and predicate in a sentence.

12. **The correct answer is C.** Because the subject of the sentence is "groups of swimming mammals," the object of the sentence should be plural (*pods*) for the nouns to agree.

13. **The correct answer is D.** The only grammatically correct option is to use a semicolon to combine the two independent clauses. Choice A is a comma splice but could be corrected with the addition of a coordinating conjunction. Choice B incorrectly uses ellipses. Choice C incorrectly uses a hyphen.

14. **The correct answer is A.** *Allude* means to "call attention to or hint at," which is the correct word to use in the context of the sentence. *Illude* and *elude* are homophones, meaning they sound the same but have different meanings. *Delude* doesn't make sense in the context of the sentence.

15. **The correct answer is D.** The word *who* is a clue that the sentence should end with a question mark.

CHAPTER

Strategies for the WritePlacer® Exam

STRATEGIES FOR THE WRITEPLACER

OVERVIEW

Understanding the WritePlacer® Exam

How to Approach the WritePlacer®

Strategies to Improve Your Writing

Sample Prompt and Essay

Summing It Up

In addition to the writing placement test, the ACCUPLACER also evaluates your writing ability with the WritePlacer exam. The WritePlacer is an untimed essay exam that is used to gauge your ability to express ideas through writing. It helps college advisors determine which writing courses you should take. In this chapter, we'll provide an overview of what to expect on the WritePlacer exam, how to approach the WritePlacer, and strategies for improving your writing in each of the six categories your writing will be evaluated on.

UNDERSTANDING THE WRITEPLACER® EXAM

The WritePlacer provides a writing prompt with a short passage and a question about the passage, and you will be asked to compose a 300–600-word response. The prompt typically asks about your general opinion or perspective on an idea or concept. You can use your own experiences, examples, understandings, and ideas to support your point of view in the essay response. The essay should be written in English. Like the rest of the ACCUPLACER, the WritePlacer is untimed, so you'll have time to outline and proofread your essay before submitting it.

The essay will receive a score between 0–8. A score of 0 indicates that the essay is not written in English, is too short, or did not address the prompt. All other scores are holistic and represent how well you perform in six writing categories:

- Purpose and focus
- Organization and structure
- Development and support
- Sentence variety and style
- Mechanical conventions
- Critical thinking

Here, we've included a sample WritePlacer prompt.

Passage

The expense of obtaining a college education has steadily increased in recent decades, leading many to wonder if the cost of higher education has reached a point where the potential benefits no longer justify the daunting expense. Some people strongly feel that the cost of a college degree is out of control, and real system-wide reform is urgently needed. Others feel that the value of a college degree justifies the price, including the enhanced earning potential and greater professional fulfillment and options of college graduates compared to nongraduates.

Assignment

Is the cost of a college education equal to its value?

Plan and write a multiparagraph essay (300–600 words) in which you develop your point of view on the above question. Support your position with reasoning and examples taken from your reading, studies, experience, or observations.

How to Approach the WritePlacer®

When you take the WritePlacer, follow these five steps to ensure your essay accurately reflects your writing ability:

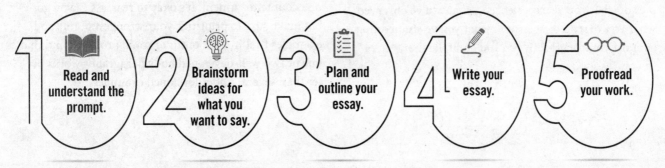

1 Read and understand the prompt.

2 Brainstorm ideas for what you want to say.

3 Plan and outline your essay.

4 Write your essay.

5 Proofread your work.

Step 1: Read and understand the prompt.

The WritePlacer evaluates your response on whether it responds directly to the prompt, so it's critical that you understand what the prompt is asking. Make sure that you read the instructions closely so that you know what to do in your essay and what to include. Be sure that you fully understand the issue at hand as well as any opposing viewpoints. Focus on the question itself and start reflecting on your own point of view.

Step 2: Brainstorm ideas for what you want to say.

It doesn't matter what your point of view is and whether or not the essay reviewers agree with you. The most important thing is that you develop a clear argument with supporting evidence and examples. Take some time to clearly articulate your point of view and why you think that way. (Hint: This should become your thesis statement!) Start listing out examples of what you've experienced, what you've observed, what you've read or seen, and what you've studied that support your perspective so you can talk about them in your essay.

Step 3: Plan and outline your essay.

Organize your ideas and examples and think about the order in which you want to present them. Cross out any that you think won't work or aren't as strong as some of the others on your list. A brief outline might look something like this.

1. Introduction + Thesis Statement
2. Reason/Example 1
   - Support 1
   - Support 2
3. Reason/Example 2
   - Support 1
   - Support 2
4. Other perspectives
   - Reasons why counterargument 1 is flawed
   - Reasons why counterargument 2 is flawed
5. Conclusion

Jotting down a brief outline of your essay can help keep you focused so that you don't veer off topic or lose track of what you're writing about. Just make sure that you regularly consult your outline as you're writing. Depending on what you have space for in your essay, you may decide to skip a paragraph, example, or a counterargument. It's okay to reassess as you go, but make sure to prioritize your strongest points and examples first in your outline. You'll probably find that one or two well-developed body paragraphs works better than several underdeveloped examples.

Step 4: Write your essay.

Once you've outlined your essay, take the time to actually write your essay. Be sure to follow through on your outline; don't change your argument or structure in the middle of writing or else you'll be stuck rewriting huge chunks of your essay. Don't forget to write the introduction and conclusion, and leave plenty of time for the last step: proofreading.

Step 5: Proofread your work.

Once you're done writing, go back and reread your essay to try and catch any grammatical errors you might have made along the way. Remember that even though you're taking the WritePlacer on the computer, there is no spelling or grammar checker available to you. As such, you'll need to read closely to catch any misspelled words, fragments, missing commas, and other errors.

STRATEGIES TO IMPROVE YOUR WRITING

In this section, we'll cover strategies for improving your writing in relation to the areas that are tested on the WritePlacer exam.

Purpose and Focus

The first dimension used to score your WritePlacer exam is purpose and focus, which refers to how well you address the topic you're given and how you present

information in a unified and coherent manner. The WritePlacer exam will always ask you to "develop your point of view," so the purpose of your response will always be the same: to develop and support an argument that directly responds to the essay prompt. As such, it is important to have a thesis statement that clearly establishes the central argument and focus of your essay.

Using a Thesis Statement

Typically, a thesis statement is a single sentence that summarizes what you'll be arguing in your essay. While you can put it in a few different places, it tends to make the most sense to place it at the end of your first paragraph. A reader should be able to tell what the main idea and purpose of your essay is just by reading the thesis statement.

HERE ARE THREE EXAMPLES OF THESIS STATEMENTS ON A SIMILAR TOPIC:

1. Despite the high costs associated, more cities need to invest in high-speed rails and other forms of transportation infrastructure that aren't centered on individual vehicles.

2. Those who support investing in high-speed rail note that development of this type of infrastructure leads to fewer emissions, increased transportation revenue, and reduced traffic.

3. It is imperative that cities invest in high-speed rail infrastructure to reduce both traffic congestion and vehicle-based emissions.

While each of these thesis statements is similar, they point to different organizational structures for essays. For instance, the first one sets the writer up to discuss "other forms of transportation infrastructure" besides just high-speed rail, while the latter two set the writer up to discuss the specific issues mentioned in the thesis, like reduced traffic and emissions.

TIP

Write your thesis statement first when planning your essay. Then, when your essay is finished, revisit your thesis statement to make sure it reflects the actual argument you wrote. If it doesn't, modify it so it does (rather than trying to change the entire essay to fit the old thesis statement).

A good thesis statement is specific, concise, and argumentative. To be specific, a thesis statement must not leave the reader with any questions as to what will be discussed. Consider these example statements.

EXAMPLE

NOT SPECIFIC: Albert Einstein is an important figure because of his many discoveries.

SPECIFIC: Because of his discoveries of the general theory of relativity, the photoelectric effect, and Brownian motion, Albert Einstein is the most important scientist of the 20th century.

The statement that is too vague leaves the reader with questions such as "An important figure to whom or in what?" and "Which discoveries?" The second, more specific thesis statement makes it clear that the argument will be about three specific scientific discoveries Einstein made. Furthermore, because this particular specific thesis statement is also divided, it previews the organization an essay might follow. In this case, the first body paragraph could be about the general theory of relativity, the second about the photoelectric effect, and the third about Brownian motion, allowing the writer to conclude by showing the relationship between the three.

To be concise, a thesis statement should say exactly what it needs to say in as few words as possible without sacrificing meaning. Wordy thesis statements that try to fit in too much information can typically be reduced by eliminating any details that are not necessary to understanding the argument. Consider these example statements.

EXAMPLE

NOT CONCISE: Because many people, especially children and those who have compromised immune systems (e.g., cancer patients), cannot get vaccinations on their own in order to have their own immunity, it is necessary for other members of the community, especially healthy adults who do not have a host of health concerns to worry about, to make sure they are vaccinated in hopes that a great enough percentage of the population is vaccinated and herd immunity can happen.

CONCISE: Because some portions of the population are unable to vaccinate, it is important that those who can vaccinate get vaccinated so that communities can achieve herd immunity.

6

TIP

Using a "divided" statement in parallel structure is a good way to preview the topics of your body paragraphs within your thesis statement.

The statement that is too wordy offers a lot of extra information that is not necessary for understanding the basic premise of the argument. Yes, the writer will want to address many of the ideas that come up in the less concise version of the thesis; however, in the introduction, where a thesis statement is usually found, it's best to stick to the most important tenets of the overall argument.

To be argumentative, a thesis statement must offer the reader the ability to agree or disagree with the thesis statement. That doesn't necessarily mean that a reader is likely to react one way or another, only that it is possible for them to do so. If the thesis statement simply offers an already known fact or reiterates common knowledge, it is not making an argument. Consider these example statements.

EXAMPLE

NOT ARGUMENTATIVE: In this novel, the author tells a fictional story about a young athlete.

ARGUMENTATIVE: In this novel, the author uses the fictional story of a young athlete as an allegory for adolescence.

In the nonargumentative statement, there is nothing to agree or disagree with—you can assume that a fictional novel about a young athlete does, in fact, tell a fictional story about a young athlete. There is nothing the author is arguing except for that which is already known, so the thesis statement does nothing to set up the information that should follow. In the argumentative example, you get a clear picture of what the writer plans to argue, which is that the novel can be considered an allegory for adolescence. A reader could, in theory, agree or disagree about the novel being an allegory for adolescence, so the thesis statement is argumentative.

Organization and Structure

Your essay will also be evaluated for the extent to which you order and connect ideas. As such, it's important that you organize your essay in a deliberate and purposeful manner. It's also essential that you use topic sentences and transitions to guide the reader through the logical progression of your ideas. These are especially important to show the reader why one idea comes first and how it prepares the reader for the next idea and so on.

Organizing Your Ideas

Your essay should be between 300–600 words and should have an introduction, body, and conclusion. Depending on the lengths of your paragraphs, you may have more than one body paragraph. An introduction typically provides an overview of the topic being discussed and will include a thesis statement, which establishes the main idea or argument of the text. Body paragraphs develop the thesis statement in more detail with evidence and analysis that support the argument. A writer will use as many body paragraphs as needed to develop the topic and accomplish their purpose. Finally, the conclusion summarizes what was discussed and reiterates key points or examples from the body paragraph(s) as well as the significance of the topic overall. Body paragraphs are essential for not only organizing your ideas but also for developing and supporting your argument, so we'll talk more about how to write a body paragraph later on in this chapter.

Using Transitions and Topic Sentences Effectively

Transitions are necessary for guiding your reader through your writing. In essays, topic sentences are a particular type of transition that can help signal for your reader how different elements of your essay can be knit together thematically. Think of a topic sentence as a mini thesis statement that occurs at the start of each paragraph. The purpose of the topic sentence is to offer a clear picture of what will be argued in that paragraph, often by gesturing to what came before to show how the two topics are linked. Consider the following example topic sentence.

> While some believe that hemp plants should be grown for medicinal and industrial uses, others believe that the potential drug-related abuses of the crop outweigh the benefits of mass cultivation.

This topic sentence gestures to what was likely discussed in the paragraph before (the medicinal and industrial uses of hemp as relates to why some support cultivating the crop) while also showing what is likely to come in the new paragraph (information on why hemp critics are concerned about drug-related abuse of the plant). When writing an essay, you'll want to have a topic sentence at the beginning of each new body paragraph.

Transition words and phrases are those that help you effectively transition between ideas. Often, these transition words or phrases will come at the start of a sentence, but that is not always the case. The following table lists common transitions.

COMMON TRANSITION WORDS AND PHRASES		
Purpose of Transition	**Example Words**	**Example Sentences**
To introduce new ideas or add to/agree with topics that have already been introduced	• additionally • coupled with • equally important • first, second, third, etc. • further • furthermore • in addition (to) • likewise • moreover • similarly	• **First**, one must understand how the structure of DNA affects genetics. • **Furthermore**, these same observations were noted at another dig site 20 km away. • The question of municipal water usage is **equally important** to the discussion of local conservation efforts.
To communicate the writer's opposition to or a limit placed upon a given idea or phrase	• as much as • by contrast • conversely • despite • however • notwithstanding • on the contrary • on the other hand • that said • while	• **Despite** new evidence, the theory remains the most prevalent in the field. • The question of parental input is, **conversely,** overemphasized in research on childhood literacy development. • **As much as** Sushmita had hoped to sleep in, the birds noisily nesting outside her window had other plans.

COMMON TRANSITION WORDS AND PHRASES

Purpose of Transition	Example Words	Example Sentences
To show a cause-and-effect relationship or communicate the conditions that influence a circumstance or idea	• as a result • as long as • because (of) • consequently • due to • hence • in case • in effect • since • then • therefore • unless • whenever • while	• I am going fishing later, **hence** the tackle box and gear. • **Consequently**, commuters were unable to reliably predict what time the trains would arrive. • Tina was upset **because of** the letters she'd found in her brother's drawer. • **Therefore**, it's important for schools to invest adequate funds into arts and music programs.
To set up an example, fact, piece of evidence, or other form of support for another concept	• by all means • especially • explicitly • for this reason • indeed • in fact • in other words • markedly • notably • significantly • to clarify • to reiterate	• The new model of the car is **by all means** a notable improvement on prior models. • **In other words**, those who wish to master a new skill should expect to devote numerous hours to being amateurish at first. • **Indeed**, Portugal was the first European nation to get actively involved in the transatlantic slave trade.
To communicate the time at which an event occurred or the timing of one event in relation to another	• after • at the present moment • frequently • in the meantime • momentarily • now • occasionally • often • once • suddenly • then • today	• I was distracted, **momentarily**, by a high-pitched shriek emitting from the far-off woods. • **Today**, the James Webb Space Telescope is known for producing the clearest images of far-off galaxies. • **Suddenly**, the doorbell rang.

COMMON TRANSITION WORDS AND PHRASES		
Purpose of Transition	**Example Words**	**Example Sentences**
To help the writer communicate a conclusion or final idea on a topic	• altogether • effectively • in any event • in conclusion • in either case • in essence • in summary • nonetheless • to conclude • to summarize • to sum up	• **In any event**, the festival proved a success despite the weather issues and a series of unfortunate technical mishaps. • **Altogether**, there are numerous factors that contribute to a feeling of loneliness, not all of them psychological. • This means that the industry as it once was is, **effectively**, over.

In addition to using transitional words or phrases, you can also connect paragraphs using repetition of a key word or phrase or by using pronouns that refer to a person or an idea mentioned in the previous paragraph.

Example of Paragraphs Connected by Transitional Words

Teenage alcoholism is a serious problem today. It is a problem that affects young people of all types, regardless of ethnic background or socioeconomic level. Alcoholism shows no discrimination in choosing its victims—it is an equal-opportunity problem.

Although the problem is far from being solved, both families and schools are taking steps to deal with alcoholism among teens.

These paragraphs are connected by the use of the transitional word *although* and the repetition of the key word *problem*. The second paragraph will continue by detailing some of the steps that are being taken to combat alcoholism.

Example of Paragraphs Connected by Repetition of a Key Word

Last summer, our whole family piled into the car and drove to Disney World in Florida. Although we had heard about the amusement park from friends who had already been there, this would be our first experience at a Disney park. We were all eager to get there, but we really did not know what to **expect**.

Our first day at Disney World went beyond any **expectations** we might have had…

These paragraphs are connected using forms of the same word. *Expect* in paragraph 1 is repeated as *expectations* in paragraph 2, allowing one thought to flow from the first paragraph to the second. The second paragraph will continue with specific things the family did at Disney World and the ways in which the trip exceeded expectations.

Development, Support, and Critical Thinking

On the WritePlacer exam, your response will also be evaluated for how well you develop and support your ideas. In argumentative writing, this refers to how well you support your claims with evidence and analysis in your body paragraphs. Because you'll be writing on the fly, you can't do research to support your claims, but you can use personal experience and things you've read or learned in class as evidence in your essay.

In this section, we also address the WritePlacer's critical thinking dimension. Critical thinking refers to your ability to analyze the issue at hand, argue your point of view, and illustrate reasoned relationships among ideas. As such, critical thinking is most evident in your ability to select appropriate evidence to support your claims and to analyze that evidence and show how it supports your claims. It can also be evident in your ability to respond to arguments you disagree with, especially if you can explain why you disagree and provide counterarguments.

It's important to write well-developed body paragraphs to demonstrate that you can organize your ideas logically, develop and support your argument, and think critically. Body paragraphs are structured in a way that helps advance the thesis statement of your essay. The sentences in a paragraph generally go in the following order. Keep in mind that while a main idea and topic sentence are often one sentence each, a writer can include multiple sentences of evidence and analysis to make the main idea stronger and thoroughly develop the paragraph.

How to Develop a Body Paragraph

1. MAIN IDEA/TOPIC SENTENCE

The first sentence should state the main idea, claim, or purpose of your paragraph. The topic sentence should tell your reader what the paragraph is about so that they know what to expect as they read. Think of topic sentences as signposts or markings that guide the reader and tell them what's coming next. In pieces of writing with multiple body paragraphs, the topic sentence helps to develop the central argument, known as the thesis statement.

2. EVIDENCE

To develop the idea outlined in the topic sentence, you should provide supporting evidence like examples, anecdotes, facts, statistics, and more. Think of supporting details as proof of your main idea and purpose. Sometimes, you'll need to present evidence followed by analysis and then more evidence followed by more analysis.

3. ANALYSIS

This is where you explain the evidence itself, why the evidence is important, and how it proves your point. Here, you should try to anticipate additional explanation and context the reader might need to understand how the evidence supports the main idea of the paragraph.

4. SUMMARY

Paragraphs often end with a summary of what was just discussed. This is where you reiterate the main idea to remind the reader of the most important takeaway from the paragraph. In a passage with several paragraphs, the last sentence of a paragraph usually summarizes what was just discussed while also functioning as a transition that prepares the reader for the next paragraph.

Let's look at a sample paragraph and break it down into parts.

EXAMPLE

<u>If consumed too frequently, the delicious sugary beverage known as soda can be detrimental to your health, especially if you don't practice good oral hygiene (M).</u> **In fact, people who drink soda on a daily basis and only brush their teeth once a day are far more likely to experience tooth decay (E).** This is because the sugar in soda interacts with the bacteria in your mouth and becomes highly acidic, causing cavities, erosion of enamel, and gum disease (A). **However, those who drink soda and consistently practice good dental hygiene—including rinsing with water after drinking soda, brushing twice daily, and flossing—show better long-term dental health than those who don't.** These healthy habits can remove the bacteria on and in between your teeth while protecting your teeth from decay (A). That way, you can still enjoy the carbonation and syrupy sweetness of soda in moderation while keeping your teeth clean and healthy (S).

The first underlined sentence in this sample paragraph is the main idea. It introduces the topic and focus of the paragraph. From this sentence, we know that we'll be reading about the effect of soda on dental health. In the next bolded sentence, we're presented with evidence of the detrimental effect soda can have on one's dental health: those who drink soda daily are more likely to have cavities. The following highlighted sentence explains why this is the case: the ingredients in soda can damage teeth. The next sentence, in bold, provides examples of good dental hygiene, and the highlighted sentence that comes after explains how these habits can mitigate the damage done by soda. Finally, the last sentence reiterates the main point of the paragraph, which is that you can still drink soda in moderation and keep your teeth clean.

Sentence Variety and Style

On the WritePlacer, it's important to vary your sentence structure to show that you have a grasp on effective ways to use vocabulary, voice, and structure. We cover vocabulary in Chapter 3: Reading Comprehension and sentence structure and voice in Chapter 5: Conventions of Syntax, Usage, and Punctuation. Here, we'll provide a few tips on how to strengthen your writing in relation to each of these categories.

Vocabulary

On the WritePlacer exam, you'll want to show that you've mastered vocabulary that is appropriate for introductory college-level writing. Strong and specific adjectives and action verbs can help you convey ideas in more detail with fewer words. Avoid using inappropriate or informal vocabulary or expressions that can significantly shift the tone of your essay. Common advice is to "show don't tell," meaning instead of saying "Climate change is bad," opt for vivid description and specific examples of why or how it's bad: "Climate change has resulted in year-round catastrophic wildfires, uncontrollable flooding, and relentless droughts, creating unpredictable weather patterns and exacerbating existing social crises."

Voice and Sentence Structure

Voice on the ACCUPLACER generally refers to your use of syntax, punctuation, point of view, word choice, and other stylistic things that make your writing your own. If you are confident in your grammatical and mechanical skills, then don't be afraid to incorporate different sentence types (compound, complex, etc.) and punctuation in your essay. For example, using semicolons to connect similar ideas rather than several short sentences all separated with periods can help break up ideas in different ways, which can add intrigue to your writing and keep the reader engaged. As we discuss in Chapter 5, try to stick with active voice instead of passive voice because the active voice is concise, clear, and direct. Keep an eye on your verb tense and mood as you write so that you don't confuse your reader with unintentional shifts. The most important thing is that you make clear and purposeful decisions in your writing to convey your ideas in ways that capture your voice as a writer.

Sentence Structure

When writers use the same sentence type over and over again in their essays, readers get bored. It can be difficult for readers to figure out how ideas are related and which information is most important. Take a look at the following paragraph, which relies too much on simple sentences.

> **EXAMPLE**
>
> Climate change has resulted in unpredictable weather patterns. There are more destructive storms. There are also more extreme drought conditions. A lack of precipitation has made wildfires worse. Several states recently had their largest fire seasons ever. There were close to 10,000 wildfires. The fires burned almost 4.5 million acres. Over 10,000 structures were destroyed. Governors realized the importance of prioritizing wildfire prevention and mitigation. Future environmental policies must prioritize this issue.

Simple sentences consist only of independent clauses, without conjunctions linking to other clauses. There are no relationships presented between sentences, and it's hard to read because it feels stilted. Using compound, complex, and compound-complex sentences can define connections between ideas and help to vary sentence length, which will make the paragraph easier to read. See the following paragraph, which uses a wider variety of sentence structures, including both independent and dependent clauses.

> **EXAMPLE**
>
> Climate change has resulted in unpredictable weather patterns, like more destructive storms and more extreme drought conditions. The lack of precipitation has exacerbated the wildfire season for several states, including Colorado, Oregon, and California. In fact, California had its largest fire season ever in 2020, with close to 10,000 wildfires. These wildfires collectively burned close to 4.5 million acres and destroyed over 10,000 structures. As a result of the widespread damage and destruction, governors have taken the initiative to prioritize wildfire prevention and mitigation in state budgets. While this increase in spending is a good first step, more research into targeted environmental policies will be needed in the coming years.

With variation in your sentences, the reader can more easily draw connections between ideas and understand why they are presented in a specific order. It also feels easier and more natural to read compared to the example composed entirely of simple sentences. Don't be afraid to use a combination of simple, compound, complex, and compound-complex sentences in your writing. See Chapter 5: Conventions of Syntax, Usage, and Punctuation to learn how to create different types of sentences while avoiding common errors.

Mechanical Conventions

On the WritePlacer, you'll be evaluated on your ability to utilize mechanical conventions, meaning the extent to which you can express your ideas in standard written English. These conventions are also a key component of the ACCUPLACER's writing placement test. We covered the conventions of standard written English in depth in Chapter 5, so we recommend reviewing that chapter in preparation for the WritePlacer exam as well.

SAMPLE PROMPT AND ESSAY

Here, we've included a sample prompt along with a sample essay response. Pay attention to the use of a thesis statement along with paragraph structure, topic sentences, and transitions.

Passage

In an effort to increase civic participation, there is a movement to reduce the voting age from 18 years old to 16 years old. Politics impact 16- and 17-year-olds just as much as 18-year-olds, and many 16- and 17-year-olds are ready and eager to vote. Most, if not all, have received civics education in school and demonstrate interest in civic engagement. By establishing voting habits earlier, lowering the voting age to 16 will increase the likelihood that people will become lifelong voters, thereby improving voter turnout and making government more representative.

Assignment

Should the voting age be lowered from 18 years old to 16 years old?

Plan and write a multiparagraph essay (300–600 words) in which you develop your point of view on the above question. Support your position with reasoning and examples taken from your reading, studies, experience, or observations.

Sample Essay (587 words)

Voting is an important act in our society. It's how you make your opinion on important issues known. While voting is limited to those who are 18 years of age and older, it's time that we as a country consider lowering the voting age to 16 years of age. Because 16-year-olds must bear the consequences of increasingly alarming political issues, such as gun violence and climate change, I believe they should be able to exercise the right to vote to elect candidates who will advocate on their behalf.

Sixteen-year-olds today have never known a world without school shooter drills, and they have a right to make their voice heard through voting in order to effect change when it comes to reducing gun violence. For example, after the school shooting in Parkland, many students turned their trauma into action, arranging to meet with local officials to talk about policies that could have prevented the shooting. Younger voters would be in a unique position to advocate for what does and doesn't work when it comes to preventing gun violence in schools because they are closer to the issue and they are the ones at risk if policies fail. In fact, in the aftermath of the shooting, some of the Parkland kids started a group called March for Our Lives that advocates for a variety of gun control policies, like a national licensing and registry program and an assault weapons bans, while encouraging Generation Z to get out and vote. This shows that younger voters can organize when it comes to important social issues and that they will do the work necessary to get behind causes and policies they believe in. As such, it's important that 16-year-olds and 17-year-olds who want to vote are given the opportunity to do so, especially when it comes to the issues that matter most to them.

In addition to social issues like gun violence, 16- and 17-year-olds also bear the greatest burden, compared to older generations, when it comes to the effects of climate change, so they should be able to have a say when it comes to how these issues are addressed by politicians today and in the future. The effects of the climate crisis are already being experienced today: my family was forced to evacuate during the Marshall Fire in Colorado. Colorado doesn't get wildfires in December, but warm temperatures and strong winds quickly fueled the spread of the fire, which ultimately destroyed more than 1,000 homes. I learned that day that climate change is real and it is here, and it is everyone's responsibility to do whatever we can to mitigate it. Numerous reports suggest that 2030 is the tipping point at which the damage caused by climate change will become irreversible. By then, current 16- and 17-year-olds will be in their mid-twenties, facing unknown and potentially disastrous repercussions if we fail to act today. Lowering the voting age to 16 years of age would bring those who are most impacted by this issue into the conversation.

Voting is essential to the preservation and well-being of our democracy. When 16-year-olds and 17-year-olds are so deeply impacted by political issues like gun violence and climate change, it's unfair that they do not have a say in how these issues are handled by the politicians who represent them. Therefore, it is critical that we consider lowering the voting age to 16 to ensure that more people are fairly represented and able to participate in making decisions about the pressing issues of our time.

SUMMING IT UP

- The WritePlacer is an untimed essay exam where you will be provided with a short passage and a writing prompt asking you to respond to the passage. You will be asked to compose a 300–600-word response in which you develop your point of view, and your essay will receive a score between 0–8. Your essay will be evaluated using six categories: purpose and focus, organization and structure, development and support, sentence variety and style, mechanical conventions, and critical thinking.

- When approaching the WritePlacer exam, follow these five steps:

  - Step 1: Read and understand the prompt.
  - Step 2: Brainstorm ideas for what you want to say.
  - Step 3: Plan and outline your essay.
  - Step 4: Write your essay.
  - Step 5: Proofread your work.

- Use a thesis statement to establish the central argument of your essay and to give your essay a sense of purpose and focus.

- Use topic sentences and transitions to clearly guide the reader through your ideas and to develop the argument over the course of your essay.

- Well-developed body paragraphs should include topic sentences, evidence, analysis, and a transition. This gives your essay a sense of structure while developing the claims and ideas that support your central argument.

- Vary your sentence structure and use of punctuation to illustrate your mastery of various stylistic conventions in English. However, make sure to avoid common grammatical and mechanical errors in the process.

PART IV
QUANTITATIVE SKILLS

CHAPTER

Arithmetic

ARITHMETIC

OVERVIEW

Understanding Arithmetic on the ACCUPLACER®

Key Concepts for Arithmetic on the ACCUPLACER®

- Math Symbols
- Numbers and Operations
- Properties and Identities
- Order of Operations
- Decimals
- Factors and Multiples
- Fractions
- Percentages

Summing It Up

Knowledge Check: Arithmetic

Answer Key and Explanations

Whether you love math or find it intimidating, the good news about math on the ACCUPLACER is that it's predictable. The ACCU-PLACER covers mathematics skills in three sections: (1) arithmetic, (2) quantitative reasoning, algebra, and statistics, and (3) advanced algebra and functions. This chapter focuses on the topics that will be addressed in the arithmetic section or that are fundamental for more advanced concepts.

UNDERSTANDING ARITHMETIC ON THE ACCUPLACER®

The arithmetic test on the ACCUPLACER covers operations involving whole numbers, fractions, decimals, and percentages. In this section, test takers are also tasked with addressing equivalents and number comparisons. To prepare you, this chapter will reintroduce you to concepts from basic math that will be necessary for arithmetic and the other quantitative sections on the exam.

In this and the two chapters that follow, we have condensed a decade (or more!) of mathematics classes into

a review that touches on most topics covered on the ACCUPLACER. That said, remember that the purpose of the exam is to accurately assess your skills so you can be placed in the right course(s) for your existing skill level. It will undoubtedly relieve nerves to review mathematics concepts before you take the ACCUPLACER, but don't stress out about improving your skills enough to place into a higher-level math course, especially if that course might not be right for you.

Chapters 7–9 will help most by illuminating what you *don't* know or may have forgotten regarding quantitative concepts. For the ACCUPLACER, it's important to make a distinction between what you've learned before (stuff you just need a "refresher" on) and what you don't know at all or have never seen before. Focus on refreshing knowledge that you've already built rather than tackling entirely new concepts, unless you feel particularly adept with them automatically.

KEY CONCEPTS FOR ARITHMETIC ON THE ACCUPLACER®

In the following sections, we'll first look at math symbols and types of numbers, including whole numbers and signed numbers. We'll also discuss number properties and how the order of operations should guide your calculations. Finally, we'll focus on decimals, fractions, and percentages and how to convert between them.

Math Symbols

Math is a language, with terms, meanings, structure, and symbols. To succeed at math, you need to understand the language. Often, the symbols used in equations can be the biggest challenge. Some, if not all, of these symbols are already familiar to you, but it's worth reviewing the symbols that go beyond addition and subtraction. We've included a table of common math symbols and their meanings here for easy reference.

MATH SYMBOLS

Symbol	Meaning	Function	Example
+	Plus sign	Addition	$5 + 3 = 8$
–	Minus sign	Subtraction	$5 - 3 = 2$
×	Times sign	Multiplication	$5 \times 3 = 15$
•	Multiplication dot	Multiplication	$5 \cdot 3 = 15$
÷	Division	Division	$10 \div 5 = 2$
.	Period	Decimal point	5.3, 7.25
%	Percent	$5\% = \dfrac{5}{100} = 0.05$	$0.5 = 50\%$ $1.25 = 125\%$
<	Strict inequality	Less than	$3 < 5$
≤	Inequality	Less than or equal to	$5 \le 5, 4 \le 5$
>	Strict inequality	Greater than	$5 > 3$
≥	Inequality	Greater than or equal to	$5 \ge 5, 5 \ge 4$
( )	Parentheses	Solve within first	$3 + (2 + 1) + 2 = 3 + 3 + 2 = 8$
[ ]	Brackets	Solve within first	$3 + [2 + 1] + 2 = 3 + 3 + 2 = 8$
x^y	Power	Exponent	$3^2 = 3 \times 3 = 9$ $3^3 = 3 \times 3 \times 3 = 27$
$\sqrt{}$	Square root	$\sqrt{a} \cdot \sqrt{a} = a$	$\sqrt{9} = 3, \sqrt{16} = 4$
π	Pi constant	Ratio between the circumference and diameter of a circle	$C = 2 \cdot \pi \cdot r$
∠	Angle	Formed by two rays	$\angle DE = 45°$
⊾	Measured angle	Formed by two rays	$\angle DEF = 60°$
∟	Right angle	Right angle = 90°	$a = 90°$
°	Degree	Interior angle measure of a circle = 360°	$a = 45°$
!	Factorial	$n! = 1 \times 2 \times 3 \times 4 \times \dots \times n$	$4! = 1 \times 2 \times 3 \times 4 = 24$

Numbers and Operations

In math, various terms exist to describe the array of numbers used for counting and calculations. The ability to distinguish between whole numbers, integers, and rational and irrational numbers can keep you from selecting incorrect answer choices on your exam.

We will discuss rational numbers, irrational numbers, and ratios in greater depth in Chapter 8. For now, just be able to recognize what the terms mean.

Signed Numbers and Basic Operations

If we lay out our number system on a line, we can see that each positive number to the right of zero has a negative counterpart to the left of zero. The following number line shows the location of some pairs of numbers: +4, –4; +2, –2; and +1, –1.

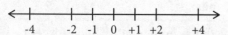

Because each number of a pair is located the same distance from zero (though in different directions), each has the same absolute value. Absolute value is symbolized by placing two vertical bars—one on each side of the number.

$$|+4| = |-4| = 4$$

The absolute value of +4 equals the absolute value of –4. Both are equivalent to 4. The absolute value of any number, positive or negative, is expressed as a positive number.

Addition of Signed Numbers

When we add two oppositely signed numbers having the same absolute value, the sum is zero.

$$(+10) + (-10) = 0$$

$$(-1.5) + (+1.5) = 0$$

$$(-0.010) + (+0.010) = 0$$

$$\left(+\frac{3}{4}\right) + \left(-\frac{3}{4}\right) = 0$$

If one of the two oppositely signed numbers is greater in absolute value, the sum is equal to the amount of that excess and carries the same sign as the number having the greater absolute value.

$$(+2) + (-1) = +1$$

$$(+8) + (-9) = -1$$

$$(-2.5) + (+2.0) = -0.5$$

$$\left(-\frac{3}{4}\right) + \left(+\frac{1}{2}\right) = -\frac{1}{4}$$

TYPES OF NUMBERS		
Number Type	**Definition**	**Examples**
Whole Numbers	Positive numbers, including 0	0, 1, 2, 73, 546
Integers	All whole numbers and negative numbers—excluding decimals and fractions	–54, –6, 0, 9, 43
Rational Numbers	Numbers that result from dividing two integers	$\frac{1}{3}, \frac{3}{5}, -\frac{7}{3}$
Irrational Numbers	All real numbers that are not rational numbers; have nonterminating, nonrepeating decimals	$\sqrt{2} = 1.41421356237\ldots$ $\sqrt{3} = 1.73205080756\ldots$

When subtracting signed numbers, keep in mind the following:

- The distance between the two numbers gives you the absolute value of the difference.
- The direction you move from the number being subtracted to get to the number from which you are subtracting gives you the sign of the difference.

EXAMPLES

Subtract –3 from +5.

Solution

Distance on the number line between –3 and +5 is 8 units.

Direction is from negative to positive—a positive direction.

Answer is +8.

Subtract –6 from –8.

Solution

Distance on number line between –6 and –8 is 2 units.

Direction is from –6 to –8—a negative direction.

Answer is –2.

Subtraction of Signed Numbers

Subtraction is the operation that finds the difference between two numbers, including the difference between signed numbers. When subtracting signed numbers, it can be helpful to refer to a number line.

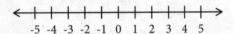

For example, if we wish to subtract +2 from +5, we can use the number line to see that the difference is +3. We give the sign to the difference that represents the direction we are moving along the number line from the number being subtracted to the number from which you are subtracting. In this case, because we are subtracting +2 from +5, we count three units in a positive direction from +2 to +5 on the number line.

 TIP

When subtracting a negative number, change the sign of the number being subtracted and follow the rules for addition.

Multiplication of Signed Numbers

Signed numbers are multiplied as any other numbers would be, with the following exceptions:

1. The product of two negative numbers is positive.

$$(-3) \times (-6) = +18$$

2. The product of two positive numbers is positive.

$$(+3.05) \times (+6) = +18.30$$

3. The product of a negative and positive number is negative.

$$\left(+4\frac{1}{2}\right) \times (-3) = -13\frac{1}{2}$$

$$(+1) \times (-1) \times (+1) = -1$$

Division of Signed Numbers

As with multiplication, the division of signed numbers requires you to observe three simple rules.

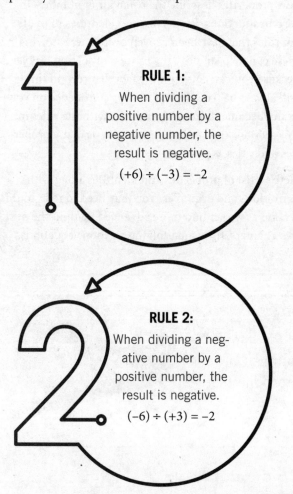

RULE 1:
When dividing a positive number by a negative number, the result is negative.
$(+6) \div (-3) = -2$

RULE 2:
When dividing a negative number by a positive number, the result is negative.
$(-6) \div (+3) = -2$

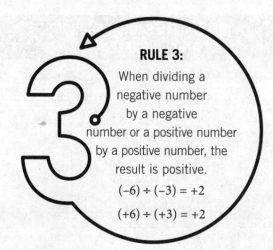

RULE 3:
When dividing a negative number by a negative number or a positive number by a positive number, the result is positive.
$(-6) \div (-3) = +2$
$(+6) \div (+3) = +2$

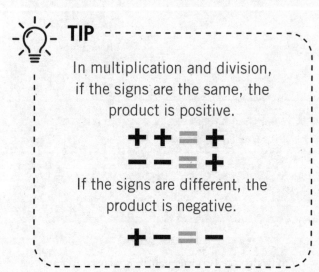

TIP

In multiplication and division, if the signs are the same, the product is positive.

$$+\ +\ =\ +$$
$$-\ -\ =\ +$$

If the signs are different, the product is negative.

$$+\ -\ =\ -$$

Comparisons and Equivalents

Sometimes, you will be asked to determine if a signed number is less than, greater than, or equal to another signed number. This may also occur when comparing fractions, decimals, percentages, or any other figures, especially between one another. As with questions involving use of a number line, you'll want to pay close attention to the sign given to the number. Where necessary, you'll also want to reduce the number to its simplest form so you can work with it more easily. Remember, unless you're working with absolute values, a positive number is always greater than a negative number.

INEQUALITIES, COMPARISONS, AND EQUIVALENCIES	
Type of Comparison	**Examples**
Greater than, less than $>$, $<$	$12 > 9$ $\dfrac{1}{4} > \dfrac{1}{8}$ $0.33 < \dfrac{1}{2}$ $x < y$
Equal to $=$	$xy = 15$ $2\dfrac{1}{8} = 2.125$ $10 \div 2 = 5$ $\dfrac{5}{25} = \dfrac{1}{5} = 0.25$
Greater than or equal to, less than or equal to $\geq$, $\leq$	$\pi r \geq 8$ $-1 \geq y \geq -10$ $2x \leq y$ $xy \leq 30$

Properties and Identities

When studying math, it's important to understand how properties describe the behavior of numbers in certain situations. Properties and identities in math are rules that have been proven over time. Knowing these can help simplify the process of solving problems because you can count on the fact that certain things will always be true. To add to your confidence on your exam, become thoroughly familiar with the rules in this section, and commit to memory as many properties and rules as possible.

Here's a list of properties and identities along with definitions and examples. You may need to refer to this section as we get into more advanced math in the next two chapters, like when solving algebraic equations.

You may also see two inequality signs used to express a range. For instance, $12 < x < 19$ expresses that x is a number greater than 12 but less than 19, while $12 \leq x \leq 19$ suggests that x may be a number between 12 and 19, but it could also be equal to either 12 or 19.

 TIP -

In inequalities, the open part of the symbol (or "mouth") should always be facing the larger number. To help you remember, imagine it like a crocodile that wants to "eat" the larger figure!

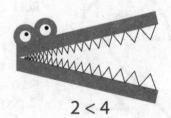

$2 < 4$

PROPERTIES AND IDENTITIES

Name	Definition	Example
Commutative Property	In addition and multiplication, order does not affect outcome	$7 + 8 = 8 + 7$ $3 \times 5 = 5 \times 3$
Distributive Property	Given an equation, $a(b + c)$, you can distribute the value of a to the value inside the parentheses	$7(2 + 8) = 7 \times 2 + 7 \times 8 = 14 + 56 = 70$
Associative Property	In addition and multiplication, changing how numbers are grouped will not change the result	$2(5 \times 4) = 5(2 \times 4) = 4(2 \times 5)$ $3 + (5 + 2) = 2 + (3 + 5) = 5 + (2 + 3)$
Identity Property	Any number added to zero will not change; any number multiplied by 1 will not change	$15 + 0 = 15$ $15 \times 1 = 15$
Reflexive Property	A number is always equal to itself	$a = a$
Symmetric Property	If $a = b$, then $b = a$	If $x = 10$, then $10 = x$
Transitive Property	If $a = b$ and $b = c$, then $a = c$	If $a = b$ and $b = 3 + 4$, then $a = 3 + 4$
Substitution Property	If $a = b$, then a can be substituted for b	If $a = 7$ and $b = 7$, then $a + 3 = 10$ and $b + 3 = 10$
Additive Identity	Any variable added to zero will remain unchanged	$x + 0 = x$
Multiplicative Property of Zero	Any number multiplied by zero equals zero	$1 \times 0 = 0$ $4,962 \times 0 = 0$
Multiplicative Inverse	Any number multiplied by its reciprocal will equal 1	$2 \times \frac{1}{2} = 1$ $12 \times \frac{1}{12} = 1$

Order of Operations

One of the most important things to know when solving math problems is where to start. You will often encounter problems that have a series of operations to perform. Fortunately, there are rules to explain what goes first. We call these rules the order of operations. The order of operations ensures that, by solving operations in this order, you'll always be able to arrive at the same correct solution. At this stage of mathematics, there are only four rules to know. They are as follows:

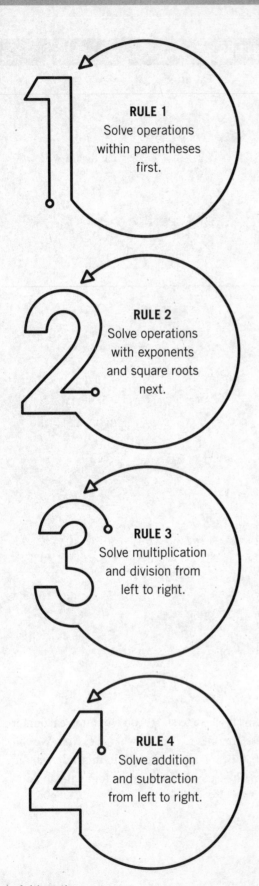

RULE 1
Solve operations within parentheses first.

RULE 2
Solve operations with exponents and square roots next.

RULE 3
Solve multiplication and division from left to right.

RULE 4
Solve addition and subtraction from left to right.

These rules inform where you should start when solving a math problem. In short, solve anything in parentheses first, going from hardest to easiest. As you go through problems using the order of operations, note each step carefully to make sure you don't skip a step or forget anything along the way. Let's look at a few examples.

EXAMPLES

$$(7 \times 2) + (8 - 2) =$$

Solution

Solve within the parentheses before adding.

$$(7 \times 2) + (8 - 2) = 14 + 6 = 20$$

$$\sqrt{81} \times 5^2 - 45 \div 9 + 14 =$$

Solution

There are no parentheses, so step one involves starting with exponents and square roots.

$$\sqrt{81} \times 5^2 - 45 \div 9 + 14 = 9 \times 25 - 45 \div 9 + 14$$

Step two is to solve multiplication and division from left to right:

$$9 \times 25 - 45 \div 9 + 14 = 225 - 5 + 14$$

Now solve addition and subtraction from left to right:

$$225 - 5 + 14 = 234$$

TIP

Remember your order of operations with the acronym **PEMDAS:**

P Parentheses

E Exponents (and Square Roots)

M Multiplication

D Division

A Addition

S Subtraction

Some learners use the mnemonic device "**P**lease **e**xcuse **m**y **d**ear **A**unt **S**ally."

Decimals

So far, we've talked extensively about whole numbers and integers, but in math, you'll frequently be working with parts of numbers in the form of decimals, fractions, and percentages. First, we'll address decimals, and then we'll move on to fractions and percentages.

When a number is written in decimal form, everything to the left of the decimal point is a whole number. Furthermore, everything to the right of the decimal point represents a part of the whole (a tenth, hundredth, thousandth, and so on). If you can count money or make change, then you already have experience with decimals. The most important step when writing decimals is placing the decimal point, since the whole system is based on its location. This chart shows place values for the number 1,236,540.132456.

As such, you could express the numbers to the left of the decimal point as 1,000,000 + 200,000 + 36,000 + 500 + 40 + 0. You could express the numbers to the right of the decimal point as

$$\frac{1}{10} + \frac{3}{100} + \frac{2}{1,000} + \frac{4}{10,000} + \frac{5}{100,000} + \frac{6}{1,000,000}.$$

When adding or subtracting decimals, you need to keep the decimal points in line. After you have lined up the decimal points, proceed with the problem the same way as with whole numbers while maintaining the location of the decimal point.

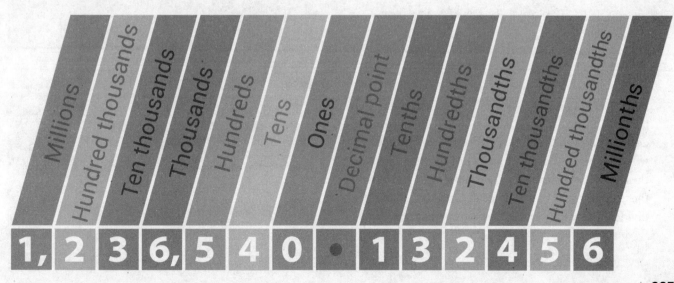

EXAMPLE

Add 36.08 + 745 + 4.362 + 58.6 + 0.0061.

Solution

$$
\begin{array}{r}
36.08 \\
745. \\
4.362 \\
58.6 \\
+ \quad 0.0061 \\
\hline
844.0481
\end{array}
$$

To keep track of the decimal places, you can also fill in the spaces with zeros.

$$
\begin{array}{r}
036.0800 \\
745.0000 \\
004.3620 \\
058.6000 \\
+ \quad 000.0061 \\
\hline
844.0481
\end{array}
$$

When multiplying decimals, ignore the decimal points until you reach the product. The placement of the decimal point depends on the sum of the places to the right of the decimal point in both the multiplier and number being multiplied.

$$
\begin{array}{r}
1.482 \quad \text{(3 places to the right of decimal point)} \\
\times \ 0.16 \quad \text{(2 places to the right of decimal point)} \\
\hline
8892 \\
14820 \\
\hline
0.23712 \quad \text{(5 places to the right of decimal point)}
\end{array}
$$

You cannot divide by a decimal because a decimal itself is a ratio. If the divisor is a decimal, you must move the decimal point to the right until the divisor becomes a whole number. Count the number of spaces you moved the decimal point in the divisor to the right and move the decimal point in the dividend (the number being divided) the same number of spaces to the right. The decimal point in the answer should be directly above the decimal point in the dividend.

$$
0.06\overline{)4.212} \quad \overset{70.2}{}
$$

In this example, the decimal point moves two spaces to the right.

Factors and Multiples

Before we can start working with fractions, we need to understand factors and multiples. A factor is a number that can be divided into a whole number evenly without leaving a remainder. The factors of any integer include 1 as well as the integer itself. Figuring out whether one number is a factor of another requires you to divide that number by another whole number that is less than itself. For example, to determine what numbers are factors of 4, we would divide 4 by the numbers in question: 1, 2, and 4 all divide into 4 evenly, without a remainder. In contrast, 3 is not a factor of 4 because when you divide 4 by 3 you do not end up with a whole number: $4 \div 3 = 1\frac{1}{3}$.

Divisibility Rules

Keep in mind the following two basic rules about factors.

RULE 1
Any integer is a factor of itself.

RULE 2
1 and –1 are factors of all integers (except 0).

RULE 3
The integer zero (0) has no factors and is not a factor of any integer.

RULE 4
A positive integer's largest factor (other than itself) will never be greater than one half the value of the integer.

Rules about Factors

1. Complementing factors are multiples. If f is a factor of n, then n is a multiple of f. For example, 8 is a multiple of 2 for the same reason that 2 is a factor of 8: because $8 \div 2 = 4$, which is an integer.

2. A prime number is a positive integer that is divisible by only two positive integers: itself and 1. Zero (0) and 1 are not considered prime numbers; 2 is the first prime number. Here are all the prime numbers less than 50:

    2 3 5 7

    11 13 17 19

    23 29

    31 37

    41 43 47

As you can see, factors, multiples, and divisibility are different aspects of the same concept.

Greatest Common Factor

To solve problems with fractions, you'll need to be able to determine the greatest common factor. The term *greatest common factor* (GCF) refers to the largest number that can be factored into two numbers cleanly (that is, without a remainder). For example, the greatest common factor of 10 and 15 is 5. For 10 and 20, the GCF is 10. How did we get those answers? Let's look at a pair of numbers.

EXAMPLE

Find the GCF for (12, 8).

Solution

Factors for 12: 1, 2, 3, 4, 6, 12

Factors for 8: 1, 2, 4, 8

The common factors—the factors common to both sets of numbers—for 12 and 8 are 1, 2, and 4. The greatest (largest) of the group is 4, so that's your answer.

 TIP

Don't be confused by the term Greatest Common Divisor as the terms *divisor* and *factor* have the same meaning. They are both numbers that can divide into something.

There may be number pairs, like (7, 13), that don't have anything other than 1 in common. When this happens, the numbers can be described as "relatively prime." Remember that a prime number is a number that is only divisible by itself and 1.

Least Common Multiple

In addition to using the greatest common factor, solving problems with fractions will also require you to find the least common multiple. The term *least common multiple* (LCM) refers to the smallest whole number into which each number in the list divides evenly. For example, the GCF of {18, 36, 63} is 9, and the LCM of {18, 36, 63} is 252.

You'll need to find the least common multiple when you need to add or subtract fractions with different denominators, as you'll need each to have the same denominator to be able to add them together. However, you will likely use greatest common factor to reduce or simplify the result.

Fractions

A fraction is a part of a whole. For instance, there are 10 dimes in a dollar, so one dime is one-tenth of a dollar—one of ten equal parts. The fraction to represent one-tenth is written $\frac{1}{10}$. The top number of a fraction is called the numerator, and the bottom number is called the denominator. The denominator tells you

 TIP

Need an easy way to remember which part of a fraction is which? Use alliteration to remember that the **d**enominator goes **d**own at the bottom.

how many equal parts the object or number is divided into, and the numerator tells you how many parts are represented.

$$\frac{3}{4} \begin{array}{l} \leftarrow \text{numerator} \rightarrow \\ \leftarrow \text{denominator} \rightarrow \end{array} \frac{7}{8}$$

A proper fraction is one in which the numerator is less than the denominator. An improper fraction is one in which the numerator is the same as or greater than the denominator. $\frac{3}{5}$ is a proper fraction, but $\frac{5}{3}$ is an improper fraction. Sometimes, you will see an integer and a fraction together. This is called a mixed number, such as $2\frac{3}{5}$.

Let's look at a few examples of how to express parts of a whole as fractions.

EXAMPLES

Divide a baseball game, a football game, and a hockey game into convenient numbers of parts. Write a fraction to answer each equation.

1. If Mitchell pitched for two innings of a baseball game (9 innings), how much of the game did he play as pitcher?

2. If Cameron was starting quarterback for three quarters of a football game but had to sit the last quarter out with an injury, how much of the whole game did they play?

3. If Naima was the goalie for two periods of a hockey game (three periods), how much of the whole game did she spend defending the goal?

Solution 1

A baseball game has nine parts (each an inning). Mitchell pitched two innings. Therefore, he played $\frac{2}{9}$ of the game as a pitcher. The denominator represents the nine parts into which the game is divided; the numerator represents the two parts we are concerned with.

Solution 2

Similarly, there are four quarters in a football game, and Cameron playing quarterback three of those quarters means they were in $\frac{3}{4}$ of the game.

Solution 3

There are three periods in hockey, and Naima was goalie for two of them. Therefore, she was goalie for $\frac{2}{3}$ of the game.

Reciprocals

When working with fractions (or any numbers), you may need to find a fraction's reciprocal. Reciprocals can be boiled down to flipping something over. Defined, a reciprocal is $\frac{1}{x}$ where x is the number in question. For example, the reciprocal of $5 = \frac{1}{5}$ or 0.2 as a decimal. The following are numbers and their reciprocals:

$$17 = \frac{1}{17}$$
$$100 = \frac{1}{100}$$
$$42 = \frac{1}{42}$$

One thing to think about with a whole number is that 17 is the same as $\frac{17}{1}$. Keep that in mind not only with reciprocals but any time you have a mix of whole numbers and fractions.

Finding the reciprocal of a fraction requires flipping the numerator and denominator. For example, to find the reciprocal of $\frac{4}{5}$, you flip the fraction over to get $\frac{5}{4}$. Here are a few other examples of reciprocal fractions.

$$\frac{1}{8} = \frac{8}{1} = 8$$
$$\frac{2}{10} = \frac{10}{2} = 5$$
$$\frac{1}{0.25} = \frac{0.25}{1} = 0.25$$

Equivalent Fractions

Fractions having different denominators and numerators might represent the same amount. These are equivalent fractions.

$$\frac{20}{10} = \frac{10}{5} = \frac{2}{1}$$

$$\frac{1}{4} = \frac{2}{8} = \frac{3}{12} = \frac{4}{16}$$

$$\frac{3}{5} = \frac{9}{15} = \frac{27}{45}$$

For a visual example, see the following circle, which has been divided into two equal parts.

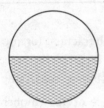

$$\frac{1 \text{ shaded}}{2 \text{ parts}} = \frac{1}{2} \text{ of the circle is shaded.}$$

The following circle is divided into four equal parts with two parts shaded.

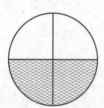

$$\frac{2 \text{ shaded}}{4 \text{ parts}} = \frac{2}{4} \text{ of the circle is shaded.}$$

This circle is divided into eight equal parts with four parts shaded.

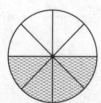

$$\frac{4 \text{ shaded}}{8 \text{ parts}} = \frac{4}{8} \text{ of the circle is shaded.}$$

In each circle, the same amount was shaded. This shows that there is more than one way to indicate one half of something.

The fractions $\frac{1}{2}$, $\frac{2}{4}$, and $\frac{4}{8}$ are equivalent fractions because they all represent the same amount. Notice that the denominator is twice as large as the numerator in every case. Any fraction you write that has a denominator that is exactly twice as large as the numerator will be equivalent to $\frac{1}{2}$.

When you cannot divide the numerator and denominator of a fraction evenly by the same whole number (other than 1), the fraction is in its simplest form.

To write equivalent fractions where the numerator is not 1 requires one more step. The quickest way to find an equivalent fraction is to divide the denominator of the fraction you want by the denominator you know. Take the result and multiply it by the numerator of the fraction you know. This becomes the numerator of the equivalent fraction.

Mixed Numbers and Improper Fractions

As noted earlier, a mixed number consists of a whole number along with a fraction. The number $4\frac{2}{3}$ is an example of a mixed number. Before combining fractions, you might need to convert mixed numbers to improper fractions (a fraction where the numerator is larger than the denominator). To convert, follow these three steps:

 Multiply the denominator of the fraction by the whole number.

 Add the product to the numerator of the fraction.

 Place the sum over the denominator of the fraction.

For example, here's how to convert the mixed number $4\frac{2}{3}$ to an improper fraction:

$$4\frac{2}{3} = \frac{(3)(4)+2}{3} = \frac{14}{3}$$

To add or subtract mixed numbers, you can convert each one to an improper fraction, then find their lowest common denominator and combine them. Alternatively, you can add together the whole numbers, and add together the fractions separately.

A fraction that has a numerator greater than the denominator is an improper fraction. Examples of improper fractions include $\frac{3}{2}$, $\frac{12}{7}$, and $\frac{9}{5}$. Improper fractions can also be in their simplest forms when the numerator and denominator cannot be divided evenly by a number other than 1.

Improper fractions can be represented as mixed numbers and vice versa. Below are a few examples of how to rename a mixed number as an improper fraction.

EXAMPLES

What is the equivalent fraction for $\frac{4}{5}$ using 10 as a denominator?

Solution

Each $\frac{1}{5}$ is equivalent to $\frac{2}{10}$; therefore, $\frac{4}{5}$ is equivalent to $\frac{8}{10}$.

Rename $\frac{3}{4}$ as equivalent fractions having 8, 12, 24, and 32 as denominators.

Solutions

$\frac{3}{4} = \frac{6}{8}$ ($8 \div 4 = 2$; $2 \times 3 = 6$)

$\frac{3}{4} = \frac{9}{12}$ ($12 \div 4 = 3$; $3 \times 3 = 9$)

$\frac{3}{4} = \frac{18}{24}$ ($24 \div 4 = 6$; $6 \times 3 = 18$)

$\frac{3}{4} = \frac{24}{32}$ ($32 \div 4 = 8$; $8 \times 3 = 24$)

Simplifying Fractions

A fraction can be simplified to its lowest terms if its numerator and denominator share a common factor. Here are a few simple examples:

$$\frac{6}{9} = \frac{(3)(2)}{(3)(3)} = \frac{2}{3}$$

(you can "cancel" or factor out the common factor 3)

$$\frac{21}{35} = \frac{(7)(3)}{(7)(5)} = \frac{3}{5}$$

(you can factor out the common factor 7)

Before you perform any operation with a fraction, always check to see if you can simplify it first. By reducing a fraction to its lowest terms, you will also simplify whatever operation you perform on it.

EXAMPLE

Rename $2\frac{1}{4}$ as an improper fraction.

Solution

The whole number 2 contains 8 fourths. Add $\frac{1}{4}$ to it to write the equivalent fraction $\frac{9}{4}$.

$2 \times 4 = 8$

$8 + 1 = 9$

Combined with the denominator, the result is $\frac{9}{4}$.

To rename an improper fraction as a mixed number, proceed backward.

EXAMPLE

Rename $\frac{9}{4}$ as a mixed number.

Solution

Divide the numerator by the denominator and use the remainder (R) as the fraction numerator:

$$9 \div 4 = 2 \text{ R1 or } 9 \div 4 = 2\frac{1}{4}$$

Adding and Subtracting Fractions

To add or subtract fractions with the same denominators, combine the numerators and keep the common denominator.

EXAMPLE

Find the difference between $\frac{7}{8}$ and $\frac{3}{8}$.

Solution

$\frac{7}{8} - \frac{3}{8} = \frac{4}{8}$ and simplified, $\frac{4}{8} = \frac{1}{2}$.

To add or subtract fractions with different denominators, you must first find the lowest common denominator, also known as the least common multiple. A common denominator is a number that can be divided by the denominators of all the fractions in the problem without a remainder. Finding the lowest common denominator is important to ensure that you have the simplest fraction.

EXAMPLE

Add the fractions $\frac{1}{4}$ and $\frac{1}{3}$.

Solution

Multiply the denominators to get $4 \times 3 = 12$. 12 can be divided by both 4 and 3:

$\frac{1}{4}$ is equivalent to $\frac{3}{12}$

$\frac{1}{3}$ is equivalent to $\frac{4}{12}$

To maintain equivalence, each numerator must be multiplied by the value used to reach the common denominator. We can now add the fractions because we have written equivalent fractions with a common denominator.

$$\frac{3}{12} + \frac{4}{12} = \frac{7}{12}$$

Therefore:
$$\frac{1}{4} + \frac{1}{3} = \frac{7}{12}$$

Seven-twelfths is in its simplest form because 7 and 12 do not have a whole number (other than 1) by which they are both divisible.

Multiplying and Dividing Fractions

When multiplying fractions, multiply numerators by numerators and denominators by denominators.

$$\frac{3}{5} \times \frac{4}{7} \times \frac{1}{5} = \frac{3 \times 4 \times 1}{5 \times 7 \times 5} = \frac{12}{175}$$

Try to work with numbers that are as small as possible. You can make numbers smaller by dividing out common factors. Do this by dividing the numerator of any one fraction and the denominator of any one fraction by the same number.

$$\frac{\overset{1}{\cancel{3}}}{\underset{2}{\cancel{4}}} \times \frac{\overset{1}{\cancel{2}}}{\underset{3}{\cancel{9}}} = \frac{1 \times 1}{2 \times 3} = \frac{1}{6}$$

In this case, we divided the numerator of the first fraction and the denominator of the second fraction by 3, while the denominator of the first fraction and the numerator of the second fraction were divided by 2.

To divide by a fraction, multiply by the reciprocal of the divisor.

$$\frac{3}{16} \div \frac{1}{8} = \frac{3}{\underset{2}{\cancel{16}}} \times \frac{\overset{1}{\cancel{8}}}{1} = \frac{3}{2} = 1\frac{1}{2}$$

Scan this QR code for a video on operations with fractions.

Percentages

A percentage (%) is a fraction or decimal number written in a different form, specifically as a number out of 100. A percentage expressed as a fraction is the number divided by 100. As an example, there are 100 cents in a dollar. One percent of $1.00, then, is one cent. Using decimal notation, we can write one cent as $0.01, five cents as $0.05, twenty-five cents as $0.25, and so forth. Instead of saying that 25 cents equal 25 hundredths of a dollar, though, we use the word percent and the form 25%. The decimal number 0.25 as a percentage, then, is written as 25% as well.

The information in this section will help you understand the relationship between decimals, fractions, and percentages and to convert numbers from one form to another.

Converting between Decimals, Fractions, and Percentages

Use the following steps to convert between decimals, fractions, and percentages.

 To change a decimal to a percentage, multiply by 100 and add the % sign.

$$0.25 = 0.25 \times 100 = 25\%$$

 The fraction bar in a fraction means "divided by." To change a fraction to a decimal, follow through on the division.

$$\frac{4}{5} = 4 \div 5 = 0.8$$

 To change a fraction to a percentage, multiply by 100, simplify, and add the percent sign (%).

$$\frac{1}{4} \times 100 = \frac{100}{4} = 25\%$$

 To change a percentage to a decimal, remove the percent sign (%) and divide the number by 100.

$$25\% = \frac{25}{100} = 0.25$$

 To change a percentage to a fraction, remove the % sign and use that number as your numerator, with 100 as your denominator, and simplify.

$$25\% = \frac{25}{100} \quad \frac{1}{4}$$

Percentage is not limited to comparing other numbers to 100. You can divide any number into hundredths and talk about percentage.

EXAMPLE

Find 1% of 200.

Solution

1% of 200 is 1/100, or 0.01, of 200.

Using decimal notation, we can calculate one percent of 200 by multiplying 200 by 0.01:

$$200 \times 0.01 = 2$$

Similarly, we can find a percentage of any number we choose by multiplying it by the correct decimal notation. For example:

Five percent of 50: $0.05 \times 50 = 2.5$

Three percent of 150: $0.03 \times 150 = 4.5$

Ten percent of 60: $0.10 \times 60 = 6$

Not all percentage measurements are between one percent and 100 percent. You might need to consider less than one percent of something, especially if that something is very large. For example, if you were handed a book 1,000 pages long and told to read one percent of it in five minutes, how much would you have to read?

$$1,000 \times 0.01 = 10 \text{ pages}$$

 TIP

With percent notation, keep in mind the following:
100% = 1, 10% = .1, 1% = .01, and percentages over 100% equate to values greater than 1. For instance, 150% = 1.5.

Quite an assignment! You might bargain to read one half of one percent, or one-tenth of one percent in the five minutes allotted to you.

Using decimal notation, we write one-tenth of one percent as 0.001, the decimal number for one thousandth. If you remember that a percent is one hundredth of something, you can see that one tenth of that percent is equivalent to one thousandth of the whole.

Here are some common percentage and fractional equivalents you should remember:

- Ten percent (10%) is one tenth $\left(\frac{1}{10}\right)$, or 0.10.

- Twelve and one-half percent (12.5%) is one eighth $\left(\frac{1}{8}\right)$, or 0.125.

- Twenty percent (20%) is one fifth $\left(\frac{1}{5}\right)$, or 0.20.

- Twenty-five percent (25%) is one quarter $\left(\frac{1}{4}\right)$, or 0.25.

- Thirty-three and one-third percent $\left(33\frac{1}{3}\%\right)$ is one third $\left(\frac{1}{3}\right)$, or 0.33$\overline{3}$.

- Fifty percent (50%) is one half $\left(\frac{1}{2}\right)$, or 0.50.

- Sixty-six and two-thirds percent $\left(66\frac{2}{3}\%\right)$ is two thirds $\left(\frac{2}{3}\right)$, or 0.66$\overline{6}$.

Solving Percentage Problems

A question involving percentages might involve one of these three tasks:

 Finding the percentage of a number

 Finding a number when a percentage is given

Finding what percentage one number is of another

Regardless of the task, three distinct values are involved: the part, the whole, and the percentage. Often, the problem will give you two of the three numbers, and your job is to find the missing value. To work with percentages, use the following formula:

$$\text{percentage} = \frac{\text{part}}{\text{whole}} \times 100$$

Once again, to know any two of those values allows you to determine the third.

Finding the Percentage

30 is what percent of 50?

In this question, 50 is the whole, and 30 is the part. Your task is to find the missing percent:

$$\text{percentage} = \frac{30}{50} \times 100$$
$$= 60\%$$

TIP

You can find a percentage with the following equation: $\text{percentage} = \left(\dfrac{\text{part}}{\text{whole}}\right) \times 100$.

That equation can be flipped around algebraically to find that

$$\text{part} = \text{whole} \times \left(\dfrac{\text{percentage}}{100}\right) \text{ or } \text{whole} = \text{part} \div \left(\dfrac{\text{percentage}}{100}\right).$$

Finding the Part

What number is 25% of 80?

In this question, 80 is the whole, and 25 is the percentage. Your task is to find the part:

$$25\% = \dfrac{\text{part}}{80} \times 100$$

In this situation, it can be helpful to change the percentage into its decimal form (.25), which then lets you drop the 100 from the equation so you can represent the percentage as a fraction, in this case $\dfrac{25}{100}$. That gives us a new form of the equation:

$$\dfrac{25}{100} = \dfrac{\text{part}}{80}$$

To solve for the missing part, cross multiply 25 and 80 and 100 with the missing part. That yields the following:

$$100(\text{part}) = 25(80)$$
$$100(\text{part}) = 2{,}000$$
$$\text{part} = \dfrac{2{,}000}{100}$$
$$\text{part} = 20$$

25% of 80 is 20. Because of the values used, there are any number of ways you could have come to that solution faster, such as by simplifying the left fraction to $\dfrac{1}{4}$, or calculating $80 \div 4$ or $80 \times .25$, but it's important that you see the full process. Let's look at how you can streamline your work in the next example.

Finding the Whole

An example of a question that requires you to find the whole might be something like "75% of what number is 150?"

In this question, 150 is the part, and 75 is the percentage. Your task is to find the whole. Here's the streamlined equation:

$$\dfrac{75}{100} = \dfrac{150}{\text{whole}}$$

Here, you can simplify the fraction on the left to $\dfrac{3}{4}$ and then cross multiply:

$$\dfrac{3}{4} = \dfrac{150}{\text{whole}}$$
$$\text{whole}(3) = 150(4)$$

Then, multiply the two diagonally situated numbers you know:

$$150 \times 4 = 600$$

Finally, divide 600 by 3, which equals 200.

75% of 200 is 150

Percent Increase and Decrease

You've likely encountered the concept of percent change with investment interest, sales tax, and discount pricing. Percent change always relates to the value before the change. Here are two simple examples.

Let's look at an example multiple-choice problem.

EXAMPLE

A computer originally priced at $500 is discounted by 10%, then by another 10%. What is the price of the computer after the second discount, to the nearest dollar?

- **A.** $400
- **B.** $405
- **C.** $425
- **D.** $450

Solution

The correct answer is B. After the first 10% discount, the price was $450 ($500 minus 10% of $500). After the second discount, which is calculated based on the $450 price, the price of the computer is $405 ($450 minus 10% of $450).

EXAMPLES

10 increased by what percent is 12?

Solution

The amount of the increase is 2.

Compare the change (2) to the original number (10).

The change in percent is $\frac{2}{10}$, or 20%.

12 decreased by what percent is 10?

Solution

The amount of the decrease is 2.

Compare the change (2) to the original number (12).

The change is $\frac{2}{12}$, or $\frac{1}{6}$ (or 16.66%).

Notice that the percent increase from 10 to 12 (20%) is not the same as the percent decrease from 12 to 10 (16.66%). That's because the original number (before the change) is different in the two questions.

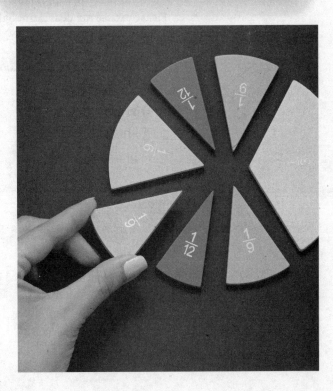

Percent-change problems typically involve tax, interest, profit, discount, or weight. In handling these problems, you might need to calculate more than one percent change.

SUMMING IT UP

- If you are having difficulties with any mathematics topic, talk to a teacher, refer to a math textbook from your school or a local library, seek out online courses (like those at Petersons.com), or look up interactive explanations for those types of problems online.

- Use the exercises in this chapter to determine what you DON'T know well. While you can study those areas if you like, recognize that it's not necessary when practicing for a placement exam like ACCUPLACER. Instead, focus energy on brushing up on what you DO already know so you can demonstrate your knowledge well.

- Review the math symbols covered in this chapter so that you're prepared when you encounter them in math problems.

- Know the different types of numbers: whole numbers, integers, rational numbers, irrational numbers, and signed numbers.

- Know how to perform basic operations with whole numbers and integers.

- Properties and identities describe how numbers behave in consistent and predictable ways, which simplifies the process of solving math problems. These will be especially important for working with algebraic expressions and equations.

- When simplifying expressions or solving equations, use the mnemonic device "Please excuse my dear Aunt Sally" to remember the order of operations:

  - **Parentheses**
  - **Exponents (and Square Roots)**
  - **Multiplication**
  - **Division**
  - **Addition**
  - **Subtraction**

7

- Decimals represent parts of numbers. Everything to the left of a decimal point is a whole number and everything to the right of a decimal point represents a part of the whole.

- A factor is a number that can be divided into a whole number evenly without leaving a remainder.

  - Multiples are similar to factors in that they are whole numbers into which a number can be divided evenly.

  - Being able to determine the greatest common factor and least common multiple of a set of numbers is important for solving problems with fractions.

- A fraction is a part of a whole and consists of both a numerator and a denominator.

  - Proper fractions are those in which the numerator is smaller than the denominator.

  - Mixed numbers are fractions accompanied by an integer.

  - Improper fractions are those in which the numerator is greater than the denominator.

  - To add or subtract fractions, they must have the same denominator.

- Percentages are fractions or decimals written in a different form. They represent parts of numbers, and you can convert between percentages, fractions, and decimals. Percentage problems may require you to find the percentage, the part, the whole, or the percent increase or decrease.

KNOWLEDGE CHECK

ARITHMETIC

20 Questions

> **Directions:** Choose the best answer. Use the space provided for any calculations.

1. $(-22) - (-18) =$

   A. -40

   B. -30

   C. -4

   D. $+13$

2. Ian received 82 points out of 100 on his recent math test. Ian didn't miss any questions completely, but a note from his teacher stated that he lost one-third of a point every time he didn't show all his work. How many total deductions did Ian have?

   A. 6

   B. 18

   C. 27

   D. 54

3. Yolanda needs to repot her collection of houseplants. Each large pot requires 1 quart of new soil, each medium pot requires a $\frac{1}{2}$ quart of new soil, and each small pot requires $\frac{1}{4}$ quart of new soil or less. The premium soil mix that she prefers contains 12 quarts of soil in each bag. If Yolanda has 15 plants in large pots, 16 in medium pots, and 12 plants that require small pots, how many bags of potting mix does she need to purchase?

   A. 1

   B. 2

   C. 3

   D. 4

4. In the expression, $166 \div 42 + (17 \times 2) - 7^2$, what operation will you perform first to simplify?

   A. $166 \div 42$

   B. $42 + (17 \times 2)$

   C. -7^2

   D. 17×2

5. $(6 \times 10 \div 15) - (3^3 + 12) =$

   A. -35

   B. -15

   C. 5

   D. 12

6. $3.41 + 5.6 + 0.873 =$

   A. 4.843

   B. 9.883

   C. 15.264

   D. 16.863

7. $3.7\overline{)2,339.86}$

   A. 62.34

   B. 63.24

   C. 632.4

   D. 634.4

8. $59.60 \div \$0.40 =$

   A. 0.149

   B. 1.49

   C. 14.9

   D. 149

9. $\dfrac{8}{15} \times \dfrac{3}{4} =$

   A. $\dfrac{1}{5}$

   B. $\dfrac{3}{10}$

   C. $\dfrac{2}{5}$

   D. $\dfrac{3}{5}$

10. $\dfrac{1}{4} \div 4\dfrac{1}{3}$

   A. $\dfrac{3}{52}$

   B. $\dfrac{5}{52}$

   C. $\dfrac{12}{52}$

   D. $\dfrac{20}{52}$

11. Three friends attend a meal at a nice restaurant together. When they receive the bill, the total is $204.60. They decide to split the bill evenly and agree that each person will leave a 20 percent tip. How much will each person pay in total for their portion of the bill plus a tip?

   A. $40.92

   B. $68.40

   C. $81.84

   D. $109.32

12. 10% of 32 =

   A. 3

   B. 3.2

   C. 3.5

   D. 4

13. A smartphone originally priced at $1,200 is discounted by 10%, then by another 10%. What is the price of the smartphone after the second discount, to the nearest dollar?

   A. $960

   B. $965

   C. $972

   D. $978

14. Duncan purchases $500 worth of cryptocurrency. The cryptocurrency's value rises by 20% during the first week, but then falls by 20% during the following week. What is the net percent change in the cryptocurrency's value?

   A. The value remains the same.

   B. The value increases by 2%.

   C. The value increases by 4%.

   D. The value decreases by 4%.

15. A recipe for 6 quarts of punch calls for $\dfrac{3}{4}$ cups of sugar. How much sugar is needed for 9 quarts of punch?

   A. $\dfrac{5}{8}$ of a cup

   B. $\dfrac{7}{8}$ of a cup

   C. $1\dfrac{1}{8}$ cups

   D. 2 cups

16. How many reams of ribbon will it take to make 45 badges if each badge uses 4 inches of ribbon, and each ream of ribbon contains 60 inches?

    A. 2
    B. 3
    C. 4
    D. 5

17. Rhea scored an 87.5% on her most recent chemistry test. She answered 56 questions correctly. How many total questions were on the test?

    A. 64
    B. 70
    C. 76
    D. 82

Questions 18–20 refer to the following scenario.

For a science experiment, Akshat is measuring the growth of chive plants given the same nutrients and soil but placed in different environments with different light conditions. Each plant started at a height of 1 cm on Day 0, meaning the day Akshat placed the chives in their new environments. Consider the table from Akshat's lab notes, then answer the questions that follow.

TOTAL HEIGHT OF CHIVES			
	Day 3	Day 6	Day 9
Environment A	1.2 cm	1.7 cm	2 cm
Environment B	2 cm	3.8 cm	5.2 cm
Environment C	2.7 cm	5 cm	8 cm

18. How many centimeters did the chives in Environment A grow between Day 3 and Day 9?

    A. 0.3 cm
    B. 0.5 cm
    C. 0.8 cm
    D. 1 cm

19. What was the combined total amount of growth in all three environments for the nine-day period?

    A. 5.2 cm
    B. 9.3 cm
    C. 12.2 cm
    D. 15.2 cm

20. By what percentage did the chives in Environment C grow from Day 0 to Day 9?

    A. 60%
    B. 160%
    C. 700%
    D. 800%

ANSWER KEY AND EXPLANATIONS

1. C	**5.** A	**9.** C	**13.** C	**17.** A
2. D	**6.** B	**10.** A	**14.** D	**18.** C
3. C	**7.** C	**11.** C	**15.** C	**19.** C
4. D	**8.** D	**12.** B	**16.** B	**20.** C

1. **The correct answer is C.** Minus negative becomes plus positive. The problem then reads:

$$(-22) + (+18) = -4$$

2. **The correct answer is D.** Ian lost one-third of a point every time he didn't show his work. To lose one total point, Ian would have neglected to show his work on three problems. Since Ian lost 18 total points to such an error, he didn't show his work $18 \times 3 = 54$ times. You can achieve the same result by dividing Ian's total number of missed points, 18, by $\frac{1}{3}$.

3. **The correct answer is C.** Create an equation to represent the different quantities of soil needed for each pot type, then add together.

$$15(1) + 16\left(\frac{1}{2}\right) + 12\left(\frac{1}{4}\right) = 15 + 8 + 3 = 26 \text{ quarts}$$

   Once you know that you need 26 quarts of soil, divide that by the number of quarts of soil (12) in each bag of potting mix.

$$26 \div 12 = 2.16\overline{6}$$

   Since Yolanda can't buy a portion of a bag, you'll need to round her purchase up to 3 bags of potting mix.

4. **The correct answer is D.** Remember PEMDAS, and you will know that the first step is to solve what is inside the parentheses first. 17×2 is the expression inside the parentheses, so it is the first thing you should solve.

5. **The correct answer is A.** Remember the order of operations as you work through the problem.

$$= (6 \times 10 \div 15) - (3^3 + 12)$$
$$= (6 \times 10 \div 15) - (27 + 12)$$
$$= (60 \div 15) - (27 + 12)$$
$$= 4 - (27 + 12)$$
$$= 4 - (39)$$
$$= -35$$

6. **The correct answer is B.**

$$\begin{array}{r} 3.41 \\ +5.6 \\ +0.873 \\ \hline 9.883 \end{array}$$

7. **The correct answer is C.**

$$\begin{array}{r} 63\,2.39 \approx 632.4 \\ 3.7\overline{)2339.8\,60} \\ \underline{222} \\ 119 \\ \underline{111} \\ 88 \\ 74 \\ \hline 146 \\ \underline{111} \\ \hline 350 \\ \underline{333} \\ \hline 17 \end{array}$$

8. **The correct answer is D.** Remember that to divide by a decimal, you must first move the decimal in the divisor to the right until it becomes a whole number, then move the decimal the same number of places in the dividend. The decimal point in the answer will be directly "above" (assuming long division notation) the decimal point in the dividend.

$$\$0.40\overline{)\$59.60} = \$4\overline{)\$596.0}^{\,149.0}$$

9. **The correct answer is C.**

$$\frac{\cancel{7}^{2}}{\cancel{15}_{5}} \times \frac{\cancel{3}^{1}}{\cancel{4}_{1}} = \frac{2}{5}$$

10. **The correct answer is A.**

$$\frac{1}{4} \div 4\frac{1}{3} = \frac{1}{4} \div \frac{13}{3} = \frac{1}{4} \times \frac{3}{13} = \frac{3}{52}$$

11. **The correct answer is C.** First, divide the bill three ways.

$$3\overline{)\$204.60} = \$68.20$$

Then, multiply by 1.2 to determine how much each person will pay after adding a 20% tip to their portion.

$$\$68.20 \times 1.2 = \$81.84$$

12. **The correct answer is B.** Convert 10% to a decimal, 0.10, and multiply the total amount by the decimal to find the answer:

$$32 \times 0.10 = 3.2$$

13. **The correct answer is C.** After the first 10% discount, the price was $1,080 ($1,200 minus 10% of $120). After the second discount, which is calculated based on the $1,080 price, the price of the smartphone is $972 ($1,080 minus 10% of $1,080).

14. **The correct answer is D.** First, the cryptocurrency rises by 20% (0.2 × $500 = $100), so the value is:

$$\$500 + \$100 = \$600$$

Then, it falls by 20% (0.2 × $600 = $120), so the final value is:

$$\$600 - \$120 = \$480$$

The difference from the original price is:

$$\$500 - \$480 = \$20$$

Knowing the difference, set up a proportion problem to determine the percentage of decrease:

$$\frac{20}{500} = \frac{x}{100}$$
$$500x = 2,000$$
$$\frac{500x}{500} = \frac{2,000}{500}$$
$$x = 4$$

15. **The correct answer is C.** First, find out how much sugar one quart of punch needs.

$$\frac{3}{4} \text{ cups} \div 6 = \frac{3}{4} \div \frac{6}{1} = \frac{\cancel{3}^{1}}{4} \times \frac{1}{\cancel{6}_{2}} = \frac{1}{8}$$

Then solve for 9 quarts of punch as follows:

$$9 \times \frac{1}{8} = \frac{9}{8} = 1\frac{1}{8}$$

16. **The correct answer is B.** Each ream of ribbon can make 15 badges, since 60 ÷ 4 = 15 , so for 45 badges, you would need 3 reams of ribbon.

17. **The correct answer is A.** Rhea scored an 87.5% by answering 56 questions correctly. You can set up an equation using what you know about calculating percentages.

$$\text{percentage} = \frac{\text{part}}{\text{whole}} \times 100$$
$$.875 = \frac{56}{\text{whole}}$$
$$\text{whole} = \frac{56}{.875}$$
$$\text{whole} = \frac{56}{1} \div \frac{7}{8}$$
$$\text{whole} = \frac{56}{1} \cdot \frac{8}{7} = \frac{448}{7} = 64$$

Alternatively, since the numbers can be difficult to work with, you can also substitute in answer choices to see what part-whole relationship yields 87.5%. Start with a choice that creates an easy-to-simplify fraction, like choice B. You would have $\frac{56}{70}$ or $\frac{4}{5}$.

That's 80%, so there would need to be fewer total questions to increase Rhea's score, thus choice A must be correct.

18. **The correct answer is C.** Make sure you're using the figures for the correct days of observation and then use subtraction to find the difference between the two:

$$2 \text{ cm} - 1.2 \text{ cm} = 0.8 \text{ cm}$$

19. **The correct answer is C.** To find the total combined growth in all three environments over the nine-day period, first find the difference between Day 9 and Day 0. All plants began at 1 cm in height. Environment A grew by 1 cm, Environment B grew by 4.2 cm, and Environment C grew by 7 cm. Combine these values for the total amount of growth across all three environments: 12.2 cm.

20. **The correct answer is C.** We know that between Day 0 and Day 9, the chives in Environment C grew to be 8 cm, a change of 7 cm. Since the starting size is 1 cm, each time the chives grew by 1 cm, that would be considered 100% growth, since a growth of 1 cm represents 100% of the original size. Since the difference between 1 cm and 8 cm is 7 cm, you can multiply 100% by 7, meaning the chives in Environment C grew by 700% over the course of 9 days.

CHAPTER

Quantitative Reasoning, Algebra, and Statistics

QUANTITATIVE REASONING, ALGEBRA

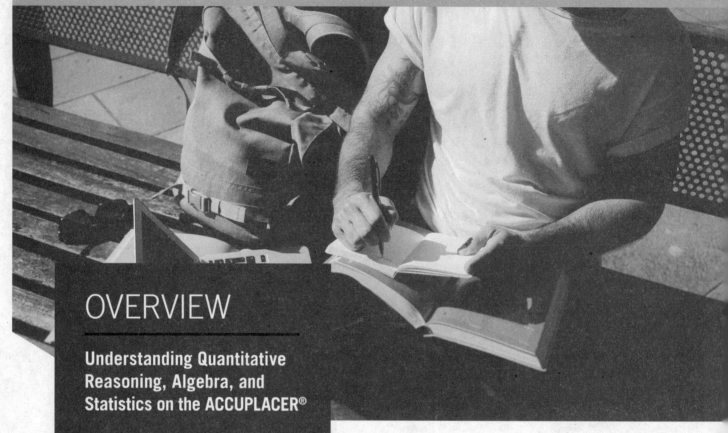

OVERVIEW

Understanding Quantitative Reasoning, Algebra, and Statistics on the ACCUPLACER®

Key Concepts for Quantitative Reasoning, Algebra, and Statistics on the ACCUPLACER®

- Rates, Ratios, and Proportions
- Exponents, Scientific Notation, and Radicals
- Basic Geometry
- Probability, Sets, and Statistics

Summing It Up

Knowledge Check: Quantitative Reasoning, Algebra, and Statistics

Answer Key and Explanations

Every single day, you use some form of quantitative reasoning. Whether you're trying to figure out how to cut a pie into 10 even pieces, determine how much you'll owe with tax on a shared restaurant bill, or calculate what percentage of your budget you spent dining out last month, using reason to figure out quantitative problems is something you do all the time. With that in mind, if you're someone who worries about math, recognize that many of the concepts we'll cover here map to real-world applications that will make the math seem quite familiar to many. In this chapter, we'll delve into numerous concepts from arithmetic, algebra, and statistics that fall under the heading of quantitative reasoning. We'll address algebraic expressions, linear equations, probability, basic geometry, and many other concepts that you will have likely already encountered in high school math courses or out in the world.

UNDERSTANDING QUANTITATIVE REASONING, ALGEBRA, AND STATISTICS ON THE ACCUPLACER®

Like the other math placement tests on the ACCUPLACER, the quantitative reasoning, algebra, and statistics test will include 20 questions and is not timed. For most questions, you will not be permitted to use a calculator. However, on the computerized test, a pop-up calculator will appear for questions when it is permitted. To simulate this computer experience, we have marked some questions with a calculator icon so that you know you are free to use your own calculator on those questions. Note that you may only use the pop-up calculator on your actual exam.

As we mentioned in the previous chapter, mathematical concepts across the three ACCUPLACER quantitative sections may overlap. For instance, you might be asked about linear equations in the quantitative reasoning, algebra, and statistics section and then again in the advanced algebra and functions section, which we'll discuss in the next chapter. We have grouped mathematical concepts according to where they are most likely to appear on the exam, but expect there to be some overlap. Accordingly, we recommend practicing all three math sections together so that you can refresh yourself on any concepts you've learned in the past. As a reminder, focus on that which is already somewhat familiar to you rather than new content to ensure that your ACCUPLACER results place you in the right math course.

KEY CONCEPTS FOR QUANTITATIVE REASONING, ALGEBRA, AND STATISTICS ON THE ACCUPLACER®

In the following sections, we'll first look at rates, ratios, and proportions, which are especially important in statistics. Then, we'll explain how to use exponents, scientific notation, and radicals to deal with very large or very small numbers. Next, we'll explore basic concepts

from geometry, particularly as they relate to algebra. Finally, we'll look at important concepts for understanding probability, sets, and statistics. All of these skills will also be crucial in forming a base of knowledge for tackling the advanced algebra and functions section of the ACCUPLACER, which is the topic of Chapter 9.

Rates, Ratios, and Proportions

Rates, ratios, and proportions can be used in multiple real-world situations, which is why they often pop up in word problems. Before looking at examples, let's review the principles of ratios and proportions as well as the different situations in which you'd need to calculate rates.

Ratios

A ratio expresses proportionate or comparative size— the size of one quantity relative to the size of another. Write a ratio by placing a colon (:) between the two numbers. Read the colon as the word *to*. For example, read the ratio 3:5 as "3 to 5." As with fractions, you can reduce ratios to lowest terms by canceling common factors. For example, given a menagerie of 28 pets that includes 12 cats and 16 dogs:

The ratio of cats to dogs is 12:16, or 3:4 ("3 to 4").

The ratio of dogs to cats is 16:12, or 4:3 ("4 to 3").

The ratio of cats to the total number of pets is 12:28, or 3:7 ("3 to 7").

The ratio of dogs to the total number of pets is 16:28, or 4:7 ("4 to 7").

Another way to think about a ratio is as a fraction. A proportion is an equation relating two ratios; it is expressed by equating two fractions, say $\frac{1}{2}=\frac{4}{8}$. Another way of saying that two ratios (or fractions) are equivalent is to say that they are "proportionate." For example, the ratio 12:16 is proportionate to the ratio 3:4. Similarly, the fraction $\frac{12}{16}$ is proportionate to the fraction $\frac{3}{4}$.

Proportions

Proportion problems are formulated when one ratio is known and one of the two quantities in an equivalent ratio is unknown. They arise when changing units of measurement or scaling up a ratio, like when preparing a recipe, among other applications. Since you can express any ratio as a fraction, you can set two equivalent ratios (also called proportionate ratios) equal to each other as fractions. For instance, the ratio 16:28 is proportionate to the ratio 4:7 because $\frac{16}{28} = \frac{4}{7}$.

If one of the four terms is missing from the equation (the proportion), you can solve for the missing term using the same method that you learned for solving percent problems in the last chapter:

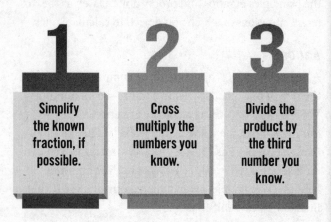

| Simplify the known fraction, if possible. | Cross multiply the numbers you know. | Divide the product by the third number you know. |

For example, if the ratio 10:15 is proportionate to 14:x, you can find the missing number by first setting up the following proportion:

$$\frac{10}{15} = \frac{14}{x}$$

Reading the ratio 10:15 as a fraction, simplify it to $\frac{2}{3}$.

$$\frac{2}{3} = \frac{14}{x}$$

Then, cross multiply the numbers you know:

$$3 \times 14 = 42$$

Finally, divide by the third number you know:

$$42 \div 2 = 21$$

The ratio 10:15 is equivalent to the ratio 14:21. You'll often encounter proportion problems as word problems. Word problems will require you to parse out the numbers and then set up the ratios so that they are proportionate in order to solve for the missing term.

Let's look at a sample problem.

EXAMPLE

Suppose there are 2 hockey sticks for every 5 pucks in the storage locker room. If the last count was 60 pucks, how many hockey sticks are in the storage room?

Solution

Let h denote the number of hockey sticks in the storage room. Here, we know that there are 2 hockey sticks for every 5 pucks. We know that there's a total of 60 pucks, but we don't know how many hockey sticks there are. However, because the number of hockey sticks is proportional to the number of pucks, we can scale up the ratio we do know to solve for the number of hockey sticks.

Set up the proportion as follows:

$$\frac{2}{5} = \frac{h}{60}$$
$$5h = 120$$
$$h = 24$$

Scan this QR code to learn more about ratios and proportions.

8

Rates

Rates represent a comparison of two quantities with different units (a kind of ratio). Rates can represent unit conversions (e.g., inches to centimeters), speed (e.g., miles per hour), cost (e.g., value per unit), and even work (e.g., task duration to total time allotted). Understanding the principals of ratios and proportions is key to calculating rates.

Rates of Speed, Time, and Distance

The basic formula used in solving problems for distance is:

$$D = RT \text{ (Distance = Rate} \times \text{Time)}$$

You can use this same formula to find rate (speed) and time.

To find rate, use $R = \dfrac{D}{T}$ (Rate = Distance ÷ Time).

To find time, use $T = \dfrac{D}{R}$ (Time = Distance ÷ Rate).

Let's look at two examples.

EXAMPLE

An aircraft flies 600 miles in 5 hours. At what rate did it complete the trip?

Solution

Here you're provided distance and time, and you're asked to determine the rate at which the distance of 600 miles can be covered in 5 hours. With the formula for calculating rate, you can see that distance will be divided by time. This creates a unit rate with the unit label of miles per hour, specifying how much distance can be covered per unit of time (every hour). Dividing the total distance by the total travel time $\left(\dfrac{600 \text{ miles}}{5 \text{ hours}} \right)$ yields a rate of 120 miles per hour (mph), communicating that for every hour of flight time, the aircraft will travel 120 miles.

We can look at another example to see how possessing the unit rate allows you to determine the different rate components.

EXAMPLE

A driver is traveling from Denver, CO, to Laramie, WY. The distance between these two cities is 128 miles. If the driver goes straight there without stopping and drives at a rate of 60 mph the entire time, how long will it take them to get to Laramie?

Solution

Here, we are given two of the variables we need: rate and distance. This means we need to solve for time. To solve for time, we'll use the $T = \dfrac{D}{R}$ and plug in the values we know.

Here, we know that the driver is traveling at a rate of 60 mph. We also know that the drive is 128 miles total. If we plug the values into our formula, we get:

$$T = \frac{128 \text{ mile}}{60 \text{ miles per hour}}$$

If we divide 128 miles by 60 mph, we get 2.13 hours (notice how the shared units—miles—cancel). Note that this is **not** the same as 2 hours and 13 minutes, but we generally know that it will take the driver a little over 2 hours to make the drive.

Rates Involving Money

Not all rates are related to speed. Rates can also involve money. For example, if you earn $30.00 in 2 hours, your rate is $15.00 per hour. The rate in a money problem represents a unit amount—such as a salary (dollars per hour) or an individual price (cost per item).

When you solve money questions, your rate formula will look like this:

$$\text{Rate (unit amount)} = \frac{\text{Total amount}}{\text{Number of units}}$$

Try out the sample question we've provided here.

EXAMPLE

If a 20-ounce bottle of juice costs $1.80, what is the cost per ounce of juice?

A. $0.09

B. $0.11

C. $0.18

D. $0.36

Solution

To solve the example shown, you must first identify the three pieces of the problem:

$$\text{Number of units} = 20 \text{ ounces}$$

$$\text{Total amount} = \$1.80$$

Unit amount (cost per ounce) = ?

Then, plug the known values into the rate formula and use it to solve for the unit amount:

$$\text{Rate (unit amount)} = \frac{\text{Total amount}}{\text{Number of units}}$$

$$= \frac{\$1.80}{20 \text{ ounces of juice}}$$

$$= \$0.09 \text{ per ounce of juice}$$

The cost per ounce of juice is $0.09, which is choice A. This dollar-to-ounce value is the unit rate.

Rates Involving Work

Another type of problem you might encounter is a work problem. The aim of a work problem is to predict how long it will take to complete a job if the number of workers increases or decreases. Work problems may also involve determining how fast pipes can empty or fill tanks. In solving pipe and tank problems, you must think of the pipes as workers.

In most work problems, a job is broken into several parts, each representing a fractional portion of the entire job. For each part represented, the numerator should represent the time actually spent working, while the denominator should represent the total time the worker needs to do the job alone. The sum of all the individual fractions must be 1 if the job is completed. The easiest way to understand this procedure is to carefully study the examples that follow. By following the step-by-step solutions, you will learn how to make your own fractions to solve both the practice problems that follow and the work problems you may find on your exam.

EXAMPLE

If Antonio does a job in 6 days and Beatrice does the same job in 3 days, how long will it take the two of them, working together, to do the job?

Solution

STEP 1: Write the fractions as follows.

$$\frac{\text{Time actually spent}}{\text{Time needed to do entire job alone}} \quad \overset{A}{\underset{6 \text{ days}}{\frac{x}{}}} + \overset{B}{\underset{3 \text{ days}}{\frac{x}{}}} = 1$$

The variable x represents the amount of time each worker will work when both work together. The number 1 represents the completed job.

STEP 2: When multiplying by 6 to get rid of the fraction, the equation becomes $\frac{6x}{6} + \frac{6x}{3} = 1(6)$, which simplifies to $x + 2x = 6$

STEP 3: Solve for x.

$$3x = 6$$
$$x = 2$$

Working together, Antonio (A) and Beatrice (B) will get the job done in 2 days.

To learn more about solving rate problems, scan this QR code.

Exponents, Scientific Notation, and Radicals

Exponents, scientific notation, and radicals all relate to ways of expressing and working with very large or very small numbers.

Exponents

An exponent represents the number of times that a number (referred to as the "base number") is multiplied by itself. In the exponential number 2^4, the base number is 2 and the exponent is 4. To calculate the value of 2^4 means to multiply 2 by itself 4 times: $2^4 = 2 \times 2 \times 2 \times 2 = 16$. An exponent is also referred to as a power, meaning you can express the exponential number 2^4 as "2 to the 4th power."

A variety of rules exist for working with exponents with different operations. Use the following table as a guide:

RULES FOR EXPONENTS	
Product	$a^m a^n = a^{m+n}$
Product of a power	$(a^m)^n = a^{mn}$
Quotient to a power	$\left(\dfrac{a}{b}\right)^n = \dfrac{a^n}{b^n}$
Quotient	$\dfrac{a^m}{a^n} = a^{m-n}$
Zero exponent	$a^0 = 1$
Negative exponent	$a^{-n} = \dfrac{1}{a^n}$
Inversion	$\left(\dfrac{a}{b}\right)^{-n} = \left(\dfrac{b}{a}\right)^n$
Fractional powers	$a^{\frac{m}{n}} = \sqrt[n]{a^m}$

EXAMPLE

Simplify the expression: $\left(\dfrac{x^2 y^4}{x^{-1} y}\right)^{-2}$

Solution

Here, apply the rules for exponents within the parentheses and then apply the –2 power. Note that a variable with no exponent is assumed to have an exponent of 1:

$$\left(\frac{x^2 y^4}{x^{-1} y}\right)^{-2} = \left(x^{2-(-1)} y^{4-1}\right)^{-2}$$
$$= \left(x^3 y^3\right)^{-2}$$
$$= x^{-6} y^{-6}$$
$$= \frac{1}{x^6 y^6}$$

Roots

The square root of a number n is a number that you "square" (multiply it by itself, or raise to the power of 2), to obtain n. The radical sign signifies square root and looks like this: $\sqrt{}$. A simple example of a square root is $2 = \sqrt{4}$ (the square root of 4) because 2×2 (or 2^2) = 4.

The cube root of a number n is a number that you raise to the power of 3 (multiply by itself twice) to obtain n. You determine higher roots (for example, the "fourth root") in the same way. Except for square roots, the radical sign will indicate the root to be taken. For example:

$2 = \sqrt[3]{8}$ (the cube root of 8) because $2 \times 2 \times 2$ (or 2^3) = 8

$2 = \sqrt[4]{16}$ (the fourth root of 16) because $2 \times 2 \times 2 \times 2$ (or 2^4) = 16

Square roots, cube roots, etc. can be expressed using fractional exponents. The following notation is used:

$$\sqrt{a} = a^{\frac{1}{2}}$$

$$\sqrt[3]{a} = a^{\frac{1}{3}}$$

$$\vdots$$

$$\sqrt[n]{a} = a^{\frac{1}{n}}$$

Using the exponent rules, we have the more general definition:

$$\sqrt[n]{a^m} = (a^m)^{\frac{1}{n}} = a^{\left(m \cdot \frac{1}{n}\right)} = \left(a^{\frac{1}{n}}\right)^m = a^{\frac{m}{n}}$$

For instance:

$$8^{\frac{2}{3}} = \left(8^{\frac{1}{3}}\right)^2 = (2)^2 = 4$$

$$16^{\frac{3}{2}} = \left(16^{\frac{1}{2}}\right)^3 = 4^3 = 64$$

Radical Expression Laws

You can simplify radical expressions using the rules provided below, some of which overlap with exponents.

$$\sqrt[n]{a} = a^{\frac{1}{n}}$$

$$\sqrt[n]{\frac{a}{b}} = \frac{\sqrt[n]{a}}{\sqrt[n]{b}}$$

$$a^{\frac{m}{n}} = \sqrt[n]{a^m}$$

$$\sqrt[nm]{a} = \sqrt[m]{\sqrt[n]{a}}$$

$$\sqrt[n]{a} \cdot \sqrt[n]{b} = \sqrt[n]{ab}$$

$$\sqrt[n]{a^n} = a$$

Scientific Notation

Scientific notation is a system for writing extremely large or extremely small numbers. In scientific notation, an integer or decimal number between 1 and 10

is written to a power of 10. For example, the number 380,000,000 can be written as 3.8×10^8. The number between 1 and 10 that you are working with is 3.8. When you count the number of zeros plus the number to the right of the decimal point, you can see that there are 8 digits. That means that the exponent is 8. A negative exponent signifies a fractional number.

To illustrate further, here's a list of numbers and their equivalents in scientific notation:

$$837,000 = 8.37 \times 10^5$$
(decimal point shifts 5 places to the left)

$$8,370 = 8.37 \times 10^3$$
(decimal point shifts 3 places to the left)

$$837 = 8.37 \times 10^2$$
(decimal point shifts 2 places to the left)

$$8.37 = 8.37 \times 10^0$$
(decimal point unchanged in position)

$$0.837 = 8.37 \times 10^{-1}$$
(decimal point shifts 1 place to the right)

$$0.0837 = 8.37 \times 10^{-2}$$
(decimal point shifts 2 places to the right)

$$0.000837 = 8.37 \times 10^{-4}$$
(decimal point shifts 4 places to the right)

Algebraic Expressions, Linear Equations, and Inequalities

Fundamentally, algebra is the manipulation of mathematical symbols. More than likely, your familiarity with the topic stems from solving for unknowns by applying various rules and procedures. Algebraic expressions, linear equations, and inequalities are useful in helping you break down and solve complex equations in algebra. We discuss them here because they are central to the quantitative reasoning, algebra, and statistics test on the ACCUPLACER, but be aware that aspects of each concept are likely to come up in the advanced algebra and functions section as well, so you will likely return to some of these concepts in Chapter 9.

Expressions and Equations

So far, you've already seen plenty of mathematical expressions: at least two values with some math operator used between them. Algebraic expressions, however, are usually used to form equations—the goal is to set two expressions equal to one another. When we're talking about algebraic expressions, know that a term is any coefficient, variable, or combination of a coefficient and a variable. In equations, at least one of the terms will be a variable—a letter such as x or y that represents a number that can vary. It does not need an exponent, but if it has one, it must be a non-negative exponent. A coefficient is the number that multiplies with a variable, such as the 2 in $2y$.

Scan this QR code to learn more about working with variables.

Standard Form

Standard form is something you've been using since you learned how to write numbers. Write the number one hundred: 100. That is standard form—the usual way you'd write a number. In addition to being the way you've written numbers all your life, standard form is also an agreed upon method of writing an equation. The standard form for equations has a couple of rules you need to know.

RULE 1

ALWAYS SET AN EQUATION EQUAL TO 0.
Example: $x = 7$ should have everything on the left of the equal sign and 0 on the right:
$x - 7 = 0$ is standard form.

RULE 2

WORK DOWN FROM THE HIGHEST EXPONENT.
Example: $7x^3 + 3x^6 - 5 + 4x^2$ should start with the highest exponent: $3x^6 + 7x^3 + 4x^2 - 5$.

Writing equations in standard form makes it easier to locate information because it is presented in a consistent order. When an equation is in standard form, you'll know what to expect and how to proceed with isolating and solving for the variable.

Evaluating Expressions through Substitution

You know that expressions can have terms, coefficients, variables, and exponents. When putting expressions into standard form, you'll often be simplifying the expression. Expressions can be simplified by combining like terms. Like terms must have the same variable (or lack thereof) and the same power (e.g., 3 and 4, $3x$ and x, $4y^7$ and $253y^7$). Sometimes, though, you'll not only be given an expression but also a value that can be substituted in for a variable to evaluate the expression. For instance, if you were told to evaluate the expression $4x^2 + 3x$ when $x = 3$, you would substitute 3 for each instance of x.

Consider this more complex example: $y = 4x + 5$. You may be asked to evaluate the equation when $x = -3$. This means plugging -3 in for x and then finding the resulting value for y:

$$y = 4x + 5$$
$$y = 4(-3) + 5$$
$$y = -7$$

The answer is $y = -7$.

Linear Equations in One Variable

As we've mentioned, algebraic expressions are usually used to form equations into two expressions that are set equal to each other. Equations contain at least one variable, most often x or y (though variables can be represented by any letter). Most equations you'll see on the test

Performing Operations to Isolate the Variable

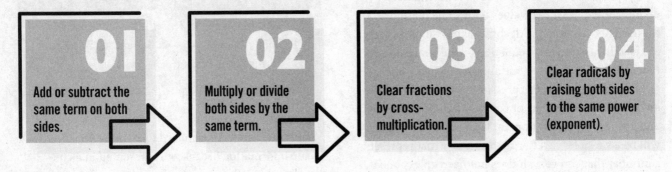

01 Add or subtract the same term on both sides.

02 Multiply or divide both sides by the same term.

03 Clear fractions by cross-multiplication.

04 Clear radicals by raising both sides to the same power (exponent).

are linear equations. In linear equations, the variables x and y don't come with exponents, and they can be graphed along the x- and y-axis of a coordinate plane.

To find the value of a linear equation's variable is to solve the equation. To solve any linear equation containing only one variable, your goal is always the same: isolate the variable on one side of the equation. To accomplish this, you may need to perform one or more of the following operations on both sides, depending on the equation.

Whatever operation you perform on one side of an equation you must also perform on the other side; otherwise, the two sides won't be equal. Performing any of these operations on both sides does not change the equality; it merely restates the equation in a different form.

Simplifying Equations

Sometimes, you need to simplify one or both sides of an equation before you can undo what's been done to the variable. This can be done through various means depending on the nature of the expression. In general, you want to isolate the target variable to one side of the equation, using standard order of operations to reach its solution. Consider the following basic example.

EXAMPLE

Simplify $3(x - 2) - 2x = 8$

Solution

Step 1: Simplify any parts of the equation, remembering to follow the order of operations (PEMDAS).

In this case, multiply the expression in parentheses by 3.

$$3x - 6 - 2x = 8$$

Step 2: Combine like terms.

Now, combine the two terms with x.

$$3x - 6 - 2x = 8$$
$$x - 6 = 8$$

Step 3: Isolate the variable by undoing what has been done to it.

To undo the subtraction of 6, add 6 to both sides.

$$x - 6(+6) = 8(+6)$$
$$x = 14$$

Simplification Methods

Here is a more detailed rundown of several simplification methods.

To find the value of the variable (to solve for x, y, or any other variable), you may need to either add a term to both sides of the equation or subtract a term from both sides. What follows are examples for each operation.

Adding the same number to both sides:

$$x - 2 = 5$$
$$x - 2 + 2 = 5 + 2$$
$$x = 7$$

Subtracting the same number from both sides:

$$y + 3 = 7$$
$$y + 3 - 3 = 7 - 3$$
$$y = 4$$

The first system isolates x by adding 2 to both sides. The second system isolates y by removing 3 from both sides.

The objective is to isolate the variable. To do this, like terms must be combined until the variable stands alone on one side of the equation. The following example isolates x by subtracting $\frac{3}{2}$ from both sides, then combining like terms and dividing by –1 to make the variable positive:

$$\frac{3}{2} - x = 12$$
$$\frac{3}{2} - \frac{3}{2} - x = 12 - \frac{3}{2}$$
$$-x = 10\frac{1}{2}$$
$$x = -10\frac{1}{2}$$

In some cases, solving for x (or y) requires that you either multiply or divide both sides of the equation by the same term. What follows are two examples.

Multiplying both sides by the same number:

$$\frac{x}{2} = 14$$
$$2 \cdot \frac{x}{2} = 14 \cdot 2$$
$$x = 28$$

Dividing both sides by the same number:

$$3y = 18$$
$$\frac{3y}{3} = \frac{18}{3}$$
$$y = 6$$

The first system isolates x by multiplying both sides by 2. The second system isolates y by dividing both sides by 3. If the variable appears on both sides of the equation, first perform whatever operation is required to position the variable on just one side—either the left or the right. The next system positions both x-terms on the left side by subtracting $2x$ from both sides:

$$16 - x = 9 + 2x$$
$$16 - x - 2x = 9 + 2x - 2x$$
$$16 - 3x = 9$$

Now that x appears on just one side, the next step is to isolate it by subtracting 16 from both sides, and then dividing both sides by –3:

$$16 - 3x = 9$$
$$16 - 3x - 16 = 9 - 16$$
$$-3x = -7$$
$$\frac{-3x}{-3} = \frac{-7}{-3}$$
$$x = \frac{7}{3}$$

Sometimes, you have to multiply a number by each of the values in parentheses when solving equations. You should usually carry out that step first, as shown in the following example.

EXAMPLE

Solve $2(x + 1) = -10$.

Solution

First use the distributive property to eliminate the parentheses:

$$2(x+1)=-10$$
$$2x+2=-10$$

Next, subtract 2 from each side:

$$2x+2-2=-10-2$$
$$2x=-12$$

Now simplify by dividing each side by 2:

$$\frac{2x}{2}=\frac{-12}{2}$$
$$x=-6$$

Simplifying and Combining Radical Expressions

For the ACCUPLACER, you should know the rules for simplifying and combining radical expressions. Look for the possibility of simplifying radicals by moving what's under the radical sign to the outside of the sign. Check inside square-root radicals for perfect squares, which are factors that are squares of nice tidy numbers or other terms. The same advice applies to perfect cubes, and so on.

Study the following three examples:

$$\sqrt{4a^2} = 2a$$

4 and a^2 are both perfect squares. Therefore, you can remove them from under the radical sign and change each one to its square root.

$$\sqrt[3]{27a^6} = 3a^2$$

27 and a^6 are both perfect cubes. Therefore, you can remove them from under the radical sign and change each one to its cube root.

$$\sqrt{8a^3} = \sqrt{(4)(2)a^3} = 2a\sqrt{2a}$$

8 and a^3 both contain perfect-square factors; remove the perfect squares from under the radical sign and change each one to its square root.

The rules for combining terms that include radicals are quite similar to those for exponents. Keep the following two rules in mind; one applies to addition and subtraction, while the other applies to multiplication and division. Each rule is followed by key examples.

RULE 1 (ADDITION AND SUBTRACTION)

If a term under a radical is being added to or subtracted from a term under a different radical, you cannot combine the two terms under the same radical.

$$\sqrt{x} + \sqrt{y} \neq \sqrt{x+y}$$

$$\sqrt{x} - \sqrt{y} \neq \sqrt{x-y}$$

$$\sqrt{x} + \sqrt{x} = 2\sqrt{x} \text{ not } \sqrt{2x}$$

RULE 2 (MULTIPLICATION AND DIVISION)

Terms under different radicals can be combined under a common radical if one term is multiplied or divided by the other, but only if the radical is the same.

$$\sqrt{x}\sqrt{x} = \left(\sqrt{x}\right)^2, \text{ or } x$$

$$\sqrt{x}\sqrt{y} = \sqrt{xy}$$

$$\frac{\sqrt{x}}{\sqrt{y}} = \sqrt{\frac{x}{y}}$$

$$\sqrt[3]{x}\sqrt{x} = ? \text{ (cannot be further simplified)}$$

Absolute Value Equations

Remember that absolute value always has the effect of removing a negative from the number inside the absolute value sign. So, not only does |5| = 5, but |–5| = 5 too.

Think of this relationship when you see an equation like this one:

$$|x| = 5$$

You can place 5 or –5 in the place of x to make this equation true. The equation $|x| = 5$ has two solutions. The equation is true if $x = 5$ or if $x = -5$.

Let's look at solving an absolute value equation problem.

EXAMPLE

What are the values for x that make the equation true?

$$|2x - 3| = 11$$

Solution

Step 1: Solve for the positive value.

If the value inside the absolute value is 11, then the equation will be true. To find x, we set $2x - 3$ equal to 11 and solve:

$$2x - 3 = 11$$
$$2x - 3 + 3 = 11 + 3$$
$$2x = 14$$
$$\frac{2x}{2} = \frac{14}{2}$$
$$x = 7$$

This is one of the solutions.

Step 2: Solve for the negative value.

If the value inside the absolute value is –11, then the equation will still be true because the absolute value will cancel the negative sign. To find x, set $2x - 3$ equal to –11 and solve:

$$2x - 3 = -11$$
$$2x - 3 + 3 = -11 + 3$$
$$2x = -8$$
$$\frac{2x}{2} = \frac{-8}{2}$$
$$x = -4$$

This is also a solution. Since both of our solutions work, we report them both (in either order):

$$x = -4 \text{ and } 7$$

Solving Algebraic Inequalities

You solve algebraic inequalities in the same manner as equations. Isolate the variable on one side of the equation, factoring and canceling wherever possible. However, one important rule distinguishes inequalities from equations.

RULE

Whenever you multiply or divide by a negative number, you must reverse the inequality symbol. Expressed in symbolic form: if $a > b$, then $-a < -b$.

The following simple example demonstrates this important rule.

$$12 - 4x < 8$$
(original inequality)

$$-4x < -4$$
(subtract 12 from both sides; inequality unchanged)

$$x > 1$$
(both sides divided by –4; inequality reversed)

Here are some additional rules for dealing with algebraic inequalities.

- Adding or subtracting unequal quantities to (or from) equal quantities:

    If $a > b$, then $c + a > c + b$

- Adding unequal quantities to unequal quantities:

    If $a > b$, and if $c > d$, then $a + c > b + d$

- Comparing three unequal quantities:

    If $a > b$, and if $b > c$, then $a > c$

- Combining the same **positive** quantity with unequal quantities by multiplication or division:

    If $a > b$, and if $x > 0$, then $xa > xb$

    If $a > b$, and if $x > 0$, then $\dfrac{a}{x} > \dfrac{b}{x}$

    If $a > b$, and if $x > 0$, then $\dfrac{x}{a} < \dfrac{x}{b}$

- Combining the same **negative** quantity with unequal quantities by multiplication or division:

    If $a > b$, and if $x < 0$, then $xa < xb$

    If $a > b$, and if $x < 0$, then $\dfrac{a}{x} < \dfrac{b}{x}$

    If $a > b$, and if $x < 0$, then $\dfrac{x}{a} > \dfrac{x}{b}$

Linear Equations in Two Variables

In the preceding section, you examined linear equations in one variable only. Now we will consider linear equations in two variables (x and y) of the form $Ax + By = C$, where A, B, and C are real numbers.

The left side of the equation ($Ax + By$) is called a linear combination of x and y. Before, you were able to find the value of the variable by isolating it on one side of the equation. This doesn't work, however, for a linear equation in two (or more) different variables. Consider the following equation, which contains two variables:

$$x + 3 = y + 1$$

The value of x is dependent on the value of y. Similarly, the value of y depends on the value of x. Without more information about either x or y, you simply cannot find the other value. However, you can express x in terms of y, and you can express y in terms of x:

$$x = y - 2$$

$$y = x + 2$$

The two equations previously shown are really the same. You can't solve it because it contains two variables. Let's look at a more complex example:

$$4x - 9 = \frac{3}{2}y$$

Solve for x in terms of y:

$$4x = \frac{3}{2}y + 9$$

$$x = \frac{3}{8}y + \frac{9}{4}$$

Solve for y in terms of x:

$$\frac{4x-9}{\frac{3}{2}} = y$$

$$\frac{2}{3}(4x-9) = y$$

$$\frac{8}{3}x - 6 = y$$

Systems of Equations

A system of equations is a set of two or more (usually just two) equations that share a set of variables.

Here's an example of a system of equations:

$$2y + 7x = 24$$

$$y + 3x = 12$$

The solution to a system of equations with two variables is an ordered pair of numbers. The ordered pair is a solution to **both** equations in the system.

For example, the solution to the system of equations above is (0, 12). With ordered pairs, the first number is the value for x and the second is the value for y. By substituting these numbers for the variables into both equations, you can check to make sure they work:

$$2(12) + 7(0) \rightarrow 24 + 0 = 24$$

$$12 + 3(0) \rightarrow 12 + 0 = 12$$

Given a system of equations, there are two different methods for finding the values of the two variables: the substitution method and the elimination method.

The Substitution Method

To solve a system of two equations using the substitution method, follow these steps (we'll use x and y here):

1. In *either* equation, isolate one variable (x) on one side.
2. Substitute the expression that equals x in place of x in the other equation.
3. Solve that equation for y.
4. Now that you know the value of y, plug it into either equation to find the value of x.

Consider these two equations:

Equation A: $x = 4y$

Equation B: $x - y = 1$

In equation B, substitute $4y$ for x, and then solve for y:

$$4y - y = 1$$

$$3y = 1$$

$$y = \frac{1}{3}$$

To find x, substitute $\frac{1}{3}$ for y into either equation. The value of x will be the same for both.

Equation A: $x = 4\left(\frac{1}{3}\right) = \frac{4}{3}$

Equation B: $x - \frac{1}{3} = 1; x = \frac{4}{3}$

The Elimination Method

Another way to solve for two variables in a system of two equations is with the elimination method, sometimes also referred to as the addition-subtraction method. Here are the steps:

1. "Line up" the two equations by listing the same variables and other terms in the same order. Place one equation above the other.
2. Make the coefficient of *either* variable the same in both equations (you can disregard the sign) by multiplying every term in one of the equations.
3. Add the two equations (work down to a sum for each term), or subtract one equation from the other, to eliminate one variable.

To learn more about solving systems of equations, scan this QR code.

Consider these two equations:

Equation A: $x = 3 + 3y$

Equation B: $2x + y = 4$

In equation A, subtract $3y$ from both sides so that all terms in the two equations "line up":

Equation A: $x - 3y = 3$

Equation B: $2x + y = 4$

To solve for y, multiply each term in Equation A by 2 so that the x-coefficient is the same in both equations:

Equation A: $2x - 6y = 6$

Equation B: $2x + y = 4$

Subtract Equation B from Equation A, thereby eliminating x, and then isolate y on one side of the equation:

$$\begin{aligned} 2x - 6y &= 6 \\ \underline{-2x - y} &= \underline{-4} \\ 0x - 7y &= 2 \\ -7y &= 2 \\ y &= -\frac{2}{7} \end{aligned}$$

Then, substitute that solution into one of the equations and solve for the value of the other variable.

Graphing

Even though graphing typically falls under the category of coordinate geometry, we'll look at the principles here to prepare you for a review of graphing linear algebraic equations.

Graphing Basics

To start, let's familiarize you with the coordinate plane. The coordinate plane (or grid) is divided into four sections. Each section is called a quadrant. The two number lines that divide the grid into quadrants are called the x-axis (the horizontal axis) and the y-axis (the vertical axis). The center of the grid, where the two axes meet, is called the origin. Any point on the plane has two coordinates that indicate its location relative to the axes. The points that are drawn on the grid

are identified by ordered pairs. In ordered pairs, the x-coordinate is always written first. The ordered pair for the origin, in the middle of the grid, is (0, 0).

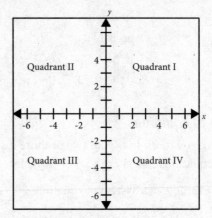

The quadrants of a grid are named in counter-clockwise order, beginning with the first quadrant in the upper right corner. For any point in the first quadrant, the coordinates are positive. The quadrant in the top left is called the second quadrant. For any point in the second quadrant, the x-coordinate is negative but the y-coordinate is positive. The quadrant in the lower left is called the third quadrant. In the third quadrant, both coordinates are negative. The quadrant in the lower right is called the fourth quadrant, and in the fourth quadrant, the x-coordinate is positive, and the y-coordinate is negative.

On the following graph, the x-coordinate of point A is 3. The y-coordinate of point A is 2. The coordinates of point A are given by the ordered pair (3, 2). Point B has coordinates (–1, 4). Point C has coordinates (–4, –3). Point D has coordinates (2, –3).

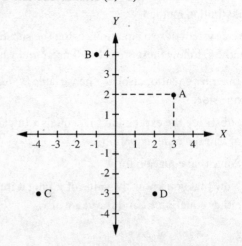

To graph a point whose coordinates are given, first locate the *x*-coordinate on the *x*-axis, then from that position, move vertically the number of spaces indicated by the *y*-coordinate.

Equations of Lines and Graphing

In a coordinate plane, a line can be defined by the equation $y = mx + b$. This is called the slope-intercept form. In this equation, you can see the following:

- The variable *m* as the slope of the line (its steepness).
- The variable *b* as the line's *y*-intercept (where the line crosses the *y*-axis).
- The variables *x* and *y*, which are the coordinates of any point on the line. Any (*x*, *y*) pair defining a point on the line can substitute for the variables *x* and *y*.

For a line with an equation of $y = 3x + 2$, the line has a positive slope of 3 and a *y*-intercept of 2. Let's review these terms and learn more about working with the slope-intercept equation.

Slope

Slope is a ratio that describes the steepness of a line.

$$\text{slope } (m) = \frac{\text{rise}}{\text{run}}$$

$$= \frac{\text{vertical change}}{\text{horizontal change}}$$

$$= \frac{\text{change in } y}{\text{change in } x}$$

To find the slope of a line from a graph, count the spaces from one point on the line to another.

Example:

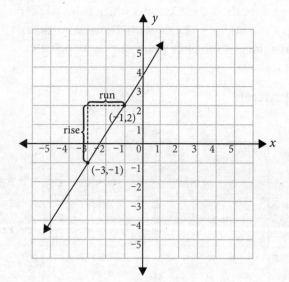

On the graph shown, count the vertical spaces and the horizontal spaces from (−3, −1) to (−1, 2).

$$\text{Slope} = \frac{\text{vertical change}}{\text{horizontal change}} = \frac{3}{2}$$

The slope of the line is $\frac{3}{2}$.

You can also calculate slope without a graph if you know two points on a line. You can find the slope of the line using the formula for slope (*m*):

$$m = \frac{y_2 - y_1}{x_2 - x_1}$$

If a line passes through points (−3, −1) and (−1, 2), let (x_1, y_1) be (−3, −1) and (x_2, y_2) be (−1, 2). Plug these values into the slope formula:

$$m = \frac{y_2 - y_1}{x_2 - x_1}$$

$$= \frac{2 - (-1)}{-1 - (-3)}$$

$$= \frac{2 + 1}{-1 + 3}$$

$$= \frac{3}{2}$$

Therefore, the slope of the line is $\frac{3}{2}$.

x	y
0	1
1	3
2	5
3	7
4	9

Keep in mind that when you plug points into the slope formula, it doesn't matter which point you name (x_1, y_1) and (x_2, y_2). The slope will be the same either way as long as you place your values appropriately in the formula.

Y-Intercepts

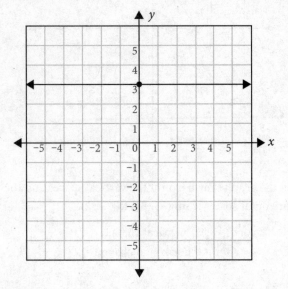

When those points are plotted, you see the following graph.

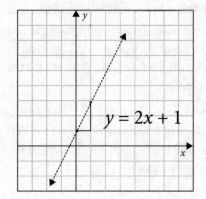

The y-intercept of a line is the y-coordinate of the point where the line crosses the y-axis. The coordinates of the y-intercept are $(0, y)$. The y-intercept of the line shown is 3, since the line crosses the y-axis at $(0, 3)$.

In any set of points on a line, you can find the y-intercept by looking for the point with an x-coordinate of 0. Each straight line crosses the y-axis only one time, so there can only be one point with an x-coordinate of 0. This point is the y-intercept.

Graphing a Line in Slope-Intercept Form

Take a look at the following equation:

$$y = 2x + 1$$

If you were to create a table to represent the points on that line, you can start with $x = 0$ as you know the corresponding y value will be 1 (since it is the y-intercept). From there, you can use the slope value in the equation to determine each successive y value. With a slope of two, each successive point on the line will rise 2 and run 1, resulting in the following table.

Graphing a Linear Equation

Another way to graph a line is to begin by rewriting the equation in slope-intercept form ($y = mx + b$). Notice that an equation written in slope-intercept form will have the y alone in the equation, so getting the y alone will be the first step. Imagine we want to graph the equation $x - 3y = 6$. To do this, we will need to subtract x from both sides of the equation, then divide by 3, as shown:

$$x - 3y = 6$$
$$-3y = -x + 6$$
$$y = \frac{1}{3}x - 2$$

Now we can simply graph the line $y = \frac{1}{3}x - 2$ the way we did previously. Start by plotting the y-intercept at $(0, -2)$. Then, rise 1 and run 3 and plot another point. Draw a straight line through the points to complete the graph.

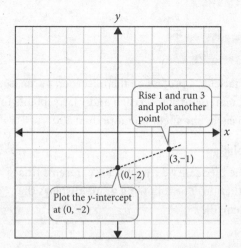

Determining Linear Equations from Slope and Points

To write the slope-intercept equation of a line when slope (m) and one point are given, you need to find the y-intercept (b).

Given the slope and a point on the line, plug these values into the slope-intercept equation and solve for b.

First, substitute the slope for m. Next, plug the coordinates of the given point into the equation for x and y. Then, solve the equation for b. Once you find b, substitute it into the equation with m.

Write the equation of the line that has a slope of −2 and passes through point (1, 5).

Solution

Start with the slope-intercept equation, and substitute in the values $m = -2$, $x = 1$, and $y = 5$. Then, solve for b.

$$y = mx + b$$
$$5 = -2(1) + b$$
$$5 = -2 + b$$
$$5 + 2 = b$$
$$7 = b$$

The slope-intercept form of the equation of the line is $y = -2x + 7$.

Parallel Lines

Two lines in the same plane are parallel if they do not intersect. The slopes of lines can be used to determine whether two lines are parallel. Two lines are parallel if they have the same slope, m.

Let's look at an example. The following graph displays the equations $y = \frac{1}{2}x + 2$ and $y = \frac{1}{2}x - 3$.

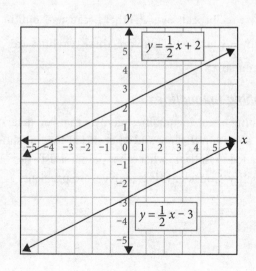

Both equations are written in the slope-intercept form, $y = mx + b$. The slope, m, of both lines is $\frac{1}{2}$. Because these two lines have the same slope, they are parallel lines.

Perpendicular Lines

Two lines are perpendicular if they intersect to form right angles. Two lines are perpendicular if their slopes are negative reciprocals of each other. This means that the product of the slopes equals −1.

For example, look at the graphs of equations $y = -2x + 2$ and $y = \frac{1}{2}x - 3$:

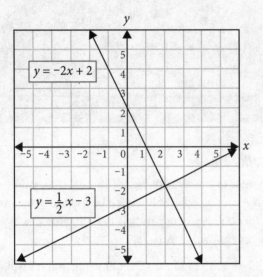

These two lines have slopes of −2 and $\frac{1}{2}$. The slopes are negative reciprocals of each other because −2 multiplied by $\frac{1}{2}$ equals −1. Therefore, these two lines are perpendicular.

Graphing Inequalities

Graphing linear inequalities requires that you determine points on the line and what side of the line should be shaded to indicate what other points satisfy the inequality. Consider this example word problem.

Charlene, a professional landscaper, purchased x small plants for $3 each and y large plants for $5 each. She spent no more than $30.

Solution

The inequality $3x + 5y \leq 30$ represents this situation. The following graph displays the inequality.

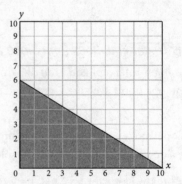

Since Charlene cannot purchase a negative number of plants, only positive values for x and y are shown. Any point in the shaded area or on the line represents a reasonable solution for the inequality.

Here's a review of how to graph inequalities with two variables, using $3x + 5y \leq 30$ as an example.

1. Graph the line for the equation $3x + 5y = 30$. Find the y-intercept by substituting 0 for x in the equation:

$$3(0) + 5y = 30$$
$$5y = 30$$
$$y = 6$$

Now find the x-intercept:

$$3x + 5(0) = 30$$
$$3x = 30$$
$$x = 10$$

2. Plot (0, 6) and (10, 0), and the line connecting them. Use a solid line as points along the line still satisfy the inequality (less than or equal to). If the inequality sign were less than or greater than, the line would be dashed.

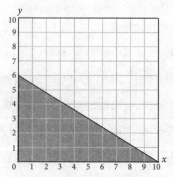

3. Choose a test point that is not on the line to decide which side of the line is shaded. If the values of the point make the inequality true, then shade the side the point is on. For example, using (0, 0) and substituting:

$$3(0) + 5(0) \le 30$$
$$0 \le 30$$

4. The point (0, 0) makes the inequality true. So, shade the side of the line containing this point.

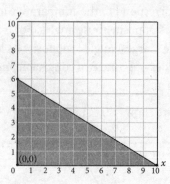

5. The points (3, 2), (5, 3), and (4, 5) are plotted on the graph.

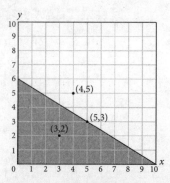

- The point (3, 2) is in the shaded region and the point (5, 3) is on the line. These points represent a reasonable number of small and large plants that the landscaper could have purchased.
- The point (4, 5) is not in the shaded region. It does not represent a reasonable solution.

Basic Geometry

You have likely already encountered the terms *point*, *line*, *line segment*, *ray*, and *angle* throughout your education. We will focus on the terminology that offers specificity to these terms in this section.

Angles

Angles are classified according to their "size" as measured using degrees. The notation m∠A is used to denote the measure of angle *A*. The following table details some basic angle terminology.

ANGLE TERMINOLOGY	
Term	**Definition**
Acute Angle	An angle with measure between 0 and 90 degrees
Right Angle	An angle with measure of 90 degrees
Obtuse Angle	An angle with measure between 90 and 180 degrees
Straight Angle	An angle with a measure of 180 degrees (a straight line)
Complementary Angles	Two angles with measures that sum to 90 degrees
Supplementary Angles	Two angles with measures that sum to 180 degrees
Congruent Angles	Two angles with the same measure

The relationships between pairs of angles are also important to recognize. We've identified these relationships in the following diagram that shows two parallel lines intersected by a transversal.

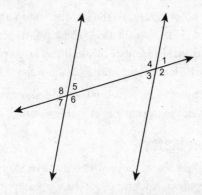

Term	Examples from Diagram
Vertical Angles	∠1 and ∠3; ∠2 and ∠4; ∠5 and ∠7; ∠6 and ∠8
Adjacent Angles	∠1 and ∠2; ∠3 and ∠4; ∠5 and ∠6; ∠7 and ∠8
Corresponding Angles	∠1 and ∠5; ∠2 and ∠6; ∠4 and ∠8; ∠3 and ∠7
Alternate Interior Angles	∠4 and ∠6; ∠3 and ∠5
Alternate Exterior Angles	∠2 and ∠8; ∠1 and ∠7

Polygons

Polygons include all two-dimensional figures formed only by line segments. Remember these two reciprocal rules about polygons:

1. If all angles of a polygon are congruent (equal in degree measure), then all sides are congruent (equal in length).

2. If all sides of a polygon are congruent (equal in length), then all angles are congruent (equal in degree measure).

A polygon in which all sides are congruent and all angles are congruent is called a regular polygon.

You can use the following formula to determine the sum of all interior angles of *any* polygon with angles that each measure less than 180° (*n* = number of sides):

$$(n - 2)(180°) = \text{sum of interior angles}$$

For regular polygons, the average angle size is also the size of every angle. But for *any* polygon (except for those with an angle exceeding 180°), you can find the average angle size by dividing the sum of the angles by the number of sides. One way to shortcut the math is to memorize the angle sums and averages for polygons with three to eight sides:

3 sides: $(3 - 2)(180°) = 180° \div 3 = 60°$

4 sides: $(4 - 2)(180°) = 360° \div 4 = 90°$

5 sides: $(5 - 2)(180°) = 540° \div 5 = 108°$

6 sides: $(6 - 2)(180°) = 720° \div 6 = 120°$

7 sides: $(7 - 2)(180°) = 900° \div 7 = 129°$

8 sides: $(8 - 2)(180°) = 1{,}080° \div 8 = 135°$

Triangles

A triangle is a three-sided shape. All triangles, regardless of shape or size, share the following properties:

- **Length of the sides:** Each side is shorter than the sum of the lengths of the other two sides.

- **Angle measures:** The measures of the three interior angles total 180°.

- **Angles and opposite sides:** Comparative angle sizes correspond to the comparative lengths of the sides opposite those angles. For example, a triangle's largest angle is opposite its longest side. (The sides opposite two congruent angles are also congruent.)

The next figure shows three particular types of triangles.

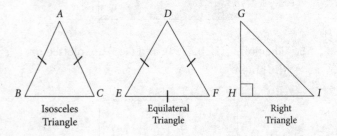

An isosceles triangle is one in which two sides (and two angles) are congruent. In the figure shown, angle *B* and angle *C* are congruent, and the sides opposite those two angles, *AB* and *AC*, are congruent. In an equilateral triangle, all three angles are congruent, and all three sides are congruent. In a right triangle, one angle is a right angle, and the other two angles are acute angles. The longest side of a right triangle (in this case, *GI*) is called the hypotenuse.

Right Triangles and the Pythagorean Theorem

In a right triangle, one angle measures 90° and each of the other two angles measures less than 90°. The Pythagorean theorem involves the relationship among the sides of any right triangle and can be expressed by the equation $a^2 + b^2 = c^2$. As shown in the next figure, the letters *a* and *b* represent the lengths of the two legs (the two shortest sides) that form the right angle, and *c* is the length of the hypotenuse (the longest side, opposite the right angle).

Pythagorean theorem: $a^2 + b^2 = c^2$

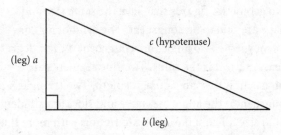

For any right triangle, if you know the length of two sides, you can determine the length of the third side by applying the Pythagorean theorem.

Quadrilaterals

A quadrilateral is a figure in a plane with four sides, each of which is a line segment. There are several common quadrilaterals (e.g., square, rectangle, parallelogram, rhombus, trapezoid) that arise in solving practical problems. As four-sided shapes, each has internal angle measures of 360 degrees. See the following table for a comparison of properties of common quadrilaterals.

COMMON QUADRILATERALS					
Property	Rectangle	Square	Parallelogram	Rhombus	Trapezoid
All sides are equal length		✔		✔	
Opposite sides are equal length	✔	✔	✔	✔	(nonparallel sides in isosceles trapezoid)
Opposite sides are parallel	✔	✔	✔	✔	(only the bases)
All angles are equal	✔	✔			
Opposite angles are equal	✔	✔	✔	✔	
Sum of two adjacent angles is 180 degrees	✔	✔	✔	✔	(base and leg angles)
Diagonals bisect	✔	✔	✔	✔	
Diagonals are perpendicular		✔		✔	

Congruency and Similarity

Two geometric figures that have the same size and shape are said to be congruent. The symbol for congruency is ≅. Two angles are congruent if their degree measure (size) is the same. Two line segments are congruent if they are equal in length. Two triangles are congruent if the angle measures and sides are all identical in size. (The same applies to figures with more than three sides.)

If a two-dimensional geometric figure, such as a triangle or rectangle, has exactly the same shape as another one, then the two figures are similar. Similar figures share the same angle measures, and their sides are proportionate (though not the same length).

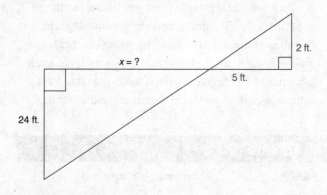

These two triangles are similar. They share an angle and both have right angles. Thus, their third angles must be equal. Because their angles are equal, their sides must be proportional. The ratio 2:5 is the same as 24:x. By creating a proportion, you can solve for x and find the missing side length as 60 ft.

Circles

Let's review some key terms related to the geometry of circles before exploring some additional characteristics of the shape.

- **Circumference:** The distance around the circle (the same as *perimeter*, but the word *circumference* applies only to circles, ovals, and other curved figures)
- **Radius:** The distance from a circle's center to any point along the circle's circumference, often represented by r

- **Diameter:** The greatest distance from one point to another on the circle's circumference (twice the length of the radius) through the center point of the circle, often represented by d
- **Chord:** A line segment connecting two points on the circle's circumference (a circle's longest possible chord is its diameter, passing through the circle's center)
- **Pi (π):** This Greek letter represents the ratio between a circle's circumference and its diameter; for all circles, the circumference divided by the diameter is π, approximated as 3.14 or $\frac{22}{7}$.

As previously noted, a circle's diameter is twice the length of its radius. The next figure shows a circle with radius 6 and diameter 12.

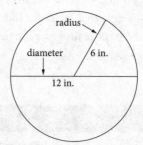

For most questions related to circles, you'll apply one, or possibly both, of two basic formulas involving circles (r = radius, d = diameter):

$$\text{Circumference} = 2\pi r, \text{ or } \pi d$$

$$\text{Area} = \pi r^2$$

With the circumference and area formulas, all you need is one value—area, circumference, diameter, or radius—and you can determine all the others. Based on the circle shown, which has a diameter of 12:

$$\text{Radius} = 6$$

$$\text{Circumference} = 12\pi$$

$$\text{Area} = \pi(6)^2 = 36\pi$$

In a coordinate plane, a circle can be graphed with the following equation:

$$(x - h)^2 + (y - k)^2 = r^2$$

where (h, k) is the coordinate of the circle's center and r is the radius.

Perimeter and Area of Planar Regions

The perimeter of a region in the plane is the "distance around." The area of a region in the plane is the number of unit squares needed to cover the shape. The following are some standard perimeter and area formulas with which you should be familiar.

PERIMETER AND AREA FORMULAS			
Region	**Illustration**	**Perimeter Formula**	**Area Formula**
Square		$P = 4s$	$A = s^2$
Rectangle		$P = 2l + 2w$	$A = l \times w$
Triangle		Sum the three lengths of the triangle.	$A = \frac{1}{2} b \cdot h$
Circle		The perimeter of a circle is called the circumference; it's found with two common expressions: $C = 2\pi r = \pi d$	$A = \pi r^2$
Arcs and Sectors of Circles		Arc length: $P = \left(\dfrac{\theta}{360°} \right) \cdot 2\pi r$	Sector area: $A = \left(\dfrac{\theta}{360°} \right) \cdot \pi r^2$

Surface Area and Volume of Solids

Two measures of interest for three-dimensional solids are surface area and volume. Conceptually, to compute the surface area of a solid, the solid is dissected and flattened out so that it can be visualized as a combination of recognizable figures whose areas can be computed using known formulas. The volume of a solid in space is the number of unit cubes needed to fill it. The following table details formulas for the surface area and volume of some common solids.

SURFACE AREA AND VOLUME FORMULAS			
Solid	**Illustration**	**Surface Area Formula**	**Volume Formula**
Cube		$SA = 6e^2$	$V = e^3$
Rectangular Prism		$SA = 2(lw + lh + wh)$	$V = lwh$
Circular Cone		$SA = \pi r^2 + \pi r \sqrt{r^2 + h^2}$	$V = \dfrac{1}{3}\pi r^2 h$
Circular Cylinder		$SA = 2\pi r^2 + 2\pi rh$	$V = \pi r^2 h$
Sphere		$SA = 4\pi r^2$	$V = \dfrac{4}{3}\pi r^3$

Coordinate Geometry

You saw elements of coordinate geometry in the algebra section earlier. Now, let's examine some more specific concepts that are likely to arise on ACCUPLACER.

Finding the Distance Between Two Points

Some questions require you to find the lengths of segments graphed on the axes. The length of a segment is the distance between its endpoints. Distance is always a positive quantity, even if one or more of the coordinates are negative.

If the endpoints of a line segment on a graph have the same *x*- or *y*-coordinates, you can determine the length of the segment just by looking at the graph and counting the units. In the next grid, for example, the distance between points A (2, 3) and B (7, 3) is 5. The distance between points C (2, 1) and D (2, –4) is also 5.

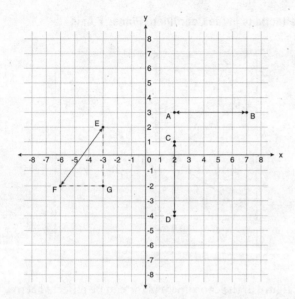

If you are asked to find the distance between two points that are not directly horizontal or vertical from each other, you can use the Pythagorean theorem. For example, to find the distance between points E and F on the preceding grid, follow these steps:

- Draw a right triangle in which line EF is the hypotenuse (as shown by the broken lines on the preceding grid).
- Determine the distance between E and G. That distance is 4. This is the length of one leg of right triangle EFG.
- Determine the distance between F and G. That distance is 3. This is the length of the other leg of a right triangle EFG.

Apply the Pythagorean theorem to find the hypotenuse of ΔEFG, which is the distance between E and F:

$$4^2 + 3^2 = c^2$$
$$16 + 9 = c^2$$
$$5 = c$$

In applying the Pythagorean theorem to the coordinate grid, you may want to use the formula for determining the distance between two points, which is a more specific way of expressing the theorem.

The distance formula is $\sqrt{(x_2 - x_1)^2 + (y_2 - y_1)^2}$, where the two points are (x_1, y_1) and (x_2, y_2).

Apply this formula to the preceding example, and you obtain the same result:

$$\sqrt{(-6 - (-3))^2 + (-2 - 2)^2}$$
$$= \sqrt{(-3)^2 + (-4)^2}$$
$$= \sqrt{9 + 16}$$
$$= \sqrt{25}$$
$$= 5$$

Transformations

A transformation is a change in the position, shape, or size of a figure. The transformed figure is called the image of the original figure. Transformations include the following:

- Translations (slides)
- Reflections (flips)
- Rotations (turns)
- Dilations (enlargement or reduction)

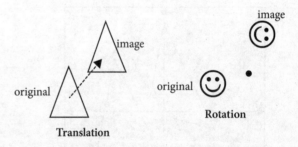

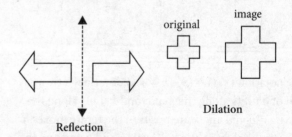

Translations

A translation, or slide, moves every point of a figure the same distance in the same direction. The object changes its location but not its orientation. That is, it does not turn or flip. The translated figure is congruent with the original.

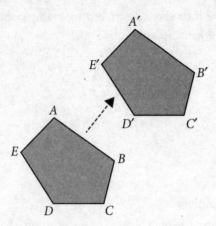

The translation in the figure maps pentagon *ABCDE* onto its image *A'B'C'D'E'*. The point *A'* is the image of point *A*. *A'* is read "A prime."

Translations in the Coordinate Plane

When a translation is applied to a figure in the coordinate plane, the *x*- and *y*-coordinates of every point in the figure each change by a fixed number of units. The resulting figure is congruent with the original.

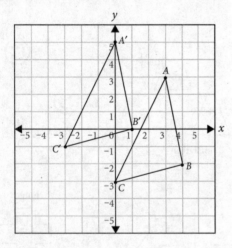

The notation $(x, y) \rightarrow (x + h, y + k)$ describes a translation of *h* units along the *x*-axis and *k* units along the *y*-axis. When *h* and *k* are positive, the figure moves *h* units to the right in the *x*-direction and *k* units up in the *y*-direction.

The figure shows a translation of $\triangle ABC$ to its image $\triangle A'B'C'$ according to the rule $(x, y) \rightarrow (x - 3, y + 2)$. Note that each point in the triangle moves 3 units to the left and 2 units up.

Reflections in the Coordinate Plane: *Y*-Axis

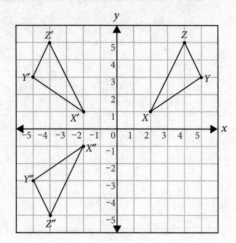

A figure in the coordinate plane can be reflected across any line.

A reflection across the *y*-axis is represented by the rule:

$$(x, y) \rightarrow (-x, y)$$

$\triangle X'Y'Z'$ is the image of $\triangle XYZ$ after a reflection across the *y*-axis. The *y*-coordinate of each point in the image is the same as the *y*-coordinate of each point in the original figure. The *x*-coordinates are opposites.

Note that the changes in the coordinates of the vertices of $\triangle XYZ$ follow the rule above:

$$X (2, 1) \rightarrow X' (-2, 1)$$

$$Y (5, 3) \rightarrow Y' (-5, 3)$$

$$Z (4, 5) \rightarrow Z' (-4, 5)$$

Reflections in the Coordinate Plane: *X*-Axis

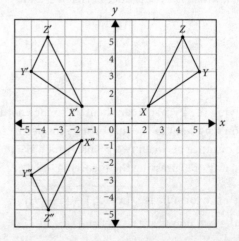

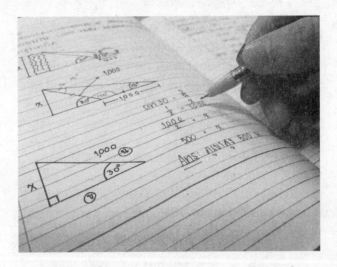

A reflection across the *x*-axis is represented by the rule:

$$(x, y) \rightarrow (x, -y)$$

$\Delta X''Y''Z''$ is the image of $\Delta X'Y'Z'$ after a reflection across the *x*-axis.

The *x*-coordinate of each point in $\Delta X''Y''Z''$ is the same as the *x*-coordinate of each point in $\Delta X'Y'Z'$.

The *y*-coordinates are opposites.

Rotations

A rotation, or turn, is a congruent transformation in which every point of an object rotates the same number of degrees about a fixed center point. The center point may be a point in the figure or a point outside the figure and is called the center of rotation.

A rotation is defined by:

- its center of rotation.
- the number of degrees the figure is turned.
- the direction of the turn (clockwise or counterclockwise).

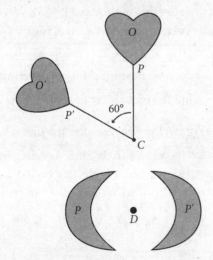

The heart in the figure shown is rotated 60° counterclockwise about point *C*. The moon could be described by a 180° rotation, either clockwise or counterclockwise, about point *D*.

Dilations

A dilation is a nonrigid transformation, meaning that it is not congruent. However, the figures in a dilation will be similar. In a dilation, a figure will either stretch (grow larger) or shrink (grow smaller) proportionally, meaning it maintains its existing shape and proportions. A dilation requires the following:

- a scale factor
- a fixed point called a center of dilation

The center of dilation determines the fixed point around which shrinking or stretching occurs, and the scale factor indicates the degree of stretching or shrinking. The three square figures that follow show the same figure stretching by 100% each time it dilates from left to right, which is the scale factor. Each dilation happens around the center of dilation in the middle of the figure.

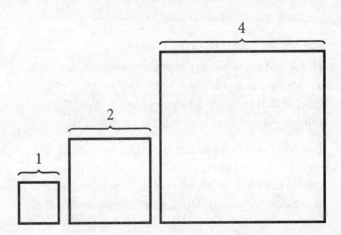

Probability, Sets, and Statistics

The ACCUPLACER can ask you to collect, describe, and analyze quantitative data in order to draw conclusions. The test will assess multiple skills to this end by asking you to work with probability, sets, and statistics.

Probability

Probability refers to the likelihood of an event occurring (or not occurring). By definition, probability ranges from 0 to 1. Probability is never negative, and it is never greater than 1. Here's the basic formula for determining probability:

$$\text{Probability} = \frac{\text{desired outcomes}}{\text{total number of possible outcomes}}$$

Probability can be expressed as a fraction, a percent, or a decimal number. The greater the probability, the greater the fraction, percent, or decimal number.

Determining Probability (Single Event)

Probability plays an integral role in games of chance, including many casino games. In the throw of a single die, for example, the probability of rolling a 5 is "one in six," or $\frac{1}{6}$, or $16\frac{2}{3}$ %. Of course, the probability of rolling a certain other number is the same. A standard deck of 52 playing cards contains 12 face cards. The probability of selecting a face card from a full deck is $\frac{12}{52}$, or $\frac{3}{13}$. The probability of selecting a queen from a full deck is $\frac{4}{52}$, or $\frac{1}{13}$. To calculate the probability of an event NOT occurring, just subtract the probability of the event occurring from 1.

Determining Probability (Two Events)

To determine probability involving two or more events, it is important to distinguish probabilities involving independent events from an event that is dependent on another one.

Two events are independent if neither event affects the probability that the other will occur. The events may involve the random selection of one object from *each of two or more groups*. Alternatively, they may involve randomly selecting one object from a group, then *replacing* it and selecting again (as in a "second round" or "another turn" of a game).

In either scenario, to find the probability of two events BOTH occurring, multiply their individual probabilities together:

probability of event 1 occurring ×
probability of event 2 occurring
=
probability of both events occurring

For example, assume that you randomly select one letter from each of two sets: {A, B} and {C, D, E}. The probability of selecting A and C $= \frac{1}{2} \times \frac{1}{3} = \frac{1}{6}$.

To calculate the probability that two events will NOT BOTH occur, subtract the probability of both events occurring from 1.

Now let's look at dependent probability. Two distinct events might be related in that one event affects the probability of the other one occurring—for example, randomly selecting one object from a group, then selecting a second object from the same group without replacing the first selection. Removing one object from the group increases the odds of selecting any particular object from those that remain.

For example, assume that you randomly select one letter from the set {A, B, C, D}. Then, from the remaining three letters, you select another letter. What is the probability of selecting both A and B? To answer this question, you need to consider each of the two selections separately.

In the first selection, the probability of selecting either A or B is $\frac{2}{4}$. But the probability of selecting the second of the two is $\frac{1}{3}$. Why? Because after the first selection, only *three* letters remain from which to select. Since the question asks for the odds of selecting both A and B (as opposed to either one), multiply the two individual probabilities: $\frac{2}{4} \times \frac{1}{3} = \frac{2}{12}$, or $\frac{1}{6}$.

For a video on probability, scan this QR code.

The number of ways of selecting k objects from a group of n objects in which order does NOT matter is called the "number of combinations of n objects taken k at a time." The formula is as follows:

$$C(n,k) = \frac{n!}{k!(n-k)!}$$

Counting Principles

Determining the *total* number of possible outcomes in an experiment, whether tossing a coin 5 times, rolling a die twice, or randomly selecting colored balls from a bin, is an important step to assessing the likelihood, or chance, of getting each possible outcome. This kind of counting includes two main concepts: combinations and permutations.

A permutation of a set of objects is an arrangement of those objects in which each object is used once and only once. For example, if you have objects labeled A, B, C, D, and E, some permutations of these objects are ABCDE and DECBA. Any unique ordering of the letters produces a different permutation. The number of ways to arrange n objects in such a manner is $n!$. You can define $n!$ as:

$$n! = n \times (n-1) \times (n-2) \times \ldots \times 3 \times 2 \times 1$$

For instance, $4! = 4 \times 3 \times 2 \times 1$.

Sometimes, we want to arrange only *some* of the objects in a given set. For instance, say we had n letters, but we only wanted to arrange k of them. This is a "permutation of n objects taken k at a time." The number of such arrangements is written as:

$$P(n,k) = \frac{n!}{(n-k)!}$$

Sometimes, the order in which objects are arranged is not relevant, like when forming a committee of 4 people from a group of 10 people in which all committee members have the same influence, or when simply selecting 5 cards randomly from a standard deck of 52 cards. To determine the number of such selections, a combination is required.

EXAMPLE

In how many ways can 4 books from a collection of 7 be arranged on a shelf?

A. 120

B. 210

C. 720

D. 840

Solution

We wish to arrange 4 of the 7 books, so we must calculate $P(7, 4)$:

$$P(7,4) = \frac{7!}{(7-4)!}$$
$$= \frac{7!}{3!}$$
$$= \frac{7 \times 6 \times 5 \times 4 \times \cancel{3} \times \cancel{2} \times \cancel{1}}{\cancel{3} \times \cancel{2} \times \cancel{1}}$$
$$= 7 \times 6 \times 5 \times 4$$
$$= 840$$

This makes the correct answer D. There are 840 ways to arrange 4 of the 7 books.

Set Notation

A set is a collection of objects. The objects in a particular set are called the members or the elements of the set. In mathematics, sets are usually represented by capital letters, and their members are represented by lower case letters. Braces, { and }, are usually used to enclose the members of a set. Thus, the set A, which has members a, b, c, d, and e and no other members, can be written as A = {a, b, c, d, e}. Note that the order in which the elements of a set are listed is not important—the set {1, 2, 3} and the set {2, 3, 1} represent identical sets.

The symbol used to indicate that an element belongs to a particular set is ∈, and the symbol that indicates that an element does not belong to a set is ∉. Thus, if B = {2, 4, 6, 8}, we can say 6 ∈ B and 7 ∉ B. If a set is defined so that it does not contain any elements, it is called the empty set, or the null set, and can be written as { } or ∅.

The union of two sets A and B, written A ∪ B, is the set of all elements that are in either A or B. The intersection of two sets, indicated A ∩ B, is the set of all elements that are in both A and B. Thus, if A = {2, 4, 6, 8, 10} and B = {1, 2, 3, 4}, we have A ∪ B = {1, 2, 3, 4, 6, 8, 10} and A ∩ B = {2, 4}. If A ∩ B = ∅, then A and B are said to be disjoint.

Statistics

Statistics requires you to bring your knowledge of probability and sets together in order to work with and analyze data.

Calculating Measures of Center and Spread

A set of data values may be summarized using measures of center and/or measures of spread. Measures of center include mean, median, and mode and represent the center of the data. Measures of spread include range and standard deviation and represent how spread out the data values are within a data set.

The Arithmetic Mean

An average or arithmetic mean is a value that is computed by dividing the sum of a set of terms by the number of terms in the collection. To find the average (arithmetic mean) of a group of n numbers, simply add the numbers and divide by n. Consider the following examples.

EXAMPLE

Find the average (arithmetic mean) of 32, 50, and 47.

Solution

$$\frac{32 + 50 + 47}{3} = 43$$

The average (arithmetic mean) of three numbers is 43. If two of the numbers are 32 and 50, find the third number.

Solution

Using the definition of arithmetic mean, write the equation:

$$\frac{32 + 50 + x}{3} = 43$$
$$32 + 50 + x = 129$$
$$82 + x = 129$$
$$x = 47$$

Median and Mode

In order to find the median of a group of numbers, list the numbers in numerical order from smallest to largest. The median is the number in the middle. For example, the median of the numbers 3, 3, 5, 9, and 10 is 5. The median and the arithmetic mean are not the same. In this problem, for example, the arithmetic mean is 30 ÷ 5 = 6.

If there is an even number of numbers, the median is equal to the arithmetic mean of the two numbers in the middle. For example, to find the median of 3, 3, 5, 7, 9, and 10, note that the two middle numbers are 5 and 7. The median, then, is $\frac{5 + 7}{2} = 6$.

The mode of a group of numbers is simply the number that occurs most frequently. Therefore, the mode of the group of numbers 3, 3, 5, 7, 9, and 10 is 3. If all of the numbers in a group only appear once, then there is no mode. A data set can have more than one mode.

EXAMPLE

What is the arithmetic mean, the median, and the mode of the following group of eight numbers?

2, 7, 8, 9, 9, 9, 10, and 10

Solution

The sum of the eight numbers is 64, so the arithmetic mean is $64 \div 8 = 8$. Since this data set has an even number of data values, the median is the arithmetic mean of the two numbers in the middle. These numbers are both 9, so the median is $\frac{9+9}{2} = 9$. The mode is the number that occurs most often, which is also 9.

Range

The range, or the spread, of a data set is the difference between the greatest and least data values. To find the range of a set of data, first write the values in ascending order to make sure that you have found the least and greatest values. Then, subtract the least data value from the greatest data value.

EXAMPLE

Celia kept track of the average price of a gallon of gas over a period of 10 years. Her data is shown in the following table. What is the range in the average price of gas?

Year	Average price/gallon in US dollars
2006	2.00
2007	2.08
2008	2.44
2009	3.40
2010	2.85
2011	2.90
2012	3.50
2013	4.20
2014	3.80
2015	3.25

Solution

Write the data in order from least to greatest:

2.00. 2.08 2.44 2.85 2.90 3.25 3.40
3.50 3.80 4.20

Subtract the least value from the greatest value:

$4.20 - 2.00 = 2.20$

$2.20 is the range (or spread) of the data.

Graphing Data Sets

Numerical data sets can be visualized in various ways. Four common types of graphs are dot plots, histograms, box plots, and scatterplots. Let's take a look at each by illustrating the data set {1, 1, 1, 2, 3, 3, 6, 6, 6, 6, 6, 10} using a dot plot, histogram, and box plot.

Dot Plots

A dot plot is plot obtained by illustrating each member of a data set as a point above the appropriate position on a number line, as follows:

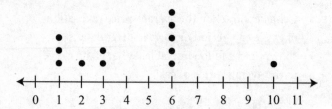

Histograms

In a histogram, bars appear above each value of the data set. The height of each bar represents the number of times that data value appears in the set. The appearance resembles a dot plot, but the bars replace the stacks of dots. The bars on a histogram always touch, may or may not appear on a number line, and will most often have labels that identify the horizontal (*x*) and vertical (*y*) axes.

Here is an example of a histogram:

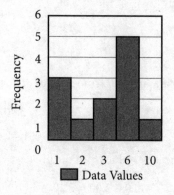

Box Plots

A box plot requires a bit more information to construct, but it tells you much more about the spread and center of a data set. Five numbers are needed to form a box plot:

- **Minimum:** This is the smallest number in the data set. Here, this number is 1.

- **First Quartile:** This is the 25th percentile, or number for which 25% of the data set is less than or equal to it. Assuming the data are arranged in increasing order, the position of the first quartile is obtained by dividing the number of values in the data set (here, 12) by 4. Doing so gives 3. So, the number in the third position from the left in the list of data is the first quartile. Here, this number is 1.

- **Median:** This is the 50th percentile. Assuming the data are arranged in increasing order, the position of the median is obtained by averaging the middle two data values since there is an even number of data in this set. (If there is an odd number of data values, it is the single value in the middle of the data set.) The middle two values are those in the 6th and 7th positions, namely 3 and 6. When you calculate the median, you get 4.5.

- **Third Quartile:** This is the 75th percentile. Assuming the data are arranged in increasing order, the position of the third quartile is obtained by dividing the number of values in the data set (here, 12) by 4 and then multiplying it by 3. Doing so gives 9. So, the number in the ninth position from the left in the list of data is the third quartile. Here, this number is 6.

- **Maximum:** This is the largest number in the data set. Here, this number is 10.

The box plot obtained is as follows:

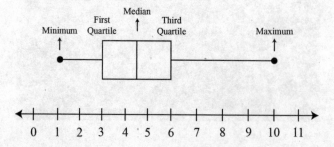

Scatterplots

A scatterplot is another type of visual presentation used to show relationships or trends in data. A scatterplot is a graph in which the *x*-axis represents the values of one variable and the *y*-axis represents the values of the other variable. Several values of one variable and the corresponding values of the other variable are measured and plotted on the graph.

If two variables have a relationship such that when one variable changes, the other changes in a predictable way, the two variables are correlated. There are typically three types of correlation: positive, negative, and no correlation.

- A **positive correlation** occurs when one variable increases and the other variable increases as well.

- A **negative correlation** occurs when one variable increases and the other decreases.

- **No correlation** occurs when there is no apparent relationship between the variables.

Generally, the more tightly packed the points are in a scatterplot, the stronger the relationship. If the data points rise from left to right, we say the relationship is positive, while if they fall from left to right, we say the trend is negative.

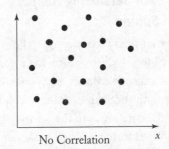

No Correlation

If there is a strong correlation in the data, it is likely that there will be a line that could be drawn on the scatterplot that comes close to all the points. This line is known as the "line of best fit." Without performing any computations, it is possible to visualize the location of the line of best fit, as the diagrams show.

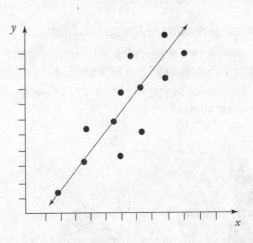

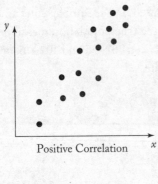

Positive Correlation

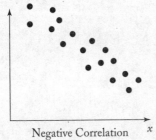

Negative Correlation

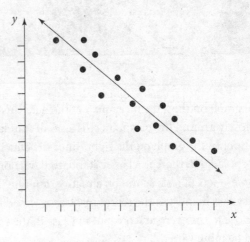

Comparing Data Sets Using Shape, Center, and Spread

Statistics questions may require you to know measures of central tendency, meaning the mean (average), median, and mode of a data set, but you will also need to be familiar with the shape, center, and spread of data. The shape of the data refers to the normal distribution curve, which we examine below. The center could be the average (arithmetic mean) or the median of the data values in the set. The spread is the range of the data, or the standard deviation of the data that describes the distance between values in a data set.

Data may be presented in tables, bar graphs, or via other methods, so it is important to be familiar with different types of data presentation.

Standard Deviation—Normal Distribution

A standard deviation describes how far the data values in a set are from the mean or how much they "deviate" from the mean. The graphs shown are both normal distribution curves.

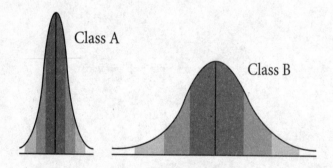

In the graph on the left, since much of the data clusters closely around the mean, there is a small standard deviation. In the graph on the right, since the data is more spread out, there is a larger standard deviation. If these were sets of tests scores on a math exam for Class A and Class B, most of the scores in Class A would be very close to the average score, but in Class B, the scores would be more varied.

Confidence Intervals and Measurement Errors

Measurement or sampling errors will usually occur when data cannot be collected about an entire population. If, for example, we are trying to determine the mean salary of people living in a city with 3.5 million people, we would probably use a smaller random sample of several hundred to several thousand people that was representative of the population. The difference between the mean salary of the actual population and that of the sample population is called a measurement or sampling error. The sampling error decreases as the sample size increases, since there is more data that should more accurately reflect the true population. Here's an example:

> A packaging company is gathering data about how many oranges it can fit into a crate. It takes a sample of 36 crates out of a total shipment of 5,540 crates. The sample mean is 102 oranges with a sampling error of 6 oranges at a 95% confidence interval.

What does the confidence interval mean? A confidence interval tells you how close the sample mean is to the actual mean of the entire population. In this case, it means that based on the sample, you can be 95% confident that the true population mean for the entire shipment is between 102 – 6 and 102 + 6, or 96 and 108 oranges per crate.

SUMMING IT UP

- The Quantitative Reasoning, Algebra, and Statistics placement test on the ACCUPLACER contains 20 questions and is not timed.

- Most questions will NOT allow you to use a calculator, but on the computerized exam, a pop-up calculator will be provided for certain questions. In this book, we have indicated which problems allow calculators using a small calculator icon ().

- Ratios are a type of fraction that can be expressed with a colon, which is read as the word *to*, so 4:1 means "4 to 1." When working with ratios, reduce to lowest terms by cancelling common factors.

- Proportions are ratios that are equivalent to one another.

- Rates are a type of ratio that allows you to compare quantities across different units.

- Use the formula Distance = Rate × Time and its equivalents, $R = \dfrac{D}{T}$ and $T = \dfrac{D}{R}$, to solve rate problems involving distance, time, or rate (speed).

- Use the following formula to address rate problems related to money:

$$\text{Rate (unit amount)} = \frac{\text{Total amount}}{\text{Number of units}}$$

- When working with rate problems involving two or more workers, pipes, or other productive elements, calculate the time actually spent on a task divided by the total time needed to complete a task alone.

- Exponents, scientific notation, and radicals are all used to deal with very large and small numbers.

- An exponent represents the number of times that a number (referred to as the "base number") is multiplied by itself.

- The square root of a number *n* is a number that you "square" (multiply it by itself, or raise to the power of 2), to obtain *n*.

- The cube root of a number *n* is a number that you raise to the power of 3 (multiply by itself twice) to obtain *n*. You determine higher roots (for example, the "fourth root") in the same way.

- In scientific notation, an integer or decimal number between 1 and 10 is written to a power of 10. For example, the number 430,000,000 can be written as 4.3×10^8.

- When working with linear equations that contain one variable, you may need to perform one or more of the following operations on both sides, depending on the equation:

  1. Add or subtract the same term on both sides.

  2. Multiply or divide both sides by the same term.

  3. Clear fractions by cross multiplication.

  4. Clear radicals by raising both sides to the same power (exponent).

- When simplifying equations, a basic process for simplification involves the following:

  1. Simplify any parts of the equation, remembering to follow the order of operations (PEMDAS).

  2. Combine like terms.

  3. Isolate the variable by undoing what has been done to it.

- Other methods for simplifying equations include using the basic operations and using the distributive property.

- Identify perfect squares, cubes, and so on to simplify and combine radical expressions.

- Remember that absolute value always has the effect of removing a negative from the number inside the absolute value sign. So, not only does $|7| = 7$, but $|-7| = 7$ too. Equations involving absolute value may therefore have more than one solution.

- When multiplying or dividing by a negative number, reverse the inequality symbol. In other words, if $a > b$, then $-a < -b$.

- Linear equations follow the pattern $Ax + By = C$ where x and y are variables corresponding to the axes and A, B, and C represent real numbers. In linear equations, the values of x and y are dependent on one another. To deal with these equations, solve for one variable or another and then express the other variable in terms of the first.

- A system of equations is a set of two or more (usually just two) equations that share a set of variables. The solution to a system of equations with two variables is an ordered pair of numbers. The ordered pair is a solution to **both** equations in the system.

- To solve systems of equations, you can use either the substitution method or the elimination method.

- In a coordinate plane, a line can be defined by slope-intercept form, which corresponds to $y = mx + b$, where m is the slope of the line and b is the y-intercept.

- Two lines in the same plane are parallel if they do not intersect.

- Two lines are perpendicular if they intersect to form right angles. Two lines are perpendicular if their slopes are negative reciprocals of each other.

- Graphing linear inequalities requires that you determine points on the line and what side of the line should be shaded to indicate what other points satisfy the inequality.

- Angles are classified according to their "size" as measured using degrees. The notation $m\angle A$ is used to denote the measure of angle A.

- Polygons include all two-dimensional figures formed only by line segments.

- A triangle is a three-sided shape. All triangles have an interior angle measure of 180 degrees. The length of a side is shorter than the sum of the lengths of the other two sides.

- In a right triangle, one angle measures 90° and each of the other two angles measures less than 90°. The Pythagorean theorem involves the relationship among the sides of any right triangle and can be expressed by the equation $a^2 + b^2 = c^2$.

- A quadrilateral is a figure in a plane with four sides, each of which is a line segment.

- Two geometric figures that have the same size and shape are said to be congruent. The symbol for congruency is $\cong$.

- If a two-dimensional geometric figure, such as a triangle or rectangle, has exactly the same shape as another one, then the two figures are similar. Similar figures share the same angle measures, and their sides are proportionate (though not the same length).

- For most questions related to circles, you'll apply one, or possibly both, of two basic formulas involving circles (r = radius, d = diameter):

  - Circumference = $2\pi r$, or πd
  - Area = πr^2

- The equation for a circle in the coordinate plane is $(x - h)^2 + (y - k)^2 = r^2$, where (h, k) is the center of the circle and r is the radius.

- The perimeter of a region in the plane is the "distance around."

- The area of a region in the plane is the number of unit squares needed to cover the shape.

- The volume of a solid in space is the number of unit cubes needed to fill it.

- The length of a segment is the distance between its endpoints. Distance is always a positive quantity, even if one or more of the coordinates are negative.

- Common types of geometric transformations include translations (slides), reflections (flips), rotations (turns), and dilations (enlargement or reduction).

- Statistics is a type of applied mathematics involving collecting, describing, and analyzing quantitative data in order to draw logical inferences from it.

- Probability refers to the statistical chances of an event occurring (or not occurring). By definition, probability ranges from 0 to 1. Probability is never negative, and it is never greater than 1. The basic formula for determining probability is:

$$\text{Probability} = \frac{\text{desired outcomes}}{\text{total number of possible outcomes}}$$

- When determining the probability of two events, it's important to determine whether the events are independent or dependent on one another, as this will affect how you calculate. You can multiply individual probabilities together to determine the probability of two events BOTH occurring.

- A set is a collection of objects. The objects in a particular set are called the members or the elements of the set.

- An average or arithmetic mean is a value that is computed by dividing the sum of a set of terms by the number of terms in the collection. To find the average (arithmetic mean) of a group of n numbers, simply add the numbers and divide by n.

- In order to find the median of a group of numbers, list the numbers in numerical order from smallest to largest. The median is the number in the middle.

- The mode of a group of numbers is simply the number that occurs most frequently.

- The range, or the spread, of a data set is the difference between the greatest and least data values.

- You can graph data sets using dot plots, histograms, box plots, and scatterplots.

- A standard deviation describes how far the data values in a set are from the mean or how much they "deviate" from the mean.

- A confidence interval tells you how close the sample mean is to the actual mean of the entire population.

QUANTITATIVE REASONING, ALGEBRA, AND STATISTICS

20 Questions

> **Directions:** In the following questions, work out each problem and mark the letter that corresponds to the correct answer. The answers and explanations will follow. Questions that allow the use of a calculator are marked with an icon (![calculator]).

1. What is the value of the following expression?

$$\frac{(5+4-27)}{9} - \frac{(3+|-1|+12)}{8}$$

   A. 0

   B. −3.75

   C. −4

   D. −4.75

2. A small banquet room contains 8 tables and 60 chairs. What is the ratio of tables to chairs in the room?

   A. $\dfrac{60}{8}$

   B. $\dfrac{4}{15}$

   C. $\dfrac{4}{17}$

   D. $\dfrac{2}{15}$

3. When you divide $\dfrac{a^2 b}{b^2 c}$ by $\dfrac{a^2 c}{bc^2}$, what is the result?

   A. $\dfrac{1}{b}$

   B. 1

   C. $\dfrac{b}{a}$

   D. $\dfrac{c}{b}$

4. If $\left|\dfrac{1}{2}x + 8\right| = 27$, what are the values of x?

   A. 9.5 and −17.5

   B. −9.5 and 17.5

   C. 38 and −70

   D. −38 and 70

5. Juan bought x discount CDs for $6 each and y discount DVDs for $4 each. He spent less than $30, not including tax. If you were to graph the inequality $6x + 4y < 30$, which point would represent a possible number of CDs and cassettes that Juan bought?

   A. (2, 5)

   B. (3, 2)

   C. (2, 8)

   D. (3, 3)

6. On a certain map, a printed distance of 1 inch represents an actual distance of 5 miles. If two towns are 30 miles apart, how many inches are between these two towns on the map?

   A. 6

   B. 30

   C. 90

   D. 180

7. $\sqrt{24} - \sqrt{16} - \sqrt{6}$ simplifies to which of the following expressions?

   A. $\sqrt{6} - 4$

   B. $4 - 2\sqrt{2}$

   C. $\sqrt{6}$

   D. $2\sqrt{2}$

8. In a group of 10 people who have salaries ranging from $75,000 to $200,000, the salary of the one person earning the maximum is increased from $200,000 to $225,000. What is true about the current mean and median salary of the 10 people as compared to before the salary increase?

   A. The mean and median remain the same.

   B. The mean increases but the median stays the same.

   C. The mean stays the same but the median increases.

   D. Both the mean and the median increase.

9. Consider n buckets arranged in a row. One marble is placed in the first one. Every successive bucket gets twice the number of marbles as the previous bucket. How many marbles will the nth bucket contain?

   A. $2n$

   B. $1 + 2(n - 1)$

   C. 2^n

   D. 2^{n-1}

10. Solve the following for b:

    $5b + 3 = 4b + 19$

    A. 4

    B. 10

    C. 12

    D. 16

11. Which of the following expressions is equivalent to $\dfrac{x^3 \left(x^2 y^3 \right)^3}{x^5 y}$?

    A. $x^{13} y^8$

    B. $x^6 y^{26}$

    C. $x^{\frac{9}{5}} y^9$

    D. $x^4 y^8$

12. If $x - y = 5$ and $x + 3y = 21$, what is the value of y?

    A. 4

    B. 5

    C. 6

    D. 8

13. One ball is drawn from a bag containing 3 white, 4 red, and 5 black balls. What is the probability that it is a white or a red ball?

    A. $\dfrac{7}{144}$

    B. $\dfrac{49}{144}$

    C. $\dfrac{3}{12}$

    D. $\dfrac{7}{12}$

14. The point of intersection of the graph $3x - 2y + 6 = 0$ with the y-axis is

    A. $(0, -3)$

    B. $(0, 3)$

    C. $(0, 6)$

    D. $(0, -6)$

15. If a square has side lengths of 6, what is the length of one of its diagonals?

   A. 36

   B. 12

   C. $6\sqrt{2}$

   D. 6

16. A rectangular box of size $100 \times 50 \times 20$ cubic cm has to be wrapped. If wrapping paper costs $1.20 per square meter, what will it cost to wrap the box?

   A. $1.20

   B. $1.92

   C. $2.04

   D. $2.40

17. 7 is to 21 as $\frac{2}{3}$ is to

   A. 3

   B. 2

   C. $\frac{4}{3}$

   D. $\frac{5}{9}$

18. If line A is parallel to the line $y = 3x - 6$, and it intersects the y-axis at point $(0, 4)$, then the equation of line A is

   A. $y = 3x - 4$

   B. $y = 4x$

   C. $y = 3x + 4$

   D. $y = 3x$

19. A cylindrical trailer is 12 feet long and has a diameter of 6 feet. How many barrels 4 feet tall and 4 feet in diameter can fit inside the trailer?

   A. 5

   B. 6

   C. 7

   D. 8

20. A set C contains 22 elements and a set D contains 35 elements. If $C \cup D$ contains 40 elements, then how many elements does $C \cap D$ contain?

   A. 13

   B. 17

   C. 18

   D. 22

ANSWER KEY AND EXPLANATIONS

1. C	5. B	9. D	13. D	17. B
2. D	6. A	10. D	14. B	18. C
3. B	7. A	11. D	15. C	19. B
4. C	8. B	12. A	16. B	20. B

1. **The correct answer is C.** Find the value as follows:

$$\frac{(5+4-27)}{9}-\frac{(3+|-1|+12)}{8}$$
$$=\frac{(5+4-27)}{9}-\frac{(3+1+12)}{8}$$
$$=-\frac{18}{9}-\left(\frac{16}{8}\right)$$
$$=-2-2$$
$$=-4$$

2. **The correct answer is D.** If there are 8 tables and 60 chairs, then the ratio of tables to chairs is 8 to 60. (Order is important, so beware of choice A.) Both 8 and 60 can be divided by 4. So, the simplest form of this ratio is $\frac{2}{15}$.

3. **The correct answer is B.** First, cancel common factors in each term. Then, you'll see that the numerator and denominator are the same, which means that the quotient must equal 1:

$$\frac{a^2b}{b^2c}\div\frac{a^2c}{bc^2}=\frac{a^2}{bc}\div\frac{a^2}{bc}=1$$

4. **The correct answer is C.** This is how your work should look:

$$\frac{1}{2}x+8=27 \qquad \frac{1}{2}x+8=-27$$
$$\frac{1}{2}x=19 \qquad \frac{1}{2}x=-35$$
$$x=38 \qquad x=-70$$

The values of x are 38 and –70.

5. **The correct answer is B.** If you were to graph the inequality $6x + 4y < 30$, then point (3, 2) would be in the shaded area of the graph. Substitute 3 for x and 2 for y to see whether the inequality is true:

$$6x+4y<30$$
$$6(3)+4(2)<30$$
$$18+8<30$$
$$26<30$$

6. **The correct answer is A.** This is a part-to-part ratio. Set up a proportion in which each fraction is a ratio of inches to miles, and be sure to keep the units consistent:

$$\frac{x}{30}=\frac{1}{5}$$
$$5x=30(1)$$
$$5x=30$$
$$\frac{5x}{5}=\frac{30}{5}$$
$$x=6$$

7. **The correct answer is A.** Although the numbers under the three radicals combine to equal 2, you cannot combine terms this way. Instead, simplify the first two terms, then combine the first and third terms:

$$\sqrt{24}-\sqrt{16}-\sqrt{6}=2\sqrt{6}-4-\sqrt{6}=\sqrt{6}-4$$

8. **The correct answer is B.** The mean of a set of numbers is defined as the average value of the set, whereas the median of a set of numbers is defined as the value of the number in the middle of the set. If any one number in the set is changed, the value of the mean changes, but the median does not unless the original median value was changed. In this case, since the number with the greatest value

is increased, the mean changes, but the median remains the same.

9. **The correct answer is D.** The first bucket gets 1 marble. The second bucket gets twice the number of the first one, which is 2^{2-1} marbles. The third bucket gets 2(2) marbles, which is 2^{3-1} marbles. The fourth bucket gets 8 marbles, which is the same as 2^{4-1}. Thus, the nth bucket will get 2^{n-1} marbles.

10. **The correct answer is D.** Isolate the variable on one side and numbers on the other. Remember to always do the same thing to both sides of the equation:

$$5b + 3 = 4b + 19$$
$$5b = 4b + 16$$
$$b = 16$$

11. **The correct answer is D.** Apply the exponent rules as follows:

$$\frac{x^3 \left(x^2 y^3 \right)^3}{x^5 y} = \frac{x^3 x^6 y^9}{x^5 y}$$
$$= \frac{x^9 y^9}{x^5 y}$$
$$= x^4 y^8$$

12. **The correct answer is A.** The question asks for the value of y, so solve the first equation for x:

$$x - y = 5$$
$$x = 5 + y$$

Now, replace x in the second equation with this result and solve the second equation for y:

$$x + 3y = 21$$
$$(5 + y) + 3y = 21$$
$$5 + 4y = 21$$
$$4y = 16$$
$$y = 4$$

13. **The correct answer is D.** There are a total of $(3 + 4 + 5) = 12$ balls. Of these, there are a total of $(3 + 4) = 7$ white or red balls. Thus, the probability of drawing a red or white ball is $\frac{7}{12}$.

14. **The correct answer is B.** To calculate the point of intersection of a line with the y-axis, we note that the point of intersection has its x-coordinate at 0. Using this information, we plug in $x = 0$ into the equation line. Thus, we have

$$3x - 2y + 6 = 0$$
$$3(0) - 2y + 6 = 0$$
$$y = 3$$

15. **The correct answer is C.** In this problem, we know that within a square a diagonal can be used to form an isosceles right triangle. Using the properties of an isosceles right triangle, you can determine the length of the hypotenuse (the diagonal of the square) to be $6\sqrt{2}$. Alternatively, use you use the Pythagorean theorem to determine the length:

$$c^2 = a^2 + b^2$$
$$c^2 = 6^2 + 6^2$$
$$c^2 = 72$$
$$c = \sqrt{36}\sqrt{2}$$
$$c = 6\sqrt{2}$$

16. **The correct answer is B.** To calculate the cost of wrapping the box, we need to first find the total amount of wrapping paper needed to wrap the box. That will be the same as the surface area of the box. The surface area of the box is twice the sum of the area of the three rectangles that make up the box. The dimensions of the rectangles are 100×50, 100×20, and 50×20, all in cm. Thus, the surface area of the box is:

$$2(100 \times 50) + 2(100 \times 20) + 2(50 \times 20)$$
$$= 16{,}000 \text{ cm sq.}$$
$$= 1.6 \text{ meter sq.}$$

The cost of wrapping would be the cost per sq. meter of wrapping times the area to be wrapped in sq. meters. Therefore, the cost of wrapping is $(1.2)(1.6) = \$1.92$.

17. **The correct answer is B.** 7 is one third of 21, and $\frac{2}{3}$ is one third of 2. You can also set up the ratios as proportions and solve for the missing whole:

$$\frac{7}{21} = \frac{\frac{2}{3}}{x}$$

$$7x = 14$$

$$x = 2$$

18. **The correct answer is C.** We need to find the equation of line A, given that it is parallel to the line $y = 3x - 6$, and it intersects the y-axis at point $(0, 4)$. Now, if line A is parallel to a given line, it has the same slope as the line, which is 3 (comparing the equation of the line with $y = mx + b$, where m is the slope of the line and b is the y-intercept). Line A intersects the y-axis at point $(0, 4)$, which means its y-intercept is 4. Thus, the equation of line A is $y = 3x + 4$.

19. **The correct answer is B.** For this problem, we first find the volume of the trailer to be filled and then find the volume of the barrels used to fill the trailer. Then, by dividing the volume of the trailer by that of an individual barrel, we will get the number of barrels that can fit into the trailer fully. The volume of a cylinder is given as $V = \pi r^2 h$, where r and h are the radius and height of the cylinder, respectively. Thus, the volume of the tank is $V_t = \pi(3)^2(12)$, which can be stated as 108π. The volume of each barrel is $V_b = \pi(2)^2(4)$, which is equivalent to 16π. The number of barrels that can fill the trailer is then stated as:

$$\frac{V_t}{V_b} = \frac{108\pi}{16\pi} = \frac{27}{4} = 6.75$$

Because the barrels cannot be divided into smaller pieces, the trailer will only be able to hold a maximum of 6 barrels.

20. **The correct answer is B.** Of the total 57 elements that comprise sets C and D, 17 must be in common (and thus present in their intersection) since otherwise their union would have more than 40 elements. Choice A is the difference of the number of elements in C and D. Choice C would imply that $C \cup D$ contains 39 elements, not 40. Choice D would imply that C is a subset of D, which is not assumed; moreover, $C \cap D$ would not include 40 elements in such case.

CHAPTER

**Advanced Algebra
and Functions**

ADVANCED ALGEBRA & FUNCTIONS

OVERVIEW

Understanding Advanced Algebra and Functions on the ACCUPLACER®

Key Concepts for Advanced Algebra and Functions on the ACCUPLACER®

- Polynomials and Factoring
- Quadratics
- Rational, Radical, Exponential, and Logarithmic Equations
- Functions
- Trigonometry

Summing It Up

Knowledge Check: Advanced Algebra and Functions

Answer Key and Explanations

By now, you've likely figured out that the math concepts you learned in basic Arithmetic and Algebra are necessary to complete the kinds of tasks that will come up in the section on advanced algebra and functions. The concepts and questions in this chapter are among the hardest quantitative questions you'll see on the ACCUPLACER. If you are someone who struggled with math or never completed more advanced math courses in high school, then there is a good chance that some of the concepts covered here will be outside your current skill set. Don't get down on yourself if this is the case; instead, remember that the ACCUPLACER is a placement test, so identifying the line between concepts you've mastered already and those you've yet to learn is precisely the goal. Focus on brushing up on what you *have* learned so you can get placed as accurately as possible.

9

UNDERSTANDING ADVANCED ALGEBRA AND FUNCTIONS ON THE ACCUPLACER®

As you work through both this chapter and the advanced algebra and functions section of the ACCUPLACER more generally, you'll likely need to revisit concepts from the last chapter on quantitative reasoning, algebra, and statistics since quantitative concepts related to advanced algebra and functions are inherently linked with these earlier skills. That said, the majority of what you'll need to know to complete tasks in the advanced algebra and functions section of the ACCUPLACER is contained in this chapter.

Just like the other quantitative ACCUPLACER placement tests, the advanced algebra and functions placement test is untimed and covers 20 questions. Test takers cannot use a calculator unless the test indicates that they are permitted to do so. On exam day, since this is a computerized exam, you'll be provided with a pop-up calculator directly in the test browser. While practicing with this book, we've mimicked this functionality by including a calculator icon to signify that you may use your own calculator for that question.

The categories assessed by questions on the ACCUPLACER advanced algebra and functions test include:

- Polynomial equations
- Quadratics
- Linear equations and applications
- Factoring
- Functions
- Radical and rational equations
- Exponential and logarithmic equations
- Geometry concepts
- Trigonometry

In the following sections, we've grouped concepts addressing these categories according to the mathematical skills you'll need to solve questions from each category. Remember, if something seems completely new, don't worry about trying to learn it before a placement exam. Just recognize that these are the types of questions you're likely to encounter in this section so you can practice any skills you *have* built in the past.

KEY CONCEPTS FOR ADVANCED ALGEBRA AND FUNCTIONS ON THE ACCUPLACER®

This section covers the majority of the concepts that will be included in the advanced algebra and functions section of the ACCUPLACER exam. Note that while we have grouped mathematics in this book according to the test where you are most likely to encounter them, you may still be asked to use other quantitative reasoning skills from the previous two chapters when completing this section of the ACCUPLACER.

Polynomials and Factoring

Polynomials and factoring relate to the manipulation of equations. In the real world, skills like these often come up in computational settings as well as in science applications.

Polynomials

A polynomial is one or more terms, each having a variable with a whole number (0, 1, 2, ...) as an exponent. A term is:

- a number (such as 2 or 4.99 or $\frac{2}{3}$ or $\sqrt{20}$)
- a variable (such as x or k)
- any combination of numbers and variables without an operation symbol (such as $5x$, $k\sqrt{3}$, abc, $\frac{h}{2}$, or $15mn^2$)

Terms make up expressions (such as $5x + 3$) and equations (such as $5x + 3 = 23$), and they also are the building blocks of polynomials, as seen here:

- $4x^6$
- $m^2 - 5m + 7$
- $9 - 2t^3$
- 17

Even the number 17 counts as a polynomial due to the implied existence of a variable and exponent. From the laws of exponents, a number with an exponent of zero is equal to 1. So, you could look at 17 in the following way: $17x^0$. This would be equivalent to 17(1) and therefore equals 17.

The following are some examples of sequences that may appear to be polynomials but are in fact in violation of some central rules.

- $\dfrac{3}{c}$ (this is a rational expression and not a polynomial)
- $\sqrt{5x}$ (this is a radical expression and not a polynomial)
- $6y^{-3}$ (this expression contains a negative exponent, equivalent to a rational expression)
- $3x^2 - 7x^{\frac{1}{2}}$ (this expression likewise contains a non-whole number exponent)

For now, let's look at an example of a more complex polynomial.

$$x^4 + 14x^3 + 15x - 7$$

This polynomial has four terms: x^4, $14x^3$, $15x$, and -7. If we focused on the second term, we have a coefficient (14), a variable (x), and an exponent (3). If you wanted to read this out loud, you'd say, "fourteen x to the third power" or "fourteen x cubed."

Simplifying Polynomials

We remember that there are several methods to consider when simplifying linear equations, and these rules still apply to polynomials of varying lengths. One of the most important aspects is combining like terms, and this can become quite complex when dealing with polynomials. However, there are clear steps and techniques that you can memorize.

In short, simplifying polynomials means organizing and combining like terms to make a polynomial as easy to read as possible. This includes putting a polynomial into standard form. Let's look at a sample polynomial that has not been simplified:

$$2x + 4x^2 - 13 + 7x - x^2 + x - 3$$

To simplify, first gather like terms:

$$4x^2 - x^2 + 2x + 7x + x - 13 - 3$$

Then, combine like terms:

$$4x^2 - x^2 = 3x^2$$

$$2x + 7x + x = 10x$$

$$-13 - 3 = -16$$

Finally, write out the expression in standard form:

$$3x^2 + 10x - 16$$

This is much easier to read—and make sense of—than the original expression.

Adding and Subtracting Polynomials

If you have two polynomials and you want to combine them through addition or subtraction, the steps are similar to what you've done already. Let's take a look:

$$(11x^2 + 14 + 3x) + (-3x^2 + 2x + 6)$$

The first step, because you have two polynomials inside of parentheses connected by addition, is to remove the parentheses:

$$11x^2 + 14 + 3x + -3x^2 + 2x + 6$$

From here, gather terms and simplify:

$$11x^2 - 3x^2 + 3x + 2x + 14 + 6$$

The resulting polynomial is:

$$8x^2 + 5x + 20$$

Let's look at the same polynomial but instead focus on subtraction. The process is essentially the same except that you need to pay careful attention to number signs.

$$(11x^2 + 14 + 3x) - (-3x^2 + 2x + 6)$$

Now that you're subtracting one polynomial from the other, remove the parentheses and distribute the negative sign to the terms inside the second set of parentheses:

$$(11x^2 + 14 + 3x) + (3x^2 - 2x - 6)$$

Now, remove the parentheses, gather like terms and combine to simplify:

$$11x^2 + 14 + 3x + 3x^2 - 2x - 6$$

$$11x^2 + 3x^2 + 3x - 2x + 14 - 6$$

$$14x^2 + x + 8$$

Multiplying Monomials

Remember that a monomial is a polynomial with only one term. For example, $7x$ is a monomial. So is $2y^2$ and $1{,}784{,}921t^{45}$. Multiplying monomials gives us the chance to combine two terms that are not alike, such as $3x^2$ and $6x^4$. Let's review multiplying exponents.

$$3x^2 (6x^4)$$

As with any polynomial equation, it's easier to solve after simplifying. With two monomials, break each monomial into its component parts:

$$3 \times 6 \text{ and } x^2 \bullet x^4$$

The first portion requires standard multiplication:

$$3 \times 6 = 18$$

As for the exponents, when you are asked to multiply, remember that if they have the same base, you will add the exponents. Therefore, $3x^2 \bullet 6x^4 = 18x^6$.

Multiplying a Polynomial and a Monomial

When multiplying a polynomial and a monomial, distribution is the key. Here's a sample problem:

$$2(x^2 + 7x + 4)$$

The first step is to distribute the 2 to the terms in the trinomial:

$$(2 \bullet x^2) + (2 \bullet 7x) + (2 \bullet 4)$$

Finish multiplying and add the terms together to present the polynomial in standard form:

$$2x^2 + 14x + 8$$

Note that even though you can factor 2 out of each term, $2x^2 + 14x + 8$ is the simplified answer. Factoring out the 2 would bring us back to the original monomial and polynomial of $2(x^2 + 7x + 4)$. We will cover factoring in more detail later on.

Multiplying Binomials

Let's start with a problem with two binomials:

$$(4x + 3)\,(2x + 9)$$

These binomials need to be multiplied together. To multiply binomials, you'll use a process called FOIL. FOIL is a mnemonic that stands for First, Outer, Inner, Last. It describes the order in which you multiply terms.

Let's apply it to the previous pair of binomials:

$$(4x + 3)\,(2x + 9)$$

Start with the first terms: $4x$ and $2x$. Multiply them together:

$$4x \bullet 2x = 8x^2$$

Then, multiply the outer terms, $4x$ and 9:

$$4x \bullet 9 = 36x$$

Continue following FOIL. Next, multiply the inner terms:

$$3 \bullet 2x = 6x$$

Then, multiply the last terms:

$$3 \bullet 9 = 27$$

Combine:

$$8x^2 + 36x + 6x + 27$$

$$= 8x^2 + 42x + 27$$

TIP

Remember **FOIL** for multiplying binomials:

F First
O Outer
I Inner
L Last

While you could have also used standard distribution to multiply the polynomial, tracking what you've multiplied can become challenging, especially as the number of terms in your polynomials grows. The mnemonic FOIL serves to remind you of the distributive property of multiplication.

There are cases wherein you can factor a trinomial (seen in the previous example) to produce two binomials, but before discussing this, we will review how to factor algebraic expressions in general.

Here are some examples of algebraic expressions that can also be factored:

$$4x + 2y = 2 \cdot (2x + y)$$

$$xz - bz = z \cdot (x - b)$$

Scan this QR code to learn more about factoring.

Factoring Numbers and Variables Out of Expressions

In some cases, all of the numbers in a polynomial can be factored out.

EXAMPLES

$$4x - 4z$$

There are two terms: $4x$ and $4z$. Each of these terms has a 4 in it, so each of these terms is divisible by 4.

Dividing $4x$ by 4 leaves x.
Dividing $4z$ by 4 leaves z.

So, factoring out the 4 leaves:

$$4x - 4z = 4(x) - 4(z)$$
$$= 4 \cdot (x - z)$$
$$= 4(x - z)$$

In this case, 4 is the largest number that can be factored out of both terms.

For some expressions, a number can be factored out, but not the entire number. In these instances, you have to pull out a factor of the number.

$$9xy - 6ab$$

Solution

The number 6 can't be factored out because 6 doesn't divide evenly into 9. Similarly, 9 can't be factored out as 9 doesn't divide evenly into 6. However, both numbers have a common factor, 3. This means that you can factor 3 out of both terms:

$$9xy = 3(3xy)$$

$$6ab = 3(2ab)$$

So, the whole expression becomes:

$$9xy - 6ab = 3(3xy - 2ab)$$

In addition to numbers, variables can also be factored out of expressions. If the same variable occurs in every term, it can be factored out.

EXAMPLE

$$11a - 5ab$$

Solution

There are no common factors for 11 and 5. However, both $11a$ and $5ab$ contain a factor of a. Therefore, you can factor out the variable, leaving the numbers as they are:

$$11a - 5ab = a(11 - 5b)$$

Sometimes, both a number and a variable can be factored out of an expression. The process for factoring out variables is essentially the same as it is for factoring out numbers.

EXAMPLE

$$8xyz - 4yb$$

Solution

Factor out the number first. Both 8 and 4 are divisible by 4, so:

$$8xyz - 4yb = 4(2xyz - yb)$$

Now, look at the variables in the parentheses. Since there is a y in both terms inside the parentheses, it can be factored out. Pull the y outside the parentheses:

$$4(2xyz - yb) = 4y(2xz - b)$$

Sometimes, you can factor an entire term from an expression.

EXAMPLE

$$4x + x$$

Solution

An x can be factored out of both terms. Note that factoring an x away from the second term leaves a 1:

$$4x + x = x(4 + 1)$$

Factoring Trinomials

Factoring a trinomial is essentially the same as multiplying binomials but in reverse. Let's look at the standard form of a trinomial and an example:

$$Ax^2 + Bx + C$$

$$x^2 + 5x + 6$$

When factoring a trinomial, the goal is to build two binomials that, when you use FOIL, recreate the trinomial.

Here's what you will see:

$$x^2 + 5x + 6 = (x + a)\,(x + b)$$

Let's expand the right side of this equation:

$$\begin{aligned} x^2 + 5x + 6 &= (x+a)(x+b) \\ &= x^2 + ax + bx + ab \\ &= x^2 + (a+b)x + ab \end{aligned}$$

What you see here is true for any trinomials that can be factored. You're looking for the values of a and b that multiply to make the C term of the standard form but also add up to the B term. In the example, ab must equal 6 and $a + b$ must equal 5.

We start by factoring the constant, 6.

$$6 : 6 \times 1$$

$$: 3 \times 2$$

Now, $6 \times 1 = 6$ but $6 + 1 = 7$. Try another pair of factors.

What about 3 × 2?

$$3 \times 2 = 6$$
$$3 + 2 = 5$$

The numbers look correct, but test it to be sure.

$$a = 3,\ b = 2$$
$$x^2 + 5x + 6 = (x + a)(x + b)$$
$$= (x + 3)(x + 2)$$
$$= (x)(x) + (x)(2) + (3)(x) + (3)(2)$$
$$= x^2 + 2x + 3x + 6$$
$$= x^2 + 5x + 6$$

Our original trinomial was $x^2 + 5x + 6$, so $(x + 2)(x + 3)$ would suffice as an answer. If the trinomial was set equal to 0 (as an equation), you would then solve for the roots (where the trinomial would intersect the x-axis if graphed) and the algebra would yield –2 and –3. We'll explore this more in the next section.

Let's look at another example. What if you are told to factor the following trinomial?

$$5x^2 + 35x + 50$$

To start, look to see if there are any common factors among 5, 35, and 50. The greatest common factor of these three numbers is 5. So, factor out a 5 from each term:

$$5(x^2 + 7x + 10)$$

From here, factor the trinomial like you did in the first example:

$$5\left(x^2 + 7x + 10\right) = (x + a)(x + b)$$
$$a + b = 7$$
$$ab = 10$$

We can factor 10 as 10 and 1 or 5 and 2. We need the factors to add to 7. Of the factors of the C term, only 5 and 2 add to 7. Substitute 5 and 2 for the a and b terms and you have your answer:

$$5(x + 5)(x + 2)$$

You now know how to factor a trinomial expression, but what about when the trinomial is an equation? We call those quadratics.

Quadratics

Quadratics take their name from *quad*, meaning "square," because in quadratics, the variable is squared. These sorts of equations come up in many real-life scenarios including those related to designing spaces or objects, calculating area, determining an object's speed, evaluating profits and loss, and much more. For this reason, quadratics are especially common in word problems.

What Is a Quadratic Equation?

In the prior section, you learned how to go about multiplying two binomials together. The resulting expression of such an operation is a special type of polynomial called a quadratic function. Simply put, a quadratic function includes one or more variables that are squared (x^2) and contains no exponents greater than this.

When set in standard form, a quadratic equation looks like the following:

$$ax^2 + bx + c = 0$$

In this particular equation type, a must be any real number other than 0. Likewise, when applicable, b and c are also real numbers. Not all quadratic equations contain a constant at the end (c), and they do not necessarily need a second x variable attached to a b coefficient. What is important is the presence of a squared variable, and these sets of restrictions allow for unique mathematical operations and graphs. We will cover them throughout this lesson.

Here are some examples of quadratic equations (trinomials):

$$x^2 + 2x + 3 = 0$$
$$3x^2 - 5x = -6$$
$$x^2 + 6x = 0$$
$$2x^2 - 8 = 0$$

Factoring Quadratic Equations

A quadratic equation can have 0, 1, or 2 solutions. Many quadratic equations can be solved by factoring. To solve a quadratic equation by factoring:

 01 Write the equation in the form: $ax^2 + bx + c = 0$

 02 Factor the expression $ax^2 + bx + c$.

03 Set each factor equal to zero and solve for x.

 04 Check that each solution makes the equation true. Do this by substituting each solution back into the equation.

 EXAMPLE

What is the solution set for this equation?

$$x^2 + 12 = 7x$$

Solution

First, organize the terms to place the equation in standard form.

$$x^2 - 7x + 12 = 0$$

Next, find factors that multiply to the C term (12) and add to the B term (–7). The factors of 12 that can add to 7 are 3 and 4. Because the B term is negative and the C term is positive, the factors will both need to be negative. The values of –3 and –4 satisfy those requirements.

$$(x - 3)(x - 4) = 0$$

When each factor is set equal to zero and you solve for x, the apparent roots of the quadratic are 3 and 4. However, you'll need to test each root to verify that it falls within the solution set for the quadratic. To do that, substitute each value into the original equation and simplify. The equation is true whether x equals 3 or x equals 4. Thus, the solution set for $x^2 + 12 = 7x$ is {3, 4}.

The Quadratic Formula

There is another method of solving quadratic equations that makes use of the quadratic formula. When graphing a quadratic, the result will be a parabola or a u-shaped graph that opens upwards or downwards. The two solutions to the quadratic formula will always mark the two locations where the arms of the parabola cross the x-axis. While not every quadratic can be factored, real roots can always be found (if there are any) using the quadratic formula.

Once again, a quadratic can be expressed in standard form as follows:

$$ax^2 + bx + c = 0$$

Remember that x is the variable, a and b are coefficients, and c is a constant. Those values can be arranged in the quadratic formula as follows:

$$x = \frac{-b \pm \sqrt{b^2 - 4ac}}{2a}$$

Notice that this formula uses a sign for plus or minus in the numerator, and this is because quadratics have two solutions, as we've previously seen. By plugging in all known values for a general quadratic into this formula, you can solve for both solutions.

Let's take the following general quadratic as an example:

$$x^2 + 6x - 8 = 0$$

In this case, $a = 1$ (as the coefficient is assumed to be 1), $b = 6$, and $c = -8$. Plugging what we have into the quadratic formula will result in this equation:

$$x = \frac{-6 \pm \sqrt{6^2 - 4(1)(8)}}{2(1)}$$

$$x = \frac{-6 \pm \sqrt{36 - 32}}{2}$$

$$x = \frac{-6 \pm \sqrt{4}}{2}$$

$$x = \frac{-6 \pm 2}{2}$$

$$x_1 = \frac{-8}{2} = -4$$

$$x_2 = \frac{-4}{2} = -2$$

Since we have to both add and subtract 2 from −6 before dividing by 2, we are left with two solutions:

$$-4 \text{ and } -2$$

These will be the points where the resultant parabola crosses the *x*-axis.

The Discriminant

The part of the quadratic formula that is underneath the square root symbol is called the discriminant ($b^2 - 4ac$). Evaluating the discriminant tells you whether a quadratic equation has two real roots, one real root, or no real roots. Let's look at some examples of how the discriminant changes for each scenario.

Positive Discriminant

If the discriminant is positive, the equation has two real roots. In other words, the equation has two different solutions.

The discriminant of the equation $2x^2 + x - 1 = 0$ is:

$$b^2 - 4ac = 1^2 - 4(2)(-1)$$

$$b^2 - 4ac = 1 + 8$$

$$b^2 - 4ac = 9$$

Since 9 is positive, the equation has two real roots. (If you looked at the whole quadratic formula, not just the discriminant, you'd see that the roots are −1 and $\frac{1}{2}$.)

Discriminant is Zero

If the discriminant is zero, the equation has one real root.

The discriminant of the equation $x^2 - 2x + 1 = 0$ is:

$$b^2 - 4ac = (-2)^2 - 4(1)(1)$$

$$b^2 - 4ac = 4 - 4$$

$$b^2 - 4ac = 0$$

The discriminant is zero, so this equation has one real root.

Negative Discriminant

If the discriminant is negative, the equation has no real roots. This is because the discriminant is under a square root symbol, and the square root of a negative number is an imaginary number, not a real number.

The discriminant of the equation $2x^2 + x + 1 = 0$ is:

$$b^2 - 4ac = 1^2 - 4(2)(1)$$

$$b^2 - 4ac = 1 - 8$$

$$b^2 - 4ac = -7$$

Since −7 is negative, the equation has no real roots, only imaginary roots.

Quadratic Inequalities

A quadratic inequality is any inequality that can be arranged so that there is a quadratic expression on one side and a zero on the other.

$$x^2 - 7x + 10 \le 0$$
$$x^2 + 7 \le 7x - 3$$

Just as you can solve for the solution set to a linear inequality, you can solve for the solution set of a quadratic inequality.

The method is a little more involved than solving a linear inequality. To solve quadratic inequalities, follow these steps:

Step 1: Rewrite the inequality so that one side equals zero and factor the quadratic.

Step 2: Solve the corresponding equation.

Step 3: Draw a number line and label the solutions.

Step 4: Test each possible solution "region" using a value from that region in the quadratic (a number before the lowest solution, between the two solutions, and after the greatest solution).

The following example demonstrates these steps.

EXAMPLE

Find the solution to $x^2 + 2x > 3$.

Solution

Use the steps for solving quadratic inequalities.

Step 1: Rewrite the inequality so that one side equals zero and factor the quadratic:

$$x^2 + 2x > 3$$
$$x^2 + 2x - 3 > 0$$
$$x^2 + 2x - 3 = 0$$
$$(x + 3)(x - 1) = 0$$

Step 2: Solve the corresponding equation (i.e., find solutions for $x^2 + 2x - 3 = 0$):

$$(x + 3)(x - 1) = 0$$
$$x + 3 = 0$$
$$x - 1 = 0$$

Step 3: Thus $x = -3$ and 1, so any regions that make the inequality true will have strict boundaries at -3 and 1.

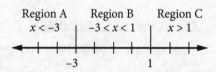

Step 4: Test each region with a value from that region and determine if the original inequality is true or false.

Pick any value from each region and test the value in the original inequality written in terms of zero ($x^2 + 2x - 3 > 0$) and determine if the solution is positive or negative. Any value that satisfies the original inequality is part of the solution set.

Region A: Test value $x = -4$

$$(-4)^2 + 2(-4) - 3 = 16 - 8 - 3$$
$$= 5 \text{ positive}$$

Region B: Test value $x = 0$

$$(0)^2 = 2(0) - 3 = -3 \text{ negative}$$

Region C: Test value $x = 2$

$$(2)^2 = 2(2) - 3 = 1 \text{ positive}$$

So, we find that the solution is positive for region A and C, where $x < -3$ and $x > 1$ or $(-\infty, -3) \cup (1, \infty)$.

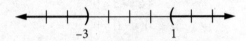

EXAMPLE

Simplify: $\dfrac{2x^2 - x}{2x^2}$

Solution

Be careful! You may want to cancel the $2x^2$ terms, but they are not factors. You can only cancel out terms that are shared by each polynomial. In the numerator, $2x^2$ cannot be factored from $-x$, but we can factor out an x from both polynomials. We can also do this in the denominator to simplify:

$$\frac{2x^2 - x}{2x^2} = \frac{x(2x-1)}{x(2x)} = \frac{2x-1}{2x}$$

In some cases, you may need to do more complicated factoring.

Rational, Radical, Exponential, and Logarithmic Equations

Rational, radical, and exponential equations all involve using the more basic algebra skills, such as finding ratios or working with exponents, to solve more advanced equations. Generally speaking, logarithms involve discussing numbers in terms of their powers of 10.

Rational Expressions and Equations

Rational expressions are formed when two polynomials form a fraction. Examples include $\dfrac{x+4}{x-1}$ and $\dfrac{2x^4 - x}{2x^6}$. Operations with rational expressions are just like the operations used with regular fractions; however, you also must pay attention to variables.

Simplifying Rational Expressions

To simplify a rational expression, cancel any common factors shared by both the numerator (the top of the fraction) and the denominator (the bottom of the fraction) of the expression.

EXAMPLE

Simplify: $\dfrac{x^2 + 3x - 4}{x^2 + 4x - 5}$

Solution

$$\frac{x^2 + 3x - 4}{x^2 + 4x - 5} = \frac{(x+4)(x-1)}{(x+5)(x-1)} = \frac{x+4}{x+5}$$

Adding and Subtracting Rational Expressions

In order to add or subtract rational expressions, you must use a common denominator just as you would with regular fractions. Then, add or subtract across the top of the fractions. When subtracting, make sure to distribute the negative to all terms in the numerator.

your final answer. Anytime there are common factors on either side of the multiplication symbol, you can cancel them out. Therefore, it is a good idea to factor as a first step.

EXAMPLE

Multiply: $\dfrac{3x^2+3}{x^2-x-2} \cdot \dfrac{x^2+2x+1}{3}$

Solution

$$\dfrac{3x^2+3}{x^2-x-2} \cdot \dfrac{x^2+2x+1}{3}$$

$$=\dfrac{\cancel{3}(x^2+1)}{\cancel{(x+1)}(x-2)} \cdot \dfrac{\cancel{(x+1)}(x+1)}{\cancel{3}}$$

$$=\dfrac{x^2+1}{x-2} \cdot \dfrac{x+1}{1}$$

$$=\dfrac{x^3+x^2+x+1}{x-2}$$

When dividing rational expressions, the first expression stays the same, but you will multiply it by the reciprocal of the second expression. You can't cross cancel until you have switched to multiplication.

TIP

A reciprocal is the inverse of a value or expression. For example, the reciprocal of 7 is $\dfrac{1}{7}$ and the reciprocal of $\dfrac{x+1}{3}$ is $\dfrac{3}{x+1}$. When you multiply a number by its reciprocal, $\dfrac{7}{1}\times\dfrac{1}{7}$, the result is always 1.

EXAMPLE

Add: $\dfrac{x+1}{x-5}+\dfrac{x+2}{x+6}$

Solution

The common denominator here will be the product of $x - 5$ and $x + 6$. In this case, you will multiply the two denominators to find a common denominator.

Now use the common denominator to add the expressions. Notice that you multiply the top and bottom of the fraction by the missing part of the common denominator:

$$\dfrac{x+1}{x-5}+\dfrac{x+2}{x+6}=\dfrac{x+1}{x-5}\left(\dfrac{x+6}{x+6}\right)+\dfrac{x+2}{x+6}\left(\dfrac{x-5}{x-5}\right)$$

$$=\dfrac{x^2+7x+6}{(x-5)(x+6)}+\dfrac{x^2-3x-10}{(x-5)(x+6)}$$

$$=\dfrac{2x^2+4x-4}{(x-5)(x+6)}$$

$$=\dfrac{2(x^2+2x-2)}{(x+5)(x+6)}$$

How much you simplify will depend on the answer choices. For instance, we did not multiply the terms on the bottom of the expression in the last example. Look at a question's answer options to decide whether to completely multiply within the numerator and denominator or factor out values as shown with the 2, etc.

Multiplying and Dividing Rational Expressions

To multiply rational expressions, multiply terms straight across as you would with simple fractions. This process was used in the previous example to find a common denominator. However, you can also use cross canceling, which can save time when simplifying

EXAMPLE

Divide: $\dfrac{x^2-x-6}{2x+1} \div \dfrac{x^2+7x+10}{3x+1}$

Solution

$$\dfrac{x^2-x-6}{2x+1} \div \dfrac{x^2+7x+10}{3x+1}$$

$$= \dfrac{x^2-x-6}{2x+1} \cdot \dfrac{3x+1}{x^2+7x+10}$$

$$= \dfrac{(x-3)\cancel{(x+2)}}{2x+1} \cdot \dfrac{3x+1}{(x+5)\cancel{(x+2)}}$$

$$= \dfrac{3x^2-8x-3}{2x^2+11x+5}$$

Division problems can also be written as complex fractions. These are fractions within a fraction. For example, the division problem above can also be presented this way:

$$\dfrac{x^2-x-6}{2x+1} \div \dfrac{x^2+7x+10}{3x+1} = \dfrac{\dfrac{x^2-x-6}{2x+1}}{\dfrac{x^2+7x+10}{3x+1}}$$

Radical Expressions and Equations

To solve radical equations, use the rules for radical expressions along with the following steps.

Step 1: Move one radical to one side of the equation and everything else to the other side.

Step 2: Eliminate the radical by raising both sides by a power that is the reciprocal of the exponent.

Step 3: Repeat steps 1 and 2 if radicals are still present.

Step 4: Solve the remaining equation.

Step 5: Check for extraneous solutions (received values that are not actual solutions).

EXAMPLE

Solve the radical equation $\sqrt{10x-4}-4=0$.

Solution

Step 1: Isolate the radical by putting it on one side:

$$\sqrt{10x-4} = 4$$

Step 2: Get rid of the radical by squaring both sides of the equation:

$$\left(\sqrt{10x-4}\right)^2 = 4^2$$
$$10x-4 = 16$$

Step 3: All radicals are eliminated, so proceed to step 4.

Step 4: Solve the remaining equation:

$$10x - 4 = 16$$
$$10x = 20$$
$$x = 2$$

Step 5: Check the solution:

$$\sqrt{10(2) - 4} - 4 = 0$$
$$\sqrt{16} - 4 = 0$$
$$0 = 0$$

The solution is $x = 2$.

Exponential and Logarithmic Equations

Exponential and logarithmic equations are related to each other by the fact that the exponential is the inverse of the logarithm and vice versa. We use this fact to solve the equations.

In an exponential equation, the variable is an exponent. For example, $4^x = 1$ and $3e^x - 1 = 2$. To solve exponential equations, express each side of the equation as a power of the same base. If the bases are the same, then the exponents can be said to be equal. For example, $2^x = 16$ becomes $2^x = 2^4$, thus $x = 4$.

Additionally, you can use logarithms. Logarithms express the relationship that:

$$y = \log_b a \Leftrightarrow b^y = a$$

For the previous example, how many 2s do you need to multiply together to get 16? If you write this in exponential and logarithmic forms, you have:

$$2^x = 16 \Leftrightarrow x = \log_2 16$$

You need $2 \times 2 \times 2 \times 2$ or four 2s. Thus, you have

$$2^4 = 16 \Leftrightarrow 4 = \log_2 16$$

When both sides of an exponential equation do not share a common base, however, you will take the log of both sides instead.

When you see e, remember that it is a special constant with an approximate value of 2.7182818. Its corresponding logarithm is called the natural log and is written as $\ln(x)$. Further, if there is no base on the log (the b in the earlier equations), it is assumed to be 10.

Here's an example where both sides of the exponential equation lack a common base.

EXAMPLE

Solve: $4(3^{3x}) = 5$

Solution

Isolate the exponential term:

$$4(3^{3x}) = 5$$
$$3^{3x} = \frac{5}{4}$$

Take log base 3 of both sides and solve:

$$\log_3(3^{3x}) = \log_3\left(\frac{5}{4}\right)$$
$$3x = \log_3\left(\frac{5}{4}\right)$$
$$x = \frac{1}{3}\log_3\left(\frac{5}{4}\right)$$

The solution is typically left in this form.

To solve logarithmic equations, use the same concept except take each side to the power of the base of the logarithm. When working with logarithms, you may find the following rules helpful.

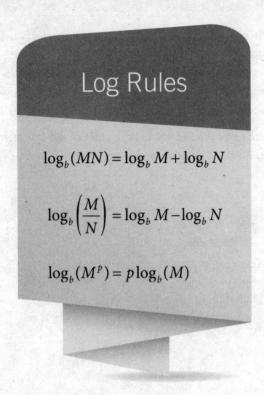

Log Rules

$$\log_b(MN) = \log_b M + \log_b N$$

$$\log_b\left(\frac{M}{N}\right) = \log_b M - \log_b N$$

$$\log_b(M^p) = p\log_b(M)$$

Functions

Functions are used to discuss and evaluate how one variable, known as an independent variable, relates to another variable, known as a dependent variable.

Definitions and Notation

Let D and R be any two sets of numbers. A function is a rule that assigns to each element of D one and only one element of R. The set D is called the domain of the function, and the set R is called the range. A function can be specified by listing all of the elements in the first set next to the corresponding elements in the second set or by giving a rule or a formula by which elements from the first set can be associated with elements from the second set.

As an example, let the set $D = \{1, 2, 3, 4\}$ and set $R = \{5, 6, 7, 8\}$. The diagram below indicates a particular function, f, by showing how each element of D is associated with an element of R.

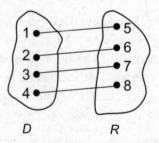

D R

This diagram shows that the domain value of 1 is associated with the range value of 5. Similarly, 2 is associated with 6, 3 is associated with 7, and 4 is associated with 8. The function f can also be described in words by saying that f is the function that assigns to each domain value x the range value $x + 4$.

Typically, the letter x is used to represent the elements of the domain and the letter y is used to represent the elements of the range. This enables us to write the equation $y = x + 4$ to express the rule of association for the function above.

Note that as soon as a domain value x is selected, a range value y is determined by this rule. For this reason, x is referred to as the independent variable, and y is called the dependent variable.

EXAMPLE

Solve: $\log(-3x) - \log(2x + 4) = 1$

Solution

Use the log rules to isolate the log term. Then take both sides to the 10th power since this is assumed to be base 10:

$$\log(-3x) - \log(2x + 4) = 1$$

$$\log\left(\frac{-3x}{2x + 4}\right) = 1$$

$$10^{\log\left(\frac{-3x}{2x+4}\right)} = 10^1$$

$$\frac{-3x}{2x + 4} = 10$$

$$10(2x + 4) = -3x$$

$$20x + 40 = -3x$$

$$23x = -40$$

$$x = \frac{-40}{23} = -\frac{40}{23}$$

Often, the rule of association for a function is written in function notation. In this notation, the symbol $f(x)$, which is read "f of x," is used instead of y to represent the range value. Therefore, the rule for our function can be written $f(x) = x + 4$. If you were asked to determine which range value was associated with the domain value of, say, 3, you would compute $f(x) = f(3) = 3 + 4 = 7$. Note that, in this notation, the letter f is typically used to stand for "function," although any other letter could also be used. Therefore, this rule could also be written as $g(x) = x + 4$. Consider the following examples.

EXAMPLES

Using function notation, write the rule for a function that associates, to each number in the domain, a range value that is 7 less than 5 times the domain value.

Solution

$$f(x) = 5x - 7$$

Use the function from the problem above to determine the range value that is associated with a domain value of −12.

Solution

$$f(-12) = 5(-12) - 7 = -60 - 7 = -67$$

If $f(x) = 8x + 9$, determine the value of $f(5)$, $f(q)$, $f(p^2)$, and $f(r + 3)$.

Solution

$$f(5) = 8(5) + 9 = 40 + 9 = 49$$

In the same way, to determine the value of $f(q)$, simply substitute q for the value of x in the rule for $f(x)$.

Therefore, $f(q) = 8q + 9$.

Similarly, $f(p^2) = 8(p^2) + 9 = 8p^2 + 9$.

Similarly, $f(r + 3) = 8(r + 3) + 9 = 8r + 24 + 9 = 8r + 33$.

Operations of Functions

Functions can be added, subtracted, multiplied, and divided. Function operations work just like operations on expressions. The notation for these operations is in the following table.

FUNCTION OPERATIONS	
Sum of f and g	$(f + g)(x) = f(x) + g(x)$
Difference of f and g	$(f - g)(x) = f(x) - g(x)$
Product of f and g	$(f \cdot g)(x) = f(x) \cdot g(x)$
Quotient of f and g	$\left(\dfrac{f}{g}\right)(x) = \dfrac{f(x)}{g(x)}$
Composite function	$(f \circ g)(x) = f(g(x))$

The new operation here is function composition. This operation allows you to find the function of another function. The input is now a function instead of a value for x.

EXAMPLE

Find $(f \circ g)(x)$ for $f(x) = 2x - x^2$ and $g(x) = x + 1$.

Solution

Replace each x in $f(x)$ with $g(x)$, then replace $g(x)$ with $x + 1$ and simplify.

$$(f \circ g)(x) = f(g(x)) = 2(g(x)) - (g(x))^2$$
$$= 2(x + 1) - (x + 1)^2$$
$$= 2x + 2 - (x^2 + 2x + 1)$$
$$= 2x + 2 - x^2 - 2x - 1$$
$$= -x^2 + 1$$

Inverse Functions

Inverse functions are based on a given function $f(x)$. The notation of an inverse to f is $f^{-1}(x)$. These functions "undo" each other. That is, $f(f^{-1}(x)) = f^{-1}(f(x)) = x$. The graphs of the two functions are the same but are reflected across the line $y = x$.

To find the inverse of a function, let $y = f(x)$, switch x and y values and then solve for y.

EXAMPLE

Find $f^{-1}(x)$ for the function $f(x) = 5x - 7$.

Solution

$$y = 5x - 7$$
$$x = 5y - 7$$
$$x + 7 = 5y$$
$$y = \frac{x + 7}{5}$$

Thus:

$$f^{-1}(x) = \frac{x + 7}{5}$$

The following graphic helps illustrate how an original function and its inverse are reflected across the line represented by $y = x$:

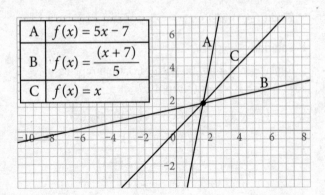

A	$f(x) = 5x - 7$
B	$f(x) = \dfrac{(x + 7)}{5}$
C	$f(x) = x$

Types of Functions

There are numerous types of functions that you may be asked to work with in either their original or inverse forms.

Linear Functions

Linear functions are functions of the form $y = f(x) = mx + b$. When graphed as a line, it will have a slope (steepness) m and y-intercept (where it crosses the y-axis) of b.

Example of Two Different Lines:
$$f(x) = -2x + 2 \text{ and } f(x) = 3x - 2$$

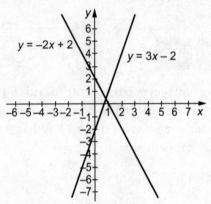

A linear function is also any function whose graph is a line. Every linear function can be written as an equation. Each equation can also be put into the form:

$y = mx + b$, where m is the slope and b is the y-intercept of the line

Quadratic Functions

A quadratic function is any function of the form $f(x) = ax^2 + bx + c$ where a, b, and c are real numbers. The shape of the graph of a quadratic function is called a parabola. It reaches a maximum or minimum height called the vertex.

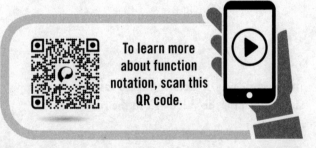

To learn more about function notation, scan this QR code.

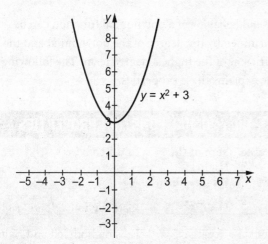

When $a > 0$, the graph opens up. When $a < 0$, the graph opens down. The x-coordinate of the vertex can be found using the formula $-\dfrac{b}{2a}$. The resulting value can then be substituted into the function to find the y-coordinate.

EXAMPLE

Find the minimum value reached by the function $f(x) = x^2 - 6x + 1$.

Solution

The minimum value is reached when:

$$x = -\frac{b}{2a} = \frac{6}{2} = 3$$

Evaluate the function for 3 to find the minimum value:

$$f(3) = 3^2 - 6(3) + 1 = 9 - 18 + 1 = -8$$

Thus, the vertex is at $(3, -8)$, and the minimum value reached by the function is -8.

Quadratic functions can be written in different forms. The *vertex form* is the most useful for determining the vertex, which will also show either the maximum or minimum value of the function.

The vertex form of a quadratic function is $y = a(x - h)^2 + k$, where the x-coordinate of the vertex is h and the y-coordinate of the vertex is k.

For example, in the function $y = (x - 3)^2 - 2$, the vertex is located at $(3, -2)$. This also means that the axis of symmetry is $x = 3$ and the minimum value of the function is -2.

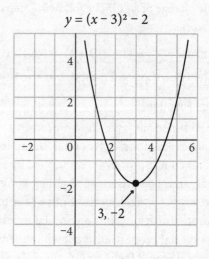

$y = (x - 3)^2 - 2$

The *factored form* of a quadratic function is the most useful for identifying the roots of the function. The factored form of a quadratic function is $y = a(x - r_1)(x - r_2)$, where r_1 and r_2 are the roots of the function. The roots may also be referred to as the x-intercepts of the graph or the zeros of the function.

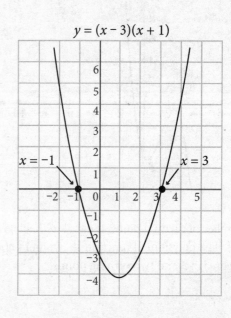

$y = (x - 3)(x + 1)$

In the example shown, the quadratic function $y = x^2 - 2x - 3$ can be rewritten as $y = (x - 3)(x + 1)$, because:

$$(x-3)(x+1) = x^2 + x - 3x - 3$$
$$= x^2 - 2x - 3$$

The roots of the function are then $x = 3$ and $x = -1$ (notice the change of sign). The following steps show why this works:

- When $x = 3$, $y = (3 - 3)(3 + 1) = (0)(4) = 0$
- When $x = -1$, $y = (-1 - 3)(-1 + 1) = (-4)(0) = 0$

Polynomial Functions

Polynomial functions have the same form as polynomial expressions. Polynomial functions have variables taken to a power, are multiplied by some coefficient, and then are added together. For example, $f(x) = -x^3 + 4x^2 - x$. Technically, both linear functions and quadratic functions are polynomial functions. But they have special properties, as shown in the previous sections. We will focus on polynomials where the degree (highest power) is 3 or greater.

The graphs of polynomial functions are curves with turning points where they change direction.

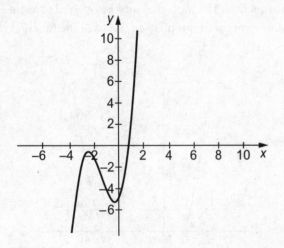

The number of turning points is equal to the degree minus 1. The polynomial function shown in the figure has a degree of 3 and two turning points.

The end behavior of a polynomial function can be determined by the degree of the polynomial and the coefficient of the highest degree term. The following table explains these properties.

POLYNOMIAL FUNCTION PROPERTIES

Degree	Sign of the Highest Degree Term	End Behavior
Even	Positive	Rises on both left and right
Even	Negative	Falls on both left and right
Odd	Positive	Falls on left, rises on right
Odd	Negative	Rises on left, falls on right

In the previous example, the polynomial function has an odd degree and a positive coefficient for the highest degree term.

Rational Functions

Rational functions are similar to rational expressions. Their domain is determined by the denominator. When the denominator is zero, the value is not included in the domain. Further, rational functions have asymptotes. The function approaches these lines but never crosses them.

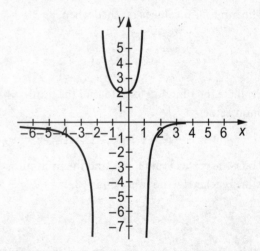

To find the vertical asymptotes of a rational function, find all values where the denominator is 0 but the numerator is not 0.

EXAMPLE

Find all vertical asymptotes of the function

$$f(x) = \frac{x^2 - x - 2}{x^2 - 2x - 3}.$$

Solution

$$f(x) = \frac{x^2 - x - 2}{x^2 - 2x - 3} = \frac{(x+1)(x-2)}{(x+1)(x-3)}$$

The denominator is 0 whenever $x = -1$ or 3. However, -1 also makes the numerator 0, so the only vertical asymptote is $x = 3$.

Horizontal asymptotes are found by looking at the degrees of the highest degree terms. The following table shows the rules for this.

HORIZONTAL ASYMPTOTE PROPERTIES

Degrees of the terms	Horizontal asymptote
The same	y = the ratio of the coefficients Ex: $y = \frac{2x^3 - 4}{5x^3}$ has horizontal asymptote $y = \frac{2}{5}$
Higher degree in the numerator	No horizontal asymptote
Lower degree in numerator	$y = 0$ is the horizontal asymptote

The function $f(x) = \frac{x^2 - x - 2}{x^2 - 2x - 3}$ has a horizontal asymptote of $y = 1$ since the degrees are the same and the coefficients are both 1.

Radical Functions

Radical functions (e.g., $y = \sqrt{x}$) are easily recognized due to the presence of the radical sign. Since the x in $y = \sqrt{x}$ cannot be negative, the graph of $y = \sqrt{x}$ only appears in the first quadrant.

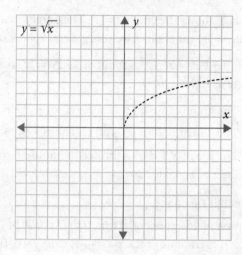

The image shows the graph $y = \sqrt{x}$. The graphs of all radical functions with even number roots have this general appearance.

Some other characteristics of square root functions are as follows:

- The graph of $y = \sqrt{x}$ is the top half of a parabola that opens sideways.
- As you travel out along the graph of $y = \sqrt{x}$, the graph keeps going higher.
- The domain and range of $y = \sqrt{x}$ are both numbers greater than or equal to zero.

Absolute Value Functions

Absolute value functions ($y = |x|$) are easily recognized due to the presence of the absolute value sign. The graphs of these functions are also distinctive due to their V shape.

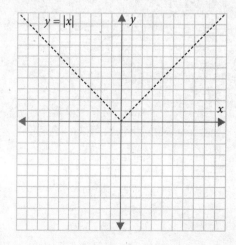

The image shows the graph $y = |x|$. The graphs of all absolute value functions have this general appearance.

Some other characteristics about absolute value functions are as follows:

- The graph of $y = |x|$ is symmetric over the y-axis.
- The domain of $y = |x|$ is all real numbers.
- The range of $y = |x|$ is limited to numbers greater than or equal to zero.

Exponential Functions

The graph of an exponential function $f(x) = b^x$ has a horizonal asymptote of the x-axis—that is, $y = 0$. If the base is a whole number, the graph rises rapidly on the right. If the base is a fraction or decimal, the graph falls quickly from left to right.

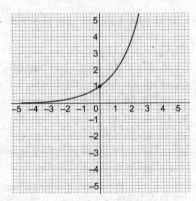

Graph of $y = 2^x$

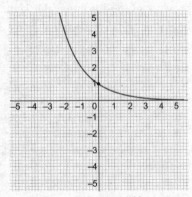

Graph of $y = \left(\frac{1}{2}\right)^x$

Logarithmic Functions

Logarithmic functions are inverse functions to exponential functions. Their graphs are a reflection across $y = x$ of the graph of the corresponding exponential function. The graph of a logarithmic function $f(x) = \log_b(x)$ has a vertical asymptote of the y-axis—that is, $x = 0$. The graph rises from left to right, but not as quickly as an exponential function.

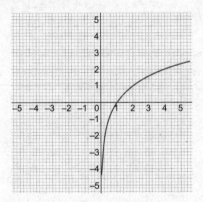

Graph of $y = \log_2(x)$

Note that if a function like that shown is translated, that is, rewritten by adding or subtracting within or outside the function, the locations of the asymptotes may change.

Trigonometry

People use trigonometry to figure out unknown angles or distances based on those that are known. Its genesis stemmed from fields like astronomy, geography, and more, where calculating unknown distances is critical.

The Three Basic Trigonometric Ratios

The three basic trigonometric ratios are sine, cosine, and tangent. You can find the sine, cosine, or tangent of an acute angle in a right triangle.

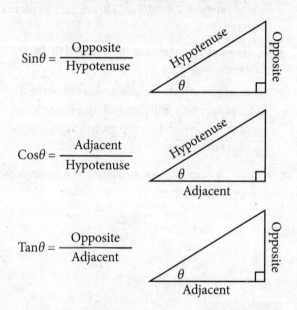

$$\text{Sin}\,\theta = \frac{\text{Opposite}}{\text{Hypotenuse}}$$

$$\text{Cos}\,\theta = \frac{\text{Adjacent}}{\text{Hypotenuse}}$$

$$\text{Tan}\,\theta = \frac{\text{Opposite}}{\text{Adjacent}}$$

Finding Trigonometric Ratios

Use **SOH**, **CAH**, **TOA** to remember how to find each ratio.

Consider $\angle B$:

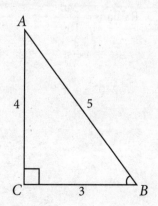

The side **opposite** or across from it is $\overline{AC}$.

The side **adjacent** or next to it is $\overline{CB}$.

The **hypotenuse** of the right triangle is $\overline{AB}$.

Find the trigonometric ratios.

Sine of $\angle B$

To find the sine of $\angle B$ think SOH:

$$\sin B = \frac{\text{Opposite}}{\text{Hypotenuse}} = \frac{AC}{AB} = \frac{4}{5}$$

Cosine of $\angle B$

To find the cosine of $\angle B$ think CAH:

$$\cos B = \frac{\text{Adjacent}}{\text{Hypotenuse}} = \frac{CB}{AB} = \frac{3}{5}$$

Tangent of $\angle B$

To find the tangent of $\angle B$ think TOA:

$$\tan B = \frac{\text{Opposite}}{\text{Adjacent}} = \frac{AC}{CB} = \frac{4}{3}$$

The measure of angle B will correspond to each of those ratios. If you were to calculate with a calculator the inverse of $\sin B = \frac{4}{5}$ $\left(\sin^{-1}\left(\frac{4}{5}\right)\right)$ or the inverses of $\cos B = \frac{3}{5}$ or $\tan B = \frac{4}{3}$, they would all reveal that angle B measures 53.13 degrees. If you input sin 53.13, you would get a ratio of 0.8, or $\frac{4}{5}$.

Unknown Lengths

If one side length and one angle measurement of a right triangle are known, all remaining sides and angle measurements can be found. Since the trigonometric ratios of most angles are irrational, a calculator (in degree mode) can be used.

In triangle ABC, $AB = 4$ cm and $\angle B$ measures 25°. Because all angles in a triangle add to 180°, the two non-right angles must add to 90°.

$$m\angle A + 25° = 90° \rightarrow m\angle A = 90° - 25° = 65°$$

Side AC is opposite to angle B and we know the hypotenuse, so use the sine ratio:

$$\frac{AC}{4} = \sin 25° \rightarrow AC = 4\sin 25° \approx 1.7 \text{ cm}$$

Side BC is adjacent to angle B and we know the hypotenuse, so use the cosine ratio:

$$\frac{BC}{4} = \cos 25° \rightarrow BC = 4\cos 25° \approx 3.6 \text{ cm}$$

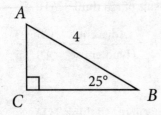

If the hypotenuse is unknown but the measure of a leg and one angle is known, the solution process is very similar. The only difference is the ratio that is used and the location of the unknown in the equation.

In triangle ABC, $BC = 2$ in. and angle A measures 35°. Side AC is adjacent to angle A and we know the opposite side, so use the tangent ratio:

$$\frac{\text{opp}}{\text{adj}} : \frac{2}{AC} = \tan 35° \rightarrow AC = \frac{2}{\tan 35°} \approx 2.9 \text{ in.}$$

Side AB is the hypotenuse and side BC is opposite angle A, so use the sine ratio:

$$\frac{\text{opp}}{\text{hyp}} : \frac{2}{AB} = \sin 35° \rightarrow AB = \frac{2}{\sin 35°} \approx 3.5 \text{ in.}$$

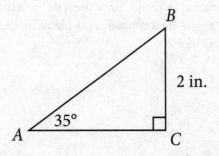

Degrees and Radians

There are two ways in which angles can be measured: degrees and radians.

Converting Degrees to Radians

While degree measures are frequently used, a radian measure is helpful in that it relates to the circumference of a circle and trigonometric functions.

- One entire revolution of a circle is equivalent to 360°. In terms of radians, one entire revolution is equivalent to 2π radians. Therefore, 2π radians = 360°.

- Half of a circle measures 180°, so half of 2π radians is π radians.

- Since angles within a circle divide the entire 2π radians proportionally, simple proportions can be used to convert an angle given in degrees to an angle in radians.

The formula for converting a measure given in degrees to a measure in radians is:

$$\text{Radians} = \frac{\text{Degrees}}{180°} \cdot \pi$$

EXAMPLE

Convert 240° to radians.

Solution

$$\text{Radians} = \frac{240°}{180°} \cdot \pi$$
$$= \frac{4}{3}\pi$$
$$240° = \frac{4}{3}\pi$$

Converting Radians to Degrees

Just as an angle measure given in degrees can be converted into an equivalent angle measure in radians, an angle measure in radians can be converted into an equivalent degree measure. The formula for converting radians to degrees is:

$$\text{Degrees} = \frac{180°}{\pi} \cdot \text{Radians}$$

EXAMPLE

Convert $\frac{5\pi}{6}$ radians to degrees.

Solution

$$\frac{180°}{\pi} \cdot \frac{5\pi}{6} = 150°$$

$$\frac{5\pi}{6} \text{ radians} = 150°$$

Arc Length

An arc is a portion of the circumference of a circle, as indicated by the shading in the example shown. Recall that the circumference of a circle, C, is the distance around the circle, which is found by multiplying the length of the radius, r, by 2π:

$$C = 2\pi r$$

The length of an arc is determined by the central angle which creates the arc. Arc length is typically represented by the variable s.

The measure of the central angle of a circle is typically represented by the Greek letter theta, which is θ.

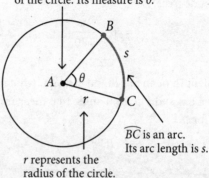

∠ BAC is a central angle of the circle. Its measure is θ.

$\widehat{BC}$ is an arc. Its arc length is s.

r represents the radius of the circle.

The radian measure θ of a central angle of a circle is defined as the ratio of the length of the arc, s, opposite of the central angle, to the radius r of the circle:

$$\theta = \frac{s}{r}$$

To find the arc length, multiply the radius of the circle by the measure of the central angle in radians:

$$s = r\theta$$

When given an angle in radian measure, substitute the angle in radians for θ, and multiply it by the radius of the circle.

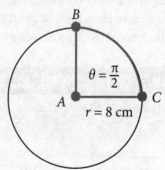

$$5 = \frac{\pi}{2} \cdot 8 = 4\pi \approx 4(3.14)$$
$$= 12.56 \text{ cm}$$

If the central angle measure is given in degrees, change the angle to radians first, and then use the arc length formula.

The formula for finding the arc length, when an angle is given in degrees, is:

$$s = r\theta \cdot \frac{\pi}{180°}$$

Find the length of an arc *BC* on circle *A*, which has a radius of 4 cm and a central angle that measures 120°. Use 3.14 for π.

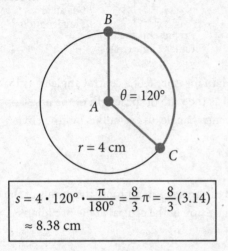

$$s = 4 \cdot 120° \cdot \frac{\pi}{180°} = \frac{8}{3}\pi = \frac{8}{3}(3.14)$$
$$\approx 8.38 \text{ cm}$$

Radian Measure and Trigonometric Functions

It pays to remember some key values for the trigonometric functions in both degrees and radians. Key values of the trigonometric ratios in the first quadrant can be derived from two special triangles (shown after the table).

KEY VALUES OF TRIGONOMETRIC RATIOS				
Degree	**Radians**	**Sine**	**Cosine**	**Tangent**
0°	0	0	1	0
30°	$\frac{\pi}{6}$	$\frac{1}{2}$	$\frac{\sqrt{3}}{2}$	$\frac{\sqrt{3}}{3}$
45°	$\frac{\pi}{4}$	$\frac{\sqrt{2}}{2}$	$\frac{\sqrt{2}}{2}$	1
60°	$\frac{\pi}{3}$	$\frac{\sqrt{3}}{2}$	$\frac{1}{2}$	$\sqrt{3}$
90°	$\frac{\pi}{2}$	1	0	undefined

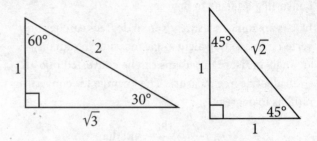

Trigonometric Functions and the Unit Circle

As in the example below, the unit circle is a circle with the center at the origin (0, 0) and a radius of 1. The central angle θ can be expressed in degrees or radians.

If an angle θ is drawn in the standard position, the terminal side of the angle will intersect the unit circle. The *x*-coordinate of the intersection point will be the cosine of θ and the *y*-coordinate of the intersection point will be the sine of θ.

In the first quadrant, both the cosine and the sine are positive. As angles rotate in the II, III, and IV quadrants, the signs of the cosine and sine change accordingly.

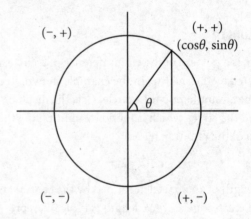

Graphs of Trigonometric Functions

Sine and cosine are periodic functions, since their patterns of *y*-values repeat every 360°.

The graphs for $y = \sin x$ and $y = \cos x$ follow. Note that the *x*-axis is measured in radians, marked with the key values $\frac{\pi}{2}$ (or 90°), π (or 180°), $\frac{3\pi}{2}$ (or 270°), and 2π (or 360°).

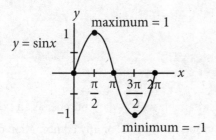

$y = \sin x$

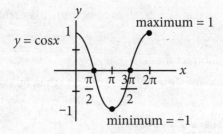

$y = \cos x$

The period of both of these graphs is 2π since that is the interval of x-values over which the function completes one cycle.

The amplitude is one-half the positive difference of the maximum and minimum values of the functions. For both these graphs, the amplitude is:

$$\frac{1}{2}\left(1-(-1)\right)=\frac{1}{2}(2)=1$$

Note that the sine function is positive between 0 and π and negative between π and 2π. The cosine function is positive between 0 and $\frac{\pi}{2}$ and between $\frac{3\pi}{2}$ and 2π and negative between $\frac{\pi}{2}$ and $\frac{3\pi}{2}$.

Amplitude and Period

You can use the equation and/or the graph of a trigonometric function to identify its amplitude and period. For an equation in the form $y = a \sin b\,\theta$ or $y = a \cos b\,\theta$, the amplitude is a and period is $\frac{2\pi}{b}$.

For the equation $y = \cos 4\theta$, the amplitude is 1 and the period is $\frac{2\pi}{4}=\frac{\pi}{2}$.

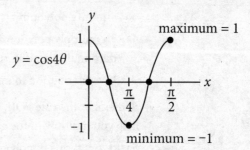

$y = \cos 4\theta$

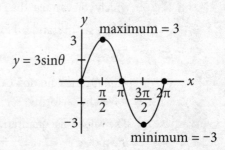

$y = 3\sin\theta$

For the equation $y = 3 \sin \theta$, the amplitude is 3 and the period is $\frac{2\pi}{1}=2\pi$.

SUMMING IT UP

- A polynomial is one or more terms, each having a variable with a whole number as an exponent.

- Terms make up expressions, and a term is a number, a variable, or any combination of numbers or variables without an operation symbol.

- One simplification method for simplifying polynomials involves combining like terms to write the expression in standard form.

    ○ Simplify polynomials in order to add or subtract them.

    ○ To multiply polynomials, break each monomial into component parts then follow standard multiplication rules.

    ○ Use distribution to multiply a polynomial and a monomial.

- Remember the rule FOIL (First, Outer, Inner, Last) when multiplying binomials. This will help you multiply in the correct order to gather and simplify terms later.

- Factor out terms in polynomials as necessary. Factor trinomials to create two binomials for which you can use the FOIL method.

- When set in standard form, a quadratic equation looks like the following:

$$ax^2 + bx + c = 0$$

- A quadratic equation can have 0, 1, or 2 real solutions. Many quadratic equations can be solved by factoring.

- The values of a quadratic equation can be arranged in the quadratic formula as follows to find the roots:

$$x = \frac{-b \pm \sqrt{b^2 - 4ac}}{2a}$$

- The part of the quadratic formula that is underneath the square root symbol is called the discriminant ($b^2 - 4ac$). Evaluating the discriminant tells you whether a quadratic equation has two real roots, one real root, or no real roots.

- A quadratic inequality is any inequality that can be arranged so that there is a quadratic expression on one side and a zero on the other. To solve quadratic inequalities, factor and then test the regions to find where the inequality is true.

- A function, f, is a rule that assigns to each element x in set A exactly one element y, denoted $f(x)$, in another set B. To compute the functional value, substitute the given value in for the variable and simplify the resulting arithmetic expression using the rules of arithmetic.

- Functions of the form $f(x) = A \cdot b^x$, where A is a nonzero real number and b is a positive real number not equal to 1, are called exponential functions.

- The inverse function (that is, the function obtained by reflecting a given function's graph over the $y = x$ line) of $f(x) = b^x$, $b > 1$, is a function called a logarithmic function, denoted as $g(x) = \log_b x$, where b is the base.

- The inverse relationship between exponentials and logarithms gives rise to $\log_a b = c$ whenever $a^c = b$.

- There are three main logarithm rules used for simplifying expressions involving the logarithms of powers, products, and quotients:

  1. the logarithm of a product is the sum of the logarithms of the individual factors

  2. the logarithm of a quotient is the difference of the logarithms of the dividend and divisor (i.e., numerator and denominator)

  3. the logarithm of the power of a quantity is the power times the logarithm of just the quantity (without the power)

- The three basic trigonometric ratios are sine, cosine, and tangent.

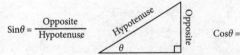 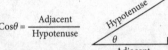 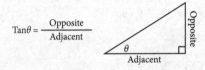

- You can use SOH, CAH, and TOA to remember each and find trigonometric ratios. If one side length and one angle measurement of a right triangle are known, all remaining sides and angle measurements can be found.

- The radian measure θ of a central angle of a circle is defined as the ratio of the length of the arc, s, opposite of the central angle, to the radius r of the circle:

$$\theta = \frac{s}{r}$$

KNOWLEDGE CHECK

ADVANCED ALGEBRA AND FUNCTIONS

Directions: In the following questions, work out each problem and mark the letter that corresponds to the correct answer. The answers and explanations will follow. Note that you may only use a calculator where indicated by an icon (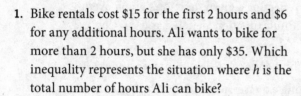).

1. Bike rentals cost $15 for the first 2 hours and $6 for any additional hours. Ali wants to bike for more than 2 hours, but she has only $35. Which inequality represents the situation where h is the total number of hours Ali can bike?

   A. $6 + 15h > 35$

   B. $6(h - 2) + 15 \leq 35$

   C. $6h + 15 < 35$

   D. $6(h + 2) + 15 \geq 35$

2. What is the equation of the line that runs perpendicular to the line $y - 2x = 0$ and passes through the point $(-4, 0)$?

   A. $y = 2x + 8$

   B. $y = \dfrac{1}{2}x - 4$

   C. $y = 2x - 4$

   D. $y = -\dfrac{1}{2}x - 2$

3. A common velocity formula is $v = \dfrac{1}{2}gt^2$, where v is velocity, t is time, and g is gravity. Which of the following correctly expresses g in terms of v and t?

   A. $g = \dfrac{2v}{t^2}$

   B. $g = 2vt^2$

   C. $g = \dfrac{2v}{t}$

   D. $g = \dfrac{v}{2t^2}$

4. What is the equation of the line passing through the points $(1, 4)$ and $(-2, 2)$?

   A. $y - 1 = \dfrac{2}{3}(x - 4)$

   B. $y + 1 = \dfrac{2}{3}(x + 4)$

   C. $y - 2 = \dfrac{2}{3}(x + 2)$

   D. $y + 2 = \dfrac{3}{2}(x - 2)$

5. Use the substitution method to solve the following system of linear equations:

$$\begin{cases} 3x + 2y = -3 \\ 2x - y = 5 \end{cases}$$

   A. $3\left(y + \dfrac{5}{2}\right) + 2y = -3$

   B. $3\left(\dfrac{5}{2} - y\right) + 2y = -3$

   C. $3x + 2(5 - 2x) = -3$

   D. $3x + 2(2x - 5) = -3$

6. Solve for x: $x^2 - 2x - 15 = 0$

   A. $+5$ or -3

   B. -5 or $+3$

   C. -5 or -3

   D. $+5$ or $+3$

7. Solve for x: $\dfrac{2}{x-2} - \dfrac{5}{x+2} = \dfrac{2}{x^2-4}$

A. $x = -4$

B. $x = -2$

C. $x = 2$

D. $x = 4$

8. Solve for x: $2x^2 + 3x = 7$

A. $x = \dfrac{3+\sqrt{65}}{4}$, $x = \dfrac{3-\sqrt{65}}{4}$

B. $x = \dfrac{-3+\sqrt{65}}{4}$, $x = \dfrac{-3-\sqrt{65}}{4}$

C. $x = \dfrac{3+\sqrt{47}}{4}$, $x = \dfrac{3-\sqrt{47}}{4}$

D. $x = \dfrac{-3+\sqrt{47}}{4}$, $x = \dfrac{-3-\sqrt{47}}{4}$

9. What is the highest point on the graph of the parabola $g(x) = -(x+4)^2 - 5$?

A. $(4, 5)$

B. $(-4, 5)$

C. $(-4, -5)$

D. $(4, -5)$

10. If $m(x) = x(x+5)$ and $n(x) = 1 - \dfrac{1}{2}x^2$, compute $(m-n)(-2)$.

A. -7

B. -6

C. -5

D. -1

11. Solve for a: $\dfrac{3}{a-7} + \dfrac{5}{a^2-13a+42} = \dfrac{7}{a-6}$

A. $a = -18$

B. $a = -9$

C. $a = 9$

D. $a = 18$

12. A soccer player kicks a ball with an initial speed of 24 feet per second from the ground. The trajectory of the ball is described by the quadratic function $h(t) = -16t^2 + 24t$, where $h(t)$ is measured in feet and t is measured in seconds. How long is the ball in the air?

A. 1 second

B. $\dfrac{3}{2}$ seconds

C. 2 seconds

D. $\dfrac{5}{2}$ seconds

13. A taxi company charges $2.25 for the first mile and $0.45 for each mile thereafter. If x stands for the number of miles a passenger travels, which of the following functions relates the length of the trip to its cost?

A. $f(x) = 2.25 + 0.45(x + 1)$

B. $f(x) = 2.25 + 0.45(1 - x)$

C. $f(x) = 2.25 + 0.45(x - 1)$

D. $f(x) = 2.25 + 0.45x$

14. Which of these functions is the result of shifting $f(x) = |x|$ down 5 units?

A. $g(x) = |x - 5|$

B. $g(x) = |x| - 5$

C. $g(x) = |x + 5|$

D. $g(x) = -5|x|$

15. Solve the equation: $x = \sqrt{16x + 225}$

A. $x = 45$

B. $x = 25$

C. $x = -9$

D. $x = -25$

16. If $f(x) = x - \dfrac{1}{x}$ and $g(x) = x + \dfrac{1}{x}$,

compute $(f \cdot g)\left(-\dfrac{1}{2}\right)$.

A. $-\dfrac{15}{4}$

B. -2

C. 0

D. $\dfrac{3}{4}$

17. To which of the following equations is $\log_4 z = 2$ equivalent?

A. $z^2 = 4$

B. $2^4 = z$

C. $4^2 = z$

D. $4^z = 2$

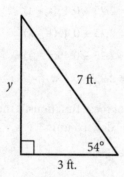

18. What is the value of y in the figure above?

A. $3 \sin 54°$

B. $7 \sin 54°$

C. $\dfrac{\cos 54°}{7}$

D. $7 \cos 54°$

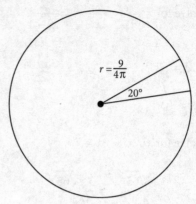

Note: Figure not drawn to scale.

19. Given the circle shown above, what is the length of the arc formed by the 20° angle?

A. $\dfrac{45}{\pi}$

B. $\dfrac{\pi}{4}$

C. $\dfrac{1}{2}$

D. $\dfrac{1}{4}$

20. The number of people living in a certain city has been growing at a constant rate of about 3.8% each year since 1980. The population in 2000 was 38,500. If y is the population of the city x years after 1980, which equation best represents this situation?

A. $y = 18,260(1.038)^x$

B. $y = 38,500(1.38)^x$

C. $y = 38,500(1.038)^x$

D. $y = 81,172(1.38)^x$

9

ANSWER KEY AND EXPLANATIONS

1. B	**5.** D	**9.** C	**13.** C	**17.** C
2. D	**6.** A	**10.** C	**14.** B	**18.** B
3. A	**7.** D	**11.** C	**15.** B	**19.** D
4. C	**8.** B	**12.** B	**16.** A	**20.** A

1. **The correct answer is B.** The cost for the first 2 hours is $15. Subtract the 2 hours from the total number of hours, h, and multiply by $6 an hour to compute the cost for the number of hours over 2. Be sure to add the initial $15 for the first 2 hours:

$$6(h-2) + 15 \le 35$$

2. **The correct answer is D.** The given line's equation can be written as $y = 2x$. Its slope is 2, so the slope of the desired line, being perpendicular to this one, is $-\dfrac{1}{2}$. Using the point-slope formula for the equation of a line, namely $y - y_1 = m(x - x_1)$, with the point $(-4, 0)$, yields:

$$y - 0 = -\frac{1}{2}(x+4)$$
$$y = -\frac{1}{2}x - 2$$

3. **The correct answer is A.** Solve for g as follows:

$$v = \frac{1}{2}gt^2$$
$$2v = gt^2$$
$$\frac{2v}{t^2} = g$$
$$g = \frac{2v}{t^2}$$

4. **The correct answer is C.** The slope of the line is:

$$m = \frac{4-2}{1-(-2)} = \frac{2}{3}$$

Using the point $(2, 2)$, the equation of the line using point-slope form is:

$$y - 2 = \frac{2}{3}(x-(-2))$$

This simplifies to:

$$y - 2 = \frac{2}{3}(x+2)$$

5. **The correct answer is D.** Solve the second equation for y:

$$y = 2x - 5$$

Substitute this in for y in the first equation:

$$3x + 2(2x - 5) = -3$$

6. **The correct answer is A.** Factoring the quadratic yields the following:

$$(x-5)(x+3) = 0$$
$$x = 5 \text{ or } -3$$

7. **The correct answer is D.** The LCD of the fractions in the equation $\dfrac{2}{x-2} - \dfrac{5}{x+2} = \dfrac{2}{x^2-4}$ is $(x-2)(x+2)$. Multiply all terms by the LCD.

$$(x-2)(x+2)\frac{2}{x-2} - (x-2)(x+2)\frac{5}{x+2} = \frac{2}{x^2-4}(x-2)(x+2)$$
$$2(x+2) - 5(x-2) = 2$$
$$2x + 4 - 5x + 10 = 2$$
$$-3x + 14 = 2$$
$$-3x = -12$$
$$x = 4$$

Remember that you should check the answer to make certain that it solves the equation.

8. **The correct answer is B.** Write the equation in standard form:

$$2x^2 + 3x - 7 = 0$$
$$a = 2, b = 3, \text{ and } c = -7$$

Then plug those values into the quadratic formula.

$$x = \frac{-3 \pm \sqrt{(3)^2 - 4(2)(-7)}}{2(2)}$$

$$x = \frac{-3 \pm \sqrt{65}}{4}$$

The solutions are:

$$x = \frac{-3 + \sqrt{65}}{4} \text{ or } \frac{-3 - \sqrt{65}}{4}$$

9. **The correct answer is C.** The vertex form for a quadratic function is $f(x) = a(x - h)^2 + k$, where the vertex is (h, k); this is the highest point on the function if a is negative, as in the given function. Here, $h = -4$ and $k = -5$, so that the vertex is $(-4, -5)$.

10. **The correct answer is C.**

$$(m - n)(-2) = m(-2) - n(-2)$$

Observe:

$$m(-2) = -2(3) = -6$$

$$n(-2) = 1 - \frac{1}{2}(-2)^2$$

$$= 1 - \frac{1}{2}(4)$$

$$= 1 - 2$$

$$= -1$$

So:

$$(m - n)(-2) = -6 - (-1) = -6 + 1 = -5$$

11. **The correct answer is C.** Note that:

$$a^2 - 13a + 42 = (a - 7)(a - 6)$$

The LCD of the fractions in the equation is:

$$(a - 7)(a - 6)$$

Multiply by the LCD:

$$(a-7)(a-6)\frac{3}{a-7} + (a-7)(a-6)\frac{5}{(a-7)(a-6)} = \frac{7}{a-6}(a-7)(a-6)$$

$$3a - 18 + 5 = 7(a - 7)$$

$$3a - 13 = 7a - 49$$

$$4a = 36$$

$$a = 9$$

Then check the solution; $a = 9$ is correct.

12. **The correct answer is B.** Solve $h(t) = 0$. The larger of the two solutions is the amount of time the ball is in the air.

$$h(t) = -16t^2 + 24t = 0$$

$$-8t(2t - 3) = 0$$

$$t = 0, \frac{3}{2}$$

The ball is in the air for $\frac{3}{2}$ seconds.

13. **The correct answer is C.** The cost for the first mile on a trip of x miles is $2.25. After this, there are still $x - 1$ miles to go, and the cost for each of these miles is $0.45. Therefore, the total cost of the trip, in dollars, is $2.25 + 0.45(x - 1)$.

14. **The correct answer is B.** Moving a function down 5 units is performed by subtracting 5 from the output, which here is $|x|$. The desired function is $g(x) = |x| - 5$.

15. **The correct answer is B.**

$$x = \sqrt{16x + 225}$$

$$x^2 = 16x + 225$$

$$x^2 - 16x - 225 = 0$$

$$(x - 25)(x + 9) = 0$$

$$x = 25, -9$$

Note when you substitute $x = -9$ into the equation, you get $-9 = 9$. This means that -9 is an extraneous solution. The only solution is 25.

16. **The correct answer is A.**

First:

$$(f \cdot g)(x) = f(x) \cdot g(x)$$

$$= \left(x - \frac{1}{x}\right) \cdot \left(x + \frac{1}{x}\right)$$

$$= x^2 - \frac{1}{x^2}$$

Then:

$$(f \cdot g)\left(-\frac{1}{2}\right) = \left(-\frac{1}{2}\right)^2 - \frac{1}{\left(-\frac{1}{2}\right)^2}$$

$$= \frac{1}{4} - \frac{1}{\frac{1}{4}}$$

$$= \frac{1}{4} - 4$$

$$= -\frac{15}{4}$$

17. **The correct answer is C.** Use the fact that $\log_b x = y$ is equivalent to $b^y = x$ to see that the given equation is equivalent to $4^2 = z$.

18. **The correct answer is B.** $\sin 54° = \frac{y}{7}$ so that $y = 7\sin 54°$.

19. **The correct answer is D.** First, we convert 20° to radians:

$$\frac{\pi \text{ radians}}{180°} \cdot 20° = \frac{\pi}{9} \text{ radians}$$

Then, we use the formula for the length of an arc, s, formed by an angle of θ radians on a circle of radius, r: $s = r\theta$. Evaluating this formula for the given radius and central angle measure, in radians, gives:

$$\frac{9}{4\pi} \cdot \frac{\pi}{9} = \frac{1}{4}$$

The length of the arc that intercepts the given central angle is $\frac{1}{4}$.

20. **The correct answer is A.** To write an exponential equation for this situation, you need to find P, the population in 1980. Use the formula for exponential growth and the known population 20 years after 1980.

$$38,500 = P(1 + 0.038)^{20}$$

$$\frac{38,500}{(1.038)^{20}} = P$$

$$18,260 \approx P$$

PART V
PRACTICE TESTS

CHAPTER

ACCUPLACER®
Practice Test 1

ACCUPLACER® PRACTICE TEST 1

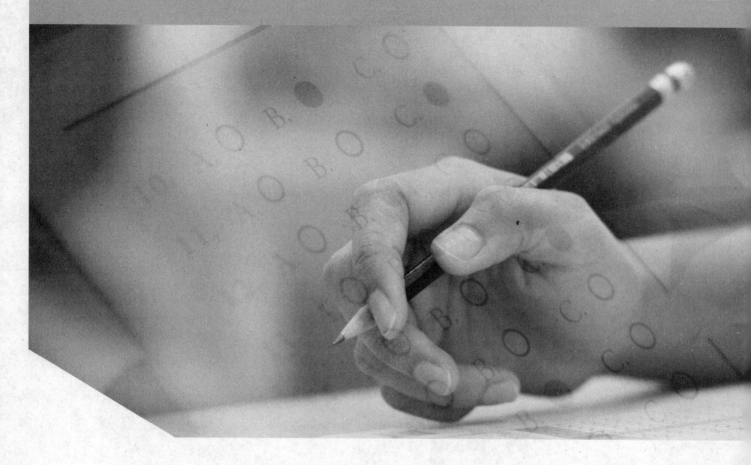

PRACTICE TEST 1

This practice test is designed to help you
recognize your strengths and weaknesses.
The questions cover information from all the
different sections of the ACCUPLACER. Use the
results to help guide and direct your study time.

10

ANSWER SHEET: ACCUPLACER® PRACTICE TEST 1

Reading

1. Ⓐ Ⓑ Ⓒ Ⓓ   5. Ⓐ Ⓑ Ⓒ Ⓓ   9. Ⓐ Ⓑ Ⓒ Ⓓ   13. Ⓐ Ⓑ Ⓒ Ⓓ   17. Ⓐ Ⓑ Ⓒ Ⓓ
2. Ⓐ Ⓑ Ⓒ Ⓓ   6. Ⓐ Ⓑ Ⓒ Ⓓ   10. Ⓐ Ⓑ Ⓒ Ⓓ   14. Ⓐ Ⓑ Ⓒ Ⓓ   18. Ⓐ Ⓑ Ⓒ Ⓓ
3. Ⓐ Ⓑ Ⓒ Ⓓ   7. Ⓐ Ⓑ Ⓒ Ⓓ   11. Ⓐ Ⓑ Ⓒ Ⓓ   15. Ⓐ Ⓑ Ⓒ Ⓓ   19. Ⓐ Ⓑ Ⓒ Ⓓ
4. Ⓐ Ⓑ Ⓒ Ⓓ   8. Ⓐ Ⓑ Ⓒ Ⓓ   12. Ⓐ Ⓑ Ⓒ Ⓓ   16. Ⓐ Ⓑ Ⓒ Ⓓ   20. Ⓐ Ⓑ Ⓒ Ⓓ

Writing

1. Ⓐ Ⓑ Ⓒ Ⓓ   6. Ⓐ Ⓑ Ⓒ Ⓓ   11. Ⓐ Ⓑ Ⓒ Ⓓ   16. Ⓐ Ⓑ Ⓒ Ⓓ   21. Ⓐ Ⓑ Ⓒ Ⓓ
2. Ⓐ Ⓑ Ⓒ Ⓓ   7. Ⓐ Ⓑ Ⓒ Ⓓ   12. Ⓐ Ⓑ Ⓒ Ⓓ   17. Ⓐ Ⓑ Ⓒ Ⓓ   22. Ⓐ Ⓑ Ⓒ Ⓓ
3. Ⓐ Ⓑ Ⓒ Ⓓ   8. Ⓐ Ⓑ Ⓒ Ⓓ   13. Ⓐ Ⓑ Ⓒ Ⓓ   18. Ⓐ Ⓑ Ⓒ Ⓓ   23. Ⓐ Ⓑ Ⓒ Ⓓ
4. Ⓐ Ⓑ Ⓒ Ⓓ   9. Ⓐ Ⓑ Ⓒ Ⓓ   14. Ⓐ Ⓑ Ⓒ Ⓓ   19. Ⓐ Ⓑ Ⓒ Ⓓ   24. Ⓐ Ⓑ Ⓒ Ⓓ
5. Ⓐ Ⓑ Ⓒ Ⓓ   10. Ⓐ Ⓑ Ⓒ Ⓓ   15. Ⓐ Ⓑ Ⓒ Ⓓ   20. Ⓐ Ⓑ Ⓒ Ⓓ   25. Ⓐ Ⓑ Ⓒ Ⓓ

Arithmetic

1. Ⓐ Ⓑ Ⓒ Ⓓ   5. Ⓐ Ⓑ Ⓒ Ⓓ   9. Ⓐ Ⓑ Ⓒ Ⓓ   13. Ⓐ Ⓑ Ⓒ Ⓓ   17. Ⓐ Ⓑ Ⓒ Ⓓ
2. Ⓐ Ⓑ Ⓒ Ⓓ   6. Ⓐ Ⓑ Ⓒ Ⓓ   10. Ⓐ Ⓑ Ⓒ Ⓓ   14. Ⓐ Ⓑ Ⓒ Ⓓ   18. Ⓐ Ⓑ Ⓒ Ⓓ
3. Ⓐ Ⓑ Ⓒ Ⓓ   7. Ⓐ Ⓑ Ⓒ Ⓓ   11. Ⓐ Ⓑ Ⓒ Ⓓ   15. Ⓐ Ⓑ Ⓒ Ⓓ   19. Ⓐ Ⓑ Ⓒ Ⓓ
4. Ⓐ Ⓑ Ⓒ Ⓓ   8. Ⓐ Ⓑ Ⓒ Ⓓ   12. Ⓐ Ⓑ Ⓒ Ⓓ   16. Ⓐ Ⓑ Ⓒ Ⓓ   20. Ⓐ Ⓑ Ⓒ Ⓓ

Quantitative Reasoning, Algebra, and Statistics

1. Ⓐ Ⓑ Ⓒ Ⓓ   5. Ⓐ Ⓑ Ⓒ Ⓓ   9. Ⓐ Ⓑ Ⓒ Ⓓ   13. Ⓐ Ⓑ Ⓒ Ⓓ   17. Ⓐ Ⓑ Ⓒ Ⓓ

2. Ⓐ Ⓑ Ⓒ Ⓓ   6. Ⓐ Ⓑ Ⓒ Ⓓ   10. Ⓐ Ⓑ Ⓒ Ⓓ   14. Ⓐ Ⓑ Ⓒ Ⓓ   18. Ⓐ Ⓑ Ⓒ Ⓓ

3. Ⓐ Ⓑ Ⓒ Ⓓ   7. Ⓐ Ⓑ Ⓒ Ⓓ   11. Ⓐ Ⓑ Ⓒ Ⓓ   15. Ⓐ Ⓑ Ⓒ Ⓓ   19. Ⓐ Ⓑ Ⓒ Ⓓ

4. Ⓐ Ⓑ Ⓒ Ⓓ   8. Ⓐ Ⓑ Ⓒ Ⓓ   12. Ⓐ Ⓑ Ⓒ Ⓓ   16. Ⓐ Ⓑ Ⓒ Ⓓ   20. Ⓐ Ⓑ Ⓒ Ⓓ

Advanced Algebra and Functions

1. Ⓐ Ⓑ Ⓒ Ⓓ   5. Ⓐ Ⓑ Ⓒ Ⓓ   9. Ⓐ Ⓑ Ⓒ Ⓓ   13. Ⓐ Ⓑ Ⓒ Ⓓ   17. Ⓐ Ⓑ Ⓒ Ⓓ

2. Ⓐ Ⓑ Ⓒ Ⓓ   6. Ⓐ Ⓑ Ⓒ Ⓓ   10. Ⓐ Ⓑ Ⓒ Ⓓ   14. Ⓐ Ⓑ Ⓒ Ⓓ   18. Ⓐ Ⓑ Ⓒ Ⓓ

3. Ⓐ Ⓑ Ⓒ Ⓓ   7. Ⓐ Ⓑ Ⓒ Ⓓ   11. Ⓐ Ⓑ Ⓒ Ⓓ   15. Ⓐ Ⓑ Ⓒ Ⓓ   19. Ⓐ Ⓑ Ⓒ Ⓓ

4. Ⓐ Ⓑ Ⓒ Ⓓ   8. Ⓐ Ⓑ Ⓒ Ⓓ   12. Ⓐ Ⓑ Ⓒ Ⓓ   16. Ⓐ Ⓑ Ⓒ Ⓓ   20. Ⓐ Ⓑ Ⓒ Ⓓ

READING

20 Questions

Directions for Questions 1–18: Read the passage(s) below and answer the question(s) based on what is stated or implied in the passage(s) and in any introductory material that may be provided.

In this passage, Sherlock Holmes and Dr. James Watson are about to reunite after a brief hiatus. Watson is contemplating his relationship with Holmes.

(1) To Sherlock Holmes she is always "the" woman. **(2)** I have seldom heard him mention her under any other name. **(3)** In his eyes she eclipses and predominates the whole of her sex. **(4)** It was not that he felt any emotion akin to love for Irene Adler. **(5)** All emotions, and that one particularly, were abhorrent to his cold, precise but admirably balanced mind. **(6)** He was, I take it, the most perfect reasoning and observing machine that the world has seen, but as a lover he would have placed himself in a false position. **(7)** He never spoke of the softer passions, save with a gibe and a sneer. **(8)** They were admirable things for the observer—excellent for drawing the veil from men's motives and actions. **(9)** But for the trained reasoner to admit such intrusions into his own delicate and finely adjusted temperament was to introduce a distracting factor which might throw a doubt upon all his mental results. **(10)** Grit in a sensitive instrument, or a crack in one of his own high-power lenses, would not be more disturbing than a strong emotion in a nature such as his. **(11)** And yet there was but one woman to him, and that woman was the late Irene Adler, of dubious and questionable memory.

(12) I had seen little of Holmes lately. **(13)** My marriage had drifted us away from each other. **(14)** My own complete happiness, and the home-centered interests which rise up around the man who first finds himself master of his own establishment, were sufficient to absorb all my attention, while Holmes, who loathed every form of society with his whole Bohemian soul, remained in our lodgings in Baker Street, buried among his old books. **(15)** He was still, as ever, deeply attracted by the study of crime, and occupied his immense faculties and extraordinary powers of observation in following out those clues, and clearing up those mysteries which had been abandoned as hopeless by the official police. **(16)** From time to time I heard some vague account of his doings: of his summons to Odessa in the case of the Trepoff murder, of his clearing up of the singular tragedy of the Atkinson brothers at Trincomalee, and finally of the mission which he had accomplished so delicately and successfully for the reigning family of Holland. **(17)** Beyond these signs of his activity, however, which I merely shared with all the readers of the daily press, I knew little of my former friend and companion.

From Arthur Conan Doyle, "A Scandal in Bohemia." Originally published in 1891.

1. The contrasts the narrator draws in paragraph 2 (sentences 12–17) between Holmes and himself are most likely meant to suggest that

    A. their friendship is merely superficial.

    B. they are different ages.

    C. the dissolution and renewal of their friendship.

    D. the narrator is engaged with the world while Holmes is mostly withdrawn.

2. The word "abhorrent" as used in sentence 5 most nearly means

    A. loathsome.

    B. enviable.

    C. antithetical.

    D. deviant.

3. The descriptive language in sentence 10 is mainly intended to

    A. establish a time period for the setting of the story.

    B. compare Holmes's mind to a high-powered lens.

    C. contrast Watson's view of love and Holmes's view on love.

    D. reinforce Holmes's view on love and emotion.

4. The reader can infer from Watson's description of Holmes that Holmes is

    A. engaged and passionate.

    B. melancholic and driven.

    C. cerebral and humorous.

    D. reserved and gregarious.

Passage 1

Truck driving is a large, predominantly male occupation, with relatively low educational requirements for entry and distinctive rules governing the terms of employment. According to data from the US Bureau of Labor Statistics (BLS) Occupational Employment Statistics (OES) survey, a nationally representative survey of nonfarm business establishments, there were approximately 1.75 million heavy and tractor-trailer truck drivers in the United States in 2017, along with 877,670 light truck or delivery services drivers and 427,000 driver/sales workers. The occupation is characterized by modest levels of education; the mode is a high school degree. There are low returns to additional education and to firm tenure for heavy and tractor-trailer truck drivers.

Truck driving is important not only because it is a large occupation, but also because it provides critically important services to the US economy. Trucks were estimated to have hauled 61 percent of the total freight (by value) transported in the United States in 2016, and this activity accounted for an estimated 3.5 percent of US gross domestic product. These estimates include both the for-hire trucking industry (firms providing motor freight services to customers who are shippers and receivers) and private carriage (firms hauling their own freight as an internal function within some other primary line of business). Trucking is the primary mode of freight transportation within the United States and a crucial component of international trade. In 2016, 65 percent of the value of goods transported between the United States and its neighboring countries (Canada and Mexico) was carried by truck.

Adapted from Steven V. Burks and Kristen Monaco, "Is the US Labor Market for Truck Drivers Broken?" *Monthly Labor Review*, US Bureau of Labor Statistics, March 2019.

ACCUPLACER® PRACTICE TEST 1

Passage 2

There came into the world a new tool—the internal-combustion engine—destined to work almost as great a change in the human life as the steam engine in its time, making possible a tool for the waterway that the waterway had never had before, making it possible to use for the highway what the highway had never had before, making necessary the alteration of the highway to suit the new tool built for it. It has never been true until now; it has just now become true that the waterway and highway have been, as regards the tools for their use, on a technical and scientific level with the railway. The Government is just putting in operation this month the first great barges for the Mississippi River intended to carry ore south and coal north, made possible because of the internal-combustion engine. The tool has come, the internal-combustion engine is altering the face of the marine world. So that we do not really need but over 6 feet of water in the northern Mississippi to carry 1,800 tons of ore in one boat. We look upon the development of the New York State barge canal with a certainty of its profitable use for the Nation, for with a 12-foot draft we know we can carry 2,500 tons in any vessel constructed for the purpose, driven by internal-combustion engines. The tool for the job and the way made ready for the tool.

I go into my shop to put up a hammer. What is the essential feature of my hammer's operation? The foundation. It may be the most powerful hammer made, but unless given a sufficient sub-structure it can only be destructive. So for the waterway, so for the highway. You may have the most perfect equipment for their use but the instrument must work in a proper environment. We must, therefore, build highways for our trucks.

Adapted from William C. Redfield, "Address by Honorable William C. Redfield, Secretary of Commerce, at Conference of Regional Chairmen of the Highway Transport Committee Council of National Defense Highway Transport Committee, Bulletin 4." Originally published October 15, 1918.

5. The main purpose of paragraph 1 in Passage 1 is to

A. establish the need for more truck drivers in the United States.

B. provide data to support the argument that more truck drivers are needed in the United States.

C. establish the minimum requirements and number of truck drivers in the United States.

D. provide evidence that characterizes educational attainment of truck drivers as well as the number of truck drivers in the United States.

6. Which conclusion can reasonably be drawn about the author of Passage 2?

A. He would oppose improvements to modernize waterways.

B. He would support future efforts to modernize society beyond waterways, railroads, and highways.

C. His knowledge of history is vast.

D. He believes the market, not government, should modernize society.

7. Which choice best describes the relationship between the two passages?

A. Passage 1 is an objective analysis of the need for truck drivers, while Passage 2 is an argument for the building of trucking infrastructure.

B. Passage 1 presents a historical perspective on trucking, while Passage 2 presents a contemporary perspective.

C. Passage 1 presents data to characterize truck drivers, while Passage 2 argues for the modernization of highways.

D. Passage 1 is an academic essay on trucking, while Passage 2 is a polemic supporting highway infrastructure.

8. Given the evidence in both passages, with which statement would the authors of both passages most likely agree?

A. Trucking is a valuable occupation for those with a high school diploma.

B. Trucking is the best way to transport goods in the United States and Canada.

C. Trucking is an important part of the current and future economy.

D. A lack of jobs may lead to the demise of trucking as a profession.

The following is excerpted from a historical zoological work on spiders.

To the philosophical entomologists I have something else to say: I have to call their attention to the consummate knowledge of the insect-killers, which vies with that of the paralyzers. I speak of insect-killers in the plural, for the Tarantula must share her deadly art with a host of other Spiders, especially with those who hunt without nets. These insect-killers, who live on their prey, strike the game dead instantaneously by stinging the nerve-centres of the neck; the paralyzers, on the other hand, who wish to keep the food fresh for their larvae, destroy the power of movement by stinging the game in the other nerve-centres. Both of them attack the nervous chain, but they select the point according to the object to be attained. If death be desired, sudden death, free from danger to the huntress, the insect is attacked in the neck; if mere paralysis be required, the neck is respected and the lower segments—sometimes one alone, sometimes three, sometimes all or nearly all, according to the special organization of the victim—receive the dagger-thrust.

Adapted from Jean-Henri Fabre, *The Life of the Spider*. Originally published in 1928.

---

9. Within the work from which this passage is excerpted, the purpose of this paragraph is to

A. summarize the tarantula's role in the ecosystems it typically occupies.

B. analyze the symbiotic relationships that exist between different types of spiders who share hunting duties.

C. present a philosophical argument to support scientific evidence the author has previously presented.

D. clarify how a category of spiders known as insect-killers hunts differently from another category of spiders known as paralyzers.

Good things come in small packages, right? Not always.

Oftentimes, what may appear to be a vibrant field of pastoral charm or gently blowing golden waves of grain are actually battlefields where small invading armies of pests threaten the nation's economic, social, and environmental well-being.

"Nearly every terrestrial, wetland, and aquatic ecosystem in the United States has been invaded by non-native species, with economic losses estimated at $137 billion per year," said Robert Nowierski, national program leader for biobased pest management at USDA's National Institute of Food and Agriculture (NIFA).

Integrated Pest Management (IPM) is an ecosystem-based strategy that focuses on long-term prevention of pests or their damage through a combination of techniques, such as biological control, habitat manipulation, modification of cultural practices, use of resistant varieties, and minimizing the use of pesticides. Benefits of IPM include greater survival of a pest's natural enemies, slower development of pesticide resistance, less pest resurgence, fewer outbreaks of secondary pests, less negative impact on the environment, and greater worker safety. In addition, many farmers report greater profits because they've reduced their expenses on pesticide.

Adapted from Scott Elliott, *Science's Big Battle Against Small Enemies.*
National Institute of Food and Agriculture, April 9, 2019.

10. In this passage, the relationship between paragraph 3 and paragraph 4 can best be described as which of the following?

   A. Paragraph 3 describes a problem, while paragraph 4 explains the government's response to the problem.

   B. Paragraph 3 offers an example of an ecological threat, while paragraph 4 extends this example.

   C. Paragraph 3 describes various ecosystems, while paragraph 4 offers a pesticide-based solution.

   D. Paragraph 3 explains the economic repercussions of non-native species, while paragraph 4 describes a holistic solution.

The principle on which experts claim to be able to detect variations and to differentiate between handwritings is based on the well-established axiom that there is no such thing as a perfect pair in nature; that, however close the apparent similarity between two things, a careful examination and comparison will reveal marked differences to those trained to detect them.

This is especially true of everything that is produced by human agency. Everyone knows how difficult it is to keep check upon and eradicate certain physical habits, such as gestures, style of walking, moving the hands, arms, tricks of speech, or tone of voice. These mannerisms, being mechanical and automatic, or the result of long habit, are performed unconsciously, and there is probably no person who is entirely free from some marked peculiarity of manner, which he is ignorant of possessing. It is a well-known fact that the subject of caricature or mimicry rarely admits the accuracy or justness of the imitation, although the peculiarities so emphasized are plainly apparent to others. Even actors, who are supposed to make a careful study of their every tone and gesture, are constantly criticized for faults or mannerisms plain to the observer, but undetected by themselves.

It is easy, therefore, to understand how a trick or a gesture may become a fixed and unconscious habit through long custom, especially when, as in the case of a peculiarity of style in handwriting, there has been neither criticism on it, nor special reason for abandoning it.

Every person whose handwriting is developed and permanently formed has adopted certain more or less distinctive peculiarities in the formation of letters of which he is generally unaware.

Adapted from Douglas Blackburn and Waithman Caddell, *The Detection of Forgery: A Practical Handbook for the Use of Bankers, Solicitors, Magistrates' Clerks, and All Handling Suspected Documents*. Originally published in 1909.

11. The third paragraph marks a shift in the passage from

    A. narrative to description.
    B. description to analysis.
    C. the general to the specific.
    D. exposition to analysis.

In 1979 with fewer than 200 plants known to exist, the Tobusch fishhook cactus was thought to be almost extinct. Thanks to the hard work and dedication of multiple partners including the Texas Parks and Wildlife Department, Texas Department of Transportation, Texas Land Conservancy, Lady Bird Johnson Wildflower Center, The Nature Conservancy and central Texas landowners, today more than 3,300 cactuses are known to exist at 105 sites across the Edwards Plateau area of Texas. As a result, the US Fish and Wildlife Service is downlisting the cactus from endangered to threatened under the Endangered Species Act (ESA).

"While the Tobusch fishhook cactus isn't completely out of the woods yet, the signs are very encouraging," said Amy Lueders, the Service's Southwest Regional Director. "Today's decision to downlist the cactus is a victory for the collaborative model of conservation that engages states, private landowners and conservation groups to play a central role in a species' recovery."

The Tobusch fishhook cactus, a small cactus armed with curved "fishhook" spines, is known to exist only on the Edwards Plateau of west-central Texas. Following the listing of the cactus under the ESA in 1979, existing populations were protected and extensive research was conducted to better determine its range and population size. The Tobusch fishhook cactus is now known to exist in eight central Texas counties: Bandera, Edwards, Kerr, Kimble, Kinney, Real, Uvalde, and Val Verde. We estimate there are about five million acres of potential habitat for the cactus in these and several adjacent counties.

Adapted from Lesli Gray, "Collaborative Conservation Efforts Put Once Near Extinct Texas Cactus on Path to Recovery, Prompt Change in Federal Protected Status." US Fish and Wildlife Services, May 15, 2018.

12. Which of the following statements provides evidence for the author's main claim?

    A. "… a victory for the collaborative model of conservation …"

    B. "… a small cactus armed with curved 'fishhook' spines …"

    C. "… the Tobusch fishhook cactus isn't completely out of the woods yet …"

    D. "… more than 3,300 cactuses are known to exist at 105 sites …"

The security of the White House and the protection of the president cannot be solved by a higher fence alone. We encourage the Secret Service and the National Park Service to think holistically in addressing the issues of threat on many levels: physical, operational, and as a wider protected zone. Any solution must be an effective combination of physical barriers and operational procedures to prevent further intrusions. However, the real opportunity lies in a comprehensive approach to the White House security zone: to clean up the accumulation of "temporary" barriers, booths, and screening facilities located on lawns, sidewalks, and roadways-including the Treasury Department, the Eisenhower Executive Office Building, and the National Park Service properties of the Ellipse (President's Park South) and Lafayette Square.

Adapted from Thomas Luebke, "White House Security: It Takes More Than a Fence." US Commission of Fine Arts, January 23, 2015.

13. The main purpose of this passage is to

    A. analyze security of the White House.

    B. propose a solution for White House security.

    C. describe facets of current White House security.

    D. critique the White House Secret Service detail.

In 1963, when anthropologists first came upon the archaeological site in Turkey now known as Göbekli Tepe, their initial analysis was that the limestone slabs jutting up from the ground were grave markers. Decades passed on the assumption that the site was little more than a cemetery abandoned sometime during the medieval period. Then, in 1994, a German archaeologist named Klaus Schmidt came upon the so-called cemetery and began looking closer on the suspicion that there might be more to it. To say that he was right is a gargantuan understatement.

What Schmidt ended up uncovering is Göbekli Tepe, an ancient gathering space, potentially religious in nature, and what is now widely considered to be the oldest human monument in the world. The discoveries scientists have made and continue to make at Göbekli Tepe, which is Turkish for "belly hill," are proof of the earliest stirrings of human civilization. The site is at least 11,000 years old, making it millennia older than some of the human monuments previously thought to be the oldest in the world, such as Stonehenge and the Great Pyramid of Giza.

14. As used toward the end of the first paragraph, the word "gargantuan" most nearly means

    A. minor.

    B. major.

    C. tiny.

    D. enormous.

Despite being very similar celestial objects, scientists have long pondered why Neptune and Uranus appear to be different colors. The planets are similar sizes, composed of similar atmospheric gasses, and have similar masses. If given this information, a scientist would hypothesize that the two planets should look alike. However, Uranus has always appeared to be a much lighter shade of blue than Neptune. So, why the difference?

In 2022, scientists finally landed on a working theory that could explain the color difference. Namely, observations taken from three different telescopes (Gemini North, the Hubble Space Telescope, and the NASA Infrared Telescope Facility) allowed scientists to create models of the two planets' atmospheres. What scientists found is that Uranus has a much thicker version of a particular type of atmospheric haze that is found on both planets. Because this haze is so dense on Uranus, it tends to make the planet's color appear blanched, such that it reads more as a deep cyan or turquoise than a true blue, like Neptune. Researchers suspect that were it not for this whitening haze, both planets would indeed appear to be about the same shade of blue.

Scientists are excited about this finding because it shows how the atmospheric models that they created from telescope observations can help address questions they have but cannot otherwise answer given our distance from the galaxy's most far-flung gas giants. They are hopeful that continued observation will yield even further insights about Uranus, Neptune, and the far edges of the Milky Way.

15. This passage is primarily about the

    A. reason Neptune and Uranus appear the same color even though they aren't.

    B. methods scientists used to determine why Neptune and Uranus are different colors.

    C. techniques scientists deploy to observe distant planets.

    D. historical reasons scientists have been interested in Neptune and Uranus.

One of the instruments that electronic music pioneer Wendy Carlos helped make famous was the Moog synthesizer. Back in 1968, she released an album called *Switched-On Bach* on which she translated the music of classical composer Johann Sebastian Bach for the Moog. Few people had used electronic sounds to compose music before that point, so hearing Bach in this new way made Carlos a sensation. Furthermore, the success of the album made the Moog synthesizer one of the definitive sounds of the 1970s, as everyone who's anyone started using it in their music. Later, producers like the Italo-disco legend Giorgio Moroder and the German band Kraftwerk would help popularize genres centered on the synthesizer sound, creating a ripple effect that still resonates today; everyone from Jay-Z to Coldplay has made modern songs directly influenced by these early electronic sounds.

16. The second sentence notes that Wendy Carlos "translated the music of classical composer Johann Sebastian Bach for the Moog." What would be an example of an equivalent idea of translation?

    A. A medical interpreter in the US translating what a doctor has said for a Japanese speaker.

    B. A child figuring out what their grandparent really means by saying a certain old-fashioned proverb.

    C. A film using captions to show what someone speaking another language is saying.

    D. A dance company creating a hip-hop dance version of a famous ballet.

While small dogs tend to have longer lifespans than big dogs, they are subject to numerous other health risks that big dogs don't typically face, such as a collapsed trachea. This is due to the pressure caused by leashed collars when they jump on walks. Similarly, jumping up on high surfaces can cause the kneecaps in small dogs to collapse.

17. This passage best supports the statement that

    A. small dogs live shorter lives.

    B. dogs' kneecaps can collapse when jumping too high.

    C. small dogs suffer health risks directly associated with jumping.

    D. big dogs never suffer collapsed tracheas.

Goffman's dramaturgical theory, or Goffman's dramaturgical model, is a sociological theory proposed by Erving Goffman in his 1959 book *The Presentation of Self in Everyday Life*. The term *dramaturgy*, which is usually associated with the world of theatre, means "the practice and theory of composing drama." Goffman borrowed from his study of the dramatic arts, saying that theatrical drama is a good metaphor to represent the way people play-act to present themselves a certain way to the rest of society.

Social interactions then, in this model, are like scenes of dialogue in which the actors (humans in a society) are constantly acting and reacting to the norms and values communicated to them by others. Whether they follow those rules and norms or not is a matter of character, manner, and temperament, all of which are curated by the individual at both the conscious and subconscious levels to create a particular version of the self to present to society. One of the ways they do so is through what Goffman calls "impression management." For instance, when a person gets dressed up and ensures that they look their best for a first date or interview, they're doing so in hopes of assuring themselves a good first impression.

18. Which statement most adequately summarizes Goffman's dramaturgical theory, as communicated by the author?

   A. People are at their most raw and unfiltered when they are pretending to be someone else, since the play-acting highlights the difference between the true self and the self they are projecting to others.

   B. Like directors do for theatrical productions, people tend to "direct" their lives down to the most minute detail.

   C. People rarely offer a true, unfiltered version of themselves; instead, they tend to act in ways that mimic how they want to be perceived or otherwise help them manage the impressions of others.

   D. Like actors on a stage, most people communicate using predetermined scripts that have little to no personal meaning.

Directions for Questions 19 and 20: The following sentences have a blank indicating that something has been left out. Beneath each sentence are four words or phrases. Choose the word or phrase that, when inserted in the sentence, best fits the meaning of the sentence as a whole.

19. In 2012, the Pulitzer Prize Fiction Jury decided that all nominees were _____ the award; therefore, they did not present a prize that year.

   A. interested in
   B. ungrateful of
   C. pleased with
   D. unworthy of

20. Though the intent of his actions was not _____, the results were devastating: a forest fire that burned down 800 acres of forest.

   A. malicious
   B. predatory
   C. exemplary
   D. benevolent

WRITING

25 Questions

> **Directions:** Read the following early essay drafts and then choose the best answer to the question or the best completion of the statement.

---

(1) The city of Boston, known today for its sports teams and baked beans, may be considered the birthplace of the American Revolution, a city that transformed itself as it became the centerpiece of the Revolutionary War. (2) In Nathaniel Philbrick's nonfiction book *Bunker Hill: A City, a Siege, a Revolution* he wrote that "in eighteen months [the] revolution transformed the city and the towns that surrounded it." (3) This transformation was necessary as the city combatted what it viewed as onerous British policies, many of which were felt especially hard by Bostonians.

(4) Prior to the Revolution, Britain's policy to the colonies and Boston was one of "salutary neglect." (5) This policy was named by Edmund Burke in an address to Parliament. (6) But this policy needed to change as the French and Indian Wars brought Great Britain enormous debt for what they viewed as helping the colonists. (7) As a result of this war, Britain was saddled with almost $22.4 billion dollars of debt in today's money. (8) Boston was viewed as a key military objective by the British because it was the main port for the importing and exporting of goods and supplies in the region and was a vital maritime center. (9) So, when Britain decided it needed money to pay its debt, they targeted the colonies, and, because of its robust economy, these policies hurt Boston the most.

(10) The British Parliament instituted a series of acts and taxes intended to help pay this debt. (11) Parliament passed the Sugar Act, a tax placed on imported sugar and molasses, the Currency Acts of 1751 and 1764, which regulated paper money in the colonies, the Stamp Act, which put a tax on all paper used in the colonies, the Townshend Acts, which placed a tax on British goods imported into the colonies, and the Tea Act which allowed tea to be shipped duty free, and which was seen as a bailout for the British East India Company. (12) Because of its importance as a commercial center, the acts instituted by the British Parliament may have stung Bostonians even more, forcing their transformation.

(13) Boston was revolutionary because it had to be. (14) These acts galvanized Boston and the American people to revolt against Britain.

---

1. Sentence 1 is reproduced below.

   The city of Boston, <u>known today for its sports teams and baked beans</u>, may be considered the birthplace of the American Revolution, a city that transformed itself as it became the centerpiece of the Revolutionary War.

   The writer is considering cutting the underlined part. Should the writer make this change?

   A. Yes, because it changes the academic tone of the piece.

   B. Yes, because it introduces two attributes that are irrelevant to Boston.

   C. No, because it provides historical context.

   D. No, because it establishes that the essay will consider Boston's impact on history.

2. Of the options given, which is the best version of the underlined portion of sentence 2 (reproduced below)?

   In Nathaniel Philbrick's nonfiction book Bunker Hill: A City, a Siege, a Revolution *he wrote that* "in eighteen months [the] revolution transformed the city and the towns that surrounded it."

   A. Nathaniel Philbrick, wrote a book called *Bunker Hill: A City, a Siege, a Revolution*, and he said that

   B. Nathaniel Philbrick, a writer, in a book called *Bunker Hill: A City, a Siege, a Revolution*, said that

   C. Nathaniel Philbrick, in his book *Bunker Hill: A City, a Siege, a Revolution*, wrote that

   D. In the novel *Bunker Hill*, Nathaniel Philbrick wrote that

3. Which sentence blurs the focus of the second paragraph and should therefore be deleted?

   A. Sentence 4

   B. Sentence 5

   C. Sentence 7

   D. Sentence 8

4. In context, which is the best version of sentence 8 (reproduced below)?

   Boston was viewed as a key military objective by the British because it was the main port for the importing and exporting of goods and supplies in the region and was a vital maritime center.

   A. (as it is now)

   B. Because it was a maritime center and the main port for importing and exporting goods and supplies in the region, Boston was considered by Britain a key military objective.

   C. A vital maritime center, Boston was the main port for importing and exporting goods and supplies in the region and was thus considered by the British a key military objective.

   D. Because it was the main port for importing and exporting goods and supplies, the British viewed Boston as a key military objective.

5. Which is the best version of sentence 11 (reproduced below)?

Parliament passed the Sugar Act, a tax placed on imported sugar and molasses, the Currency Acts of 1751 and 1764, which regulated paper money in the colonies, the Stamp Act, which put a tax on all paper used in the colonies, the Townshend Acts, which placed a tax on British goods imported into the colonies, and the Tea Act which allowed tea to be shipped duty free, and which was seen as a bailout for the British East India Company.

A. (as it is now)

B. Parliament passed the Sugar Act, a tax placed on imported sugar and molasses; the Currency Acts of 1751 and 1764, which regulated paper money in the colonies; the Stamp Act, which put a tax on all paper used in the colonies; the Townshend Acts, which placed a tax on British goods imported into the colonies; and the Tea Act, which allowed tea to be shipped duty free and which was seen as a bailout for the British East India Company.

C. Parliament passed the Sugar Act, a tax placed on imported sugar and molasses, the Currency Acts of 1751 and 1764, which regulated paper money in the colonies, the Stamp Act, which put a tax on all paper used in the colonies, the Townshend Acts, which placed a tax on British goods imported into the colonies, and the Tea Act which allowed tea to be shipped duty free—and which was seen as a bailout for the British East India Company.

D. Parliament passed many acts such as the Sugar Act, a tax placed on imported sugar and molasses, the Currency Acts of 1751 and 1764, which regulated paper money in the colonies, the Stamp Act, which put a tax on all paper used in the colonies, the Townshend Acts, which placed a tax on British goods imported into the colonies, and the Tea Act which allowed tea to be shipped duty free, and which was seen as a bailout for the British East India Company.

(1) Legends surround the poet. (2) He is called the Banished Immortal. (3) This legend states that his behavior in heaven was so notorious that he was kicked out and sent to Earth, there to spend all eternity wandering among people. (4) Another legend, this of his death—which seems to negate the whole immortal thing—tells of him chasing the moon while leaping from boat to boat, eventually falling in and drowning. (5) Such a tale jibes with his poems, many of which celebrate the moon. (6) Who is this man?

(7) His name is Li Bai, and to some critics he is considered the greatest Chinese poet. (8) In fact every student in China, during their school years, memorizes his poem "Quiet Night Thought." (9) In America, he is called Li Po.

(10) The poet Li Bai lived in China from 701–762 C.E. and was one of two major poets writing during the Tang Dynasty, sometimes referred to as the Golden Age of Chinese Poetry. (11) He was born in the ancient Chinese frontier, present day Kyrgyzstan, where his family prospered in business. (12) At the age of five, his father moved the family to the central Chinese city of Jiangyou in Sichuan Province. (13) As a boy he read extensively, particularly in the Confucian classics, while also indulging his love of sword fighting and taming wild birds. (14) At the age of twenty, he attempted to find work with Su Ting, a royal inspector and governor in Chengdu, sending along several of his poems. (15) Su Ting was impressed with the young man and introduced him to some local officials, but the officials, upon finding that his father was a businessman from the frontier, had Li Bai dismissed. (16) He would try again with other officials and continually be dismissed. (17) He also couldn't take the civil service exam because his family was not affiliated with the aristocracy or officialdom. (18) Though he acquired a series of minor government jobs, he was never happy, and in 724 C.E. he set out on the road to wander and write poetry. (19) Li Bai's poems are a compendium of his life: places he visited, friends he saw on journeys, his dreams, current events, and descriptions from nature.

6. Which choice most effectively combines sentences 2 and 3 (reproduced below)?

   He is called the Banished Immortal. This legend states that his behavior in heaven was so notorious that he was kicked out and sent to Earth, there to spend all eternity wandering among people.

   A. He is called the Banished Immortal, which indicates that his notorious behavior got him kicked out of heaven and sent to Earth and then he lived on Earth for all eternity.

   B. His nickname, the Banished Immortal, came about because of a tale in which he was kicked out of heaven and sent to Earth, there to spend all eternity wandering among people.

   C. His moniker, the Banished Immortal, derives from a legend in which he was kicked out of heaven, banished to Earth, and there forced to spend all eternity wandering among people.

   D. His moniker, the Banished Immortal, derives from a legend in which he was kicked out of heaven, sent to Earth, and forced to spend eternity wandering among people.

7. Which is the best version of sentence 5 (reproduced below)?

   Such a tale jibes with his poems, many of which celebrate the moon.

   A. Such a tale conforms with his poems, many of which celebrate the moon.

   B. Such a tale coincides with his poems, many celebrating the moon.

   C. Such a tale is in accord with his poems, many of which are a celebration of the moon.

   D. Such a tale accords with his poems, as many celebrate the moon.

8. Which is the best version of sentence 8 (reproduced below)?

   In fact every student in China, during their school years, memorizes his poem "Quiet Night Thought."

   A. (as it is now)

   B. In fact every student in China during their school years memorizes his poem "Quiet Night Thought."

   C. In fact, every student in China, during their school years, memorizes his poem "Quiet Night Thought."

   D. In fact, every student in China, during their school years memorizes his poem "Quiet Night Thought."

9. In context, which is the best version of sentence 12 (reproduced below)?

   At the age of five, his father moved the family to the central Chinese city of Jiangyou in Sichuan Province.

   A. (as it is now)

   B. At the age of five, his family moved to the central Chinese city of Jiangyou in Sichuan Province.

   C. At the age of five, Li Bai moved with his family to the central Chinese city of Jiangyou in Sichuan Province.

   D. Li Bai moved with his family to the central Chinese city of Jiangyou in Sichuan Province.

10. Which choice results in the most effective transition from sentence 16 to sentence 17 (reproduced below)?

    He would try again with other officials and continually be dismissed. He also couldn't take the civil service exam because his family was not affiliated with the aristocracy or officialdom.

    A. He would try again with other officials continually be dismissed. Additionally, he couldn't take the civil service exam because his family was not affiliated with the aristocracy or officialdom.

    B. He would try again with other officials but continually be dismissed. Additionally, he couldn't take the civil service exam because his family was not affiliated with the aristocracy or officialdom.

    C. He would try again with other officials and continually be dismissed. However, he couldn't take the civil service exam because his family was not affiliated with the aristocracy or officialdom.

    D. He would try again with other officials continually be dismissed, but he also couldn't take the civil service exam because his family was not affiliated with the aristocracy or officialdom.

(1) *Salvelinus fontinalis*, the little salmon of the fountain, is the Latin taxonomic name of the Eastern Brook Trout. (2) The little salmon of the fountain, like all trout, require four things for survival: cold water, food, safety, and a place to spawn. (3) All across America, brook trout are threatened by a manmade contraption called a culvert.

(4) Culverts, which pass beneath roads and trails throughout the northeast, allow water to flow under a road. (5) Culverts come in many shapes and sizes round, elliptical, flat-bottomed, pear-shaped, or box-like. (6) Whatever their shape, they do have some benefits. (7) Because, they prevent road erosion, which can be a costly fix. (8) Additionally, proper use of culverts can improve water quality and allow forestry operations, such as logging, to continue as roads allow access to deeper parts of the forest. (9) Although culverts have some positive impacts, they inhibit the movement of fish upstream to the cold water refuge and breeding grounds they need, which ultimately hurts fish populations. (10) The recent development and use of culverts, while not malicious, had unintended environmental costs on the brook trout. (11) Although culverts have a long history, used by ancient Romans and early American settlers, it is the most recent version that is so distressing to the northeast.

(12) What is the problem? (13) Some culverts do not allow for brook trout passage upstream. (14) When water gets low in the summertime, the bottom of the culvert is exposed, water no longer flowing, and the fish are unable to pass. (15) This restricts brook trout from the gravel base streambed, found upstream, needed to contain their eggs and allow them to spawn. (16) It also, similarly, restricts fish from the headwaters of streams, where the water is generally cooler and more well oxygenated, both necessities during the hot months of July and August. (17) If you see a culvert you can be sure that the fish in the stream, the Eastern Brook Trout, is probably absent from the stream, unless someone is trying to "daylight" it.

(18) The process of removing a culvert from a stream is known as daylighting, a step that some environmental and fishing organizations have undertaken to make fish passage possible. (19) One example of this is the efforts of the organization Trout Unlimited who have with the University of New Hampshire developed a New England Culvert Program with the mission of "restoring in-stream connectivity."

(20) It is through the efforts of groups like this one that the Eastern Brook Trout may once again flourish in the rivers and streams of New England.

11. Which is the best version of sentence 5 (reproduced below)?

    Culverts come in many shapes and sizes round, elliptical, flat-bottomed, pear-shaped, or box-like.

    A. (as it is now)

    B. Culverts come in many shapes and sizes; round, elliptical, flat-bottomed, pear-shaped, or box-like.

    C. Culverts come in many shapes and sizes: round, elliptical, flat-bottomed, pear-shaped, or box-like.

    D. Culverts come in many shapes and sizes, some of which are round, elliptical, flat-bottomed, pear-shaped, or box-like.

12. In context, which is the best version of the underlined portion of sentence 7 (reproduced below)?

    <u>Because,</u> they prevent road erosion, which can be a costly fix.

    A. (as it is now)

    B. For example,

    C. However,

    D. At the same time,

13. Which is the most logical placement for sentence 11 (reproduced below)?

Although culverts have a long history, used by ancient Romans and early American settlers, it is the most recent version that is so distressing to the northeast.

A. (as it is now)

B. Before sentence 4

C. Before sentence 6

D. Before sentence 9

14. Which is the best version of the underlined portion of sentence 14 (reproduced below)?

When water gets low in the summertime, the bottom of the culvert is exposed, <u>water no longer flowing</u>, and the fish are unable to pass.

A. (as it is now)

B. water no longer is flowing

C. preventing water flow

D. which does prevent the water from flowing

15. Which version of sentence 18 (reproduced below) makes the best introductory sentence to paragraph 4?

The process of removing a culvert from a stream is known as daylighting, a step that some environmental and fishing organizations have undertaken to make fish passage possible.

A. (as it is now)

B. Environmental and fishing organizations, in a process called daylighting, have taken steps to make fish passage possible; to do this they must remove culverts.

C. Daylighting, the process of removing culverts, has recently been undertaken by both environmental and fishing organizations in an attempt to make fish passage possible.

D. Some environmental and fishing organizations have undertaken steps to make fish passage possible by removing culverts, a process known as daylighting.

16. Sentence 19 is reproduced below.

One example of this is the efforts of the organization Trout Unlimited who have with the University of New Hampshire developed a New England Culvert Program with the mission of "restoring in-stream connectivity."

The writer is considering adding the following text as the next sentence. Should they do so?

Their efforts have so far resulted in an increase in wetland permits, improved stream habitats, and more thorough assessment of stream crossings for long-term analysis and intervention.

A. Yes, because it elaborates on the example provided in sentence 19.

B. Yes, because it establishes the historical period in which the New England Culvert Program was established.

C. No, because it introduces details that are irrelevant to the paragraph's focus on culverts.

D. No, because it fails to explain whether these things have had an impact on the brook trout population.

(1) In 2005, Jeff Howe and Mark Robinson editors for *Wired Magazine*, defined a revolutionary way to use technology; they called it crowdsourcing, and defined it as outsourcing a task to a large, undefined group of people through an open call. **(2)** Though aspects of crowdsourcing existed prior to this time and offline, since that momentous year crowdsourcing has taken on a new life, adopted, it seems at times, by everyone.

(3) Not all of crowdsourcing have been good. **(4)** As criminals have adapted to new technology, some of them have taken to crowdsourcing to commit crimes, furthering their criminal enterprises. **(5)** A particular type of crime using crowdsourcing is called a "crime flash mob" in which groups of individuals, using online platforms such as Facebook and Twitter, arrange to descend upon a shop or store, creating mass confusion. **(6)** In this confusion, some members of the crowd, in some cases many members of the crowd, proceed to steal goods, while the shop keeper or store owner cannot contain the sheer size of the descending people. **(7)** This technique was recently used by a group in London who descended on a Victoria's Secret, stealing tens of thousands of dollars worth of goods. **(8)** One innovative bank robber in Seattle advertised on Craigslist for a lucrative construction job, worth $28.50 an hour. **(9)** Potential employees responding to the ad were asked to wear yellow safety vests, safety goggles, respirator masks, and blue shirts, and were told to stand at a specific corner. **(10)** Unbeknownst to the job seekers, an armored car was delivering to a Bank of America on that exact corner, at that exact time. **(11)** The bank robber, dressed like all the other potential employees, pepper sprayed the armored car guards, stole the money, and fled. **(12)** When police were notified, they had hundreds of suspects. **(13)** To counter this, some government entities have incorporated technology into their crime fighting repertoire, using Facebook and other social media to out criminals to uncover criminal activity. **(14)** In 2011, government officials in Vancouver, Canada, used social media to identify numerous suspects who had, in the wake of the Vancouver Canucks loss in the 2011 Stanley Cup Finals, taken to the streets and destroyed thousands of dollars of goods.

(15) It is not just government and criminals who have used crowdsourcing, but private corporations. Goldcorp, a Canadian mining company, was frustrated that their geologists could not uncover gold on a piece of property they were prospecting. **(16)** The company decided to post all the data sets online and offer a $500,000 reward if anyone could find the gold. **(17)** One enterprising citizen uncovered the gold cache for Goldcorp, which resulted in them finding a gold strike worth $3 billion. **(18)** Money well spent.

17. Which is the best version of the underlined portion of sentence 1 (reproduced below)?

    In 2005, Jeff Howe and Mark <u>Robinson editors for</u> Wired Magazine, <u>defined</u> *a revolutionary way to use technology; they called it crowdsourcing, and defined it as outsourcing a task to a large, undefined group of people through an open call.*

    A. (as it is now)
    B. Robinson editors for *Wired Magazine* defined
    C. Robinson—editors for *Wired Magazine* defined
    D. Robinson, editors for *Wired Magazine*, defined

18. Which is the best version of the underlined portion of sentence 3 (reproduced below)?

    Not all of <u>crowdsourcing have been good</u>.

    A. (as it is now)
    B. crowdsourcing has been good
    C. crowdsourcing was good
    D. crowdsourcing will be good

19. Which is the best version of the underlined portion of sentence 7 (reproduced below)?

    This technique was recently used by a group in London who descended on a Victoria's Secret, stealing tens of thousands of <u>dollars worth of goods</u>.

    A. (as it is now)
    B. dollar's worth of goods
    C. dollars of goods
    D. dollars worth

20. Which is the best version of sentence 8 (reproduced below)?

    One innovative bank robber in <u>Seattle advertised</u> on Craigslist for a lucrative construction job, worth $28.50 an hour.

    A. (as it is now)
    B. Seattle; he advertised
    C. Seattle, advertised
    D. Seattle placed an advertisement

21. Which is the best version of the underlined portion of sentence 17 (reproduced below)?

    One enterprising citizen uncovered the gold cache for Goldcorp, which <u>resulted in them</u> finding a gold strike worth $3 billion.

    A. (as it is now)
    B. resulted in Goldcorp
    C. resulted in the citizen
    D. resulted in him

(1) What do you want to be when you grow up? (2) Such an innocuous question, but one, I'm sure, every child has heard. (3) When I was young, I wanted to be, in successive order: a Musketeer, a member of Robin Hood's Merry Men, and, finally, an explorer.

(4) I tried once to join the French Foreign Legion, thinking this the modern day equivalent of the Musketeers, but when I did some inquiry I discovered that the French Foreign Legion was a landing spot for many criminals, this Legion gave us the word nom de guerre, because so many men, hiding from criminal activities, needed to change their name upon enlisting and needed "war names." (5) I was neither criminal or Frenchman, plus I was frightened, so I begged off this choice.

(6) My next choice, and this did occur sequentially, was to be one of Robin Hood's Merry Men. (7) Nothing could be better, I thought, then days spent stomping in the woods and seeking adventure. (8) I spent much of my free time hiking anyway. (9) I didn't want to steal from rich or from poor, and I had no money, so this idea quickly dissolved with the Musketeers.

(10) Finally, I hit upon exploration. (11) I would discover rivers and mountains and new lands filled with undiscovered people. (12) I would, like my heroes, be inducted into the Royal Geographic Society. (13) The Royal Geographic Society is a United Kingdom "learned society" for geographers and the study of the world's geography. (14) But, alas, once again, I was stifled, as I discovered an inherent fear of frogs. (15) If I was afraid of frogs, what would happen when I came upon an anaconda? (16) The city—with its safety and restaurants and lack of frogs—was the place for me.

(17) As one can infer, my choices were based mostly upon my reading: Alexander Dumas, Howard Pyle, and the biographies of men like Richard Burton, David Livingstone, and Henry Morton Stanley, all my bibles. (18) My decision not to become any of these things has only recently been rectified with a visit to Disneyworld, for here, in the Magical Kingdom, I was able to be Robin Hood and a Mouseketeer, which was close enough to a Musketeer, and I spent the day exploring all the vast lands of Epcot Center. (19) Finally, the dreams of my youth were fulfilled.

(20) It's now your turn to think about how you will fulfill the dreams of your youth.

22. Which is the best version of the underlined portion of sentence 4 (reproduced below)?

I tried once to join the French Foreign Legion, thinking this the modern day equivalent of the Musketeers, but when I did some inquiry I discovered that the French Foreign Legion was a landing spot for many criminals, this *Legion gave us the word nom de guerre, because so many men, hiding from criminal activities, needed to change their name upon enlisting and needed "war names."*

A. (as it is now)

B. criminals. The

C. criminals—the

D. criminals, but the

23. Which is the best version of the underlined portion of sentence 5 (reproduced below)?

I was neither criminal or Frenchman, plus I was frightened, so I begged off this choice.

   A. (as it is now)

   B. I was either criminal or Frenchman,

   C. I was neither criminal nor Frenchman,

   D. I was criminal, Frenchman,

24. Which choice most effectively combines sentences 12 and 13 (reproduced below)?

I would, like my heroes, be inducted into the Royal Geographic Society. The Royal Geographic Society is a United Kingdom "learned society" for geographers and the study of the world's geography.

   A. (as it is now)

   B. I would, like my heroes, be inducted into the Royal Geographic Society, a United Kingdom "learned society" for geographers and the study of the world's geography.

   C. I would, like my heroes, be inducted into the Royal Geographic Society; the Royal Geographic Society is a United Kingdom "learned society" for geographers and the study of the world's geography.

   D. I would, like my heroes, be inducted into the Royal Geographic Society; it is a United Kingdom "learned society" for geographers and the study of the world's geography.

25. Sentence 20 is reproduced below.

It's now your turn to think about how you will fulfill the dreams of your youth.

The writer is considering cutting this sentence. Should the writer make this decision?

   A. No, the sentence effectively transitions to the next section of the essay.

   B. No, the sentence sums up the main idea of the excerpt.

   C. Yes, the sentence is redundant to the passage as a whole.

   D. Yes, the sentence is irrelevant to the passage as a whole.

ARITHMETIC

20 Questions

Directions: Choose the best answer. Use the space provided for any calculations.

---

1. $57 \div 19 =$

    A. 2

    B. 3

    C. 4

    D. 38

2. Which of the following is equivalent to $\frac{2}{3} \div \frac{4}{5}$?

    A. $\frac{8}{15}$

    B. $\frac{5}{6}$

    C. $\frac{6}{5}$

    D. $\frac{15}{8}$

3. Which of the following statements is true?

    A. $0.2 < 0.3 < 0.29$

    B. $0.2 < 0.29 < 0.3$

    C. $0.29 < 0.2 < 0.3$

    D. $0.3 < 0.29 < 0.2$

4. In a 2016 senate election, 900,000 votes were cast. In 2018 in the same state, 720,000 votes were cast in a senate race. Between 2016 and 2018, the number of votes cast

    A. increased by 180%.

    B. decreased by 180%.

    C. decreased by 25%.

    D. decreased by 20%.

5. Which of the following is equivalent to $\frac{107}{11}$?

    A. $9\frac{7}{11}$

    B. $9\frac{8}{11}$

    C. $10\frac{7}{11}$

    D. $99\frac{7}{11}$

6. On the following number line, which two points represent |2|?

    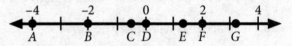

    A. A and F

    B. A and B

    C. B and F

    D. D and G

7. What is $\frac{1,688}{101}$ rounded to the nearest integer?

    A. 15

    B. 16

    C. 17

    D. 168

8. What is the value of $\frac{52}{1,000} - \frac{3}{100}$?

    A. $\frac{11}{500}$

    B. $\frac{41}{500}$

    C. $\frac{49}{900}$

    D. $\frac{49}{1,000}$

9. What is the value of 0.093 + 6.75 + 0.816?

   A. 1.584
   B. 6.5611
   C. 7.559
   D. 7.659

10. A housing development with 45 homes builds an additional 15 homes. To the nearest percent, what is the percent increase in the number of homes in the development?

    A. 3%
    B. 30%
    C. 33%
    D. 34%

11. Which of the following has the greatest value?

    A. 25% of 16
    B. 30% of 10
    C. 50% of 12
    D. 80% of 5

12. Which of the following statements is NOT true?

    A. $\frac{37}{8} = 4\frac{5}{8}$
    B. $\frac{9}{20} = 0.45$
    C. $6.6 = 6\frac{2}{3}$
    D. $6\% = 0.06$

13. What is $\frac{78}{120}$ expressed as a percent?

    A. 0.65%
    B. 15.40%
    C. 58%
    D. 65%

14. What is the value of 18 ÷ 0.4?

    A. 4.5
    B. 7.2
    C. 45
    D. 72

15. What is the value of $\frac{117}{150} - \frac{8}{25}$?

    A. $\frac{23}{50}$
    B. $\frac{31}{50}$
    C. $\frac{109}{125}$
    D. $\frac{11}{10}$

16. Which is the best estimate of 211^2?

    A. 420
    B. 4,200
    C. 40,000
    D. 42,000

17. Which is the best approximation of $\frac{120}{159}$?

    A. $\frac{2}{3}$
    B. $\frac{3}{4}$
    C. $\frac{4}{5}$
    D. $\frac{5}{6}$

18. What is 2.5217 rounded to the nearest thousandth?

    A. 2.521
    B. 2.522
    C. 2.5227
    D. 2.5217

19. Sita has $1,300 in her savings account and withdraws 40% of it. What is the amount of Sita's withdrawal?

   A. $52
   B. $325
   C. $520
   D. $780

20. A carton contains 6 cans of motor oil. If 45 cans of oil must be packed into cartons, how many cartons will be completely filled?

   A. 5
   B. 7
   C. 8
   D. 9

QUANTITATIVE REASONING, ALGEBRA, AND STATISTICS

20 Questions

> **Directions:** In the following questions, work out each problem and mark the letter that corresponds to the correct answer. The answers and explanations will follow. You are only permitted to use a calculator where indicated by a symbol (🖩).

1. Which of the following is equivalent to $15.7 - (18 - 2) \div 0.5$?

   A. 7.7

   B. −0.6

   C. −8.6

   D. −16.3

2. The Statue of Liberty in New York is 305 feet high. What is the height of the Statue of Liberty in meters? (1 meter = 3.28 feet)

   A. 93 meters

   B. 930 meters

   C. 1,000.4 meters

   D. 10,004 meters

3. Which of the following is equivalent to $\frac{1}{4^{-3}}$?

   A. $-\frac{1}{64}$

   B. $-\frac{1}{12}$

   C. $\frac{1}{64}$

   D. 64

4. The rental fee for a compact car is $0.18 per mile. Gasoline averages $0.10 per mile. Which of the following represents total cost in dollars, including gasoline, of driving the rental car m miles?

   A. $0.10m + 0.18$

   B. $0.18m + 0.10$

   C. $0.28m$

   D. $0.018m$

5. A rectangular plot of land is twice as long as it is wide. The length of each longer side is more than 60 yards and, at most, 75 yards. Which inequality below expresses the perimeter, P, of the plot in yards?

   A. $180 < P < 225$

   B. $180 < P \le 225$

   C. $240 < P < 300$

   D. $240 < P \le 300$

6. A bag contains 20 red marbles, 20 blue pebbles, 10 green marbles, and 10 green pebbles. What is the probability of randomly choosing two objects of the same color, without replacement?

   A. $\frac{19}{59}$

   B. $\frac{19}{60}$

   C. $\frac{19}{177}$

   D. $\frac{116}{177}$

7. The circumference of a circle is 12π. What is the area of the circle?

   A. 36

   B. 36π

   C. 144

   D. 144π

8. If Albie dives off a platform that is 10 feet above the water level to a depth of 8 feet below the water level, how far has he descended in feet?

   A. 2 feet

   B. 10 feet

   C. 18 feet

   D. 80 feet

9. What is the number of liters in 600 milliliters? (1 liter = 1,000 milliliters)

   A. 600,000

   B. 60,000

   C. 6,000

   D. 0.6

10. The average distance from the earth to the sun is about 150 million kilometers. How is this distance expressed in scientific notation?

    A. 1.5×10^6 km

    B. 1.5×10^7 km

    C. 1.5×10^8 km

    D. 1.5×10^9 km

11. Lori bought some cookies for $2 each and muffins for $3 each. She bought twice as many muffins as cookies and spent $16. How many cookies did Lori buy?

    A. 2

    B. 3

    C. 4

    D. 6

12. Which of the following is the equation of the line that passes through the point (0, 1) and is perpendicular to the line shown below?

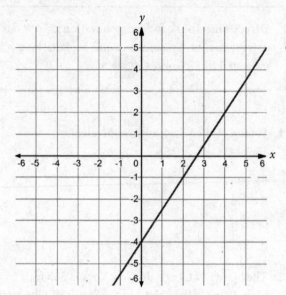

   A. $y = \dfrac{3}{2}x - 4$

   B. $y = \dfrac{3}{2}x + 1$

   C. $y = -\dfrac{2}{3}x + 1$

   D. $y = -\dfrac{2}{3}x - 4$

13. An automobile dealer sold an average of 23 cars per week over a two-week period and then averaged 27.5 cars per week for the next 4 weeks. How many cars per week did the dealer sell, on average, over the entire 6-week period?

   A. 8.42 cars

   B. 25.25 cars

   C. 26 cars

   D. 156 cars

14. In the graphic below, rectangle *ABCD* lies in the *xy*-plane, and the coordinates of vertex *D* are (−4, −3). Rectangle *ABCD* is reflected across the *x*-axis and then rotated 90° clockwise about the origin to produce rectangle *A′B′C′D′*, where vertex *D′* corresponds to vertex *D* of rectangle *ABCD*. What are the coordinates of *D′*?

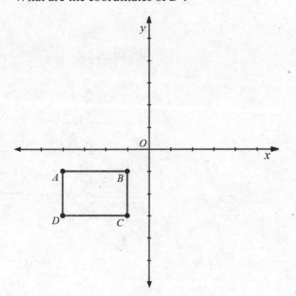

A. (−4, 3)

B. (−3, 4)

C. (3, 4)

D. (4, 3)

15. Which of the following is equivalent to $\dfrac{-7}{-14-(-7)}$?

A. 1

B. $\dfrac{1}{3}$

C. $-\dfrac{1}{2}$

D. −1

16. Juan works 6 hours per day for 10 days and is paid $1,080. What is Juan's hourly wage?

A. $1.80

B. $18.00

C. $60.00

D. $108.00

17. Which is equivalent to $2^{\frac{2}{3}}$?

A. $\dfrac{1}{2}$

B. $\dfrac{4}{3}$

C. $\sqrt{8}$

D. $\sqrt[3]{4}$

18. $(3u^4 - 6u^2 + u) + (-u^5 - 2u^2 + 9) =$

A. $-u^5 + 3u^4 - 4u^2 + u + 9$

B. $-u^5 + 3u^4 - 8u^2 + u + 9$

C. $-u^5 + 3u^4 - 8u^2 + 9u$

D. $u^5 + 3u^4 - 4u^2 + u - 9$

19. If the point $(p, 26)$ lies on the line $-x + \dfrac{y}{2} = 10$, then what is the value of p?

A. 3

B. 6

C. 42

D. 72

ACCUPLACER® PRACTICE TEST 1

20. The table below shows a survey of 75 high school students. Each student was asked how they travelled to school most often. If a student who takes a school bus most often is randomly selected, what is the probability that the student is a freshman or a sophomore?

SURVEY OF 75 HIGH SCHOOL STUDENTS			
	Walk or car	School bus	Total
Seniors	6	11	17
Juniors	9	15	24
Sophomores	2	12	14
Freshmen	4	16	20
Total	21	54	75

A. 0.07

B. 0.37

C. 0.45

D. 0.52

ADVANCED ALGEBRA AND FUNCTIONS

20 Questions

Directions: In the following questions, work out each problem and mark the letter that corresponds to the correct answer. The answers and explanations will follow. You are only permitted to use a calculator where indicated by a symbol (🔢).

1. If $y = mx - 7$ is satisfied by $x = -2$, $y = 15$, then what is the value of m?

   A. -22

   B. -11

   C. -4

   D. 11

2. If you know a train's velocity and the distance traveled, what formula would you use to directly compute the time of the trip?

   A. $v = dt$

   B. $t = \dfrac{v}{d}$

   C. $t = \dfrac{d}{v}$

   D. $d = vt$

3. When $9x^2 + 30x + 16$ is factored into two monomials, which of the following monomials is a factor?

   A. $3x$

   B. $(3x - 4)$

   C. $(3x + 2)$

   D. $(9x + 4)$

4. Using the quadratic formula to solve the following equation, which would be a correct intermediate result?

   $$4x^2 - 2x + 3 = 0$$

   A. $\dfrac{2 \pm \sqrt{4 - 48}}{8}$

   B. $\dfrac{-2 \pm \sqrt{4 - 48}}{8}$

   C. $\dfrac{2 \pm \sqrt{-2 - 48}}{8}$

   D. $\dfrac{2 \pm \sqrt{4 - 48}}{4}$

5. Function f is defined by $f(x) = \dfrac{-4x}{3} + 3$. What is the value of $f(3A + 2)$?

   A. $\dfrac{-4A}{3} + 3$

   B. $-4A + \dfrac{1}{3}$

   C. $-4 + 3$

   D. $\dfrac{-4A + 1}{3}$

6. What, if any, is a real solution to $\dfrac{\sqrt{151 + x}}{3} - 6 = -2$?

   A. -7

   B. 105

   C. 425

   D. There is no real solution.

7. For which of the following equations are $x = 2$ and $x = -\dfrac{1}{2}$ both solutions?

   A. $2x^2 + 5x + 2 = 0$

   B. $2x^2 - 5x - 2 = 0$

   C. $2x^3 - 7x^2 + 4x + 4 = 0$

   D. $2x^3 + 9x^2 + 12x + 4 = 0$

8. If $\log_6 (-4x) = 2$, then what is the value of x?

   A. -16

   B. -9

   C. 9

   D. 16

9. The surface area of a cube can be found by adding the areas of each face of the cube. What is the length of one edge of a cube whose surface area is 54 square inches?

   A. 3 in.

   B. $3\sqrt{6}$ in.

   C. 9 in.

   D. 9 in.^{2}

10. Which values of x satisfy the inequality $8 - 5x \geq 2$?

    A. $x \geq \dfrac{6}{5}$

    B. $x \leq \dfrac{6}{5}$

    C. $x \geq 2$

    D. $x \leq 2$

11. The perimeter of a square must be at least 244 meters and less than 420 meters. Which inequality for the length in meters l of a single side satisfies this condition?

    A. $61 \leq l < 105$

    B. $61 \leq l \leq 105$

    C. $244 \leq l < 420$

    D. $2\sqrt{61} \leq l < 2\sqrt{105}$

12. Which of the expressions below is equivalent to $-10x^2 + 6x + 4$?

    A. $(x - 1)(10x + 4)$

    B. $(2x + 2)(-5x + 2)$

    C. $-2(x - 1)(5x + 2)$

    D. $-2(-x - 1)(5x + 2)$

13. Which of the following could NOT be the graph of a function $y = f(x)$?

A.

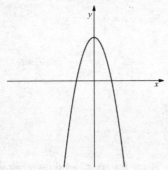

B.

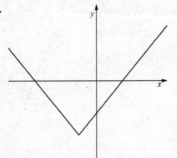

C.

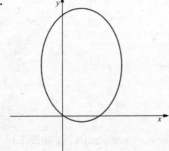

D.

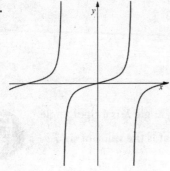

14. Which point is the reflection of the point $(2, -3)$ about the x-axis?

A. $(-3, 2)$

B. $(-2, 3)$

C. $(-2, -3)$

D. $(2, 3)$

15. The operating expenses for Tatianna's Tavern can be modeled by the function $c(m) = 2,600 + 1,100m$, where m is the number of months that the restaurant is open, and $c(m)$ is the operating cost in dollars. What is the cost of operations for three months?

A. $2,930

B. $3,300

C. $5,900

D. $11,100

16. Which is the graph of $y = -\sqrt[3]{x}$?

A.

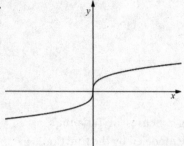

B.

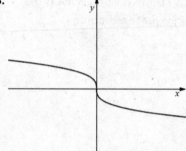

C.

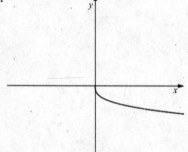

D.

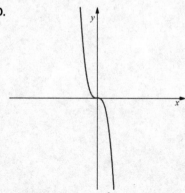

17. What is the solution to the following system of equations?
$$2x + 3y = 7$$
$$5x + 7y = 9$$

A. $x = \dfrac{13}{2}; y = -2$

B. $x = 2; y = -\dfrac{1}{7}$

C. $x = -22, y = 17$

D. $x = -76, y = 53$

18. Given $m\angle A = m\angle B$, are the triangles shown below congruent or similar? What is the value of x?

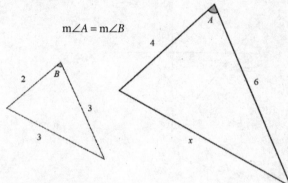

A. Congruent; $x = 4$

B. Congruent; $x = 6$

C. Similar; $x = 4$

D. Similar; $x = 6$

19. Which of the following equations is equivalent to $b^{(x+3)} = 5$, where b is a constant greater than 1?

A. $x = \log_b (5) - 3$

B. $x = \log_b (5 - 3)$

C. $x = \log_5 (b) - 3$

D. $x = \log_5 (b - 3)$

20. In triangle XYZ, angle X is a right angle. If $\tan Z = \dfrac{8}{15}$, what is the value of $\sin Z$?

A. 1

B. $\dfrac{8}{17}$

C. $\dfrac{15}{17}$

D. Not enough information is provided to determine $\sin Z$.

ANSWER KEYS AND EXPLANATIONS
Reading

1. D	5. D	9. D	13. B	17. C
2. A	6. B	10. D	14. D	18. C
3. D	7. C	11. C	15. B	19. D
4. B	8. C	12. D	16. D	20. A

1. **The correct answer is D.** Compared with the withdrawn Holmes, the narrator (Watson) has been engaged in the world during their hiatus. As he states in sentence 14, he had been married and was in "complete happiness," while Holmes had "remained in our lodgings […] buried among his old books," leaving the house only when beckoned to solve crimes.

2. **The correct answer is A.** *Loathsome* is a synonym for *abhorrent*.

3. **The correct answer is D.** Watson states that Holmes had a "cold, precise" mind (sentence 5) and that "[a]ll emotions, and that one particularly, were abhorrent" to Holmes. Holmes was a "perfect reasoning and observing machine" (sentence 6). In sentence 9, Watson states that for a "trained reasoner to admit such intrusions into his own delicate and adjusted temperament was to introduce a distracting factor." Sentence 10 extends this analogy by introducing a foreign body, "grit," into two things that are delicate and adjusted: "a sensitive instrument" and a "high-power" lens. All of these details add up to reinforce Watson's description of Holmes's view on love and emotion in the sentences prior.

4. **The correct answer is B.** The reader can infer Holmes's drive from his accomplishments when Watson states that Holmes solved the "Trepoff murder" or the "singular tragedy of the Atkinson brothers" and offered help to the "reigning family of Holland" (sentence 16). Holmes's reclusiveness is apparent as Watson states that he has "seen little of Holmes lately" (sentence 12); Holmes "loathed every form of society" (sentence 14). None of the other answers contain adjectives that can both be supported by details of the passage.

5. **The correct answer is D.** The passage characterizes the educational attainment of truck drivers by pointing out the "relatively low educational requirements" and that the "mode is a high school degree," while also providing evidence of the number of truck drivers in the United States.

6. **The correct answer is B.** The author celebrates progress, stating that "the foundation" and "substructure" must be built for the modernization and economic benefit of society. He also discusses how "the way [should be] made ready for the tool." By making the way ready, the author implies that modernization should be a priority to keep pace with technology. You can eliminate choice A because while the author supports the modernization of waterways, his focus is ultimately on the development of highways. The passage does not include evidence of that author having a "vast" knowledge of history (choice C). Choice D is incorrect because, as a government employee, it's reasonable to infer he would support the government's endeavors. Also, he praises the "Government" that is modernizing waterway transportation.

7. **The correct answer is C.** Passage 1 characterizes truck drivers, stating their "mode" of educational attainment and noting that the gender disparity in the profession leans toward men. Passage 2 is an argument for highway infrastructure change, characterized by reason—the comparison to the waterways, the logic behind the hammer example—as well as emotional appeals, such as the appeal to workers with the imagery of the hammer. Although Passage 1 is objective in the presentation of the data, choice A is incorrect because there is no analysis present. The reverse of choice B is true. Passage

1 offers a more contemporary (2019) perspective, while Passage 2 presents a historical argument for needed infrastructure changes that was written approximately a century prior (1918). Choice D is incorrect because Passage 2 is not a polemic, but a well-reasoned argument, using the examples of waterway infrastructure changes to support needed highway infrastructure changes.

8. **The correct answer is C.** Passage 1 states "Truck driving is important not only because it is a large occupation, but also because it provides a critically important service to the US economy." Passage 2, while not as blatant in its appraisal, compares highway infrastructure to waterway infrastructure, which the author states is "profitable use for the Nation." Though the author of Passage 1 may agree with choice A, there is no evidence that the author of Passage 2 would agree with this answer. Choice B is incorrect because neither passage provides a "best way." Passage 1 is a statistical look at truck drivers in the United States, while Passage 2 celebrates advances in waterways and pushes for new highways for trucks. Choice D is incorrect because both passages suggest the future of trucking is robust, not lacking.

9. **The correct answer is D.** Close reading reveals that the purpose of this paragraph is to clarify how a category of spiders known as insect-killers hunts differently from another category of spiders known as paralyzers. Though the tarantula is mentioned, there is no attempt to summarize its role in the ecosystem (choice A) beyond describing the type of hunting it does. Similarly, though the author mentions the word *philosophical*, presenting a philosophical argument (choice C) is not the purpose of the paragraph. You might infer from the passage that insect-killers and paralyzers might have a symbiotic relationship, but this is far more vague an answer than the correct one.

10. **The correct answer is D.** Paragraph 3 explains the economic repercussions ($137 billion per year) of non-native species, and paragraph 4 describes a holistic solution based on "a combination of techniques, such as biological control, habitat manipulation, modification of cultural practices,

use of resistant varieties, and minimizing the use of pesticides." Choice A is incorrect because paragraph 4 does not offer any evidence that IPM is the "government's response" to non-native species. Choice B is incorrect because paragraph 3 does not present a specific example, and paragraph 4 does not extend this because an example is not provided. Choice C is incorrect as paragraph 3 does not describe various ecosystems, merely stating that three ecosystems are threatened, while paragraph 4 specifically states that the solution is found in "minimizing the use of pesticides."

11. **The correct answer is C.** The first two paragraphs detail many general points of comparison such as "gestures, style of walking, moving the hands, arms, tricks of speech, or tone of voice," "the subject of caricature," and "actors." None of these are presented in detail but are provided as general examples to support the author's initial claim. The authors then transition in the third paragraph to the specific example of "handwriting," which they continue to develop in the subsequent paragraph. Choice A is incorrect because there is no narrative present in this passage. Choice B is incorrect because the authors do not describe different things in the first two paragraphs but merely present examples to support their claim that "there is no such thing as a perfect pair in nature." Choice D is incorrect because the authors do not offer exposition. In sentence 1, they state their claim that "there is no such thing as a perfect pair in nature," and they spend the rest of the passage supporting this claim by presenting examples such as "gestures, style of walking, moving the hands, arms, tricks of speech, or tone of voice," and, eventually, handwriting.

12. **The correct answer is D.** The author's main claim in this passage is that protections made for the Tobusch fishhook cactus have been successful. The statement "…3,300 cactuses are known to exist at 105 sites" provides evidence to support the claim, as the original number in 1979 was 200. This is a significant increase. Choice A shows a stated opinion, but that opinion doesn't constitute evidence. Choice B is a description of the cactus and does not provide

evidence for the claim. Choice C is speculating on the future and providing a warning.

13. **The correct answer is B.** The writer proposes a "holistic" approach that addresses three different levels of security: "physical, operational, and as a wider protected zone." He also proposes a cleaning up of "barriers, booths, and screening facilities." Choice A is incorrect because the author does not analyze White House security. The reader may infer that this was done prior to this excerpt, but the analysis does not appear in this passage. Choice C is incorrect because the author does not describe "facets" of White House security, focusing instead on one facet, the "higher fence." The author also states in this passage that there are other facets, such as "physical barriers" and "occupational procedures" that are not described here. Choice D is incorrect because the author does not critique the White House Secret Service detail, merely the proposal of a higher fence.

14. **The correct answer is D.** The word *gargantuan* means "enormous, vast, or massive."

15. **The correct answer is B.** The main idea of this passage is that while Neptune and Uranus have similar compositions, they appear different colors, and scientists have recently determined that the reason has to do with a particular haze on both planets being thicker on Uranus. The passage contradicts choice A. Choices C and D do not adequately encompass the passage's main idea.

16. **The correct answer is D.** Every answer given provides an example of something either being translated or needing translation—your job is to figure out which matches the context used in the passage. The passage describes Carlos taking Bach's original music and creating an electronic version of the same compositions using a Moog synthesizer. The answer that best matches is choice D, since a dance company using a famous choreographer's ballet and doing a hip-hop interpretation of it would be a very similar act of translation. Reading between the lines

of what someone is saying (choice B) and making something understandable across language barriers (choices A and C) are two different concepts of translation that are valid but do not match the context here.

17. **The correct answer is C.** The only statement that can be fully supported by evidence presented in the passage is the one that says small dogs suffer health risks directly associated with jumping. The second and third sentences provide examples of jumping injuries that are especially prominent in small dogs.

18. **The correct answer is C.** The most adequate summarization of Goffman's theory, as communicated by the author of the passage, reads "People rarely offer a true, unfiltered version of themselves; instead, they tend to act in ways that mimic how they want to be perceived or otherwise help them manage the impressions of others."

19. **The correct answer is D.** A prize is a measure of worth, and, in this case, since no book was awarded the prize, it can be assumed the jury thought the nominees were "unworthy." While it can also be assumed that a nominee would be interested in an award, choice A is incorrect because the sentence turns in a different direction on the word *therefore*. There must be a causal relationship between the first part of the sentence and the second part, and "interested in" does not have a relationship to the jury not awarding a prize. Choice B is incorrect because there is no indication that the jury thought the nominees were "ungrateful." If the jury was pleased with the nominees, they would have selected one, so choice C cannot be correct either.

20. **The correct answer is A.** The word *though* at the beginning of the sentence suggests a disparity between intent and outcome. The outcome was "a forest fire that burned down 800 acres of forest," a bad outcome. Therefore, the missing word must suggest the opposite of good intentions—in this case, *malicious*.

Writing

1. A	**6.** D	**11.** C	**16.** A	**21.** B
2. C	**7.** D	**12.** B	**17.** D	**22.** B
3. B	**8.** C	**13.** B	**18.** B	**23.** C
4. D	**9.** C	**14.** C	**19.** C	**24.** B
5. B	**10.** B	**15.** A	**20.** A	**25.** D

1. **The correct answer is A.** Yes, the writer should make this change because the phrase changes the academic tone of the piece. The author makes multiple choices that help establish an academic tone for the piece as a whole, such as citing a work from a noted historian and listing the policies associated with the beginning of the American Revolution in paragraph 3. Choice B is not the best answer because while partially correct in that "sports teams" and "baked beans" are irrelevant to the piece as a whole, they are not irrelevant to Boston as the sentence states. Choice C is incorrect because the underlined words provide contemporary rather than historical context. Choice D is incorrect because there is no reference to the historical impact of baked beans or sports teams in Boston.

2. **The correct answer is C.** This question assesses a writer's ability to signal into quotes, which is accomplished most effectively in choice C. Choice A is stilted and introduces an unnecessary comma after the subject. Choice B is incorrect because of its wordiness and the rhythmic stunting of the appositive "a writer." Choice D is incorrect because the book is not a novel.

3. **The correct answer is B.** Sentence 5, while an interesting historical fact, does not contribute to the development of this paragraph and in fact blurs its progression. Sentence 4 is necessary as it introduces the concept of "salutary neglect," which would stand in sharp contrast to the future policies the British instituted. Sentence 7 is needed as it explains the economic consequences of the French and Indian War, which would lead to the policies that Britain instituted. Sentence 8 is imperative as it continues to develop the idea that Boston, as "the main port for

the importing and exporting of goods and supplies in the region and as a vital maritime center" would suffer from these policies.

4. **The correct answer is D.** Since it can be inferred that as "the main port for importing and exporting goods and supplies" Boston is a "vital maritime center," this last phrase is unnecessary, making the best version of the sentence choice D. As it stands, the given sentence is unnecessarily wordy and there are too many words between "Boston" and its strategic importance. Choice B increases the wordiness of the sentence. Choice C remains wordy as the phrase "a vital maritime center" is already inferred.

5. **The correct answer is B.** A compound-complex sentence such as this needs to clearly establish modifications. Choice B most effectively does this by separating the British policies with semicolons. Choice C does little to change the sentence, merely adding an em dash at the end. In choice D, the writer has added "many acts" to the sentence, believing that the adjective "many" will help the reader, but saying that there were a lot of them does little to help the reader understand the modifications.

6. **The correct answer is D.** Choice D correctly combines both sentences, while adding the key word *moniker*. While choice C bears close resemblance to choice D, it unnecessarily adds the word *there*, which results in faulty parallel structure. Choices A and B are unnecessarily wordy.

7. **The correct answer is D.** This question asks a writer to choose between similar words—*conforms*, *coincides*, and *accord*—while also choosing the best ending phrase. In this case, "as many celebrate" is less wordy and clearly modifies *poems*. Choice A is incorrect as *conforms* means to be "similar" or

"identical," which is not the exact word needed. *Coincide* (choice B) means to "occupy the same place in space and time"; again, this is not the meaning the writer intended. Choice C correctly uses the word *accord*, but the end phrase is needlessly wordy compared with that of choice D.

8. **The correct answer is C.** This question asks a writer to be aware of comma placement. Choice A misses the necessary comma after the opening phrase "in fact." Choice B omits all necessary commas. Choice D needs a comma after "during their school years."

9. **The correct answer is C.** Choice C adds specificity by indicating Li Bai rather than using a dangling modifier while also preserving the necessary phrase "at the age of five."

10. **The correct answer is B.** This question asks a writer to consider the relationship between two sentences. Only choice B smoothly transitions between the related ideas of Li Bai's failure with the officials and his inability to take the civil service exam. Choice A is incorrect because there needs to be a conjunction between the actions of trying with other officials and being dismissed. Choice C is incorrect because *however* indicates a shift and contrast or contradiction; there is no contrast here. Choice D is incorrect for a similar reason; the word *but* also indicates a contrast or contradiction.

11. **The correct answer is C.** This question requires a writer to be familiar with the grammatical use of the colon to introduce a list, which is used correctly in choice C. Choice A improperly leads into the list of culvert shapes and sizes. Choice B incorrectly uses a semicolon, as it does not connect two independent clauses. Choice D effectively introduces the list but does so in a less concise manner compared to choice C.

12. **The correct answer is B.** Sentence 6 states "they do have some benefits." A writer would need to assess the correct transition from sentence 6 to sentence 7. Sentence 7 presents an example of one of the benefits, so "For example," is the best transition.

13. **The correct answer is B.** Placing the sentence at the beginning of the second paragraph allows it to function as an effective transition between the ideas of each paragraph. Placing the sentence before sentence 6 (choice C) would disrupt the transition from describing "shapes" in sentence 5 to sentence 6, which states "Whatever its shape." Likewise, to place this sentence before sentence 9 (choice D) would similarly disrupt the transition from sentence 8, the "positive impacts," to sentence 9, which introduces the negative impacts.

14. **The correct answer is C.** The phrase "preventing water flow" is meant to modify what happens when the bottom of the culvert is exposed. This phrase places emphasis on the activity—the fact that the water is prevented from flowing. As such, the use of the word *preventing* adds clarity and enhances the chronology. Choices A and B both place unnecessary emphasis on the noun *water*. Choice D is incorrect because it is needlessly wordy compared with the correct answer.

15. **The correct answer is A.** As the sentence is currently written, it effectively transitions from the mention of the term *daylight* in the previous paragraph to discussing the term in paragraph 4.

16. **The correct answer is A.** Choice A provides an elaboration of the efforts of the New England Culvert Program. By presenting examples of how the program has already made improvements, the writer provides further evidence of the positive impact of the example. Choice B is incorrect because, while the date 2017 is mentioned, it does not provide historical context. Choice C is incorrect because the details are relevant for the whole paragraph. Choice D is incorrect because, although it does fail to explain the impact on the brook trout population, the paragraph does not intend to explain the impact, but rather the efforts.

17. **The correct answer is D.** Being editors at *Wired Magazine* gives Howe and Robinson a degree of credibility, making their position as editors important for that sentence. The reader needs to know that "editors for Wired Magazine" is modifying Jeff Howe and Mark Robinson and thus this phrase needs to be between two commas, an appositive. As written, the sentence is missing a comma after "Robinson." Choice B fails to separate the

nonessential information between the compound subject of the sentence and the verb *defined*. To use em dashes (choice C), they would need to be present on both sides of the parenthetical information.

18. **The correct answer is B.** Choice B displays the only correct verb usage in tense and subject-verb agreement. Choice A incorrectly attributes a plural verb with the singular noun phrase "all of crowdsourcing." Choices C and D both use incorrect verb tenses.

19. **The correct answer is C.** By eliminating the word *worth*, choice C offers the greatest concision while maintaining the meaning of the phrase. Choice A uses the word *worth*, adding an unnecessary word as its meaning is inferred from "tens of thousands of dollars." Choice B incorrectly makes *dollar* possessive. Choice D is incorrect because it eliminates the necessary phrase "of goods."

20. **The correct answer is A.** The sentence, as it stands, is the best answer. Choice B adds a semicolon incorrectly as the first part of the sentence is the subject of the independent clause. Choice C places a comma where none is needed. While grammatically correct, choice D uses three words—"placed an advertisement"—where one, the much stronger verb *advertised,* will do.

21. **The correct answer is B.** The difficulty of this questions lies in understanding the ambiguity of the pronoun *them*. A reader will be unsure if *them* refers to the "citizen" or "Goldcorp." The best decision a writer can make to reduce ambiguity is to repeat the antecedent—in this case "Goldcorp." Choices C and D are both incorrect as Goldcorp found the strike, not the citizen.

22. **The correct answer is B.** The information about the "nom de guerre" and the definition of the term should be its own sentence. The original sentence is

a run-on with a comma splice. Choice C incorrectly uses an em dash. Choice D adds the coordinating conjunction *but*, but the relationship is not one of contrasts as that word suggests.

23. **The correct answer is C.** As the sentence is written, *neither* and *or* do not agree. The correct usage is "neither … nor," making choice C the best answer. Choice B introduces the incorrect relationship of "either … or," which does not fit the writer's sentence. Choice D eliminates any "neither … nor" construction, which results in an unclear, grammatically incorrect sentence.

24. **The correct answer is B.** While the sentence as it is written is grammatically correct, it is not the best option because it takes the reader out of the purpose of this paragraph. The best decision would be to combine it in some way with sentence 12. Choices B, C, and D all do this, but choices C and D retain, essentially, the same two independent clauses, making them wordy (both repeat "the Royal Geographic Society is a") and not subordinate to the first mention of the Royal Geographic Society. This leaves choice B as the most effective combination as it uses sentence 13, in abbreviated form, to modify the Royal Geographic Society, an essential piece of information as the society might be unfamiliar to readers.

25. **The correct answer is D.** The sentence should be cut as it is irrelevant to the passage's purpose and tone. Choice A is incorrect because a decision on transitioning cannot be made unless the rest of the essay is present. Choice B is incorrect because it doesn't sum up the passage but moves in another direction. Choice C is incorrect because the sentence, or a version of the sentence, does not appear elsewhere in the essay and so cannot be redundant.

Arithmetic

1. B	5. B	9. D	13. D	17. B
2. B	6. C	10. C	14. C	18. B
3. B	7. C	11. C	15. A	19. C
4. D	8. A	12. C	16. D	20. B

1. **The correct answer is B.** Multiplication is the inverse operation of division. To divide 57 by 19, we must find the number such that, when the number is multiplied by 19, the product is 57. In symbols, this can be expressed as $19 \times ? = 57$. The answer is $19 \times 3 = 57$, which is the inverse of $57 \div 19 = 3$.

2. **The correct answer is B.** To perform division on two fractions, invert the divisor (the fraction to the right of the division sign), and multiply the two fractions:

$$\frac{2}{3} \div \frac{4}{5} = \frac{2}{3} \times \frac{5}{4}$$

To multiply, multiply the numerators to get the numerator of the product, and multiply the denominators to get the denominator of the product:

$$\frac{2}{3} \times \frac{5}{4} = \frac{2 \times 5}{3 \times 4} = \frac{10}{12}$$

The solution is $\frac{10}{12}$, which can be reduced to $\frac{5}{6}$.

3. **The correct answer is B.** $0.2 = \frac{2}{10} = \frac{20}{100}$ is less than $0.29 = \frac{29}{100}$, and $\frac{29}{100}$ is less than $0.30 = \frac{30}{100}$.

4. **The correct answer is D.** Because the number of votes in the later year is less than the number in the earlier year, the number of votes cast decreased, so we can immediately eliminate choice A. To determine the percent decrease, first calculate the difference:

$$900,000 - 720,000 = 180,000$$

Then, divide this difference by the number of votes in the earlier year, and multiply by 100 to get the percent change.

$$\frac{180,000}{900,000} \times 100 = 0.2 \times 100 = 20$$

The number of votes cast decreased by 20%.

5. **The correct answer is B.** To rewrite $\frac{107}{11}$ as a mixed number, first divide 107 by 11 to get 9 with a remainder of 8 ($107 = 11 \times 9 + 8$). The whole number part of the equivalent mixed number is the quotient, 9. To obtain the fractional part, use the remainder, 8, as the numerator; the denominator of the fractional part is the same as the denominator of the original fraction, 11. So, $\frac{107}{11} = 9\frac{8}{11}$.

6. **The correct answer is C.** The figure |2| represents the absolute value of 2, which is reflected by both +2 and –2. Therefore, you need the answer that matches these two points on the number line, *B* and *F*.

7. **The correct answer is C.** Since you're asked to round, notice that the difference between $\frac{1,688}{101}$ and $\frac{1,688}{100}$ is not large. The latter fraction is equivalent to 16.88, so we would expect our answer to be close to 16.88 and between 16 and 17, which eliminates choices A and D. $16 = \frac{1,616}{101}$ while $17 = \frac{1,717}{101}$. $\frac{1,688}{101}$ is closer to $\frac{1,717}{101}$ than $\frac{1,616}{101}$. Therefore, the given fraction, $\frac{1,688}{101}$, would be rounded to 17.

8. **The correct answer is A.**

$$\frac{52}{1,000} - \frac{3}{100} = \frac{52}{1,000} - \frac{30}{1,000}$$

$$= \frac{22}{1,000}$$

$$= \frac{11}{500}$$

9. **The correct answer is D.** Moving right to left, starting with the thousandths column three digits to the right of the decimal point, find the value as follows:

ANSWERS: ACCUPLACER® PRACTICE TEST 1

The sum in the thousandths place is $3 + 0 + 6 = 9$.

In the hundredths place, $9 + 5 + 1 = 15$; record 5 and carry 1 to the tenths column.

In the tenths place, the carried $1 + 0 + 7 + 8 = 16$; record 6 and carry 1 to the ones column.

In the ones place, the carried $1 + 0 + 6 + 0 = 7$. Hence, $0.093 + 6.75 + 0.816 = 7.659$.

10. **The correct answer is C.** To determine the percent increase, divide the numerical increase, 15, by the number of homes before the new homes were added, 45; then, multiply this quotient by 100.

$$\frac{15}{45} \times 100 = 0.333.. \times 100 = 33.333...$$

To the nearest percent, the percent increase in the number of homes is 33%.

11. **The correct answer is C.** Convert all of the percents into numbers.

$$25\% \text{ of } 16 = \frac{25}{100} \times 16 = \frac{400}{100} = 4$$

$$30\% \text{ of } 10 = \frac{30}{100} \times 10 = \frac{300}{100} = 3$$

$$50\% \text{ of } 12 = \frac{50}{100} \times 12 = \frac{600}{100} = 6$$

$$80\% \text{ of } 5 = \frac{80}{100} \times 5 = \frac{400}{100} = 4$$

So 50% of $12 = 6$ is the greatest of these.

12. **The correct answer is C.** $\frac{2}{3}$ is the repeating decimal $0.666...$ (also written as $0.\overline{6}$), where the sixes continue without end. So, $6\frac{2}{3} = 6.666...$, which, rounded to the nearest tenth, is 6.7. This means that choice C is not a true statement.

13. **The correct answer is D.** This is equivalent to the question, "78 is what percent of 120"? To determine what percent of 120 is 78, you'll need to divide 78 by 120 and multiply by 100. First, reduce the fraction by a factor of 6 to yield $\frac{13}{20}$, and then solve as follows:

$$\frac{13}{20} \times 100 = 0.65 \times 100 = 65$$

14. **The correct answer is C.** To divide 18 by 0.4, first multiply both numbers by 10 to clear the decimal from 0.4. Multiplying the dividend and divisor by the same number does not affect the value of the quotient. So $18 \div 0.4 = 180 \div 4 = 45$ (because $180 = 4 \times 45$).

15. **The correct answer is A.**

$$\frac{117}{150} - \frac{8}{25} = \frac{117}{150} - \frac{8 \times 6}{25 \times 6}$$

$$= \frac{117}{150} - \frac{48}{150}$$

$$= \frac{69}{150} = \frac{23}{50}$$

16. **The correct answer is D.** $211^2 = 211 \times 211$. Since the question asks for an estimate, note that it is fairly easy to calculate 200×211, as shown:

$$200 \times 211 = 200 \times (200 + 11)$$
$$= (200 \times 200) + (200 \times 11)$$
$$= 40{,}000 + 2{,}200$$
$$= 42{,}200$$

Observe that 200×211 is close enough to 211×211 to make 42,000 a reasonable estimate of 211^2.

17. **The correct answer is B.** Observe that $\frac{120}{159}$ is close to $\frac{120}{160} = \frac{3}{4}$. So $\frac{3}{4}$ is a good approximation for $\frac{120}{159}$.

18. **The correct answer is B.** The thousandths place is three digits to the right of the decimal point; in the numeral 2.5217, that is 1. To round to the nearest thousandth, check the digit to the right of the thousandths place. If that digit is 5 through 9, increase the digit in the thousandths place by 1 (if the digit to be increased is 9, change it to 0 and increase the next digit to the left by 1). If that digit is 0 through 4, leave the thousandths digit alone. Then, "truncate" by removing all of the digits to the right of the thousandths place. In this case, the digit to the right of the thousandths place, 7, is greater than 5. So, change the thousandths digit to 2 and truncate to get 2.522.

19. **The correct answer is C.** To find 40% of 1,300, multiply 1,300 by 0.40: $1{,}300 \times 0.40 = 520$.

20. **The correct answer is B.** Divide the number of cans
to be packed by the number that fits in a carton:

$45 \div 6 = 7$ with a remainder of 3

$(45 = (6 \times 7) + 3)$

Quantitative Reasoning, Algebra, and Statistics

1. D	**5.** B	**9.** D	**13.** C	**17.** D
2. A	**6.** A	**10.** C	**14.** C	**18.** B
3. D	**7.** B	**11.** A	**15.** A	**19.** A
4. C	**8.** C	**12.** C	**16.** B	**20.** D

1. **The correct answer is D.** Following order of operations, first perform operations within parentheses:

$$15.7 - (18 - 2) \div 0.5 = 15.7 - 16 \div 0.5$$

Then, perform the division:

$$15.7 - 16 \div 0.5 = 15.7 - 32$$

Finally, subtract:

$$15.7 - 32 = -16.3$$

2. **The correct answer is A.** To convert feet to meters, divide by 3.28:

$$\frac{305}{3.28} = 92.99 \approx 93$$

3. **The correct answer is D.** Negative exponents create fractions. Thus,

$$\frac{1}{4^{-3}} \text{ equals } \frac{1}{\left(\frac{1}{4^{-3}}\right)}, \text{ or } \frac{1}{\left(\frac{1}{64}\right)}.$$

Dividing 1 by $\frac{1}{64}$ yields 64. The same result can be achieved by flipping the fraction to remove the negative on the exponent.

4. **The correct answer is C.** The total cost per mile, including both the rental fee and gas, is $0.18 + $0.10 = $0.28. Therefore, the cost in dollars of driving the rental car m miles is $0.28 times the number of miles, or $0.28m$.

5. **The correct answer is B.** Let L equal the length of a longer side. Because the plot is twice as long as it is wide, the shorter sides have length $\frac{L}{2}$. The perimeter of the rectangular plot is the sum of the lengths of the four sides, therefore:

$$P = L + L + \frac{L}{2} + \frac{L}{2} = 3L$$

The information we are given about the length of the longer sides is expressed by this inequality (note that the words "at most" in the question imply less than or equal to):

$$60 < L \le 75$$

Multiply through by 3 to get:

$$180 < 3L \le 225$$

Since $P = 3L$, we have $180 < P \le 225$.

6. **The correct answer is A.** First, observe that there are 20 objects of each color in the bag, and a total of 60 objects. The probability of picking an object of any color on the first try is $\frac{20}{60} + \frac{20}{60} + \frac{20}{60} = 1$. On the second try, there are 19 objects of the same color as the first left in the bag, out of a total of 59 objects. The probability of choosing two objects of the same color, without replacement, is $1 \times \frac{19}{59} = \frac{19}{59}$.

7. **The correct answer is B.** The formula for the circumference of a circle is $C = 2\pi r$, where C is the circumference and r is the radius of the circle. We are given that $C = 12\pi$, so we have $12\pi = 2\pi r$. Divide both sides of this equation by 2π to get $r = 6$. A circle with radius r has area πr^2, so the area of the given circle is $\pi \times 6^2$ or 36π.

8. **The correct answer is C.** To get the total vertical distance of Albie's dive, add the distance from the platform to the water's surface, 10 feet, to the distance from the water's surface to the bottom of the dive, 8 feet:

$$10 + 8 = 18 \text{ feet}$$

9. **The correct answer is D.** To calculate the number of liters in 600 milliliters, divide the number of milliliters by 1,000:

$$\frac{600}{1,000} = \frac{6}{10} = 0.6$$

10. **The correct answer is C.** 150 million km = 150 × 1,000,000 = 150 × 10^6 km

    To write 150 × 10^6 in scientific notation, observe that:

    $$150 = 1.5 \times 100 = 1.5 \times 10^2$$

    Therefore:

    $$150 \text{ million} = 150 \times 10^6 = 1.5 \times 10^2 \times 10^6 = 1.5 \times 10^8 \text{ km}$$

11. **The correct answer is A.** Let c be the number of cookies Lori bought. Lori bought twice as many muffins (m) as cookies, so she bought $2c$ muffins. The total cost of Lori's purchase is the number of cookies times the cost of a cookie, plus the number of muffins times the cost of a muffin:

    $$2c + 3m = 16$$
    $$2c + 3(2c) = 16$$
    $$8c = 16$$
    $$c = 2$$

12. **The correct answer is C.** The slopes of perpendicular lines are negative reciprocals of each other. The slope of the line in the graph is $\frac{3}{2}$. Therefore, the slope of any line perpendicular to the line shown is $-\frac{2}{3}$, and the equation is $y = -\frac{2}{3}x + b$, where b is the y-intercept of the perpendicular line. We are given that $(0, 1)$ lies on the perpendicular, so its y-intercept is 1. Hence, the equation of the perpendicular line is $y = -\frac{2}{3}x + 1$.

13. **The correct answer is C.** First, calculate the total number of cars sold over the six-week period. The dealer averaged 23 cars per week for the first two weeks, so they sold 2 × 23 = 46 cars over that period. Over the next four weeks, they sold 4 × 27.5 = 110 cars. The total number of cars sold over six weeks is 46 + 110 = 156. To determine the average weekly sales, divide the total sold by the number of weeks: 156 ÷ 6 = 26 cars.

14. **The correct answer is C.** When rectangle $ABCD$ is reflected across the x-axis, point D is translated from $(-4, -3)$ to $(-4, 3)$. Then, after the rectangle is rotated 90° clockwise about the origin, D is translated from $(-4, 3)$ to $(3, 4)$.

15. **The correct answer is A.**

    $$\frac{-7}{-14-(-7)} = \frac{-7}{-14+7} = \frac{-7}{-7} = 1$$

16. **The correct answer is B.** To determine the hourly wage, first determine how many hours Juan worked to earn $1,080. Multiply the number of days by the number of hours per day: 10 × 6 = 60. Juan worked 60 hours. Divide the number of dollars by the number of hours worked to calculate dollars per hour: $\frac{1,080}{60} = 18$. Juan's hourly wage is $18.00.

17. **The correct answer is D.** In general, if r is a real number, and m and n are integers with $n \neq 1$,

    $$r^{\frac{m}{n}} = \left(\sqrt[n]{r}\right)^m = \sqrt[n]{r^m}$$

    Hence:

    $$2^{\frac{2}{3}} = \sqrt[3]{2^2} = \sqrt[3]{4}$$

18. **The correct answer is B.** First, write the terms in order of decreasing exponents:

    $$(3u^4 - 6u^2 + u) + (-u^5 - 2u^2 + 9)$$
    $$= -u^5 + 3u^4 - 6u^2 - 2u^2 + u + 9$$

    Then, combine the two u^2 terms:

    $$-u^5 + 3u^4 - 8u^2 + u + 9$$

19. **The correct answer is A.** Substitute 26 for y in the given equation:

    $$-x + \frac{26}{2} = 10$$

    This is equivalent to:

    $$-x + 13 = 10$$
    $$x = 3$$

20. **The correct answer is D.** The table shows that a total of 54 surveyed students ride a school bus. Of those bus riders, 12 are sophomores and 16 are freshmen, so a total of 28 of the bus riders are either freshmen or sophomores. The requested probability is 28 ÷ 54, or approximately 0.52.

Advanced Algebra and Functions

1. B	5. B	9. A	13. C	17. C
2. C	6. A	10. B	14. D	18. D
3. C	7. C	11. A	15. C	19. A
4. A	8. B	12. C	16. B	20. B

1. **The correct answer is B.** The value of m can be found by substituting 15 for y and –2 for x. This yields $15 = m(-2) - 7$. Adding 7 to both sides of this equation results in $22 = m(-2)$. Dividing both sides by –2 then gives us the final result: $-11 = m$.

2. **The correct answer is C.** We want an equation that is equivalent to $v = \dfrac{d}{t}$, and because we want to be able to calculate the time (t) directly, we want the value t isolated on one side of the equation. To get this, first multiply both sides of the given equation by t to arrive at $vt = d$. Then divide both sides by v, resulting in $t = \dfrac{d}{v}$.

3. **The correct answer is C.** Factoring the equation $9x^2 + 30x + 16$ results in $(3x + 2)(3x + 8)$; the first of these monomials matches choice C.

4. **The correct answer is A.** Substitute $a = 4$, $b = -2$, $c = 3$ into $\dfrac{-b \pm \sqrt{b^2 - 4ac}}{2a}$.

5. **The correct answer is B.** Replace x with the value $3A + 2$:

$$f(3A+2) = \frac{-4(3A+2)}{3} + 3$$

$$= \frac{-12A - 8}{3} + 3$$

$$= -4A - \frac{8}{3} + 3$$

$$= -4A + \frac{1}{3}$$

6. **The correct answer is A.** Begin by adding 6 to both sides of the equation, and then multiply both sides by 3 to get $\sqrt{151 + x} = 12$. Squaring both sides results in $151 + x = 144$, or $x = -7$.

7. **The correct answer is C.** Replace x with both values:

$$2(2)^3 - 7(2)^2 + 4(2) + 4 = 16 - 28 + 8 + 4 = 0$$

and

$$2\left(-\frac{1}{2}\right)^3 - 7\left(-\frac{1}{2}\right)^2 + 4\left(-\frac{1}{2}\right) + 4 = -\frac{1}{4} - \frac{7}{4} - 2 + 4 = 0$$

8. **The correct answer is B.** Convert the given logarithmic equation in exponential form:

$$6^2 = -4x$$

Then, divide both sides by –4:

$$x = \frac{6^2}{-4} = \frac{36}{-4} = -9$$

9. **The correct answer is A.** A cube has 6 faces. Each face of a cube with total surface area 54 in^2 is a square with area 9 in.^{2} ($54 \div 6 = 9$). The length of one edge of the cube is the length of a side of this square, so the length is $\sqrt{9}$ or 3 inches.

10. **The correct answer is B.** Start by subtracting 8 from both sides to arrive at $-5x \geq -6$. Then, divide both sides by –5, remembering you must reverse the inequality from $\geq$ to $\leq$.

11. **The correct answer is A.** The perimeter of a square with sides of length l is $4l$. To satisfy the stated conditions, the inequality $244 \leq 4l < 420$ must be true. Dividing by 4 yields $61 \leq l < 105$.

12. **The correct answer is C.** Begin by factoring –2 out of $-10x^2 + 6x + 4$ to get $-2(5x^2 - 3x - 2)$. Then, factor the quadratic to arrive at $-2(x - 1)(5x + 2)$.

13. **The correct answer is C.** Because a function has at most one output for each input, each x-value on the graph of $f(x)$ must correspond to only one y-value. Some x-values on this graph—for instance, $x = 0$—have two corresponding y-values. Choices A, B, and

D all pass the "vertical line test" and could be the graphs of functions.

14. **The correct answer is D.** In general, when (x, y) is reflected across the x-axis, its image is $(x, -y)$. For the given point $x = 2$ and $y = -3$, the reflection is $(2, -(-3))$, or $(2, 3)$.

15. **The correct answer is C.** Using the specified function, at three months it would be $c(3) = 2,600 + 1,100(3) = 2,600 + 3,300 = \$5,900$.

16. **The correct answer is B.** When x is negative, $\sqrt[3]{x}$ also is negative, so $-\sqrt[3]{x}$ is positive. When x is positive, $\sqrt[3]{x}$ also is positive, so $-\sqrt[3]{x}$ is negative.

17. **The correct answer is C.** Multiply the first equation by 5 to get $10x + 15y = 35$, then multiply the second by -2 to get $-10x - 14y = -18$. Add the two equations to eliminate the x terms, resulting in $15y - 14y = 35 - 18$, or $y = 17$. Substituting 17 for y in the first equation gives $2x + 3(17) = 7$, which simplifies to $x = -22$. Choices A and D satisfy the first equation but not the second. Similarly, choice B satisfies the second equation but not the first.

18. **The correct answer is D.** By the side-angle-side theorem, if an angle of one triangle is congruent to any angle of the second triangle, and the lengths of the sides including these angles are proportional, then the triangles are similar. We are given that angles A and B are congruent, and the corresponding sides are proportional: $\frac{4}{2} = \frac{6}{3}$. Because the triangles are similar, x and 3 must share this proportionality: $\frac{4}{2} = \frac{6}{3} = \frac{x}{3}$. Hence $x = 6$.

19. **The correct answer is A.** In general, if $b^x = y$, where $b > 0$ and $b \neq 1$, then $x = \log_b(y)$. In the case of the equation $b^{(x+3)} = 5$, we have $x + 3 = \log_b(5)$, which is equivalent to $x = \log_b(5) - 3$.

20. **The correct answer is B.** In right triangle XYZ, if $\tan Z = \frac{8}{15}$, then by the definition of the tangent function, the ratio of the leg opposite $\angle Z$ to the leg adjacent to $\angle Z$ is $\frac{\text{opposite}}{\text{adjacent}} = \frac{8}{15}$. That means $\triangle XYZ$ is congruent or similar to a right triangle with legs of lengths 8 and 15. By the Pythagorean theorem, a right triangle with legs of lengths 8 and 15 has a hypotenuse of length 17 (because $8^2 + 15^2 = 17^2$). The value of $\sin Z$ is the ratio of the length of the leg opposite $\angle Z$ to the hypotenuse, which is $\frac{8}{17}$.

SCORE YOURSELF: ACCUPLACER® PRACTICE TEST 1

Add up the total number of questions you answered correctly for each section, then compare your scores against the section charts below, which roughly recreate the scoring bands used by the ACCUPLACER. For more information on how the scoring bands relate to specific skills, see the extended scoring charts at the end of each answer and explanation section in Chapter 2.

Reading

Total Number of Correct Answers: _____ /20

Total # of Correct Answers	Approximate ACCUPLACER Score
8 or fewer	200–236
9–11	237–249
12–14	250–262
15–17	263–275
18–20	276–300

Writing

Total Number of Correct Answers: _____ /25

Total # of Correct Answers	Approximate ACCUPLACER Score
9 or fewer	200–236
10–13	237–249
14–17	250–262
18–21	263–275
22–25	276–300

Arithmetic

Total Number of Correct Answers: _____ /20

Total # of Correct Answers	Approximate ACCUPLACER Score
8 or fewer	200–236
9–11	237–249
12–14	250–262
15–17	263–275
18–20	276–300

Quantitative Reasoning, Algebra, and Statistics

Total Number of Correct Answers: _____ /20

Total # of Correct Answers	Approximate ACCUPLACER Score
8 or fewer	200–236
9–11	237–249
12–14	250–262
15–17	263–275
18–20	276–300

Advanced Algebra and Functions

Total Number of Correct Answers: _____ /20

Total # of Correct Answers	Approximate ACCUPLACER Score
8 or fewer	200–236
9–11	237–249
12–14	250–262
15–17	263–275
18–20	276–300

LEVEL <u>UP</u>
YOUR
TEST PREP

- Access to **entire course catalog** (prep for 185+ tests and exams)

- 5,000+ flashcards, practice tests, interactive lessons, and videos

- Access to our **mobile app** to study on the go

- Live, on-demand **tutoring** with top-notch tutors

- Test-taking **tips and strategies** to earn your best score

- **Essay review** for applications, scholarships, and assignments

All-inclusive subscriptions provide access to every course, along with subject-based tutorials and videos to refresh your memory.

LEVEL UP TODAY!

CHAPTER

ACCUPLACER®
Practice Test 2

ACCUPLACER® PRACTICE TEST 2

PRACTICE TEST 2

This practice test is designed to help you
recognize your strengths and weaknesses.
The questions cover information from all the
different sections of the ACCUPLACER. Use the
results to help guide and direct your study time.

ANSWER SHEET: ACCUPLACER® PRACTICE TEST 2

Reading

1. Ⓐ Ⓑ Ⓒ Ⓓ   5. Ⓐ Ⓑ Ⓒ Ⓓ   9. Ⓐ Ⓑ Ⓒ Ⓓ   13. Ⓐ Ⓑ Ⓒ Ⓓ   17. Ⓐ Ⓑ Ⓒ Ⓓ
2. Ⓐ Ⓑ Ⓒ Ⓓ   6. Ⓐ Ⓑ Ⓒ Ⓓ   10. Ⓐ Ⓑ Ⓒ Ⓓ   14. Ⓐ Ⓑ Ⓒ Ⓓ   18. Ⓐ Ⓑ Ⓒ Ⓓ
3. Ⓐ Ⓑ Ⓒ Ⓓ   7. Ⓐ Ⓑ Ⓒ Ⓓ   11. Ⓐ Ⓑ Ⓒ Ⓓ   15. Ⓐ Ⓑ Ⓒ Ⓓ   19. Ⓐ Ⓑ Ⓒ Ⓓ
4. Ⓐ Ⓑ Ⓒ Ⓓ   8. Ⓐ Ⓑ Ⓒ Ⓓ   12. Ⓐ Ⓑ Ⓒ Ⓓ   16. Ⓐ Ⓑ Ⓒ Ⓓ   20. Ⓐ Ⓑ Ⓒ Ⓓ

Writing

1. Ⓐ Ⓑ Ⓒ Ⓓ   6. Ⓐ Ⓑ Ⓒ Ⓓ   11. Ⓐ Ⓑ Ⓒ Ⓓ   16. Ⓐ Ⓑ Ⓒ Ⓓ   21. Ⓐ Ⓑ Ⓒ Ⓓ
2. Ⓐ Ⓑ Ⓒ Ⓓ   7. Ⓐ Ⓑ Ⓒ Ⓓ   12. Ⓐ Ⓑ Ⓒ Ⓓ   17. Ⓐ Ⓑ Ⓒ Ⓓ   22. Ⓐ Ⓑ Ⓒ Ⓓ
3. Ⓐ Ⓑ Ⓒ Ⓓ   8. Ⓐ Ⓑ Ⓒ Ⓓ   13. Ⓐ Ⓑ Ⓒ Ⓓ   18. Ⓐ Ⓑ Ⓒ Ⓓ   23. Ⓐ Ⓑ Ⓒ Ⓓ
4. Ⓐ Ⓑ Ⓒ Ⓓ   9. Ⓐ Ⓑ Ⓒ Ⓓ   14. Ⓐ Ⓑ Ⓒ Ⓓ   19. Ⓐ Ⓑ Ⓒ Ⓓ   24. Ⓐ Ⓑ Ⓒ Ⓓ
5. Ⓐ Ⓑ Ⓒ Ⓓ   10. Ⓐ Ⓑ Ⓒ Ⓓ   15. Ⓐ Ⓑ Ⓒ Ⓓ   20. Ⓐ Ⓑ Ⓒ Ⓓ   25. Ⓐ Ⓑ Ⓒ Ⓓ

Arithmetic

1. Ⓐ Ⓑ Ⓒ Ⓓ   5. Ⓐ Ⓑ Ⓒ Ⓓ   9. Ⓐ Ⓑ Ⓒ Ⓓ   13. Ⓐ Ⓑ Ⓒ Ⓓ   17. Ⓐ Ⓑ Ⓒ Ⓓ
2. Ⓐ Ⓑ Ⓒ Ⓓ   6. Ⓐ Ⓑ Ⓒ Ⓓ   10. Ⓐ Ⓑ Ⓒ Ⓓ   14. Ⓐ Ⓑ Ⓒ Ⓓ   18. Ⓐ Ⓑ Ⓒ Ⓓ
3. Ⓐ Ⓑ Ⓒ Ⓓ   7. Ⓐ Ⓑ Ⓒ Ⓓ   11. Ⓐ Ⓑ Ⓒ Ⓓ   15. Ⓐ Ⓑ Ⓒ Ⓓ   19. Ⓐ Ⓑ Ⓒ Ⓓ
4. Ⓐ Ⓑ Ⓒ Ⓓ   8. Ⓐ Ⓑ Ⓒ Ⓓ   12. Ⓐ Ⓑ Ⓒ Ⓓ   16. Ⓐ Ⓑ Ⓒ Ⓓ   20. Ⓐ Ⓑ Ⓒ Ⓓ

Quantitative Reasoning, Algebra, and Statistics

1. Ⓐ Ⓑ Ⓒ Ⓓ 5. Ⓐ Ⓑ Ⓒ Ⓓ 9. Ⓐ Ⓑ Ⓒ Ⓓ 13. Ⓐ Ⓑ Ⓒ Ⓓ 17. Ⓐ Ⓑ Ⓒ Ⓓ

2. Ⓐ Ⓑ Ⓒ Ⓓ 6. Ⓐ Ⓑ Ⓒ Ⓓ 10. Ⓐ Ⓑ Ⓒ Ⓓ 14. Ⓐ Ⓑ Ⓒ Ⓓ 18. Ⓐ Ⓑ Ⓒ Ⓓ

3. Ⓐ Ⓑ Ⓒ Ⓓ 7. Ⓐ Ⓑ Ⓒ Ⓓ 11. Ⓐ Ⓑ Ⓒ Ⓓ 15. Ⓐ Ⓑ Ⓒ Ⓓ 19. Ⓐ Ⓑ Ⓒ Ⓓ

4. Ⓐ Ⓑ Ⓒ Ⓓ 8. Ⓐ Ⓑ Ⓒ Ⓓ 12. Ⓐ Ⓑ Ⓒ Ⓓ 16. Ⓐ Ⓑ Ⓒ Ⓓ 20. Ⓐ Ⓑ Ⓒ Ⓓ

Advanced Algebra and Functions

1. Ⓐ Ⓑ Ⓒ Ⓓ 5. Ⓐ Ⓑ Ⓒ Ⓓ 9. Ⓐ Ⓑ Ⓒ Ⓓ 13. Ⓐ Ⓑ Ⓒ Ⓓ 17. Ⓐ Ⓑ Ⓒ Ⓓ

2. Ⓐ Ⓑ Ⓒ Ⓓ 6. Ⓐ Ⓑ Ⓒ Ⓓ 10. Ⓐ Ⓑ Ⓒ Ⓓ 14. Ⓐ Ⓑ Ⓒ Ⓓ 18. Ⓐ Ⓑ Ⓒ Ⓓ

3. Ⓐ Ⓑ Ⓒ Ⓓ 7. Ⓐ Ⓑ Ⓒ Ⓓ 11. Ⓐ Ⓑ Ⓒ Ⓓ 15. Ⓐ Ⓑ Ⓒ Ⓓ 19. Ⓐ Ⓑ Ⓒ Ⓓ

4. Ⓐ Ⓑ Ⓒ Ⓓ 8. Ⓐ Ⓑ Ⓒ Ⓓ 12. Ⓐ Ⓑ Ⓒ Ⓓ 16. Ⓐ Ⓑ Ⓒ Ⓓ 20. Ⓐ Ⓑ Ⓒ Ⓓ

READING

20 Questions

Directions for Questions 1–18: Read the passage(s) below and answer the question(s) based on what is stated or implied in the passage(s) and in any introductory material that may be provided.

Jane Austen's Pride and Prejudice follows the experiences of the Bennet family and the events surrounding the Bennet family's attempts to find their daughters husbands. In the following passage, Mr. and Mrs. Bennet discuss the arrival of wealthy Mr. Bingley.

(1) It is a truth universally acknowledged, that a single man in possession of a good fortune, must be in want of a wife.

(2) However little known the feelings or views of such a man may be on his first entering a neighborhood, this truth is so well fixed in the minds of the surrounding families, that he is considered the rightful property of some one or other of their daughters.

(3) "My dear Mr. Bennet," said his lady to him one day, "have you heard that Netherfield Park is let at last?"

(4) Mr. Bennet replied that he had not.

(5) "But it is," returned she; "for Mrs. Long has just been here, and she told me all about it."

(6) Mr. Bennet made no answer.

(7) "Do you not want to know who has taken it?" cried his wife impatiently.

(8) "You want to tell me, and I have no objection to hearing it."

(9) This was invitation enough.

(10) "Why, my dear, you must know, Mrs. Long says that Netherfield is taken by a young man of large fortune from the north of England; that he came down on Monday in a chaise and four to see the place, and was so much delighted with it, that he agreed with Mr. Morris immediately; that he is to take possession before Michaelmas, and some of his servants are to be in the house by the end of next week."

(11) "What is his name?"

(12) "Bingley."

(13) "Is he married or single?"

(14) "Oh! **(15)** Single, my dear, to be sure! **(16)** A single man of large fortune; four or five thousand a year. **(17)** What a fine thing for our girls!"

(18) "How so? **(19)** How can it affect them?"

(20) "My dear Mr. Bennet," replied his wife, "how can you be so tiresome! **(21)** You must know that I am thinking of his marrying one of them."

(22) "Is that his design in settling here?"

(23) "Design! **(24)** Nonsense, how can you talk so! **(25)** But it is very likely that he may fall in love with one of them, and therefore you must visit him as soon as he comes."

From Jane Austen, *Pride and Prejudice*. Originally published in 1813.

1. The relationship between the aphorism in sentence 1 and the rest of the passage is that the aphorism

   A. posits that people with money are despised when they move, while the rest of the passage contradicts this.

   B. instigates the plot of the story, while the rest of the passage characterizes Mr. Bingley.

   C. makes a statement foreshadowing the plot of the story, while the rest of the passage initiates the plot.

   D. establishes the narrator's wisdom and ability to tell the forthcoming story.

2. Based on the passage, Netherfield Park can best be characterized as

   A. the town where the Bennets live.

   B. an opulent house.

   C. a large park.

   D. the neighborhood where the Bennets live.

3. The main purpose of sentences 10–23 is to

   A. suggest Mrs. Bennet's plan.

   B. scold Mr. Bennet.

   C. order Mr. Bennet to visit Mr. Bingley.

   D. characterize Mrs. Bennet.

4. In context, the word "design" in sentences 22 and 23 most likely means

   A. a plan or drawing produced to show the look and function of an object.

   B. to conceive and plan out in the mind.

   C. to have as a purpose.

   D. to build for a specific function or end.

11

Passage 1

It is very important that teachers should realize the importance of habit, and psychology helps us greatly at this point. We speak, it is true, of good habits and of bad habits; but, when people use the word "habit" in the majority of instances it is a bad habit which they have in mind. They talk of the smoking-habit and the swearing-habit and the drinking-habit, but not of the abstention-habit or the moderation-habit or the courage-habit. But the fact is that our virtues are habits as much as our vices. All our life, so far as it has definite form, is but a mass of habits—practical, emotional, and intellectual—systematically organized for our weal or woe, and bearing us irresistibly toward our destiny, whatever the latter may be.

I believe that we are subject to the law of habit in consequence of the fact that we have bodies. The plasticity of the living matter of our nervous system, in short, is the reason why we do a thing with difficulty the first time, but soon do it more and more easily, and finally, with sufficient practice, do it semi-mechanically, or with hardly any consciousness at all. Our nervous systems have "grown" to the way in which they have been exercised, just as a sheet of paper or a coat, once creased or folded, tends to fall forever afterward into the same identical folds.

Habit is thus a second nature; for the acquired habits of our training have by that time inhibited or strangled most of the natural impulsive tendencies which were originally there. Ninety-nine hundredths or, possibly, nine hundred and ninety-nine thousandths of our activity is purely automatic and habitual, from our rising in the morning to our lying down each night. Our dressing and undressing, our eating and drinking, our greetings and partings, our hat-raisings and giving way for ladies to precede, nay, even most of the forms of our common speech, are things of a type so fixed by repetition as almost to be classed as reflex actions. To each sort of impression we have an automatic, ready-made response. My very words to you now are an example of what I mean; for having already lectured upon habit and printed a chapter about it in a book, and read the latter when in print, I find my tongue inevitably falling into its old phrases and repeating almost literally what I said before.

Adapted from William James, *Talks to Teachers on Psychology; And to Students on Some of Life's Ideals*. Originally published in 1899.

Passage 2

The process of learning, which consists in the acquisition of habits, has been much studied in various animals. For example: you put a hungry animal, say a cat, in a cage which has a door that can be opened by lifting a latch; outside the cage you put food. The cat at first dashes all round the cage, making frantic efforts to force a way out. At last, by accident, the latch is lifted and the cat pounces on the food. Next day you repeat the experiment, and you find that the cat gets out much more quickly than the first time, although it still makes some random movements. The third day it gets out still more quickly, and before long it goes straight to the latch and lifts it at once. Or you make a model of the Hampton Court maze, and put a rat in the middle, assaulted by the smell of food on the outside. The rat starts running down the passages, and is constantly stopped by blind alleys, but at last, by persistent attempts, it gets out. You repeat this experiment day after day; you measure the time taken by the rat in reaching the food; you find that the time rapidly diminishes, and that after a while the rat ceases to make any wrong turnings. It is by essentially similar processes that we learn speaking, writing, mathematics, or the government of an empire.

Adapted from Bertrand Russell, *The Analysis of Mind*. Originally published in 1921.

5. The main purpose of the first paragraph in Passage 1 is to

A. greet educators and students and show gratitude for the opportunity to speak.

B. explore the word "habit" etymologically.

C. broaden the audience's understanding of habits.

D. inspire the audience to embrace their habits because it is their destiny.

6. The main purpose of Passage 2 is to offer

A. criticism.

B. justification.

C. a counterargument.

D. exemplification.

7. Which choice best describes the relationship between the two passages?

A. Passage 1 mainly discusses how habits are learned, while Passage 2 discusses the nature of habits.

B. Passage 1 presents a critique of bad habits, while Passage 2 celebrates the development of habits.

C. Passage 1 focuses on the development of habits in humans, while Passage 2 focuses on the development of habits in animals.

D. Passage 1 discusses the nature of habits, while Passage 2 explores how the way animals learn habits relates to human learning.

8. Given the evidence in both passages, with which statement would the authors of both passages most likely agree?

A. Forming habits is a natural part of being a conscious being.

B. Habits are harder to break for some people than others.

C. There is no need to put effort into forming habits.

D. Most people have too many bad habits.

Georg Wilhelm Friedrich Hegel (1770–1831) is one of the most prominent German philosophers of all time. Though his dense works are notorious for giving today's philosophy students headaches, his complex ideas were so revolutionary that they founded the basis of most modern philosophy, including serving as inspiration to prominent thinkers like Karl Marx, Søren Kierkegaard, and Michel Foucault. Hegel developed a way of thinking known as the dialectic, which involved investigating how contradictions between two seemingly true things, termed a thesis and antithesis, can reveal an even higher level of truth. The process of thinking through the contradiction between thesis and antithesis and its implications was known as the "Hegelian dialectic" and the idea was that engaging in dialectical thinking helped advance knowledge over time.

Hegel's most illustrative example of the dialectic involves the idea of power. The concept is often termed the "master/slave" dialectic, and it describes a dialectical thought process, which imagines the power dynamic that would exist between an enslaved person and the person who enslaves them. Sometimes also referred to as the "Lordship and Bondage" dialectic, the concept is essentially that the two cannot exist without the other. Let's call the thesis the idea that a person cannot be enslaved without another person forcing them to do so. No one would choose to be a slave, most likely, so they can only become one if someone else exerts power over them. Meanwhile, the antithesis is the idea that the person who forces another person to be their slave cannot feel that sense of power over another without a person to force into slavery. Their existence as "master" over a slave only happens so long as the slave exists. Therefore, the power of one does not exist without the antithetical power of the other. This master/slave dialectic is thus meant to reveal a greater truth about the nature of power.

9. How might you summarize the primary contradiction of the master/slave dialectic?

   A. Power can be both given and taken away.

   B. No one wants to be a slave, yet some people are enslaved.

   C. Power is also weakness.

   D. Neither the slave nor the master can exist without the other.

Most people think of an image when they hear the word *art*. Whether it's an elaborate oil painting, a thoughtful photograph, an intricate drawing, or even a sculpture, art is understandably most often considered the realm of the visual. This does not mean, of course, that no art exists outside of traditional visual art media and discourses. It does mean that conceptual artists like Jenny Holzer have free range to interrogate the idea of what art is by introducing elements that others might not initially think of as visual.

In Holzer's case, the two elements she plays with most in her conceptual artworks are text and the built environment. Specifically, Holzer is known for projecting written statements in a bold font onto buildings, posting messages as neon signage, integrating poetry into places where more direct communication usually appears, or otherwise finding ways to introduce text into the spaces of everyday life. Holzer has also been known to display her signature alongside these works, creating an additional thoughtful play on the idea of the artist's signature as a type of visual representation that is both text and personal doodle.

One of Holzer's go-to methods for her conceptual works is LED signs like those one would find throughout the architecture of everyday life. Other places her works have turned up include parking meters, T-shirts, billboards, placards, and anywhere else one might find text. In every act, Holzer's goal is to get her viewer to pause and think about the visual messages we receive every day; what are their true contents, where are they situated, and how do we respond to them?

10. In which of the following places can you infer you would be *least likely* to see a piece of Jenny Holzer's artwork?

   A. Hanging as an oil painting in a private art gallery

   B. Graffitied on a subway car

   C. Painted into a parking spot

   D. Scrolling across an LED sign at the airport

A nomad is essentially a wanderer; it's a word for those who do not make their home in one permanent place. Many times, nomadic peoples have been living this way for years as a way to continuously find resources or match the ebbs and flows of seasons, weather patterns, and animal migration. There are many nomadic people groups still scattered across the world, including the Kochi of Afghanistan, the Pokot of Kenya and Uganda, the Nukak-Maku of Colombia, and the Sarakastsani of Greece, to name just a few.

One such group with a centuries-long tradition of nomadic living are the Bedouin, primarily of Jordan, Iraq, and Syria, but also prominent in other areas throughout northern Africa and the Arabian Peninsula. Bedouins are particularly adapted to life in the desert, having a keen understanding of how to navigate the landscape and rely on sources of water along the way, such as the Nile in Egypt. Rather than being connected to one particular nation or culture, Bedouins are bonded by their shared nomadic tradition.

Bedouins predominantly live in tribes of animal herders, meaning that they move animals with them from place to place and raise them. This is often how the tribes earn their livelihood, as they sell food and wares related to their chosen form of animal stewardship wherever they go. However, not all Bedouin tribes raise the same animals; in fact, the species of animal that a tribe chooses to raise often dictates how they are classified by other Bedouin tribes and where they can choose to live. A nomadic tribe raising goats and sheep is likely to live somewhere like Syria or Iraq, whereas those who raise cattle do well in the southern part of the Arabia Peninsula, such as in Saudi Arabia. In the Sahara and other deserts, Bedouin camel tribes dominate.

11. Where are you NOT likely to find Bedouin encampments?

   A. Egypt
   B. Saudi Arabia
   C. Jordan
   D. South Africa

The following is adapted from an American history textbook. In this passage, the author has been enumerating some of the issues that arose during the rapid suburbanization process of the mid-20th century.

Redlining was a formalized process to help banks make determinations about mortgage applications. From 1934 onward, maps were created to divide every major city in the US into sections based on a neighborhood's suitability for mortgages. Under redlining, neighborhoods considered less likely to be profitable for mortgage lenders, which were also those inhabited by large communities of color, were drawn in "red," deeming them least desirable. People consequently couldn't get favorable mortgages for homes in redlined areas, yet they were the only areas with racial covenants that allowed certain populations (mainly people of color) to live there. White families were thus free to take part in expanding suburbanization, while families of color were largely left out. Therefore, understanding how redlining contributed to housing segregation along racial lines is critical for understanding the generational wealth gaps that contribute to racial inequality today.

12. If a neighborhood was "redlined," what did this mean?

   A. Banks considered the neighborhood a more desirable place to issue mortgages.

   B. Banks issued more mortgages to that neighborhood than any other.

   C. Banks considered the neighborhood an undesirable place to issue mortgages.

   D. No housing developments were allowed in these neighborhoods.

The following is adapted from the introduction to an encyclopedia of mushrooms.

The world of fungi goes far beyond the portobello and shiitake mushrooms that most of us are more likely to encounter on a dinner plate than growing wild in the woods. The term *mushroom* describes fungus that has fruited and can release spores. There are roughly 14,000 species of mushrooms, also known as toadstools, described in nature so far, though some scientists suspect there could be millions more as of yet undiscovered. Of those thousands, as many as 20 are potentially lethal to humans while hundreds more are known to be poisonous. Still others are known to have medicinal qualities. There's so much to discover inside the weird, wide world of mushrooms!

---

13. It would be accurate to describe the tone of this passage as

   A. contemptuous.

   B. dispassionate.

   C. somber.

   D. enthusiastic.

Animal sanctuaries are places where man is passive and the rest of Nature active. A sanctuary is the same thing to wild life as a spring is to a river. In itself a sanctuary is a natural "zoo." But it is much more than a "zoo." It can only contain a certain number of animals. Its surplus must overflow to stock surrounding areas. And it constitutes a refuge for all species whose lines of migration pass through it. So its value in the preservation of desirable wild life is not to be denied. Of course, sanctuaries occasionally develop troubles of their own; for if man interferes with the balance of nature in one way he must be prepared to interfere in others. But all experience shows that an easily worked system will ensure a maximum of gain and a minimum of loss.

Adapted from William Wood, *Draft of a Plan for Beginning Animal Sanctuaries in Labrador.* Originally published in 1913.

---

14. Based on the passage, Wood most likely put the word "zoo" in quotation marks to

   A. acknowledge a place of refuge for threatened animals.

   B. satirize society's conception of a zoo.

   C. emphasize the paradox of using the term to refer to a natural place.

   D. indicate the inclusion of dialogue.

> *In the excerpt below, Frederick Douglass describes what it was like to be a free man after his time as a slave had finally ended.*
>
> My free life began on the third of September, 1838. On the morning of the fourth of that month, after an anxious and most perilous but safe journey, I found myself in the big city of New York, a FREE MAN—one more added to the mighty throng which, like the confused waves of the troubled sea, surged to and fro between the lofty walls of Broadway. Though dazzled with the wonders which met me on every hand, my thoughts could not be much withdrawn from my strange situation. For the moment, the dreams of my youth and the hopes of my manhood were completely fulfilled. The bonds that had held me to "old master" were broken. No man now had a right to call me his slave or assert mastery over me. I was in the rough and tumble of an outdoor world, to take my chance with the rest of its busy number. I have often been asked how I felt when first I found myself on free soil. There is scarcely anything in my experience about which I could not give a more satisfactory answer. A new world had opened upon me. If life is more than breath and the "quick round of blood," I lived more in that one day than in a year of my slave life. It was a time of joyous excitement which words can but tamely describe. In a letter written to a friend soon after reaching New York, I said: "I felt as one might feel upon escape from a den of hungry lions." Anguish and grief, like darkness and rain, may be depicted; but gladness and joy, like the rainbow, defy the skill of pen or pencil. During ten or fifteen years I had been, as it were, dragging a heavy chain which no strength of mine could break; I was not only a slave, but a slave for life. I might become a husband, a father, an aged man, but through all, from birth to death, from the cradle to the grave, I had felt myself doomed. All efforts I had previously made to secure my freedom had not only failed but had seemed only to rivet my fetters the more firmly, and to render my escape more difficult. Baffled, entangled, and discouraged, I had at times asked myself the question, May not my condition after all be God's work, and ordered for a wise purpose, and if so, Is not submission my duty? A contest had in fact been going on in my mind for a long time, between the clear consciousness of right and the plausible make-shifts of theology and superstition. The one held me an abject slave—a prisoner for life, punished for some transgression in which I had no lot nor part; and the other counseled me to manly endeavor to secure my freedom. This contest was now ended; my chains were broken, and the victory brought me unspeakable joy.
>
> Adapted from Frederick Douglass, *My Escape from Slavery*. Originally published in 1881.

15. What might you logically expect to come next in the narrative?

    A. Information on what Douglass did during his first few weeks as a free man

    B. The story of how, when, and where Douglass was born

    C. A historical background on slavery

    D. Data on how many people escaped slavery in the years leading up to the Civil War

The following is excerpted from a cultural exploration of different festivals from around the world.

One such singular festival is the Nakizumo Baby Crying Festival, an annual event that takes place in Tokyo, Japan. Translated into English, Nakizumo means "Naki Sumo," which is a hint as to what occurs at this unorthodox event. Namely, two sumo wrestlers enter a ring, each carrying a baby. The objective is to be the first sumo wrestler to get your opponent's baby to cry while also soothing your own baby to keep them from crying. Contests like this go on throughout the festival's events.

While this may seem a bit wacky from an outsider perspective, the event is steeped in a nearly 400-year-old tradition. Specifically, the festival is linked with the long held Japanese belief that getting a baby to have a hard cry will help ensure they stay healthy. One related saying, "Naku-ko wa sodatsu," translates to "the child who cries grows up," meaning that the Japanese see crying as essential for childhood development. There are also some regions of Japan that share further beliefs about crying babies, such as the idea that the sound of a baby's cry can ward off evil spirits.

You might think that it's easy enough to get a baby to cry during this festival, but it can actually be quite tough when the festival atmosphere is laidback and celebratory. Babies tend to pick up on the energy around them, so they aren't always fast to cry when everyone around them is having fun. When this happens, the sumo wrestlers must resort to other measures to bring on the waterworks, such as startling the babies with loud sounds, donning scary costumes and masks, and contorting their faces into grimaces. It's a battle of the tears, and whoever cries first (or loudest, if they both start at once) wins!

16. The purpose of paragraph 3 is to

A. describe the folkloric beliefs behind the Nakizumo Baby Crying Festival.

B. introduce the concept of cultural festivals generally.

C. explain how the Nakizumo Baby Crying Festival got its name.

D. illustrate what sumo wrestlers do when neither baby will cry.

Patients deserve to know the list price of the drugs they need, because many of them will pay the list price or a share of it. For the 47 percent of Americans with high-deductible health plans, the price they'll see in ads essentially is the price, until they hit their deductible. Every single Medicare Part D plan requires coinsurance for particularly expensive drugs, which can range up to 30 percent of a drug's list price.

Drug companies even sometimes advertise drugs that insurance rarely covers, knowing patients may go ask their doctor about a drug without knowing its unaffordable list price. One of the most commonly advertised drugs, which treats plaque psoriasis, carries a list price of $3,400 a month, but is only covered by one of the 25 standalone Medicare Part D plans in the Washington, D.C. area. For the majority of Part D beneficiaries around D.C., the list price is the price for that drug.

The majority of Americans struggling to afford their drugs are put in that position because they're paying based on high list prices. It's not an exaggeration to say that suggesting list prices don't matter is essentially suggesting there is no problem with high drug costs at all. You don't need a poll to know that very few American seniors or patients with serious illnesses would agree with that sentiment.

Adapted from John O'Brien, *"Why Putting List Prices in Drug Ads Matters."* Health and Human Services blog, May 17, 2019.

17. The author's point of view in this passage is one of a(n)

A. expert arguing for greater public transparency on drug prices.

B. patient arguing against greater public transparency on drug prices.

C. politician summarizing a new law on drug prices.

D. professor explaining a concept for pharmacology students.

Tinker v. Des Moines was a Supreme Court case that established the legal precedent for free speech in public schools following the silent protests of multiple 11-year-old students at a public school in Des Moines. The plan was for a group of students to wear black armbands in silent protest against the war in Vietnam, but when the school got wind of this plan, they took preemptive measures against it to ensure no armbands were worn. When some students returned to school with black armbands, they were suspended until they agreed to shed the bands. Of course, most students agreed to shed the bands, but their parents swiftly took to the courts and filed a First Amendment lawsuit. The court's decision ruled in favor of the students (7–2), asserting that school officials possessed no absolute power over students and that minors did not surrender their constitutional rights at the door of the classroom.

18. Based on the information in the passage, *Tinker v. Des Moines*

A. involved the silent protests of parents of students at a Des Moines public school.

B. established the legal precedent for punishing schools that suspend students due to wardrobe choices.

C. had more to do with the war at hand than it did with the suspended students.

D. held the opinion that students do not surrender their First Amendment rights when they arrive at school.

Directions for Questions 19 and 20: The following sentences have a blank indicating that something has been left out. Beneath each sentence are four words or phrases. Choose the word or phrase that, when inserted in the sentence, best fits the meaning of the sentence as a whole.

19. I was left there, feeling exhilarated but _____, as the solution I was grappling with sat out there on the edge of consciousness, my mind trying to figure it out.

   A. unsettled

   B. frightened

   C. ecstatic

   D. somber

20. With the _____ a small portion of the population, most have embraced the restrictions deemed necessary by public safety officials following the massive eruption.

   A. permission for

   B. exception of

   C. approval to

   D. cooperation from

WRITING

25 Questions

> **Directions:** Read the following early essay drafts and then choose the best answer to the question or the best completion of the statement.

(1) It's sometimes called mirroring people or understanding the other side. (2) Carl Rogers, a noted psychologist, believed it imperative in productive discussion and debate. (3) Carl Rogers lived from 1902–1987. (4) It's called empathy, a term you might be familiar with and which science has been trying to understand in recent years.

(5) Thirty years ago, the discovery of mirror neurons may have helped neuroscientists unlock the key to understanding empathy. (6) The discovery of mirror neurons, one researcher suggested, would do for neuroscience what the discovery of DNA did for biology. (7) It is through these mirror neurons, measurable through fMRI, that scientists are getting quantitative data and, thus, a better understanding of empathy.

(8) Mirror neurons may have never been discovered if not for the careful ear of an Italian neuroscientist named Giacomo Rizzolatti. (9) Rizzolatti's lab, located in Parma, Italy, was diligently experimenting on macaque monkeys, trying to uncover the part of the brain that was triggered when a monkey reached for something. (10) The monkeys had an electrode permanently implanted in their brain which would signal to a computer whenever a section of the brain, called F5, was active. (11) Rizzolatti's team was hoping to uncover this part of the brain and, sometime in the future, possibly help people who had lost the use of their hands, through disease or traumatic injury. (12) He was in between experiments and was preparing for the next one, while a monkey was sitting, quietly waiting for his next task. (13) Rizzolatti turned his back and reached for something. (14) Suddenly, Rizzolatti's ear started buzzing. (15) The monkey's brain had gone crazy when Rizzolatti reached because the monkey's neurons were triggered. (16) These would become known as mirror neurons and were the first inkling that empathy could be measured and understood.

(17) Though there is some debate about this apocryphal story—one story suggests it was another scientist in the Parma lab reaching for a peanut; another story credits it to yet another scientist, this one reaching for ice cream—whatever the genesis, the findings were the same: the monkeys, training to reach, had neurons that were triggered when their trainers reached. (18) This was the discovery of mirror neurons.

(19) In recent years, three trends in the studying of mirror neurons have manifested. (20) First is the studying of mirror neurons for insights into autism. (21) Second is the studying of the development of mirror neurons in infants. (22) And, finally, is the studying of mirror neurons to develop more refined descriptions of what they are. (23) The importance of mirror neurons for developing empathy is best summarized by Marco Iacoboni, himself a neuroscientist studying mirror neurons: "The more we investigate the properties of mirror neurons, the more we understand how these cells help us to be empathetic and fundamentally attuned to other people. (24) This is perhaps the most important finding of all, and it is a beautiful one."

1. Which sentence should be eliminated from the first paragraph to preserve its cohesiveness?

   A. Sentence 1
   B. Sentence 2
   C. Sentence 3
   D. Sentence 4

2. In context, which version of sentence 4 (reproduced below) best transitions to the second paragraph?

   It's called empathy, a term you might be familiar with and which science has been trying to understand in recent years.

   A. It's called empathy, a term coined thirty years ago and one which you might be familiar with and which science has been trying to understand in recent years.
   B. It's called empathy, a term you might be familiar with and which science has been trying to understand, recently making some important discoveries.
   C. It's called empathy, a term you might be familiar with and which science has been trying to understand in recent years, succeeding three decades ago.
   D. It's called empathy, a term you might be familiar with and which science has been trying to understand in recent years; in the past three decades, science has made some major gains in understanding empathy thanks to the discovery of mirror neurons.

3. Which choice most effectively combines sentences 12 and 13 (reproduced below)?

   He was in between experiments and was preparing for the next one, while a monkey was sitting, quietly waiting for his next task. Rizzolatti turned his back and reached for something.

   A. (as it is now)
   B. A monkey, sitting quietly, awaited his next task when Rizzolatti turned his back and reached for something.
   C. Rizzolatti, in between experiments, turned his back to reach for something while a monkey, sitting quietly, awaited his next task.
   D. In between experiments, Rizzolatti turned his back while a monkey was sitting quietly, waiting for his next task.

4. Which is the best version of sentence 17 (reproduced below)?

   Though there is some debate about this apocryphal story—one story suggests it was another scientist in the Parma lab reaching for a peanut; another story credits it to yet another scientist, this one reaching for ice cream—whatever the genesis, the findings were the same: the monkeys, training to reach, had neurons that were triggered when their trainers reached.

   A. (as it is now)

   B. Though there is some debate about this apocryphal story—some suggest it was another scientist in the Parma lab reaching for a peanut; other stories credit it to yet another scientist, this one reaching for ice cream—whatever the genesis, the findings were the same: the monkeys, training to reach, had neurons that were triggered when their trainers reached.

   C. Though there is some debate about this apocryphal story, some suggest it was another scientist in the Parma lab reaching for a peanut; another story credits it to yet another scientist, this one reaching for ice cream, whatever the genesis, the findings were the same: the monkeys, training to reach, had neurons that were triggered when their trainers reached.

   D. Though there is some debate about this apocryphal story—some suggest it was another scientist in the Parma lab reaching for a peanut; another story credits it to yet another scientist, this one reaching for ice cream—whatever the genesis, the findings were the same that the monkeys, training to reach, had neurons that were triggered when their trainers reached.

5. Which is the best version of sentence 18 (reproduced below)?

   This was the discovery of mirror neurons.

   A. (as it is now)

   B. This was the discovery of mirror neuron's.

   C. Mirror neurons had been discovered.

   D. This was a eureka moment when mirror neurons were discovered.

6. In context, which is the best version of sentence 22 (reproduced below)?

   And, finally, is the studying of mirror neurons to develop more refined descriptions of what they are.

   A. (as it is now)

   B. And, lastly, is the studying of mirror neurons to develop more refined descriptions of what they are.

   C. Third is the studying of mirror neurons to develop more refined descriptions of what they are.

   D. And, ultimately, there is the studying of mirror neurons to develop more refined descriptions of what they are.

(1) Native American reservations dot the American landscape, 326 of them stretching from Maine to California, from Florida to Oregon. (2) The first reservation, established in New Jersey in 1758, was called Edgepillock, but is now known as Indian Mills and is located in Shamong Township. (3) Since that date, Native Americans and various governments have tangled over legal tensions inherited in this reservation system.

(4) Legal tensions arise because of the confused web of sovereignty—essentially the question of who is in power. (5) The courts have tried to straighten things out, but have only confused things further. (6) For example, in 1978, the Supreme Court case *Oliphant v. Suquamish* stripped a tribe's ability to arrest and prosecute non-Indians who commit crimes on Indian land: if victim and perpetrator were non-Indian, a state officer makes the arrest; if the perpetrator is non-Indian and the victim an enrolled member, a federal agent must make the arrest. (7) If an enrolled member is the perpetrator, a tribal officer can make the arrest, but the case still goes to federal court. (8) This leads to conflicts with reservation law and federal law, as it's often unclear who has power to arrest. (9) Extending this example, there was the case of Helen and Russell Bryan. (10) Helen, because of her Indian heritage, had ancestral land in the village of Squaw Lake, on the north side of Leech Lake Reservation in Minnesota, where she and her husband put a small, two-bedroom trailer. (11) One day, the Bryans noticed a man on their property, the county tax man, who assessed them a total of $147. (12) The Bryans fought the right of their property to be taxed, going all the way to the Supreme Court. (13) In *Russell Bryan vs. Itasca County*, the Supreme Court ruled in favor of the Bryans, that as the Minneapolis Tribune declared, "States Forbidden to Tax on Reservations."

(14) Because tribes possess a limited tribal sovereignty, laws on tribal lands differ from those of the surrounding area, which has led to some interesting developments, like the rise of gambling and casinos on Indian reservations.

7. Which is the best version of the underlined portion of sentence 3 (reproduced below)?

Since that date, Native Americans and various governments have tangled over legal tensions <u>inherited</u> in this reservation system.

- **A.** (as it is now)
- **B.** inherent
- **C.** invested
- **D.** indelible

8. At the end of paragraph 2, the writer wants to emphasize the "confused web of sovereignty" idea expressed in sentence 4. Which of these options for an additional sentence best accomplishes that goal?

- **A.** You can guess how that worked out!
- **B.** *Oliphant v. Suquamish* and *Bryan v. Itasca County* are just two of numerous court cases.
- **C.** The question of sovereignty, crucially, remained the pinnacle of each case.
- **D.** Sovereignty is the idea of a "self-governing state" according to Merriam-Webster's Dictionary.

9. In context, which is the best decision regarding the underlined portion of sentence 9 (reproduced below)?

Extending this example, there was the case of Helen and Russell Bryan.

A. (as it is now)

B. For example, there was

C. An example of this was

D. Another example of blurry authority was

10. Which is the best decision regarding the underlined portion of sentence 14 (reproduced below)?

Because tribes possess a limited tribal sovereignty, laws on tribal lands differ from those of the surrounding area, which has led to some interesting developments, like the rise of gambling and casinos on Indian reservations.

A. Leave it as it is now.

B. Revise it to "some interesting developments occurred."

C. Revise it to "causing interesting developments."

D. DELETE it

(1) Alzheimer's disease, in 2015, affected approximately 29.8 million people worldwide. (2) It generally does not present as a full-blown syndrome, but rather as isolated symptoms such as short-term memory loss and subtle problems with attentiveness, planning, and abstract thinking. (3) Frequently, these early symptoms lead doctors to suspect a small stroke or tumor. (4) Eventually, these small lapses in memory or cognitive distortions coalesce into profound global dementia. (5) By the end, an Alzheimer's patient is completely dependent on caregivers as language is reduced to simple phrases, simple tasks become impossible, apathy and exhaustion become extreme, and eventually, the patient is bedridden and unable to feed themselves. (6) Alzheimer's disease is characterized by the loss of neurons and synapses in the cerebral cortex. (7) This loss results in atrophy of these regions of the brain and the subsequent brain malfunctions.

(8) The cause for most Alzheimer's cases remains unknown, though several hypothesis have been suggested. (9) One hypothesis suggests that there is a genetic heritability to this disease, known as early onset familial Alzheimer's disease. (10) However, most cases of Alzheimer's are termed sporadic, with both environmental and genetic risk factors. (11) Another hypothesis, termed the amyloid hypothesis, proposes that extracellular amyloid beta deposits are the fundamental cause of the disease. (12) Another hypothesis, called the cholinergic hypothesis, suggests that Alzheimer's disease is the result of reduced synthesis between a neurotransmitter. (13) Another hypothesis, this one environmentally based, suggests that air pollution may be a contributing factor to the disease's development.

(14) The nature of the disease can severely hurt the caregiver as well, as a loved one descends into the cognitive fog of Alzheimer's. (15) To see a loved one lose their memories, their identity, and ultimately their physical voice is too much for some. (16) Dr. Oliver Sacks, a noted neurologist, wrote "As a physician, I have seen this all too often—sometimes an elderly husband or wife will sacrifice their own health and die before the incapacitated loved one they are caring for."

11. Which is the best version of the underlined portion of sentence 5 (reproduced below)?

By the end, an Alzheimer's patient is completely dependent on caregivers as language is reduced to simple phrases, simple tasks become impossible, apathy and exhaustion become extreme, and eventually, the patient is bedridden and unable to feed themselves.

A. (as it is now)

B. For example,

C. During the final stages,

D. As the patient approaches death,

12. Which choice most effectively combines sentences 6 and 7 (reproduced below) at the underlined portion?

Alzheimer's disease is characterized by the loss of neurons and synapses in the cerebral cortex. This *loss results in atrophy of these regions of the brain and the subsequent brain malfunctions.*

A. cortex; and this

B. cortex—this

C. cortex, this

D. cortex, and this

13. Which is the best version of the underlined portion of sentence 8 (reproduced below)?

The cause for most Alzheimer's cases remains unknown, though several hypothesis *have been suggested.*

A. (as it is now)

B. hypotheses

C. effects

D. questions

14. Sentence 11 is reproduced below.

Another hypothesis, termed the amyloid hypothesis, proposes that extracellular amyloid beta deposits *are the fundamental cause of the disease.*

The writer is considering adding the following text after the underlined portion.

—*protein fragments usually broken down and eliminated but which in Alzheimer's patients form a hard, insoluble plaque*—

Should the writer make the addition there?

A. Yes, because it offers the reader figurative language, allowing the reader to see the process.

B. Yes, because it explains a process likely unfamiliar to the reader.

C. No, because it introduces details that are irrelevant to the paragraph's focus on explaining. potential causes of Alzheimer's disease.

D. No, because it creates an unnecessarily wordy sentence.

15. Sentence 13 is reproduced below.

Another hypothesis, this one environmentally based, suggests that air pollution may be a contributing factor to the disease's development.

The writer is considering adding the following text after sentence 13.

The associated study, published by Yang and Moulton in the 2012 issue of Journal of Environmental and Public Health, *is still in the early stages.*

Should the writer make the addition there?

A. No, because it adds unnecessary information.

B. No, because it blurs the purpose of this paragraph.

C. Yes, because this hypothesis is so different from the previous ones, it's important to attribute it and say it's in the early stages.

D. Yes, because by citing a source, the author of this essay strengthens their own credibility.

(1) In many parts of the world such as Antarctica, Greenland, and the peaks of high mountains, temperatures remain frigid year-round. (2) It is in such places that glaciers are born. (3) Glaciers are slow-moving masses of ice and play a key role in the earth's ecosystem—as a potential water source, as a historical record of Earth's climates, and recently as a tourist marvel as cruise ships flock to Alaska so adventurous tourists can seek out the mysterious "jade berg," a green iceberg made from the refraction of light through ice. (4) Yet, despite their key role, glaciers are in trouble as global climate change threatens their survival.

(5) Glaciers, improbably, start off as a single snowflake. (6) Once a snowflake hits the ground, it clumps with other snowflakes, creating a surface layer and air gaps, accumulating and eventually compressing, if this accumulated snowflake mass survives one melt season, it turns into a grainy material that scientists call firn. (7) This process is repeated, increasing pressure and building the snow mound, until the ice field becomes approximately 66 feet thick, when it spreads out under her own weight and begins to shift and move. (8) The glacier may continue to move, several inches a year or a hundred feet a day.

(9) Glacial speed might be an oxymoron, but glaciers can move as a result of two factors: thickness and temperature. (10) The thicker a glacier is, the faster it moves thanks to the pull of gravity. (11) In addition, warmer weather melts the under layer of a glacier, increasing the amount of meltwater and increasing glacial speed. (12) As you can imagine, a moving glacier, weighing several million tons, can wreak havoc on a landscape, widening and deepening valleys, flattening forests, and grinding boulders to dust. (13) Some of our landscape features, such as kettle ponds and glacial erratics, are the result of the last ice age, when huge glaciers moved across the earth. (14) Glacial erratics are pieces of rock that differ from the size and type of rock native to the area in which they rest; kettle ponds are made when retreating glaciers leave behind blocks of dead ice, which become surrounded by sediment and, as the ice melts, leaving behind a depression called a kettle hole.

16. Which is the best version of the underlined portion of sentence 4 (reproduced below)?

    Yet, despite their key role, glaciers are in trouble as global climate change threatens their survival.

    A. (as it is now)

    B. And,

    C. For example,

    D. Lastly,

17. Which is the best version of the underlined portion of sentence 6 (reproduced below)?

    Once a snowflake hits the ground, it clumps with other snowflakes, creating a surface layer and air gaps, accumulating and eventually compressing, if this accumulated snowflake mass survives one melt season, it turns into a grainy material that scientists call firn.

    A. (as it is now)

    B. compressing; if

    C. compressing—if

    D. compressing, but if

18. Which is the best version of the underlined portion of sentence 7 (reproduced below)?

    This process is repeated, increasing pressure and building the snow mound, until the ice field becomes approximately 66 feet thick, when it spreads out under <u>her own weight</u> and begins to shift and move.

    A. (as it is now)
    B. their own weight
    C. his or her own weight
    D. its own weight

19. In context, which is the best version of sentence 9 (reproduced below)?

    Glacial speed might be an oxymoron, but glaciers can move as a result of two factors: thickness and temperature.

    A. (as it is now)
    B. Glacial speed, an oxymoron, because glaciers can move as a result of two factors: thickness and temperature.
    C. Glacial speed is an oxymoron; in fact, glaciers can move as a result of two factors: thickness and temperature.
    D. Glacial speed might be an oxymoron, but glaciers can move as a result of two factors thickness and temperature.

20. Which is the best version of the underlined portion of sentence 14 (reproduced below)?

    Glacial erratics are pieces of rock that differ from the size and type of rock native to the area in which they rest; kettle ponds are made when retreating glaciers leave behind blocks of dead ice, which become surrounded by sediment and, as the ice melts, <u>leaving behind</u> a depression called a kettle hole.

    A. (as it is now)
    B. producing
    C. recreate
    D. form

(1) Have you ever noticed someone wearing a fitness tracker? (2) This "wearable tech" gives us data on our everyday activities. (3) It tells us how much we move, how many calories we burn, what we eat, and how much (and how well) we sleep. (4) Our trackers tell us what we do in an average day. (5) But ultimately, what purpose does all of this data serve?

(6) Fitness trackers themselves do serve an important purpose; in many cases, they aggregate and present valuable information that we can use to make informed decisions about our health. (7) Or if you're less active than you'd like to be, they can provide a gentle reminder (maybe a gentle buzz or a friendly push notification) to get you up and moving a little more. (8) This data can give you a baseline picture of your overall health and activity. (9) However, this information is only moderately useful at best if you're not using it as part of a doctor-approved wellness regime. (10) Trackers can give you a general overview of what you're doing that's good for your body, but without any kind of medical guidance or structure, the data is just being stored and rudimentarily analyzed without any great effect.

(11) Then there's accuracy. (12) Trackers can measure the number of steps you take, based on a built-in pedometer, and some can measure your heart rate, but how accurate is that data? (13) These trackers are often imprecise at best when it comes to tracking sleep quality especially, leaving users with only an inkling as to their actual behaviors.

21. The writer wants to add a sentence to the beginning of paragraph 1. Which of the following would be the most effective first sentence for this essay?

   A. In recent years, the fitness tracking industry has trained itself up to become a billion-dollar business with tech that is miles ahead of similar devices from just a few years ago.

   B. Activity trackers are available in all shapes and sizes, offering such considerable variety that they can allow users to follow the latest tech trend and accessorize fashionably.

   C. The accuracy of fitness trackers is questionable, and such a flaw may stand as the major impediment to their widespread adoption by the average consumer and the medical community.

   D. It seems like fitness trackers are ubiquitous these days, popping up in every context: at work, school, the gym, and the doctor's office.

22. Within the context of the passage, where would the following sentence best be placed in paragraph 2?

   For example, if your fitness tracker tells you you're getting a less-than-optimal amount of sleep, you can program your desired bedtime to improve the quality of your shut-eye.

   A. Before sentence 6

   B. After sentence 6

   C. After sentence 7

   D. After sentence 8

23. In context, which information would be best inserted after sentence 9?

   A. A quote from a doctor about the effectiveness of fitness trackers

   B. A personal story about how the writer uses a fitness tracker

   C. Sales figures for the top brands of fitness trackers

   D. A quote from a commercial that advertises fitness trackers

24. In context, what is the best revision to sentence 10 (reproduced below)?

Trackers can give you a general overview of what you're doing that's good for your body, but without any kind of medical guidance or structure, the data is just being stored and rudimentarily analyzed without any great effect.

A. Data from your fitness tracker is stored and offered without any real medical guidance or structure.

B. What's good for your body is what a fitness tracker can track, but it is not the whole picture.

C. Although it's great for a general overview, fitness trackers without any kind of medical guidance or structure lack an essential feature: usefulness.

D. Without any medical guidance or structure, fitness tracker data as of yet gives little but a basic overview of your health.

25. Which of the following would be an effective closing sentence for this essay?

A. Although fitness trackers remain a popular gadget for the masses, the dangers are too great to ignore.

B. As it stands, fitness trackers are popular because they're so effective, and they're so effective because they present exactly what we need to know to make smart health decisions.

C. Right now, fitness trackers are popular for good reason, but they shouldn't be the last word in wellness.

D. Because fitness trackers are so popular right now, we can expect to see them become even bigger sellers in the near future.

ARITHMETIC

20 Questions

> **Directions:** Choose the best answer. Use the space provided for any calculations.

1. $6 + (9 \div 3)^2 \times 2 =$

   A. 24

   B. 30

   C. 78

   D. 162

2. $3\frac{1}{4} \times 8\frac{2}{5} =$

   A. $11\frac{13}{20}$

   B. $24\frac{1}{10}$

   C. $27\frac{3}{10}$

   D. $54\frac{3}{5}$

3. What is the sum of 74.55 and 6.98, to the nearest integer?

   A. 80

   B. 81

   C. 82

   D. 520

4. 140 is what percent of 40?

   A. 3.50%

   B. 28.60%

   C. 350%

   D. 700%

5. Which of the following statements is true?

   A. $2.7 > 2.74 > \frac{11}{4} > 2\frac{4}{5}$

   B. $2.74 > 2.7 > 2\frac{4}{5} > \frac{11}{4}$

   C. $\frac{11}{4} > 2\frac{4}{5} > 2.74 > 2.7$

   D. $2\frac{4}{5} > \frac{11}{4} > 2.74 > 2.7$

6. What is the remainder when 708 is divided by 7?

   A. 0

   B. 1

   C. 7

   D. 8

7. $1\frac{3}{8} \times 4\frac{1}{6} =$

   A. $4\frac{3}{48}$

   B. $5\frac{5}{16}$

   C. $5\frac{13}{24}$

   D. $5\frac{35}{48}$

8. Which is equivalent to 0.25%?

   A. $\frac{1}{40}$

   B. $\frac{1}{4}$

   C. $\frac{25}{100}$

   D. $\frac{25}{10,000}$

9. Which of the following inequalities is true?

   A. $\frac{3}{4} < \frac{3}{5}$

   B. $\frac{3}{4} > \frac{19}{24}$

   C. $\frac{3}{4} < \frac{12}{9}$

   D. $\frac{6}{5} > \frac{7}{6}$

10. If 4,100 is increased by 65%, what is the result?

    A. 1,435
    B. 4,165
    C. 6,765
    D. 26,650

11. Which of the following is equivalent to $\frac{3}{20}$?

    A. 3.2
    B. 0.6
    C. 0.15
    D. 0.015

12. On a 15-mile expedition, Melissa traveled $\frac{2}{5}$ of the distance by mountain bike and paddled $\frac{1}{3}$ by canoe. If Melissa walked for the remainder of the trip, how many miles did she walk?

    A. 4 miles
    B. $\frac{45}{8}$ miles
    C. $\frac{75}{8}$ miles
    D. 11 miles

13. To the nearest integer, what is the product of 49.3 and 9.4?

    A. 59
    B. 463
    C. 464
    D. 4,634

14. A movie theater has 275 seats. For a blockbuster debut, the theater pre-sold 220 tickets. What percent of the available tickets were pre-sold?

    A. 125%
    B. 80%
    C. 55%
    D. 20%

15. Given the points labeled W, X, Y, and Z on the number line below, which of the following correctly associates each point with an approximate number?

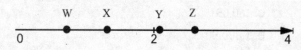

    A. $W = \frac{3}{4}$; $X = \frac{4}{3}$; $Y = \frac{23}{11}$; $Z = 2.6$

    B. $W = \frac{4}{3}$; $X = \frac{3}{4}$; $Y = \frac{23}{11}$; $Z = 2.6$

    C. $W = \frac{3}{4}$; $X = \frac{4}{3}$; $Y = 2.6$; $Z = \frac{23}{11}$

    D. $W = \frac{4}{3}$; $X = \frac{3}{4}$; $Y = 2.6$; $Z = \frac{23}{11}$

16. A gallon of milk costs $3.84. If a customer pays for three gallons of milk with a $20 bill, how much change will the customer receive?

    A. $8.48
    B. $11.52
    C. $16.16
    D. $18.85

17. A baker combines 155 cups of flour with 62 cups of sugar to bake a large batch of cookies. How many total cups of these ingredients does the baker use?

    A. 93
    B. 117
    C. 217
    D. 227

18. Which of the following is greater than 2.75?

   A. $2\dfrac{8}{100}$

   B. $2\dfrac{3}{4}$

   C. $\dfrac{13}{4}$

   D. 2.075

19. What is the value of 16.005 ÷ 100?

   A. 0.16005

   B. 1.6005

   C. 160.05

   D. 1,600.50

20. Burt's pickup truck carries $2\dfrac{1}{2}$ cubic yards of soil when it is filled to capacity. If the truck is $\dfrac{2}{5}$ full when he starts, how much will it cost Burt to fill up the remaining space with soil at \$16 per cubic yard?

   A. \$9.60

   B. \$16

   C. \$24

   D. \$40

QUANTITATIVE REASONING, ALGEBRA, AND STATISTICS

20 Questions

Directions: In the following questions, work out each problem and mark the letter that corresponds to the correct answer. The answers and explanations will follow. You are only permitted to use a calculator where indicated by a symbol ( ).

---

1. $\dfrac{3}{4} \div \dfrac{4}{7} - 3\dfrac{1}{2} =$

   A. $-\dfrac{43}{14}$

   B. $-\dfrac{35}{16}$

   C. 1

   D. $\dfrac{77}{16}$

2. A jar contains twenty balls, numbered 1 through 20. Sasha picks a ball at random, records the number on the ball, and returns the ball to the jar. Sasha repeats this process twice more, recording a total of three numbers. How many possible outcomes (simple events) does this experiment have?

   A. 20

   B. 60

   C. 400

   D. 8,000

3. A basketball arena holds 8,000 spectators. Which equation below might approximate the number of spectators, S, in the arena in the minutes after a sold-out game ends? (The variable t is the number of minutes after the end of the game.)

   A. $S = t - 8{,}000$

   B. $S = -\dfrac{2}{5}t - 8{,}000$

   C. $S = 25t + 8{,}000$

   D. $S = -250t + 8{,}000$

4. Given triangle ABC below, with right angle A and lengths of sides AC and BC as shown, what is the value of x?

   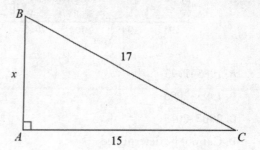

   A. 2

   B. 7

   C. 8

   D. 12

5. What is the solution to the system of equations below?

   $$x - 2y = 16$$
   $$4x + y = 1$$

   A. $(2, -7)$

   B. $(9, -2)$

   C. $\left(\dfrac{5}{3}, \dfrac{3}{20}\right)$

   D. $\left(\dfrac{5}{3}, -\dfrac{3}{20}\right)$

ACCUPLACER® PRACTICE TEST 2

6. The bar graph below shows the population of trout in a lake from 1985 to 2015. In which decade shown was the percent decrease in trout population the greatest?

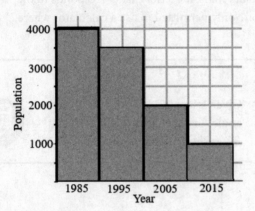

A. 1985–1995

B. 1995–2005

C. 2005–2015

D. Cannot be determined

7. Which exponential expression below is equivalent to $\dfrac{4}{\sqrt{3}}$?

A. $2 \times 3^{-\frac{1}{2}}$

B. $4 \times 3^{-\frac{1}{2}}$

C. $4 \times 3^{\frac{1}{2}}$

D. 4×3^{-2}

8. When lit, a foot-long candle loses $\dfrac{1}{2}$ inch in length every 3 hours. How many hours will it take for the candle to be completely spent? (1 foot = 12 inches)

A. 18

B. 24

C. 36

D. 72

9. An isosceles triangle has two sides of length m and one side of length n. Which is the correct equation for the perimeter, P, of the triangle?

A. $P = m + n$

B. $P = 2m + n$

C. $P = mn$

D. $P = \dfrac{mn}{2}$

10. Which expression below equals 11?

A. $16 + |-8 + 6 \div 2|$

B. $16 - |8 + 6 \div 2|$

C. $16 - |-8 + 6 \div 2|$

D. $16\, |-(-8 + 6) \div 2|$

11. Which number below is equivalent to $\dfrac{3}{4} - 4^{-2}$?

A. $\dfrac{-5}{4}$

B. $\dfrac{5}{8}$

C. $\dfrac{11}{16}$

D. $16\dfrac{3}{4}$

12. Solve for x: $\dfrac{3x}{7} = \dfrac{9}{14}$

A. $\dfrac{3}{14}$

B. $\dfrac{27}{98}$

C. $-\dfrac{3}{2}$

D. $\dfrac{3}{2}$

13. Which two lines are perpendicular?

A. $x + 3y = 6$ and $-3x + y = 2$

B. $2x + 4y = 16$ and $-2x + 4y = 6$

C. $x - 2y = 6$ and $6x - 3y = 24$

D. $2x - 8y = 16$ and $-3x + 12y = 6$

14. Which of the following is equivalent to the expression below?

$$-6x(-3x - 2) + 3(-8x + 3)$$

   A. $3(6x^2 - 4x + 3)$

   B. $3(6x^2 - 36x + 3)$

   C. $x(18x - 6) + 9$

   D. $3(3x - 1)(2x - 3)$

15. In a genetics study, a family is selected at random from the set of families with three children where at least one parent has eyes that are not brown. Observing the eye colors of the first-, second-, and third-born children, where B denotes brown eyes and O denotes any other color, the possible outcomes are: {BBB, BBO, BOB, BOO, OBB, OBO, OOB, OOO}. Assume that each of these outcomes is equally likely. What is the probability that the family has exactly two children that do not have brown eyes, given that the first-born child does not have brown eyes?

   A. $\dfrac{1}{4}$

   B. $\dfrac{3}{8}$

   C. $\dfrac{1}{2}$

   D. $\dfrac{5}{8}$

16. The table below gives estimated populations of the six New England states in 2018. Which is greater, the median or the mean population of these states?

NEW ENGLAND STATES IN 2018	
State	Population
Connecticut	3,572,665
Maine	1,338,404
Massachusetts	6,902,149
New Hampshire	1,356,458
Rhode Island	1,057,315
Vermont	626,299

   A. The median is greater than the mean.

   B. The mean is greater than the median.

   C. The median and the mean are equal.

   D. Not enough information is provided to determine which is greater.

17. How many cubic feet of concrete are needed to pour the floor of a rectangular basement that is 6 inches thick and 80 feet long by 60 feet wide? (1 foot = 12 inches)

   A. 2,400 ft.³

   B. 4,800.5 ft.³

   C. 9,600 ft.³

   D. 28,800 ft.³

18. The population of a colony of bacteria doubles every day. If P is the initial population of the colony, which expression below represents the population after n days?

   A. $2Pn$

   B. Pn^2

   C. $P2^n$

   D. P^{2n}

19. There are 72 cards in a deck. If 54 of the cards are red and the rest of the cards are black, what is the ratio of red cards to black cards in the deck?

    A. 3 to 1
    B. 1 to 4
    C. 4 to 1
    D. 3 to 4

20. Elsa earns $390 per week on a summer job and saves two-thirds of her earnings every week. If she works $14\frac{1}{2}$ weeks, how much will Elsa save?

    A. $1,820
    B. $1,885
    C. $3,770
    D. $8,482.50

ADVANCED ALGEBRA AND FUNCTIONS

20 Questions

Directions: In the following questions, work out each problem and mark the letter that corresponds to the correct answer. The answers and explanations will follow. You are only permitted to use a calculator where indicated by a symbol (⌨).

1. Which of the following linear equations is satisfied by all the x, y pairs listed in the table?

x	y
-2	$3\frac{1}{2}$
4	2
12	0

A. $y = \dfrac{1}{4}x - 3$

B. $y = \dfrac{1}{4}x + 3$

C. $y = \dfrac{-x}{4} + 3$

D. $y = \dfrac{-x + 3}{4}$

2. The graph below shows the price, in dollars, of topsoil as a function of the number of cubic yards purchased at a co-op. Which equation below accurately represents the price, p, of topsoil if 10 or more cubic yards, c, are purchased?

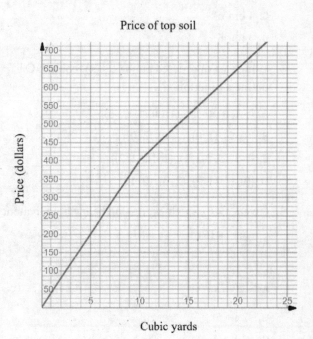

Price of top soil

Cubic yards

A. $p = 25c$

B. $p = 40c$

C. $p = 25c + 150$

D. $p = 25c + 400$

3. Which of the following trinomials is equivalent to $(A - B)^2$, where $A = nx$ and $B = m$, and n and m are positive integers?

   A. $36x^2 + 60x + 25$

   B. $36x^2 + 60x - 25$

   C. $36x^2 - 60x + 25$

   D. $36x^2 - 60x - 25$

4. Which of the following values of x satisfies the equation below?

   $$x^2 - 2x + 1 = 25$$

   A. -1

   B. $\dfrac{5}{2}$

   C. 4 or -6

   D. -4 or 6

5. Which set of ordered pairs $(x, f(x))$ could NOT define a function f?

   A. $\{(-1, 0), (5, 5), (11, 0), (17, -5)\}$

   B. $\{(0, 0), (1, 0), (2, 0), (3, 0)\}$

   C. $\{(-2, 2), (-1, 1), (1, 1), (2, 2)\}$

   D. $\{(0, 0), (1, 2), (2, 3), (0, 1)\}$

6. Given $x \neq 0$, which expression below is equivalent to $\dfrac{-6x^3 + 15x}{3x}$?

   A. $\dfrac{-2x^2 + 5}{x}$

   B. $-2x + 5$

   C. $-2x^2 + 5$

   D. $-2x^3 + 5x$

7. Simplify the following expression:

   $$2\left(-5p + \frac{9}{2}\right)^2$$

   A. $50p^2 + \dfrac{81}{2}$

   B. $50p^2 - 45p + \dfrac{81}{2}$

   C. $-50p^2 - 90p + \dfrac{81}{2}$

   D. $50p^2 - 90p + \dfrac{81}{2}$

8. If the value of a used car whose price is initially $10,000 decreases by 10% each year, what will be the value of the car after three years?

   A. $6,460

   B. $7,000

   C. $7,290

   D. $8,100

9. One leg of a right triangle has a length of 6 centimeters, and the hypotenuse is 10 centimeters long. What is the length of the other leg of this triangle?

   A. 4 cm

   B. 8 cm

   C. $\sqrt{136}$ cm

   D. 64 cm

10. Given △*ABC* shown below, with length *AB* = 5 and length *AC* = 7, if sin *B* = 0.70, what is the value of sin *C*?

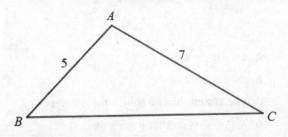

A. $\dfrac{1}{10}$

B. $\dfrac{1}{5}$

C. $\dfrac{1}{2}$

D. $\dfrac{5}{7}$

11. Which of the following steps should be used to solve $\dfrac{2}{5}x + 6 = 9$?

A. Multiply both sides by $\dfrac{5}{2}$, then subtract 6 from both sides.

B. Subtract 6 from both sides, then divide both sides by $\dfrac{5}{2}$.

C. Subtract 9 from both sides, then multiply both sides by $\dfrac{5}{2}$.

D. Subtract 6 from both sides, then multiply both sides by $\dfrac{5}{2}$.

12. Which graph below is the graph of the equation $y = -\dfrac{5}{3}x + \dfrac{3}{2}$?

A.
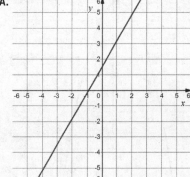

B.
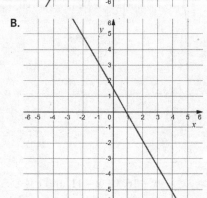

C.
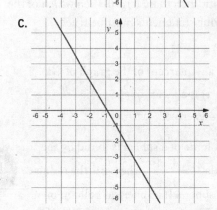

D.
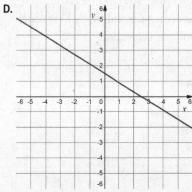

13. Which of the following functions corresponds to the graph shown below?

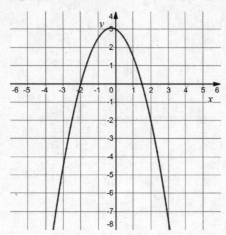

A. $y = x^2 - \dfrac{1}{2}x + 3$

B. $y = x^2 - 2x + 3$

C. $y = -x^2 - 2x + 3$

D. $y = -x^2 - \dfrac{1}{2}x + 3$

14. If $f(x) = 3x^5 - 9x + 16x^2 + x - 11$, and c is a constant such that $f(c) = 0$, then which of the following statements must be true?

A. $f(0) = c - 11$

B. c is a y-intercept of the graph of $f(x)$.

C. $(x - c)$ is a factor of $f(x)$.

D. $-c$ is a zero of $f(x)$.

15. The volume of a sphere is found by the formula $V = \dfrac{4}{3} \pi r^3$, where r is the radius of the sphere. If a spherical balloon of radius 3 inches expands to a radius of 6 inches as air is pumped in, by how much has its volume increased?

A. 36 in.³

B. 252 in.³

C. 252π in.³

D. 288π in.³

16. What is the solution to the following system of equations?

$$9x + 3y = 15$$
$$-3x - y = -5$$

A. $x = -2; y = 1$

B. $x = 1; y = -2$

C. The system has no solution.

D. All (x, y) such that $y = 5 - 3x$

17. Which of the inequalities below is a solution to $x^2 + 5x - 36 > 0$?

A. $-4 < x < 9$

B. $-9 < x < 4$

C. $x > -9$ or $x < 4$

D. $x < -9$ or $x > 4$

18. Solve for x when $x = \sqrt{-2x + 21} + 3$.

A. –2

B. 6

C. –2 or 6

D. There is no real solution.

19. The graph of $f(x) = -a^x$, where a is a constant, is shown below. Which of the following inequalities best describes possible values of a?

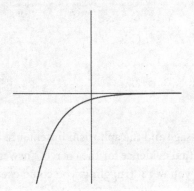

A. $0 < a < 1$

B. $a > 1$

C. $0 \le a \le 1$

D. $-1 \le a \le 1$

20. What is the equation of the circle shown below?

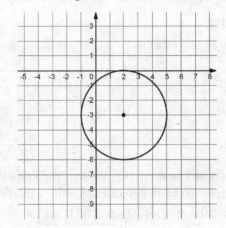

A. $(x - 2)^2 + (y + 3)^2 = 3$

B. $(x + 2)^2 + (y - 3)^2 = 9$

C. $(x - 2)^2 + (y + 3)^2 = 9$

D. $(x - 3)^2 + (y + 2)^2 = 9$

ANSWER KEY AND EXPLANATIONS
Reading

1. C	**5.** C	**9.** D	**13.** D	**17.** A
2. B	**6.** D	**10.** A	**14.** C	**18.** D
3. A	**7.** D	**11.** D	**15.** A	**19.** A
4. C	**8.** A	**12.** C	**16.** D	**20.** B

1. **The correct answer is C.** Whether you know that the term aphorism describes something like "a witty observation disguising a general truth" or not, you should still be able to surmise how the first sentence relates to the passage as a whole. The numerous details in the passage—from Mr. Bingley's wealth to his moving to the neighborhood to Mrs. Bennet's order at the end for her husband to visit Mr. Bingley—initiate the plot. Looking back at the first sentence after reading, it should be clear that it foreshadows what is to come. Choice A is incorrect because the aphorism does not state nor suggest that a wealthy man is "despised." Choice B is incorrect because Mr. Bingley is just introduced as a person with money; he is not characterized in full. While choice D uses the correct definition of an aphorism, it's a superficial reading of one's ability to tell a story, as wisdom does not necessarily correlate to storytelling ability.

2. **The correct answer is B.** All indications are that it is an opulent house or estate. We know that Mr. Bingley "let" the house, and the dialogue in sentence 10 specifically states that Mr. Bingley is to take "possession" of the house. The inference that it is opulent comes from the description of Mr. Bingley as wealthy, "a young man of large fortune" who earns "four or five thousand a year." The word *park* in the title might confuse some readers into choosing C, but this is an incorrect characterization based on information the reader is given in sentences 2 and 3.

3. **The correct answer is A.** One could argue that any of the choices are factually true, so your task in this case is to determine which describes the main purpose of the sentences indicated. The details of

the passage and the aphorism in sentence 1 provide contextual evidence for the correct answer. That said, if you were struggling, you could execute a process of elimination. First, eliminate choices B and C because the wording refers more to what Mrs. Bennet's motivations as a character might be in this scene rather than the author's purpose for the dialogue, which is what your question asks. You can then eliminate choice D because we do not get enough details about Mrs. Bennet specifically for this answer to be correct.

4. **The correct answer is C.** All of the choices correctly define the word *design*, which is why the question specifies that you should pay attention to context. In sentence 22, Mr. Bennet is asking if Bingley's purpose in moving is to acquire a wife, which makes choice C the best option.

5. **The correct answer is C.** The author broadens the understanding of habits by including both good and bad habits that might influence one's "destiny." The passage does not contain a greeting (choice A), nor is there an attempt to explore the etymology of the word *habit* (choice B). Choice D is incorrect because the author does not inspire the audience, though he does state that habits are bearing us "irresistibly toward our destiny."

6. **The correct answer is D.** Based on both the preponderance of sentences in Passage 2 that are used as examples of the concepts from Passage 1 and the lack of criticism, justification, or counterargument, we can safely select choice D, since *exemplification* is another way of saying that the purpose is to provide examples.

7. **The correct answer is D.** Passage 1 discusses the nature of habits, the good and the bad, their inevitability, and even the author's own delving into habits, when he writes, "My very words to you now are an example of what I mean." Passage 2 uses the development of habits in cats and rats to show how habits and learning form. Choice A is incorrect because it reverses the two passages. The author of Passage 1 does not critique bad habits (choice B) or focus on the development of habits in humans (choice C), so neither statement can be true for both passages.

8. **The correct answer is A.** Both passages focus on natural habit formation in conscious beings—humans, of course, but also rats and cats. While Passage 1 mentions that some habits are "bad," there is no mention of whether habits are difficult to break or not (choice B), and the authors do not suggest that people have too many bad habits (choice D). While both passages do suggest that habits form naturally, neither claims that no effort is needed to form a habit (choice C).

9. **The correct answer is D.** The correct answer is a restatement of one of the key sentences in the passages, which reads, "Sometimes also referred to as the 'Lordship and Bondage' dialectic, the concept is essentially that the two cannot exist without the other."

10. **The correct answer is A.** Paragraphs 2 and 3 both make it clear that Holzer most often chooses nontraditional places for her works. For instance, paragraph 3 states: "Other places her works have turned up include parking meters, T-shirts, billboards, placards, and anywhere else one might find text." While it is true that some of Holzer's works have appeared in museums, this is not mentioned in the passage. Your most logical inference based on the information you are given is that Holzer's work is less likely to turn up in a traditional art space, like hanging as an oil painting in a private art gallery, than in the nontraditional places listed.

11. **The correct answer is D.** Egypt (choice A), Saudi Arabia (choice B), and Jordan (choice C) are all mentioned in the passage as places where Bedouin tribes are likely to be found. You could also infer that since

South Africa is not in "northern Africa and the Arabian Peninsula," as mentioned in paragraph 2, it must not be as likely a place to find Bedouin people.

12. **The correct answer is C.** The maps used to divide cities into sections based on their suitability for mortgages involved using a literal red pen to draw lines around those neighborhoods deemed least suitable for mortgage lending. Therefore, choices A and B represent the opposite of the truth. Choice D is false because there was still housing development in redlined neighborhoods; it was just harder to do so with favorable financial backing.

13. **The correct answer is D.** In this passage, the author's word choice and sentence structure reveal a great deal of enthusiasm for the topic of mushrooms. For instance, at the end of the passage, you'll find an enthusiastic exclamation: "There's so much to discover inside the weird, wide world of mushrooms!" Other terms that might name the tone of this passage include *informative*, *celebratory*, *appreciative*, and *light-hearted*.

14. **The correct answer is C.** The author used the word *zoo* immediately following the word *natural*, which is an inherent paradox; a zoo is an artificial establishment created to mimic the natural world. Choice A is incorrect because a specific place is not acknowledged; rather, the author explains the concept of a sanctuary. Choices B and D are not supported by the details of the passage.

15. **The correct answer is A.** After describing what it was like to be free for the first time, the reader can logically expect that Douglas's narrative will go on to describe how he spent his first few weeks as a free man. In a personal narrative, Douglass is highly unlikely to switch to a more informative tone, such as by giving a historical account (choice C) or sharing data on slavery (choice D). Information on Douglas's place and time of birth (choice B) is more likely to have come earlier in his narrative, if at all.

16. **The correct answer is D.** The purpose of paragraph 3 is to illustrate what sumo wrestlers do when they can't get a baby to cry during the festival. Most of the other choices discuss the topics of other paragraphs, such as the explanation of the festival's

name (choice C) in paragraph 2 and the description of the folklore behind the festival (choice A) in paragraph 2. There is no attempt in this excerpt to make a general introduction to cultural festivals (choice B).

17. **The correct answer is A.** If it isn't immediately obvious to you that this passage represents the point of view of an expert arguing for greater transparency on drug prices, pay attention to what the passage *doesn't* do. The author makes no attempt to summarize a law (choice C) or explain a concept from pharmacology (choice D). It is clear that the author is making an argument, but there is no evidence that the author is against greater public transparency on drug prices (choice B). You can confirm your answer by noting that the tone is indeed that of an expert who is familiar with the subject.

18. **The correct answer is D.** This is a main idea question that asks you to identify the statement that correctly summarizes the main idea of the passage. In this case, the main idea is that *Tinker v. Des Moines* held the opinion that students did not surrender their First Amendment rights whenever they entered

a school building. You could verify this answer by noting that it essentially rephrases the final sentence of the brief passage.

19. **The correct answer is A.** The word *unsettled* denotes worry and unease, which the writer is feeling while standing on the "edge" of a solution with their "mind trying to figure it out." Choice B doesn't make sense because if the writer was frightened, then they wouldn't be "trying to figure it out." The word *ecstatic* is too similar to the word *exhilarated* to be separated by the word *but*, thus eliminating choice C. The word *somber* is antithetical to the word *exhilarated*, so it could be a possible fit, but if the writer was on the edge of a solution they were "grappling with," then they would be less likely to be gloomy than unsettled.

20. **The correct answer is B.** Each of the phrases grammatically fits the sentence, but only "exception of" fits the logical meaning of the whole sentence, since the word *most* in the second clause indicates that the "small portion of the population" mentioned is an exception to the majority.

Writing

1. C	**6.** C	**11.** C	**16.** A	**21.** A
2. D	**7.** B	**12.** D	**17.** B	**22.** B
3. C	**8.** C	**13.** B	**18.** D	**23.** A
4. A	**9.** D	**14.** B	**19.** A	**24.** D
5. A	**10.** A	**15.** C	**20.** D	**25.** C

1. **The correct answer is C.** In sentence 3, the information that "Carl Rogers lived from 1902–1987" is irrelevant to the paragraph. Sentence 1 is important because it introduces the topic of the essay. Sentence 2 extends the importance of this concept by citing an expert while also connecting neuroscience to psychology. Sentence 4 introduces the key term discussed in the essay while also transitioning to the next paragraph.

2. **The correct answer is D.** This question assesses your ability to determine which sentence is the most concise, conveys the necessary information, and most successfully transitions between two paragraphs. While choice D is the longest sentence, it does the best job of providing all the necessary information (three decades, mirror neurons) while also using syntax that flows well and is easily understood. Choice A is wordy without adding any new information or improving clarity. Choices B and D do not use the phrase "mirror neurons," which is important to transition to the next paragraph. In addition, choice B doesn't provide the historical context of thirty years.

3. **The correct answer is C.** Choice C best retains the important information from both sentences while presenting a better order of events. While there is nothing grammatically incorrect about leaving the sentence as is, the better choice to retain the rhythm of the sentences is to eliminate the simple sentence "Rizzolatti turned his back and reached for something." Choice B inverts the order, making the monkey first and Rizzolatti second, which impedes the narrative chronology. Choice D eliminates Rizzolatti reaching for something, which is integral to understanding the discovery.

4. **The correct answer is A.** This sentence is the best the way it is. Choice B misses the agreement of "some suggest" and "other stories." Choice C is less effective because it eliminates the em dashes, which are necessary as the provided information is tangential to the meaning of the sentence. Choice D eliminates the necessary colon, which provides a needed explication at the end.

5. **The correct answer is A.** The way the sentence is written is a simple and effective declarative sentence that emphasizes the importance of this discovery. Choice B has an incorrect possessive, "neuron's." Choice C eliminates the word *this*, which inhibits the transition from sentence 17 that details the serendipitous discovery of mirror neurons. Choice D becomes wordy with the addition of "a eureka moment."

6. **The correct answer is C.** This question assesses a writer's ability to present a chronological list while maintaining parallelism. Since the previous two sentences used "First" and "Second," this sentence should maintain this pattern. Only the sentence in choice C does this.

7. **The correct answer is B.** The word *inherent* is an adjective meaning "existing in something as a permanent, essential, or characteristic attribute." In this case, the reservation system has "characteristic attributes" based on the ambiguity of who is in power. *Inherited* (choice A) means "to receive as an heir." A superficial reading might lead to this answer, as one might make the case that, though not monetary, the reservation system inherited this legal tangle. However, the correct idiom would be "inherited by" which makes the answer grammatically incorrect as well. *Invested* (choice C) means to "expend money with the

expectation of achieving a profit." *Indelible* (choice D) means "making marks that cannot be removed."

8. **The correct answer is C.** As sentence 4 implies, the focus of the paragraph is the issue of sovereignty; choice C concludes the paragraph by referencing both sovereignty and the cases that have come to complicate the issue. Choice A lacks a clear antecedent and appropriate tone for the passage. Choice B is a limited summary of the paragraph. Choice D would effectively blur the point of the paragraph by offering an unnecessary definition.

9. **The correct answer is D.** The key to this question is considering your options in the context of what comes before sentence 9. Choice D correctly states that this is "another example" to add to the *Oliphant v. Suquamish* example, furthering the author's claim that these court cases lead to the "confused web of sovereignty." Choice A is incorrect because, as written, the example is not being extended; rather, the writer is offering another example. Choice B does not consider that the writer already provided another example, the case of *Oliphant v. Suquamish*. Choice C is incorrect because using "an example of this" does not clearly define what the "this" is, since the pronoun's antecedent would be ambiguous.

10. **The correct answer is A.** The underlined portion should remain as it is. If the underlined portion is deleted, the modifying phrase at the end of the sentence "like the rise of gambling and casinos on Indian reservations" would be dangling. Choice B creates an independent clause and thus a run-on sentence. Choice C is not a cause-and-effect relationship but rather, as choice A states, a potential outcome.

11. **The correct answer is C.** The introductory phrase "During the final stages," best captures the chronological progression of a disease that appears in stages. Choice B is incorrect because it is not providing an example but merely continuing with the chronological progression. Choices A and D both bring the disease to the "end" or "approach[ing]" death, but in context, there is no suggestion that the patient is near death; rather, the patient is in the later stages of the disease.

12. **The correct answer is D.** Choice C is not grammatically correct as it forms a run-on sentence with a comma splice. Choice D provides the best sentence combination. The word *and* is integral in making the connection between the first part of the sentence and the second. In other words, "the loss of neurons and synapses in the cerebral cortex" and the resultant "atrophy" should be linked with the conjunction *and*. While choice A also makes use of *and* before this, a coordinating conjunction should not follow a semicolon when connecting two independent clauses.

13. **The correct answer is B.** The correct plural form of *hypothesis* is *hypotheses*. There is no need to change the term itself (choices C and D), but the plural form of the word is necessary.

14. **The correct answer is B.** Adding a simple description of a process likely unfamiliar to the reader is the best choice here as it allows the reader to understand the process. Choice A is incorrect because the description does not utilize figurative language. Choice C is incorrect because the details are relevant, adding a description of a process that explains one of the hypotheses. Though the sentence is certainly longer, choice D is incorrect because the information is valuable for clarifying the topic of the sentence.

15. **The correct answer is C.** In context, the "environmentally based" hypothesis is much different from the other ones detailed. A reader might wonder about the accuracy of this study or how it was conducted. By offering the authors and journal of publication and by noting that it is still in the early stages, the writer is qualifying the hypothesis' inclusion in the paragraph. Choices A and B are, then, incorrect because the information would be necessary and would still retain the paragraph's focus on delineating and describing some hypotheses. Choice D is true but is not the best answer because the additional details mentioned in choice C are the main reason for the addition.

16. **The correct answer is A.** *Yet* means "but at the same time," which is the relationship between sentence 3, which explores all the ways glaciers are valuable, and sentence 4, which tells the reader they are threatened. Choice B is incorrect because *and* is used to indicate connection, which is not the best choice here as the

previous sentence spoke of the potential benefits and uses of glaciers while sentence 4 details their threat. Choice C is incorrect because the writer is not presenting an example. Choice D is incorrect because sentence 4 is not part of a list or sequence.

17. **The correct answer is B.** Choice A is a run-on sentence with a comma splice. Choice D is incorrect because the word *but* is indicative of a contrast, and none is present; in fact, the latter portion of this sentence adds explication not contrast. Choice C is a possibility, so the writer needs to choose which is better, the semicolon of choice B or the em dash of choice C. An em dash is generally used to set aside parenthetical phrases or clauses in a sentence. In this case, the latter part of the sentence, which reads "if this accumulated snowflake mass survives one melt season, it turns into a grainy material that scientists call firn," is a complete sentence, so the better choice is the semicolon.

18. **The correct answer is D.** This choice asks a writer to choose the correct pronoun. In this case, the noun "snow mound" is singular, so it must take a singular pronoun. Since a snow mound is an object rather than a being, the proper pronoun is *it*.

19. **The correct answer is A.** The sentence is an explication, explaining why "glacial speed" is an oxymoron. The current sentence is the best option among those available. Choice B is a fragment, lacking a verb. Choice C is incorrect because there is no error that needs correcting, which the words *in fact* imply. Choice D is missing punctuation before the two factors, thickness and temperature.

20. **The correct answer is D.** This question requires you to determine appropriate verb tense and word choice given the context of the paragraph. While *form* and *producing* (choice B) have similar meanings, only *form* is in the proper tense given the rest of the sentence. *Recreate* (choice C) means to "create again," and in this case, the creation is original. As written (choice A), the sentence contains an incorrect verb tense.

21. **The correct answer is A.** The writer is trying to establish the popularity of fitness trackers and the caliber of the technology, purposes that can be presaged by discussing the growth of the industry and a rapid advance in technology. Choice B emphasizes aesthetics over rates of adoption to displace the intended focus of the paragraph. Choice C, while offering a preview of a later topic of the passage, is not discussed in the first paragraph. Choice D speaks to popularity, but it creates redundancy with the existing sentence 1.

22. **The correct answer is B.** The writer is giving examples of how fitness trackers can help you improve your health, so it makes sense to insert this after sentence 6. Sentence 7 gives an example as well, but it's written as if it's a continuation ("Or if. . ."), so the new sentence would work better coming before sentence 7.

23. **The correct answer is A.** The writer is trying to make the case that fitness trackers aren't necessarily medically sound on their own, so information about how doctors feel about fitness trackers would be an effective addition here. This is an informative essay, not a personal one, so choice B would be inappropriate. The writer is not comparing or describing particular fitness trackers, so sales figures (choice C) do not fit with the context, and marketing information about fitness trackers (choice D) would only serve the writer's purpose if the quote could be contrasted with an expert assessment of fitness trackers' effectiveness.

24. **The correct answer is D.** Of the given options, choice D preserves the meaning while tightening the sentence. Choice A changes the sentence by ignoring its first part. Choice B is wordy and repetitive ("fitness tracker can track"). Choice C overstates the writer's criticism as it has been established that fitness trackers are useful, only that their medical value is currently limited.

25. **The correct answer is C.** Choice A suggests that the writer's main point is that fitness trackers are dangerous, which is not supported by the passage. Choice B ignores the drawbacks that the writer mentioned throughout the passage. Choice C summarizes the popularity of fitness trackers but also highlights the writer's concerns about using them as absolute indicators of wellness. Choice D introduces new information and isn't relevant to the rest of the passage.

Arithmetic

1. A	5. D	9. D	13. B	17. C
2. C	6. B	10. C	14. B	18. C
3. C	7. D	11. C	15. A	19. A
4. C	8. D	12. A	16. A	20. C

1. **The correct answer is A.** This question requires you to use the order of operations. To find the value of $6 + (9 \div 3)^2 \times 2$, first evaluate the part of the expression within parentheses: $9 \div 3 = 3$, so $6 + (9 \div 3)^2 \times 2 = 6 + 3^2 \times 2$. Next, evaluate any numbers raised to a power: $3^2 = 9$, so $6 + 3^2 \times 2 = 6 + 9 \times 2$. Always evaluate multiplication and division before addition and subtraction, so multiply 9 by 2 next to get $6 + 9 \times 2 = 6 + 18$. Now perform the addition to get the final answer, 24.

2. **The correct answer is C.** Write each mixed number as a fraction, then multiply the numerators and denominators:

$$3\frac{1}{4} \times 8\frac{2}{5} = \frac{13}{4} \times \frac{42}{5} = \frac{546}{20}$$

This reduces to $\frac{273}{10}$. Convert the fraction to a mixed number:

$$\frac{273}{10} = 27\frac{3}{10}$$

3. **The correct answer is C.** The sum of 74.55 and 6.98 is 81.53. Because the decimal part, 0.53, is greater than 0.5, round up to get the nearest integer, 82. Choice A is the sum of 74 and 6, but the decimal parts of the given numbers cannot be ignored. Choice B is incorrect because the nearest integer is determined by rounding up in this case. Choice D is the nearest integer to the *product* of 74.55 and 6.98.

4. **The correct answer is C.** To determine what percent of 40 is 140, divide 140 by 40 and multiply by 100:

$$\frac{140}{40} \times 100 = 3.5 \times 100 = 350$$

So 140 is 350% of 40.

5. **The correct answer is D.** To compare the numbers, convert them to fractions with a common denominator of 100:

$$2\frac{4}{5} = \frac{14}{5} = \frac{280}{100}$$

$$\frac{11}{4} = \frac{275}{100}$$

$$2.74 = \frac{274}{100}$$

$$2.7 = \frac{270}{100}$$

Compare the numerators:

$$280 > 275 > 274 > 270$$

Hence:

$$2\frac{4}{5} > \frac{11}{4} > 2.74 > 2.7$$

6. **The correct answer is B.** Divide 708 by 7 to get 101 with a remainder of 1:

$$708 = (7 \times 101) + 1$$

7. **The correct answer is D.** Write each mixed number as a fraction. Then, multiply the numerators and denominators, and reduce:

$$1\frac{3}{8} \times 4\frac{1}{6} = \frac{11}{8} \times \frac{25}{6} = \frac{275}{48}$$

Convert the fraction to a mixed number:

$$\frac{275}{48} = \frac{240+35}{48} = 5\frac{35}{48}$$

8. **The correct answer is D.**

$$0.25\% = \frac{0.25}{100} = \frac{0.25 \times 100}{100 \times 100} = \frac{25}{10,000}$$

Choice A equals 2.5%. Choices B and C equal 25%.

9. **The correct answer is D.** To compare fractions in an inequality, convert them into fractions with a common denominator and compare the numerators:

$$\frac{6}{5} = \frac{36}{30} > \frac{7}{6} = \frac{35}{30}$$

10. **The correct answer is C.** First, calculate 65% of 4,100:

$$0.65 \times 4{,}100 = 2{,}665$$

This is the amount of the increase.
Add to 4,100 to get:

$$4{,}100 + 2{,}665 = 6{,}765$$

11. **The correct answer is C.** Convert your fraction so that the denominator is 100 by multiplying both numerator and denominator by 5. Then, you're able to see how to convert to an equivalent decimal.

$$\begin{aligned} \frac{3}{20} &= \frac{3 \times 5}{20 \times 5} \\ &= \frac{15}{100} \\ &= 0.15 \end{aligned}$$

12. **The correct answer is A.** To determine how many miles Melissa traveled by bicycle and canoe, multiply those fractions by the total distance:

$$\frac{2}{5} \times 15 = \frac{30}{5} = 6$$

and

$$\frac{1}{3} \times 15 = \frac{15}{3} = 5$$

Melissa biked 6 miles and paddled 5 miles, which means she walked the remaining 4 miles $(15 - 6 - 5 = 4)$.

13. **The correct answer is B.** The product of 49.3 and 9.4 is $49.3 \times 9.4 = 463.42$, which rounds to 463.

14. **The correct answer is B.** To determine what percent of 275 is 220, divide 220 by 275 and multiply by 100:

$$\frac{220}{275} \times 100 = 0.8 \times 100 = 80$$

So 80% of the available tickets were pre-sold.

15. **The correct answer is A.** First, we have to make sense of the variables in terms of their location on the number line. Start with W and X and observe that:

W: $\frac{3}{4} < 1$

X: $1 < \frac{4}{3} < 2$

Then, consider the options given for Y and Z and observe that:

Y: $2 < \frac{23}{11} < 3$ (because $2 = \frac{22}{11}$ and $3 = \frac{33}{11}$)

Z: $2 < 2.6 < 3$

That means $\frac{3}{4}$ is the left-most point on the number line, W, and $\frac{4}{3}$ is next to the right, X.

To distinguish between $\frac{23}{11}$ and 2.6, note that:

$\frac{23}{11} = 2 + \frac{1}{11}$ and $2.6 = 2 + \frac{6}{10}$

Since $\frac{6}{10} > \frac{1}{11}$, this means that:

$2 + \frac{6}{10} > 2 + \frac{1}{11}$ or $2.6 > \frac{23}{11}$

So $\frac{23}{11}$ and 2.6 are the right-most points, Y and Z, and 2.6 lies to the right of $\frac{23}{11}$. Only choice A associates the points W, X, Y, and Z with the numbers in accordance with the inequalities above.

16. **The correct answer is A.** If one gallon of milk costs $3.84, then 3 gallons cost $3.84 \times 3 = \$11.52$. To calculate the change back from $20, subtract the cost: $20 - \$11.52 = \$8.48$.

17. **The correct answer is C.** The word *total* indicates that the number of cups of flour that should be added to the number of cups of sugar.
$155 + 62 = 217$ total cups of ingredients.

18. **The correct answer is C.** Convert 2.75 to a fraction with denominator 4:

$$2.75 = 2\frac{75}{100} = \frac{275}{100} = \frac{11}{4}$$

Note that:

$$\frac{13}{4} > \frac{11}{4}$$

So:

$$\frac{13}{4} > 2.75$$

19. **The correct answer is A.** To divide a decimal number by 10^n, where n is a positive integer, move the decimal point n digits to the left. In this case, $16.005 \div 10^2 = .16005 = 0.16005$.

20. **The correct answer is C.** To determine how much soil Burt needs to buy, note that:

$$1 - \frac{2}{5} = \frac{5}{5} - \frac{2}{5} = \frac{3}{5}$$

If the truck is initially $\frac{2}{5}$ full, then Burt must add $\frac{3}{5}$ of the truck's capacity to fill it. We are given that the truck's capacity is $2\frac{1}{2}$ cubic yards. Compute $\frac{3}{5}$ of $2\frac{1}{2}$ by multiplying:

$$1 - \frac{2}{5} = \frac{5}{5} - \frac{2}{5} = \frac{3}{5}$$

$$\frac{3}{5} \times 2\frac{1}{2} = \frac{3}{5} \times \frac{5}{2}$$

$$= \frac{15}{10}$$

$$= \frac{3}{2}$$

Burt must purchase $\frac{3}{2}$ yd³ of soil, at \$16 per cubic yard:

$$\frac{3}{2} \times \$16 = \frac{3 \times \$16}{2}$$

$$= \frac{\$48}{2}$$

$$= \$24$$

Quantitative Reasoning, Algebra, and Statistics

1. B	5. A	9. B	13. A	17. A
2. D	6. C	10. C	14. A	18. C
3. D	7. B	11. C	15. C	19. A
4. C	8. D	12. D	16. B	20. C

1. **The correct answer is B.** First, perform the division by inverting $\frac{4}{7}$ and multiplying:

$$\frac{3}{4} \div \frac{4}{7} = \frac{3}{4} \times \frac{7}{4} = \frac{21}{16}$$

Placing this into the equation, we now have:

$$\frac{21}{16} - 3\frac{1}{2} = \frac{21}{16} - \frac{7}{2}$$

Multiply the numerator and denominator of $\frac{7}{2}$ by 8:

$$\frac{21}{16} - \frac{7}{2} = \frac{21}{16} - \frac{56}{16} = \frac{-35}{16}$$

2. **The correct answer is D.** There are 20 possible outcomes for the first trial and, for each of those outcomes, 20 possible outcomes for the second trial. For each of those pairs of outcomes, there are 20 possible outcomes for the third trial. Hence, there are a total of $20 \times 20 \times 20 = 8{,}000$ possible outcomes.

3. **The correct answer is D.** All the choices are linear equations of the form $S = mt + b$. Assuming there are 8,000 spectators in the arena when the game ends, we expect b to be 8,000 because $S = 8{,}000$ when $t = 0$. We also expect the slope, m, to be negative because S is decreasing as spectators leave the arena. Choice D, in which $b = 8{,}000$ and $m = -250$, fits these requirements.

4. **The correct answer is C.** If a and b are the lengths of the legs of a right triangle and c is the length of the hypotenuse, then the Pythagorean theorem states that $a^2 + b^2 = c^2$. In the given triangle, we have $a = x$, $b = 15$, and $c = 17$. Solve $x^2 + 15^2 = 17^2$ for x. Subtract 15^2 from both sides to get:

$$x^2 = 17^2 - 15^2 = 289 - 225 = 64$$

If $x^2 = 64$ then $x = 8$ or $x = -8$. Only $x = 8$ makes sense here.

5. **The correct answer is A.** If $4x + y = 1$, then $y = -4x + 1$. Substitute $-4x + 1$ for y in $x - 2y = 16$:

$$x - 2(-4x + 1) = 16$$
$$x + 8x - 2 = 16$$
$$9x - 2 = 16$$

Add 2 to both sides of $9x - 2 = 16$ and divide by 9 to get $x = 2$. Substitute 2 for x in $4x + y = 1$:

$$4(2) + y = 1$$

Solve for y to get $y = -7$. So the solution of the given system is $x = 2$, $y = -7$.

6. **The correct answer is C.** The percent decrease from 2,000 trout to 1,000 is 50%, greater than that for the other decades.

7. **The correct answer is B.** The figure can be rewritten as:

$$\frac{4}{\sqrt{3}} = 4 \times \frac{1}{3^{\frac{1}{2}}} = 4 \times 3^{-\frac{1}{2}}$$

8. **The correct answer is D.** Let H equal the number of hours it will take for all 12 inches to burn away. We are given the ratio of one-half inch per 3 hours, or:

$$\frac{\left(\frac{1}{2}\right)}{3}$$

That implies:

$$\frac{\left(\frac{1}{2}\right)}{3} = \frac{12}{H}$$

Cross-multiply:

$$\frac{1}{2}H = 36$$

Multiply both sides by 2 to get $H = 72$. It will take 72 hours for the candle to burn completely.

9. **The correct answer is B.** The perimeter is the sum of the lengths of the sides, $m + m + n = 2m + n$.

10. **The correct answer is C.** Following the order of operations within the absolute value symbols first:

$$16 - \left| -8 + 6 \div 2 \right| = 16 - \left| -8 + 3 \right|$$
$$= 16 - \left| -5 \right|$$

The absolute value of –5 is 5, so:

$$16 - \left| -5 \right| = 16 - 5 = 11$$

11. **The correct answer is C.** The expression can be rewritten as:

$$\frac{3}{4} - 4^{-2} = \frac{3}{4} - \frac{1}{4^2}$$
$$= \frac{3}{4} - \frac{1}{16}$$
$$= \frac{12}{16} - \frac{1}{16}$$
$$= \frac{11}{16}$$

12. **The correct answer is D.** Multiply both sides of the given equation by $\frac{7}{3}$ then simplify each side:

$$\frac{3x}{7} \cdot \frac{7}{3} = \frac{9}{14} \cdot \frac{7}{3}$$
$$\frac{\cancel{3}x}{\cancel{7}} \cdot \frac{\cancel{7}}{\cancel{3}} = \frac{63}{42}$$
$$x = \frac{63}{42}$$
$$x = \frac{3 \cdot 21}{2 \cdot 21}$$
$$x = \frac{3}{2}$$

13. **The correct answer is A.** If two lines are perpendicular, their slopes, m, will be negative reciprocals. Write each of the equations in slope-intercept form to find the slopes of the equations.

The two equations for choice A can be written in slope-intercept form as follows:

$x + 3y = 6$	$-3x + y = 2$
$-x + x + 3y = -x + 6$	$3x - 3x + y = 3x + 2$
$3y = -x + 6$	$y = 3x + 2$
$\dfrac{3y}{3} = \dfrac{-x + 6}{3}$	
$y = -\dfrac{1}{3}x + 2$	

14. **The correct answer is A.** First, perform the multiplication within the given expression:

$$-6x(-3x - 2) + 3(-8x + 3)$$
$$= 18x^2 + 12x - 24x + 9$$

Combine the x terms to get $18x^2 - 12x + 9$. Factoring out 3 yields $3(6x^2 - 4x + 3)$.

15. **The correct answer is C.** We are given that the first-born child does not have brown eyes, so our subset sample space is the 4 equally likely outcomes of {OBB, OBO, OOB, OOO}. In two of these outcomes, OBO and OOB, the family has exactly two children whose eyes are not brown. The probability is the number of selected outcomes divided by the total number of (equally likely) outcomes, or $\frac{2}{4} = \frac{1}{2}$.

16. **The correct answer is B.** The median is the middle value. Because there are an even number of populations, find the median of the middle two values. The middle two numbers are 1,338,404 and 1,356,458. Add these numbers and divide by 2:

$$\frac{1,338,404 + 1,356,458}{2} = 1,347,431$$

So 1,347,431 is the median population of the six states. To see that the mean population must be greater than 1,347,431, observe that the total population of the six states must be greater than 12 million. This can be calculated quickly by rounding each state's population *down* to the nearest million; from the top of the list, $3 + 1 + 6 + 1 + 1 + 0 = 12$ (million). If the total population of six states is greater than 12,000,000, then the mean population is greater than $\frac{12,000,000}{6} = 2,000,000$, which is greater than 1,347,431. (In fact, the mean population is 2,475,548 when calculated more precisely.) Choices A and C are incorrect because the mean is greater. Choice D is incorrect because the data necessary to calculate the median and mean populations are provided.

17. **The correct answer is A.** The volume of a 3-dimensional rectangle, or prism, is the product of its depth or thickness, its length, and its width. To solve for the volume in feet, first convert 6 inches to feet: $\frac{6}{12} = \frac{1}{2}$ foot. The volume of the floor is then:

$$\frac{1}{2} \text{ foot} \times 80 \text{ feet} \times 60 \text{ feet} = 2{,}400 \text{ cubic feet}$$

18. **The correct answer is C.** Recognize the pattern:

After 1 day, the population is $2P$.

After 2 days, $2 \times 2P$.

After 3 days, $2 \times 2 \times 2P$, etc.

After n days, the population is $2^n \times P$. The expression in choice A represents what the population would be if it increased by $2P$ daily. Choices B and D can be verified as incorrect by substituting 1, 2, 3, and so on for n.

19. **The correct answer is A.** If there are 72 cards in the deck, of which 54 are red and the rest black, then there are $72 - 54 = 18$ black cards. The ratio of red cards to black cards is 54 to 18. Divide both numbers by 18 to reduce this ratio to 3 to 1.

20. **The correct answer is C.** First, calculate Elsa's weekly savings:

$$\$390 \times \frac{2}{3} = \$260$$

Multiply by $14\frac{1}{2}$ to determine her total savings:

$$14\frac{1}{2} \times \$260 = \$3{,}770$$

Advanced Algebra and Functions

1. C	5. D	9. B	13. D	17. D
2. C	6. C	10. C	14. C	18. B
3. C	7. D	11. D	15. C	19. A
4. D	8. C	12. B	16. D	20. C

1. **The correct answer is C.** All three x, y pairs satisfy the equation $y = \dfrac{-x}{4} + 3$. Placing the values of each pair of variables in the equation produces:

$$3\frac{1}{2} = \frac{-(-2)}{4} + 3$$

$$2 = \frac{-4}{4} + 3$$

$$0 = \frac{-12}{4} + 3$$

Note that $y = \dfrac{-x}{4} + 3$ is equivalent to $y = -\dfrac{1}{4}x + 3$. Although (12, 0) *does* satisfy the equation for choice A, this answer is incorrect because $\dfrac{1}{4}(-2) - 3$ equals $-3\dfrac{1}{2}$ not $3\dfrac{1}{2}$.

2. **The correct answer is C.** The line to the right of $c = 10$ includes the points (10, 400) and (20, 650). The slope of this line is:

$$\frac{600 - 400}{20 - 10} = \frac{250}{10} = 25$$

Using the point (10, 400), the point-slope form of the equation of the line is $p - 400 = 25(c - 10)$; this is equivalent to $p = 25c + 150$. Choice A is incorrect because (10, 400) and other points on the line to the right of $c = 10$ do not satisfy $p = 25c$.

3. **The correct answer is C.** Substituting the variables, we get $(nx - m)^2$, which becomes:

$$n^2x^2 - 2mnx + m^2$$

Because n and m are positive, $-2mn < 0$; also, $m^2 > 0$ for all m. Choice C has a negative coefficient on x (-60) and a positive constant term (25):

$$36x^2 - 60x + 25 = (6x - 5)^2$$

4. **The correct answer is D.** Start by subtracting 25 from both sides of the equation to get $x^2 - 2x - 24 = 0$. The left-hand side of the equation can be factored, producing $(x + 4)(x - 6) = 0$. Therefore, the solutions to the quadratic equation are $x = -4$ and $x = 6$.

5. **The correct answer is D.** This set contains both (0, 0) and (0, 1), but by the definition of a function, $f(0)$ can have only one value.

6. **The correct answer is C.** The expression $\dfrac{-6x^3 + 15x}{3x}$ can be rewritten as $\dfrac{-6x^3}{3x} + \dfrac{15x}{3x}$, which can be reduced to $-2x^2 + 5$.

7. **The correct answer is D.** The given expression, $2\left(-5p + \dfrac{9}{2}\right)^2$, can be expanded to:

$$2\left(25p^2 + 2\left(\frac{-45}{2}\right)p + \frac{81}{4}\right)$$

which can be reduced to $50p^2 - 90p + \dfrac{81}{2}$.

8. **The correct answer is C.** The value of the car after three years will be $\$10{,}000 \times 0.9 \times 0.9 \times 0.9 = \$7{,}290$.

9. **The correct answer is B.** If a and b are the lengths of the legs of a right triangle, and c is the length of the hypotenuse, then the Pythagorean theorem states that $a^2 + b^2 = c^2$. In the given triangle, we have $a = 6$ and $c = 10$. Solve the equation $6^2 + b^2 = 10^2$ for b. Subtract 6^2 from both sides to get:

$$b^2 = 10^2 - 6^2 = 100 - 36 = 64$$

If $b^2 = 64$, then $b = 8$ or $b = -8$; only $b = 8$ makes sense here.

10. **The correct answer is C.** By the law of sines:

$$\frac{\sin B}{7} = \frac{\sin C}{5}$$

Substituting 0.70 for sin B, we have:

$$\frac{0.70}{7} = \frac{\sin C}{5}$$

Multiply both sides by 5 to get:

$$\begin{aligned}\sin C &= \frac{5(0.70)}{7}\\ &= \frac{3.50}{7}\\ &= \frac{35}{70}\\ &= \frac{1}{2}\end{aligned}$$

11. **The correct answer is D.** Subtracting 6 first puts the constant term on the right side, then multiplying by $\frac{5}{2}$ removes the coefficient from x (that is, it makes the coefficient equal to 1).

12. **The correct answer is B.** Note that this graph has a slope of $-\frac{5}{3}$ and a y-intercept of $\frac{3}{2}$.

13. **The correct answer is D.** The parabola on the graph opens down, so the coefficient on x^2 must be negative. This eliminates choices A and B because the graphs of those functions would open upward. The graph shown includes the point $(-2, 0)$, which satisfies $y = -x^2 - \frac{1}{2}x + 3$ but does not satisfy $y = -x^2 - 2x + 3$, which is the only other choice with a negative coefficient on x^2.

14. **The correct answer is C.** If c is a zero of a polynomial function $f(x)$, as we are given, then $(x - c)$ must be a factor of $f(x)$.

15. **The correct answer is C.** The initial volume of the balloon is $V = \frac{4}{3}\pi 3^3$, which can also be expressed as 36π cu. in. The final volume is $V = \frac{4}{3}\pi 6^3$ or 288π cu. in. The increase is the difference:

$$288\pi - 36\pi = 252\pi \text{ cu. in.}$$

16. **The correct answer is D.** Multiply the second equation by 3 to get $-9x - 3y = -15$. Adding that to the first equation results in the identity $0 = 0$. That means the system has an infinite number of solutions. Either equation simplifies to $y = 5 - 3x$.

17. **The correct answer is D.** To find values of x satisfying $x^2 + 5x - 36 > 0$, first solve $x^2 + 5x - 36 = 0$. Factor $x^2 + 5x - 36$ to get $(x + 9)(x - 4)$. This tells us that $x^2 + 5x - 36 = 0$ when $x = -9$ or $x = 4$. These values demarcate three intervals: $x < -9$, $-9 < x < 4$, and $x > 4$. Test values from each interval to confirm that $x < -9$ or $x > 4$ satisfies $x^2 + 5x - 36 > 0$. The intervals for choices A, B, and C all include the value $x = 0$. Substituting 0 for x in the left side of the given inequality gives $0^2 + 5(0) - 36$. This expression is equal to -36, which is not greater than 0.

18. **The correct answer is B.** Subtract 3 from both sides of the equation to get $x - 3 = \sqrt{-2x + 21}$. Squaring both sides gives $x^2 - 6x + 9 = -2x + 21$. Gather all of the terms on the left to get $x^2 - 4x - 12 = 0$, which factors to $(x - 6)(x + 2) = 0$. Testing the solutions to this factored equation in the original given equation reveals that $x = 6$ satisfies the equation, but -2 does not. Substituting $x = -2$ on the right side yields $\sqrt{25} + 3$, which is not equal to -2.

19. **The correct answer is A.** When a is positive but less than 1, all values of a^x are positive, so $-a^x$ is always negative. For $0 < a < 1$, as x approaches $-\infty$, $-a^x$ approaches $-\infty$, as we see on the left side of the graph. As x increases in a positive direction, $-a^x$ approaches 0, as we see on the right. The values $a = 0$ and $a = 1$ are excluded because 0^x is undefined and 1^x is the constant 1.

20. **The correct answer is C.** The general formula for a circle on the xy-plane, centered at (h, k) with radius r, is $(x - h)^2 + (y - k)^2 = r^2$. The circle shown is centered at $(2, -3)$ with radius 3, so the equation is $(x - 2)^2 + (y - (-3))^2 = 3^2$, which can be rewritten as $(x - 2)^2 + (y + 3)^2 = 9$.

SCORE YOURSELF: ACCUPLACER® PRACTICE TEST 2

Add up the total number of questions you answered correctly for each section, then compare your scores against the section charts below, which roughly recreate the scoring bands used by the ACCUPLACER. For more information on how the scoring bands relate to specific skills, see the extended scoring charts at the end of each answer and explanation section in Chapter 2.

Reading

Total Number of Correct Answers: _____ /20

Total # of Correct Answers	Approximate ACCUPLACER Score
8 or fewer	200–236
9–11	237–249
12–14	250–262
15–17	263–275
18–20	276–300

Writing

Total Number of Correct Answers: _____ /25

Total # of Correct Answers	Approximate ACCUPLACER Score
9 or fewer	200–236
10–13	237–249
14–17	250–262
18–21	263–275
22–25	276–300

Arithmetic

Total Number of Correct Answers: _____ /20

Total # of Correct Answers	Approximate ACCUPLACER Score
8 or fewer	200–236
9–11	237–249
12–14	250–262
15–17	263–275
18–20	276–300

Quantitative Reasoning, Algebra, and Statistics

Total Number of Correct Answers: _____ /20

Total # of Correct Answers	Approximate ACCUPLACER Score
8 or fewer	200–236
9–11	237–249
12–14	250–262
15–17	263–275
18–20	276–300

Advanced Algebra and Functions

Total Number of Correct Answers: _____ /20

Total # of Correct Answers	Approximate ACCUPLACER Score
8 or fewer	200–236
9–11	237–249
12–14	250–262
15–17	263–275
18–20	276–300

NOTES

NOTES

NOTES